Unmaking the West

Unmaking the West

"WHAT-IF?" SCENARIOS THAT
REWRITE WORLD HISTORY

Philip E. Tetlock,
Richard Ned Lebow, &
Geoffrey Parker, *Editors*

THE UNIVERSITY OF MICHIGAN PRESS   ANN ARBOR

Copyright © by the University of Michigan 2006
All rights reserved
Published in the United States of America by
The University of Michigan Press
Manufactured in the United States of America
⊗ Printed on acid-free paper

2009   2008   2007   2006   4   3   2   1

A CIP catalog record for this book is available from the British Library.

Library of Congress Cataloging-in-Publication Data

Unmaking the West : "what-if" scenarios that rewrite world history /
     Philip E. Tetlock, Richard Ned Lebow, and Geoffrey Parker, editors.
        p.   cm.
     Includes bibliographical references and index.
     ISBN-13: 978-0-472-11543-3 (cloth : alk. paper)
     ISBN-10: 0-472-11543-X (cloth : alk. paper)
     ISBN-13: 978-0-472-03143-6 (pbk. : alk. paper)
     ISBN-10: 0-472-03143-0 (pbk. : alk. paper)
      1. Imaginary histories.   2. World history.   I. Tetlock, Philip.
   II. Lebow, Richard Ned.   III. Parker, Geoffrey, 1943–

   D21.3.U56   2006
   909—dc22   2006010054

Contents

Maps

Figure

Acknowledgments

The idea for this book dates back to March 1997. Philip Tetlock had just arrived at The Ohio State University and gave an after-dinner talk at the Mershon Center about his long-running research project on counterfactual thought experiments. His presentation intrigued Geoffrey Parker, who had also written on "what if," and they began to discuss how historians might address these questions in a more "scientific" or at least more open-minded way. Being rather undertheorized himself, Parker suggested convening a panel of better-informed historians to find out. Tetlock therefore approached Richard Ned Lebow, Director of the Mershon Center, who also had a serious scholarly interest in the proposed agenda, for financial support. At a meeting of the three of us to formulate a proposal in May 1997, the idea emerged of using the rise of the West as a test case—a particularly demanding test case, as readers will soon discover—of the power of counterfactual thought exercises to clarify the causal assumptions and expand the imaginative range of historical scholarship.

In November 1997, many of the authors represented in the book, together with Jeremy Black, Robert Cowley, Carole Fink, Richard Hamilton, Richard Herrmann, Edward Ingram, Ira Lapidus, Randolph Roth and Arthur Waldron, met at Mershon for a three-day workshop on "Alternative Histories of the Rise of the West." In the light of those discussions, the three editors decided to commission chapters for a volume on "unmaking the West." Some were procedural, but most were substantive, focusing on what workshop members had identified as the "turning points" at which the rise of the West could have been prevented, halted, or reversed.

The editors composed a series of ever-longer and more complex directives to the authors. Several faltered under the burden, but stronger shoulders and more cunning pens swiftly replaced them until, two years later, we had drafts of almost all the chapters. The editors then convened a second workshop at the Mershon Center at which Kenneth Andrien, Alan Beyerchen, Robert Cowley, Carter Findley, Richard Hamilton, Ira Lapidus, Charles Long, Patricia Seed, and Sanjay Subrahmanyam joined the authors for another three days of lively debate.

Our first debt, therefore, is to the colleagues who attended these workshops and provided valuable ideas, suggestions, and references and especially to the authors who accepted more editorial direction—from more editors—than any scholar should have to endure. We would also like to thank three other colleagues who provided insights and material that assisted us: Timothy Barnes, Richard W. Bulliet, and Sabina MacCormick. Next we thank the staff of the Mershon Center, who handled arrangements for the conferences, especially Ann Powers and Beth Russell, who provided logistical support; Andrew Mitchell and Katherine Becker of the Ohio State University History Department for editorial assistance; Katie Mongeon and Carol Chapman of the University of California, Berkeley; our friend and colleague, Joel Mokyr, of Northwestern University, for his critical assistance in introducing us to Chris Collins and the University of Michigan Press; and the two anonymous reviewers for that press whose comments have helped us to sharpen our arguments and presentation. Finally, we acknowledge our indebtedness to institutions. The Social Science Research Council offered valuable seed money support at an early phase through its MacArthur Foundation supported Committee on International Security. And without Colonel Ralph Mershon, whose magnificent bequest to The Ohio State University created the Mershon Center, this project could never have been realized.

Preface

The Editors

Unmaking the Middle Kingdom

Imagine a book that began:

We Chinese take our primacy for granted. We are one of the oldest civilizations in the world and the oldest continuous culture in existence. Every day, our much sought after manufactures, specialty agricultural goods, and products of popular and high culture are exported to every corner of the globe. Our language and culture have spread far beyond the river valleys where they originated; currently, almost two billion non-Han people speak or understand standard Chinese. It is the universal language of science, transportation, and business. With the exception of a minor European country and its former New World colony along the banks of the Zian-te Lo-rent River, schoolchildren everywhere begin studying Chinese in their first year of school. Almost a third of all Han live overseas, intermingled with the peoples of the islands and archipelagoes south of us or in the new continents they colonized. New Guangzhou, whose twelve million people are spread out in the valleys and hills of what was once a desert bordering the far side of the great ocean, rivals Beijing in size and wealth. Its free and easy lifestyle, suitable to an automobile culture in a sun-drenched climate, seems to have an irresistible appeal to our own youth.

Did this have to be? Could China have failed to achieve the cultural and political unity that gave it a jump start on other regions of the world? Could anything have prevented our country from developing the techno-logical, military, economic, political, and cultural dominance it currently enjoys? Could some other region—say India, the Ottoman Empire, or even Europe—have achieved this primacy instead? Many people will refuse to take such questions seriously. We Han are a practical people, not given to flights of fancy: our language does not even include "would have been" tenses. Some of our scholars have a further objection to claims that rest on "counterfactuals"—"what-if" statements about the past and the different outcomes to which they might have led in the pres-ent. The honorable historian En Hao Kar once compared counterfactual argument to mah-jongg: both are parlor games played by old women with time on their hands. Perhaps such a dismissive response is excessive. If counterfactual probing of the past can be done rigorously, we could evaluate the contingency of developments that led up to today's world and thus understand more fully why events unfolded as they did.

To this end we convened a panel of prominent scholars with diverse expertise. Most are historians of Chinese imperial expansion under the Great Khans and their successors, but some study public health, science, religion, language, and literature, while others are experts on non-Han cultures. We asked our panel to identify the developments and turning points in China and abroad that they thought most responsible for the shape of the modern world and to consider plausible "minimal rewrite" counterfactuals: tiny changes that might have forestalled these develop-ments or led to different outcomes at key turning points. They were fur-ther asked to consider "second-order counterfactuals": subsequent devel-opments that might have returned the initiative to the Central Nation.

There was a lively debate about key developments and turning points. Concerning China, a consensus developed that three turning points proved critical: first, if a typhoon had sunk the fleet that invaded and con-quered Nippon, it would have deprived China of the base it needed for the naval exploration of the New World; second, the overthrow of the Great Khans by a native, inward-looking, "Ming" dynasty, after barely one hundred years of rule, would have ended overseas expansion; and, finally, the failure to adopt the phonetic alphabet introduced to China by European visitors would have prevented the development of a simple sys-tem of printing and the rapid spread of ideas. Our non-Han scholars came up with even more fanciful possibilities, the most extreme of which was to suppose that the Great Khan's armies had returned eastward just

*before they conquered Europe, leaving Christianity as the dominant reli-
gion of the region and creating conditions under which coastal kingdoms
in Western Europe might conduct their own overseas explorations. Not
even that alternative history, however, could unmake the primacy of the
Middle Kingdom.*

The preceding paragraphs reflect an alternative world in which China, not
Western Europe, became the locus of worldwide colonial expansion and
industrialization and achieved a corresponding degree of political, economic, military, and cultural hegemony. It is unlikely that any of the present editors—born in Canada, France, and Britain—would have participated in such a comparative counterfactual study except as token
representatives of subordinate and backward regions. But many things are
possible in counterfactual worlds, and it is not out of the question that one
or more of our ancestors might have migrated to China instead of to the
United States either seeking economic opportunity or fleeing oppression.

Entertainment aside, why have we opened our book with a *double*
counterfactual—imaginary people in an imaginary world envisioning an
alternative world that bears a mischievous resemblance to our own, the
actual, world? The primary value of such an exercise, we suggest, is
humility. The world we inhabit is but one of a vast array of possible
worlds that might have been brought about if some deity could, as
Stephen J. Gould once speculated, rerun the tape of history over and
over. Psychologists have documented a widespread human tendency,
known as "hindsight bias," to see the future as more contingent than the
past: that is, once we know what has happened, it is difficult to recall
how unsure we used to be about the future. The authors of *The 9/11
Commission Report,* who had to deal with the phenomenon at first hand,
expressed the problem with exemplary clarity.

> In composing this narrative, we have tried to remember that we
> write with the benefit and the handicap of hindsight. Hindsight
> can sometimes see the past clearly—with 20/20 vision. But the path
> of what happened is so brightly lit that it places everything else
> more deeply into shadow. . . . As time passes, more documents
> become available, and the bare facts of what happened become
> still clearer. Yet the picture of *how* those things happened becomes
> harder to reimagine, as that past world, with its preoccupations
> and uncertainty, recedes and the remaining memories of it become
> colored by what happened and what was written about it later.[1]

As the editors write this preface in October 2004, all political observers agree that the outcome of the U.S. presidential election only a few weeks ahead is "too close to call"; and yet, as *you* read these same words, the outcome (whatever it may be) will seem almost inevitable. How could your editors (like everyone else) have been so dumb that they failed to predict the correct result when the signs were so clear and the trend so obvious?

Experimental research has shown that the more people try to transport themselves by acts of imagination into counterfactual worlds, and the more richly they embellish those scenarios, the more likely they are to realize that history could indeed have taken a different course. "Unmaking the Middle Kingdom," therefore, aims to shake our readers free of hindsight bias in order to become more receptive to the premise of our book: that it is worth allocating greater mental energy to the possibility that what happened in the past did not necessarily have to happen; that we must always grant contingency its due.

There is a remarkably broad and deep consensus across branches of human knowledge, as diverse as cosmology and evolutionary biology and economics and political science, that counterfactual thought experiments form an indispensable tool for drawing thoughtful lessons from the past, above all for giving us a nuanced sense of the degree of inevitability in what happened.[2] Moreover, the consensus extends to practitioners. Business schools and military academies include what-if scenarios as integral parts of their rigorous training for running corporations or winning wars. Governments set up special commissions in the wake of national catastrophes (such as the terrorist attacks on September 11, 2001) in order to ascertain what went wrong and what reforms might have averted disaster.[3] Financial analysts likewise devote close study to market meltdowns to assess what they could reasonably have foreseen and, by implication, what they should do to control future risk exposure. For all of these experts, the key question is not whether they are going to conduct counterfactual thought experiments but whether they are going to conduct such thought experiments well or poorly. Failing to acknowledge this fact is virtually a guarantee that one will conduct them poorly.

We leave it to others to explain why historians continue to mount organized scholarly resistance to counterfactual thought experiments and why only they still deny the need to undertake counterfactual reasoning in order to establish the probable causes of a given outcome. Instead, in this volume we apply counterfactual reasoning to an unusually challenging and ideologically charged set of historical puzzles: the debate over the rise of the West that has engaged many leading intellectuals for over a century. But our approach is different—we believe radically different—from those of our scholarly predecessors. The editors represent an interdisciplinary team that is collectively as interested in the cognitive processes of observing and drawing causal lessons from history as in the historical record itself. We shall show that history looks different when our initial question is factual (why did x occur?) as opposed to "counterfactual" (why did alternatives to x fail to occur?). Framed factually, the central question in the "rise of the West" debate—one repeatedly asked in the past—is: "How did so few Europeans, working from seemingly unpromising beginnings in the first half of the last millennium, manage so quickly in the second half to surpass all other peoples on the planet in wealth and power?" Our central questions are very different. We ask:

- How close did we come to alternative worlds in which the West failed to rise, perhaps as the result of events internal to the West (such as an even more lethal black death or the failure to achieve an Industrial Revolution)?
- How close did external events (such as a successful Mongol invasion or stronger resistance to European expansion by Native American, African, or Asian states) come to preventing or derailing the rise of the West?
- Could the rise of the West have taken a different form—perhaps more benign, perhaps more malign?

Applying counterfactual history to this particular controversy poses three special analytical challenges. In the first place, controversy surrounds the question of how to define *the West*. Some, such as Victor Davis Hanson (chap. 2), define it as a set of moral and cultural ideas, a recipe for creating more civilized or advanced societies that, once followed, ensures the dominance of those societies. Others see the West as merely a geographical expression: in chapter 3, for example, Barry Strauss imagines an alternative Western civilization that rested on Persian and German rather than Greek and Roman foundations and yet eventually resembled actual Western civilization in most respects. Most of our authors, however, assume a West centered first on Greece and Rome, then on Latin Christendom, and only since the nineteenth century on Western Europe and North America. We agree. And, although we reject the exaggerated Eurocentrism of Charles Murray's book *Human*

Accomplishment, for the purposes of this volume we equate the Western heartland between 1400 and 1940—the period covered by most of the chapters in this volume—with Murray's "polygon": a relatively compact area lying between Naples, Marseilles, Taunton, Glasgow, Jutland, and Wroclaw (see map 1). Those whose accomplishments defined the West in this period (in the sciences as well as the arts) came overwhelmingly from Britain, France, Germany, Italy, and the Low Countries. The epicenter of this area may have changed over time—from Italy in the fifteenth century to the Low Countries in the sixteenth and seventeenth, France and Britain in the eighteenth, and France, Britain, and Germany thereafter—but only after 1940 did North American accomplishments become significant.[4] Although at least a dozen definitions of *the West* have been offered by different scholars, we prefer a geographical entity with the polygon at its center.[5]

The second analytical challenge arises from the fact that what-if scenarios, whether or not they are related to the rise of the West, are widely identified with microhistories in which the crucial variable is killing or sparing a key player or a different outcome to a specific battle or power struggle. Most counterfactual histories therefore take the form of essays or novels. Extending counterfactual history to a macrohistorical controversy, such as the debate over the rise of the West, requires not only far more space but also a major conceptual stretch. It is not enough to show that a different victor would have emerged on a particular battlefield. Counterfactually weakening the West means not just delaying or preventing the emergence of (say) the British Empire; it means making sure that the change does not merely shift power to another part of Western Europe or North America. To unmake the West, one must rule out not just the specific form that Western hegemony took: one must eliminate *all* members of the large set of possible forms that Western hegemony could have taken. The complexity can quickly become staggering. The counterfactual historian confronts metastasizing networks of counterfactual inference about how "if x had happened, then probably y would have followed, and if y, then possibly . . ." The number of nodes of uncertainty thus has the potential to expand exponentially. But through this torturous process we discover historians' most deeply thought-through answers to the "West versus the rest" debate: for eventually these "second-order counterfactuals" must either bring alternative histories back to something resembling our world, affirming the inevitability of Western dominance in some form, or else allow alternative histories to stray into

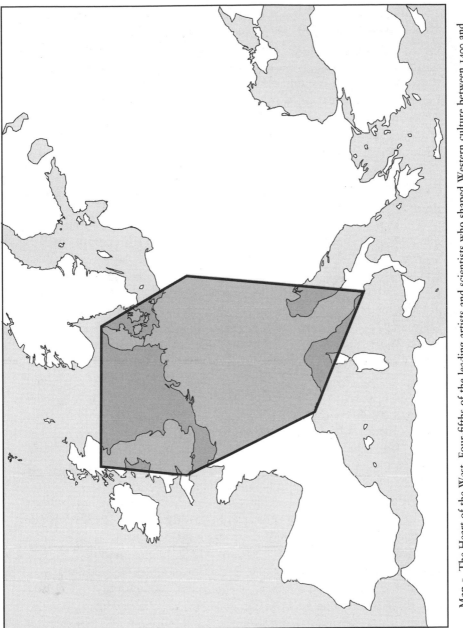

Map 1. The Heart of the West. Four-fifths of the leading artists and scientists who shaped Western culture between 1400 and 1940 grew up in the area within the shaded polygon. (Courtesy of Charles Murray, *Human Accomplishment: The Pursuit of Excellence in the Arts and Sciences, 800 B.C. to 1950* [London and New York: HarperCollins, 2003], 295–303 and 508–88.)

worlds that look and feel entirely different from our own, affirming the capriciousness of Western dominance.

A third challenge in applying counterfactual history to the rise of the West debate arises from the powerful ideological bias of many of the debaters. Surveys of professional historians have shown that observers who lean toward the political Right are more likely to maintain that things had to work roughly as they did and that Western dominance has been in the historical cards for a long time (sometimes as far back as a thousand years). Insofar as these observers tolerate explicit counterfactuals at all, they favor second-order counterfactuals—which bring history back on track in fairly short order—that concede that, yes, this or that surface cause could have taken on a different value and rerouted events briefly, but deeper forces would have returned history to something much like the trajectory we are now on.[6] To these scholars, the West achieved geopolitical dominance because it exemplified distinctive cultural values and possessed unique political assets that conferred a long-term competitive advantage in creating and applying new technologies.[7] The West won because it got certain things right—displaying more respect for property rights, implementing a clear separation of church and state, granting greater freedom to launch independent inquiry—that the rest got wrong. For them, any attempt to imagine counterfactual scenarios in which Western primacy is easily undone by minor twists of fate—a botched assassination here or a delayed invention there—will fail for the simple reason that the roots of the success of the West and of the failure of the rest lie deeply embedded in the mores, folkways, and institutional habits of the relevant societies.[8]

By contrast, observers on the political Left tend to deride such thinking as "triumphalist." They find the rise first of Europe and then of North America to global dominance during the last five hundred years as just as improbable as it seemed to our imaginary Chinese panelists. For them, the rise of the West was an accident of history, and Western hegemony a fluke, a one in a million shot that can be readily undone—at least in our imaginations—by altering minor background conditions as late as the seventeenth or eighteenth centuries: if a key individual had died slightly earlier or later, or if the weather had been cloudier or windier, "we" would find ourselves in a very different world. These scholars also deny that there is anything superior about Western culture when it is compared with the spirituality and communal solidarity of many African and Asian societies.

Such an outlook makes it relatively easy to conjure up what-if scenarios that slow or even reverse the rise of the West or that facilitate the rise to dominance of other civilizations in China or India or the Islamic world.[9] In this view, Western dominance was the by-product of natural forces that reflect no credit on Western civilization: geographical accidents such as the location of mountains and coastlines, geological accidents such as the ready availability of coal or gold or arable land, climatological accidents such as the timing of ice ages or the directions of ocean currents, and biological accidents (not always so accidental) that affect the susceptibility of various population groups to lethal diseases.[10]

Each side has been quick to mock the other: gloating "it had to be" counterfactuals from the triumphalist Right have crossed swords with bad loser "could have been a contender" counterfactuals from the multiculturalist Left. Counterfactual historians, in our view, earn their keep if they can check such partisan overconfidence by reminding us of just how many intricately interconnected assumptions scholars need to make to justify claims about the inevitable or improbable rise and fall of civilizations. We see enormous intellectual value—perhaps, indeed, the greatest service counterfactual historians can render—in unearthing the labyrinthine logical complexity of "what-if" assumptions underpinning the often all too confident claims about why the West, and not one of the rest, rose to global hegemony. We all need to be reminded that the greater the number of probabilistic "if-then" linkages in our arguments the more these sources of uncertainty add up and so the more vulnerable our conclusions become. And nowhere is it more useful to be reminded of this oft-neglected logical truism than in highly politicized controversies.[11]

To more cynical readers who suspect this book of being yet another collection of what-if stories by frustrated historians (or, worse, social scientists) who wish they were novelists, we reply that not all counterfactual thought experiments are equally subjective and therefore equally speculative. We believe—and will explain why we believe—that such experiments must be conducted in a careful manner, must make rigorous use of evidence in support of their claims, and must not differ in fundamental ways from so-called factual history. To achieve these ends, all chapters incorporate three exacting quality-control questions designed expressly to neutralize the most common objections to counterfactual history.

- *How little needs to change for history to take an alternate road and thus justify an examination of events from a counterfactual vantage point?* (The "minimal-rewrite rule"—which favors causes that require little tampering with the actual historical record—looms large in most chapters here.)[12]

- Assuming it is plausible to introduce some counterfactual alterations into the original flow of events, *how strong a case can be made as to the direction that subsequent events would have taken,* and, once engaged in projecting alternative futures for possible worlds, *how far "down the road" is it prudent to try to project what would have happened?*

- Reflecting back on the entire exercise, *how easy or difficult is it to identify ways in which the exercise either undermines or reinforces the particular interpretations of history one held at the outset?*

This volume includes ten essays that examine individual events that we believe critically affected the rise of the West: the possible destruction of Greek culture by Persia in the fifth century BC (by Victor Davis Hanson and Barry Strauss, who view the same counterfactual from diametrically opposing standpoints), a Roman decision not to crucify Christ (by Carlos M. N. Eire), a Catholic modern England (by Eire again, and then by Jack A. Goldstone and Carla Gardina Pestana, who explore an alternate set of pathways to the same counterfactual outcome and also reach diametrically opposing conclusions), the emergence of a more robust China (by Robin D. S. Yates and Kenneth Pomeranz), a failed transition to the Industrial Revolution (by Joel Mokyr), and a Nazi victory in World War II (by Holger H. Herwig).

The choice of these topics (rather than others) reflects not only their perceived prominence but also the editors' ability to find scholars willing to write chapters about them: our sample of turning points is thus neither random nor representative. Nevertheless, each chapter addresses a common theme: the relative ease or difficulty of redirecting history at each juncture so as to slow, halt, or perhaps even reverse the powerful historical forces that allowed a remarkably small number of Europeans to exert great sway over most of the planet. Taken together, the essays to some extent reconcile the triumphalist Right and the multiculturalist Left because (crudely stated) they conclude that:

- Prior to about AD 1500, it is easy to throttle the baby in its cradle: there seem to be innumerable possibilities for redirecting history so that the West never "rises."

- Beyond this date, it becomes progressively more difficult to find single junctures at which it is plausible to suppose that "but for this" events would have led the world down a markedly different path. By the eighteenth century, in order to derail Western expansion one needs to advance increasingly complex what-if scenarios that tinker with history at multiple junctures and stretch the credulity and patience of even indulgent readers.

- After 1800, it is virtually impossible to halt or reverse the rise of the West (although one can easily envisage it being either more benign or more malign.)

Although the volume covers a lot of ground, it does not attempt to examine global history over the past twenty-five hundred years—such an enterprise would have required many volumes—nor does it aspire to provide a definitive study of the rise of the West. Our goals are far more modest: on the one hand, we seek to provide new perspectives on an old problem, new insights into existing explanations, and new questions that lead to a more sophisticated research agenda; and, on the other hand, by doing so we want to demonstrate the utility—indeed, the necessity—of using properly constructed counterfactual tools to study history.

NOTES

1. *The 9/11 Commission Report. Final Report of the National Commission on Terrorist Attacks upon the United States* (New York: Norton, 2004), 339.

2. The technical definition of *counterfactual* is "any subjunctive conditional assertion in which the antecedent is known to be false." See James Fearon, "Counterfactuals and Hypothesis Testing in Political Science," *World Politics* 43 (1991): 169–95; and G. King, R. O. Keohane, and S. Verba, *Designing Social Inquiry: Scientific Inference in Qualitative Research* (Princeton: Princeton University Press, 1994).

3. *The 9/11 Commission Report* is full of what-if speculations: see, for example, pages 44–46 in chapter 1, 315–23 in chapter 9, and all of chapter 11, entitled "Foresight and Hindsight."

4. Charles Murray, *Human Accomplishment: The Pursuit of Excellence in the Arts and Sciences, 800 B.C. to 1950* (London and New York: HarperCollins, 2003), especially chapters 11 and 13. Although we respect Murray's energy in assembling data on the accomplishments of Western artists and scientists, we reject his argument that their achievements dwarfed those of other civilizations because he lacks comparable data: see, for example, his admission that he could not evaluate Chinese scientific and technological accomplishments. One problem is the "lack of translations for works in non-Roman alphabets," he claims on

page 603, note 11—an inadmissible excuse in any case—but Murray fails even to use easily available Western-language works. Thus he dismisses "Joseph Needham's seven-volume account of Chinese science and technology" as "microscopic" (259). Murray seems unaware that each "volume" is divided into parts (volume 5, for example, has thirteen parts, most of them larger than his own book) and seeks specifically to show the extent to which Chinese inventions preceded and often surpassed Western ones.

5. For the twelve versions, see Norman Davies, *Europe: A History* (Oxford: Oxford University Press, 1996), 22–25. See also the illuminating discussion of how the West has been constructed, deconstructed, and reconstructed in Jonathan Clark, "Is There Still a West? The Trajectory of a Category," *Orbis* 48 (2004): 577–91; and *Our Shadowed Present: Modernism, Postmodernism, and History* (Stanford: Stanford University Press, 2004), chap. 7.

6. Philip E. Tetlock and Richard Ned Lebow, "Poking Counterfactual Holes in Covering Laws: Cognitive Styles and Historical Reasoning," *American Political Science Review* 95 (2001): 829–43.

7. See Gale Stokes, "The Fates of Human Societies: A Review of Recent Macrohistories," *American Historical Review* 106 (2001): 355–71.

8. See the various degrees of triumphalism displayed in the following (arranged in chronological order): Douglass C. North and Robert Paul Thomas, *The Rise of the Western World: A New Economic History* (Cambridge: Cambridge University Press, 1973); William H. McNeill, *The Pursuit of Power: Technology, Armed Force, and Society since A.D. 1000* (Chicago: University of Chicago Press, 1982); Eric L. Jones, *The European Miracle: Environments, Economies, and Geopolitics in the History of Europe and Asia*, 2nd ed. (Cambridge: Cambridge University Press, 1987); Jean Baechler, John A. Hall, and Michael Mann, eds., *Europe and the Rise of Capitalism* (Oxford: Basil Blackwell, 1988); Felipe Fernández-Armesto, *Millennium: A History of the Last Thousand Years* (New York: Charles Scribner's Sons, 1995); David Landes, *The Wealth and Poverty of Nations* (New York: Norton, 1997); Alfred W. Crosby, *The Measure of Reality: Quantification and Western Society, 1250–1600* (Cambridge: Cambridge University Press, 1997); David Gress, *From Plato to NATO: The Idea of the West and Its Opponents* (New York: Free Press, 1998); Jacques Barzun, *From Dawn to Decadence: 500 Years of Western Cultural Life* (New York: HarperCollins, 2000); and Murray, *Human Accomplishments.*

9. Peter Gran, *Beyond Eurocentrism: A New View of Modern World History* (Syracuse, NY, 1996); David Herlihy, *The Black Death and the Transformation of the West* (Cambridge: Harvard University Press, 1997); Bobby S. Sayyid, *A Fundamental Fear: Eurocentrism and the Emergence of Islamism* (London: Zed Books, 1997); Jared Diamond, *Guns, Germs, and Steel: The Fates of Human Societies* (New York: Norton, 1997).

10. This pattern of opinion is consistent with the hypothesis that those on the Left are more interested in counterfactuals that puncture "Western triumphalism." But, in an ironic twist, the latest addition to the debunkers of counterfactual history, Richard Evans, has posited the opposite relationship between ideology and receptivity to what-if scenarios. Evans asserts that it is "young fogey," "New Right" historians such as Niall Ferguson who are most eager to embrace

scenarios that undo the unmaking of their beloved British Empire (Richard J. Evans, "Telling It Like It Wasn't," *Historically Speaking*, March 2004, 11–15). The contradiction may be superficial since both generalizations are consistent with E. H. Carr's "bad loser" hypothesis, as well as a sizable body of psychological research (Neal Roese, "Counterfactual Thinking," *Psychological Bulletin* 121 (1997): 133–48). Both the Carr and Evans arguments do, however, border on the ad hominem. We should not forget that even the most bloody-minded radicals and reactionaries occasionally stumble on the truth—and that arguments must be addressed on their merits, no matter how tempting the name-calling shortcuts.

11. A large research literature attests to how insensitive people are to the compounding of sources of uncertainty in complex narratives and scenarios—a phenomenon sometimes labeled cascaded inference. See Philip E. Tetlock, *Expert Political Judgment: How Good Is It? How Can We Know?* (Princeton: Princeton University Press, 2005).

12. Philip Tetlock and Aaron Belkin, in their edited volume *Counterfactual Thought Experiments in World Politics* (Princeton: Princeton University Press, 1996), 21, coined the term *minimal-rewrite rule,* but the concept goes back to 1906 and Max Weber's "Objective Possibility and Adequate Causation in Historical Explanation," in *The Methodology of the Social Sciences* (Glencoe, NY: Free Press, 1949), 164–88. Tetlock and Belkin also lay out a taxonomy of logical, historical, and theoretical tests for thought experiments.

CHAPTER I

Counterfactual Thought Experiments

WHY WE CAN'T LIVE WITHOUT THEM &
HOW WE MUST LEARN TO LIVE WITH THEM

Philip E. Tetlock and Geoffrey Parker

Anything that has been condemned by Carr, Thompson, and Hobsbawm must have something to recommend it, especially if on the other side of the argument we have such distinguished supporters and practitioners of the counterfactuals technique as Edward Gibbon, Winston Churchill, Thomas Carlyle, Sir Lewis Namier, Hugh Dacre, Harold Nicolson, Isaiah Berlin, Ronald Knox, Emil Ludwig, G. K. Chesterton, H. A. L. Fisher, Conrad Russell and the utterly delightful Gwyneth Paltrow.

—Andrew Roberts, *What Might Have Been*

If we could replay the game of life again and again, always starting at the left wall [the first single-celled organism] and expanding thereafter in diversity, we would get a right tail almost every time, but the inhabitants of this region of greatest complexity would be wildly and unpredictably different in each rendition—and the vast majority of replays would never produce (on the finite scale of a planet's lifetime) a creature with self-consciousness. Humans are here by the luck of the draw, not the inevitability of life's direction or evolution's mechanism.

—Stephen Jay Gould, *Full House*

Counterfactual history polarizes scholars. Edward Hallett Carr's influential book *What Is History?* is one of many works—mostly by Anglo-Saxon academics—that disparage it as a dead end, a parlor game, even a methodological rat hole.[1] They see no point in fretting over how history would have unfolded in hypothetical worlds that no one can ever visit or document: we should simply accept that we will never know what would have happened if, say, the Persians had won at Salamis, Christ had not been crucified, or Hitler had perished with millions of other unlucky infantrymen in World War I. History is hard enough as it is—as it actually is, these critics pointedly remind us—without self-indulgent diversions into "alternative realities," "imaginary universes," and "possible worlds." More recently, Richard J. Evans, Professor of Modern History at Cambridge, has accused historians who indulge in counterfactual history of using it merely as a device to prop up their ideological prejudices, "discovering" that events in these empirically inaccessible worlds dovetail suspiciously conveniently with their ideological preconceptions.[2]

Other historians, by contrast, see the counterfactual approach as an indispensable tool. Moreover, they embrace the approach for a remarkable range of reasons—from the positivist to the humanist. At the positivist end of the continuum, we find economic historians and econometricians, as well as other social science methodologists, who use counterfactuals in a targeted fashion to test particular hypotheses about, say, the impact of technologies on economic growth or the effects of change in diplomatic or military strategy on the outcomes of crises or wars. These scholars insist that, like it or not, we are all counterfactual historians. There is absolutely no logical way to make causal inferences without simultaneously making assumptions about how events would have unfolded if the causal factors we consider crucial had taken on different forms. At the humanist end of the continuum, we find scholars who use counterfactuals in a far more speculative fashion to infuse lost possibilities with fresh narrative life—to give us some imaginative sense for how different life would have been if, say, the Persians had won at Salamis or the Spanish Armada had prevailed in the English Channel. Their agenda is to save us from the cognitive tyranny of hindsight bias: to prevent the world that did happen from obstructing our view of the panorama of possible worlds that could have sprung into being but for tiny twists of fate, to sharpen our appreciation of how uncertain almost everyone was about what would happen before they learned what did happen, and to sensitize us to the intricate complexity and probabilistic character of the causal processes that produced the world we happen to inhabit.[3]

It seems unlikely that the debate between proponents and opponents of counterfactual history will ever be resolved at a purely philosophical level. Whether it proves a passing fad, as skeptics such as E. H. Carr and

Richard Evans have predicted, or a durable tool, as proponents such as Hugh Trevor-Roper and Niall Ferguson have argued, will ultimately hinge on how useful workaday historians find such methods of analysis in solving the puzzles that they deem worthy of study. In this pragmatic spirit, we devote the bulk of our volume to a small number of specific counterfactual case studies, not to metaphysical speculation on free will versus determinism or epistemological speculation on the "knowability" of the mysterious alternative worlds that are so central to what-if histories. The proof of this pudding will largely be in the eating, not in the philosophical recipe.

We could end at this point and let the volume speak for itself. But recent exchanges in the scholarly literature have revealed so much confusion about the aims and methods of counterfactual history that we feel bound to lay out the assumptions underlying this volume as well as the guidelines and methodology followed by our contributors. We therefore divide the remainder of this introductory chapter into three principal sections. The first makes the foundational case for counterfactual history as an essential complement to actual history: it demonstrates why we cannot live without it. The second section explains why, if counterfactual history is so indispensable, so many thoughtful historians have denounced and even ridiculed the genre. We examine the three principal objections advanced by critics who feel that counterfactual history is beyond methodological redemption: it is hopelessly arbitrary (because it offers no principles for winnowing out which of the infinity of possible what-ifs warrant our attention), it is hopelessly speculative (because it gives us no way of determining who was right), and it is hopelessly self-serving (because, in the absence of reality checks, it leaves us free to invent whatever what-if scenarios we wish to prop up our prejudices).[4] We acknowledge these grounds for concern—counterfactual arguments, like all historical arguments, can be constructed sturdily or shoddily— but we use the objections of the critics not for their intended purpose of banishing counterfactual history from the realm of acceptable scholarship but rather to advance our own agenda of articulating acceptable standards of evidence for counterfactual thought experiments.

The third section lays that agenda out: we posed a series of procedural questions that called on our contributors to clarify whether each of the three main objections leveled against counterfactual history applies to their case studies. We argued that good thought experiments should possess certain qualities, and we prevailed on all our contributors to be unusually explicit about how they conducted theirs. We believe that thought experiments should be approached in the same spirit in which scientists are supposed to approach laboratory experiments: be prepared to cry "foul" if we detect methodological flaws but, when we cannot find fault, be prepared to change our minds in response to what the exercises reveal.[5]

Why We Are All (Like It or Not) Counterfactual Historians

Our argument for the unavoidability of counterfactual history has two parts: one logical and the other psychological. The logical argument builds on the work of a long line of scholars who assert the impossibility of avoiding counterfactual history if we hope to go beyond *bare descriptions of what happened* to *explanations of why certain things rather than others happened*. Whenever we draw a cause-effect lesson from the past, we commit ourselves to the claim that, if key links in the causal chain were broken, history would have unfolded otherwise.[6] Here we make common cause with economic historians and political methodologists. The psychological argument builds on work in cognitive science to warn of the dangers of the hindsight bias: the powerful tendency of human beings to start forgetting, as soon as we learn what happened, how unpredictable the world looked beforehand and to dedicate ourselves to forging chains of reasons that make what happened appear to be the inevitable outcome of prior causes.[7] This bias toward retrospective determinism should not be dismissed as mere posturing. People often convince themselves that they saw it coming all along and hold to this position even when they know objective records of earlier statements could belie their claims.[8] Shattering hindsight complacency is the best way to make us appreciate how uncertain everything seemed before everyone became contaminated by outcome knowledge.

We draw on both arguments to challenge the claim by opponents of counterfactual history that hindsight—knowing the eventual winners and losers of historical struggles—provides the only sure standard for distinguishing significant from insignificant historical forces. We propose instead that a balanced appraisal of history requires striking what philosophers call a "reflective equilibrium" between factual and counterfactual methods of framing our questions about what had to be and what could have been.[9] To level the playing field for testing rival hypotheses— whether derived from studies of specific historical cases or from lapidary social science "laws"—it is essential to balance any inquiry that begins with the factual query "why did the observed outcome occur?" with the complementary counterfactual query "why did the many possible alternatives to the observed outcome fail to occur?"[10]

The Logical Case for Counterfactual History

Critics err when they insinuate that counterfactual history is as superfluous to serious scholarship as (say) parlor games. This is easily demonstrated because whenever we make the apparently factual claim that factor x made a critical causal contribution to outcome y we *simultaneously* make the counterfactual claim that, in a logical shadow universe with factor x deleted, outcome y would not have occurred. Since it is impossible to rerun history to test this proposition, and since all similar cases in the real world to which we might turn for comparison will be only imperfectly similar, we are stuck with doing counterfactual history: with trying to infer the workings of the shadow universe using the best analytical and imaginative tools we can muster.

History can be rendered counterfactual free only if those who study it are prepared to eschew all causal inference and limit themselves to strictly descriptive narratives of what happened. This precludes smuggling in causal claims under the guise of verbs such as *influenced, shaped, responded, transformed, triggered, molded,* and *precipitated.* Putting to one side the feasibility of purging all but the blandest narratives of all allusions to causality, this prohibition bars us from drawing the sorts of lessons from history that both scholars and policymakers want to draw: Did this policy work or were we just lucky? Did this policy fail or were we just unlucky, sabotaged by a quirky concatenation of bad breaks? Historical figures, such as the duke of Wellington, cannot have it both ways—dismissing Clausewitz's book *On War* because "it is useless to speculate upon supposed military movements which were never made, and operations which never took place" and then going on to say of the battle of Waterloo: "I do not think it would have done if I had not been there." Neither can historians such as E. H. Carr and Richard Evans have it both ways—ridiculing counterfactual history in one place and covertly using it in others.[11]

But even scholars sympathetic to counterfactual history may not fully appreciate how ubiquitous what-if reasoning is in historical narratives. For instance, counterfactual arguments play just as critical a role for those who take a deterministic perspective on the rise of the West (what happened was inevitable) as for those who take an antideterministic stand (what happened could easily have been otherwise). The latter, who depict major outcomes as easily undone with a trivial tweaking of antecedents, feel little pressure once embarked on a train of inference to keep history close to the reality track. They often organize their arguments into pyramidal structures layered with increasingly higher order counterfactuals in which hypothetical worlds diverge increasingly radically from our world. In chapter 2, for example, Victor Davis Hanson treats an initial what-if conjecture ("if Themistocles had been ousted as commander of the Athenian fleet before the battle of Salamis in 480 BC, the Athenians would have adopted a different strategy") as the foundation for second-order counterfactuals that push the hypothetical world farther from the actual ("without Themistocles, the Athenians would have adopted a different strategy and therefore would have lost the battle"), which in turn provides the foundation for third- and fourth-order counterfactuals that take us even farther from the world we inhabit ("if the Athenians had lost, all Greece would have fallen, and if Greece had fallen to the Persians then key ideas in the Western canon would have been lost, probably forever").[12]

By contrast, those who take strongly deterministic positions—who depict major outcomes as difficult to "undo" with minor alterations of background conditions—often invoke "reversionary" counterfactuals that attenuate rather than amplify deviations from reality. They insist that, even if we grant the first-order counterfactual that "if x had been different, then some alternative outcome, y, would have occurred," history would have been but briefly derailed and quickly put back on track by the intercession of equilibrium-restoring causal forces. Thus, in chapter 3, Barry Strauss grants Hanson that it was in no sense inevitable that Themistocles had to command the Athenian fleet, but he is not convinced that an alternative commander would have failed to repel the Persian onslaught. Strauss displays more faith in the talent pool available to the Athenian polity than does Hanson (who suspects that all plausible alternatives to Themistocles would have proved not up to this task). Strauss also provides several layers of reversionary argument: his second-order counterfactual suggests that even after defeat at Salamis the Greeks might still have mounted an effective resistance on the mainland, his third-order counterfactual suggests that if that failed the Athenians might have mounted a counteroffensive from their Sicilian colonies, and his fourth-order defense maintains that even if the Persian empire had successfully been extended into the western Mediterranean with a Pax Persica rather than a Pax Romana key ideas identified with Greece would have been independently discovered by other peoples at later times.[13]

We focus on the chapters by Hanson and Strauss because they anchor relatively extreme endpoints on the determinism continuum, which ranges from the completely contingent to the totally foreordained. Most of our contributors—and probably most historians—take more moderate positions: the extent to which outcomes can be "unmade" hinges on exactly where and when those outcomes pop up in the historical flow of events.

We do not believe it possible to formalize the profoundly intuitive process by which seasoned observers come to the conclusion that history has locked in certain possibilities and locked out others, but we can examine a simple game that captures some of the basic causal intuitions likely to be activated at varying points in the narratives that follow.

The game, known as Polya's urn, starts with an urn containing one red and one blue ball.[14] Players are instructed to remove one ball, at random, and return it to the urn, accompanied by an additional ball of the same color. And they repeat this procedure until they have filled the urn. If the urn starts out with one red and one blue ball, then the odds of picking either color start out even, but after a player takes a red ball, and returns both it and a like-colored ball, the odds shift. There are now two red balls and one blue, so on the next move the odds of picking red are 2 to 1. And if a red ball is picked again and returned with a mate, there will be three red balls to one blue ball and the chances of picking a red ball will have risen from 50 to 75 percent in just two moves. If one keeps picking in accord with the prevailing chances, which increasingly favor red, the odds climb so swiftly that red balls will soon overwhelm. It will be easy to forget that the odds of the urn going "red" or "blue" were once even.

The counterfactual turning points for imagining alternative outcomes to a given Polya urn game are thus clustered in the early phases of the game, and much the same can be said for many historical processes, be they the emergence of a religious movement (Carlos M. N. Eire on Christ or the origins of the Church of England) or of a dynamic economy (Joel Mokyr on the Industrial Revolution and Kenneth Pomeranz on China) or of a military power. Once things start moving in any particular direction, they pick up momentum, increasing the odds of further movement in the same direction and rapidly transforming the improbable into the inevitable. Disputes over historical causality often revolve around disagreements over how to separate those moments when alternative outcomes seem evenly balanced, as at the beginning of the Polya urn game, from those when trends seem so self-reinforcing that they feel unstoppable.

The Polya urn game captures recurring themes in debates over the rise of the West to which we shall return in our concluding chapter. Here, however, it is worth highlighting three of these themes.

(a) Initial unpredictability and massive potential for random effects. At the start of the process, it is impossible to predict the final ratio of red to blue balls: it could range from 99.99 percent red to .01 percent red. Early draws, which have a massive random element, have a disproportionate effect on which of possible equilibria will ultimately emerge. This is where we find the greatest potential for small causes to have big effects (also known as butterfly effects).[15] Accidental events early in the sequence do not inevitably cancel each other out and should not be dismissed as mere "noise." Drawing just a few blue balls in succession early on can jump-start a positive feedback loop in which blue begets blue, thereby locking history into a predominantly blue future.

Some historians see signs that small Western advantages had already begun to compound and reinforce each other in positive feedback loop fashion as far back as twenty-five hundred years ago in ancient Greece or more recently in fifteenth-century Europe, setting the stage for the dramatic overseas expansion of the Iberian powers. But there are serious divisions of professional opinion here. Other historians see little evidence that European civilization was on the fast track to global dominance that far back in the past. Other powers—Islam, China, and even the Mongols—could have been equally or more promising contenders. The strongest proponents of this view argue that the more we focus our magnifying lens on the early stages of this mysterious process the clearer it becomes how much hinges on seemingly endless tiny details of the "Cleopatra's nose" variety: the wiliness of Themistocles, the vacillations of Pontius Pilate, or William of Orange's narrow brushes with death in battle.

(b) A steady increase in inflexibility (and reduced potential for butterfly effects). Later draws contribute only minutely to the distribution of balls in the Polya urn, and the distribution settles into an equilibrium range. It is relatively straightforward to determine when things have settled into a stable equilibrium range in Polya-urn thought experiments. The sampling parameters are well defined. Those conditions are, however, rarely satisfied in history, and thus debates over when trends became irreversible are notoriously difficult to resolve. A key point of contention in the rise of the West debate concerns roughly when the geopolitical balance favoring the West settled into an equilibrium range and when it ceases to be useful to look for close-call counterfactuals that produce lasting effects that cannot be easily undone by equilibrium-restoring second-order counterfactuals. The zone of most active controversy hovers between AD 1500 and 1800. If we go back five hundred or more years, most observers find it easy to think of what-if scenarios that either enfeeble the West or empower one of the rest; by contrast, after 1800 virtually everyone concedes that it is well-nigh impossible to come up with such scenarios.

(c) Potential path inefficiency. In the long run, the locked-in path may leave most of us poorer and more miserable than the alternative paths would have left us. Invincible optimists aside, the odds are that we do not inhabit the best of all possible worlds, and there is even a reasonable chance that we have slipped into the lower end of the distribution of once possible worlds—the ontological slums. This insight will come as no shock to those who feel victimized by Western colonialism and believe that but for the forces of chance their civilizations could have been "contenders."[16] But the potential for regret is not limited to the third world. Things could have gone far better (and perhaps worse) for every definable subgroup of humans on which we care to shine the counterfactual spotlight. By reminding us of paths not taken, counterfactual history can stoke a powerful array of what-if emotions ranging from regret to relief.[17] What did "we" or "they" do right or wrong? What could we or they have done differently? What should be done now? Who owes what to whom? When we concentrate our explanatory efforts on the great impersonal forces that push history onto one path or another, we short-circuit, for better or for worse, these morally, emotionally, and angst-laden debates.

The Psychological Case for Counterfactual History

Historical observers—be they card-carrying historians or historically minded social scientists—are human beings, creatures of bounded rationality, whose minds are subject to the same principles of cognitive functioning as those of ordinary mortals.[18] Indeed, the very term *historical observer* is misleading insofar as it implies an objective encoding of reality. The world is too complex to understand without the aid of simplifying assumptions. The conclusions we cull from the past are inevitably a difficult to disentangle mixture of what is actually historically present ("bottom-up" or "data-driven" information processing in the jargon of cognitive science) and what we expect to find ("top-down" or "theory-driven" information-processing). Although the relative importance of these two modes of thinking shifts from one observer to the next, and from one context to the next, it is a safe bet that one's initial mind-set at the commencement of the inquiry—the presuppositions behind the questions one deems worth posing—will be a potent determinant of the channels down which one pursues it. Where we begin our search determines, in no small measure, what we discover.[19]

Drawing on relevant work in cognitive science, we derive two propositions concerning the power of initial mind-sets to steer historical analysis down certain pathways rather than others. The first is the *framing postulate*. At the outset of any study, we confront a choice of mind-set so fundamental that it is almost always made on the basis of automatic cognitive habits rather than on principled philosophical positions of historical causality. We can frame our starting-point questions so that the focus is on either the actual world ("Why did the observed outcome occur, and when in the course of events did it become irreversible?") or on the set of alternative or counterfactual worlds ("Why did the once viable alternatives to the observed outcome fail to occur, and when did they become impossible?").[20]

From a narrowly logical point of view, making a big fuss about alternative framings of historical questions is odd because, far from being contradictory, factual and counterfactual framings are complementary. As soon as one decides that x has become inevitable (a probability of 1.0), one answers the question "At what point did $\sim x$ outcomes become impossible?" (a probability of zero). Likewise, as soon as one estimates the likelihood of Western geopolitical domination at time y to be 1 in 3, one estimates the likelihood of alternatives to Western domination to be 2 in 3.

Logical complementarity does not, however, imply psychological compatibility. There is often a palpable tension between these two ways of teasing insights from the past: both thoughtful introspection and experimental evidence tell us that factual and counterfactual framings of historical questions trigger qualitatively different mental processes in historical observers. Factual framings produce searches for deterministic "what made it happen" accounts of the past, whereas counterfactual framings produce searches for antideterministic accounts that keep pushing back the last possible moment when something else could have happened.[21]

Scholars who opt for a factual framing of their opening questions find it natural to devote the bulk of their explanatory energy to the tectonic forces that inexorably pushed history down the only path it could have taken. Applied to the rise of the West debate, this framing puts the spotlight on a fundamental fact of our world—Western dominance—and invites analysts to mobilize their favorite explanatory themes in ways that render the victorious ascent of Europe (and later Europe and North America) the likely, and eventually the inevitable, result of powerful forces working on well-specified background conditions. The resulting deterministic accounts emphasize now familiar themes: deeply rooted traditions of property rights, greater separation of church and state, stronger incentives to explore scientific questions and engineer technological spin-offs, and a competitive state system that punished laggards. Whatever the exact balancing of causal forces in the portfolio of explanations, there is a common (albeit usually implicit) cutoff point for inquiry: one has done a good job when one has pieced together an account that convinces thoughtful readers that things pretty much had to work out when, where, and how they did.[22]

By contrast, scholars who frame their questions counterfactually shift the spotlight from what happened to what could have happened. They find it natural to devote most of their energy to exploring the myriad alternative paths that history could have taken and to understanding why these once possible worlds became impossible. This framing encourages the question "How close did history come to serving up a different menu of outcomes?" Is it possible, with minimal tampering, to undo Western dominance—to redirect events so that Europe never "rises" (e.g., because of a shift in tactics at Salamis that permits the Persians to defeat the Athenians) or so that its rise is nipped in the bud by merciless invaders (such as the Mongols in the thirteenth century)? And then, within European civilization, how easy is it to eliminate—by accident or disease or other quasi-random mechanisms—one of the multitude of necessary conditions for jump-starting the positive feedback cycle of scientific investigation, technical innovation, and commercial and military application that underlay the exponential expansion of European influence? Finally, assuming European ascendancy, could it have taken a more malign or benign form than it did? Might not one of the many internal bids to achieve European hegemony—say by Nazi Germany and its allies—have succeeded, thus further brutalizing the nature of Western world domination? Alternatively, had the Spanish Hapsburgs heeded those who, like Fray Bartolomé de Las Casas, urged an end to servitude in the Americas and the humane treatment of all subjects of the crown, might the Europeans have sought partnerships rather than profits in the New World?[23]

Whatever the exact character of these counterfactual worlds, there is again a common (albeit usually implicit) cutoff point for inquiry: one has done a good job when one has convinced thoughtful readers that, right up to the last minute, things did not have to work out as they did. Nevertheless, we are by no means agnostic on which framing bias poses the more serious threat to scholarship. Our second guiding hypothesis, the *hindsight-bias postulate,* identifies good reasons for believing that observers of the past are prone to rely too much on factual frames and to slight, even ignore, counterfactual frames.[24] Factual framing, which takes the real world as its starting point, comes more naturally to most of us than counterfactual framing, which requires constructing alternatives to that world.

Experimental work in cognitive science reinforces our suspicion that counterfactual arguments often need a special boost to get a fair hearing. Work on hindsight bias shows that as soon as observers learn the outcome of an historical process they begin to reorganize their understanding of causal forces at work so that the outcome appears more retrospectively foreseeable than it was prospectively.[25] In one ingenious study, the experimenters told participants about a battle in nineteenth-century India between the Gurkhas and the British in which there were good reasons to expect either side to win. Terrain and weather favored the former; training and equipment favored the latter. Some participants were then told that the British won, others were told that the Gurkhas won, and still others were told nothing. Significantly, those participants given outcome information not only convinced themselves that "their" outcome was more likely than the other possibility; they erroneously recollected that they knew all along which outcome would happen! "Outcome knowledge" thus contaminated observers' perceptions of the past, making it exceptionally difficult for them to recall what they once thought possible, even probable. The ironic result is that events experts deem improbable ex ante are often judged by those same experts as overdetermined ex post.[26]

This well-replicated effect is no hothouse flower that survives only in the rarefied environs of psychological laboratories. There is no shortage of real-world examples. Few in the early 1980s predicted the rise of the East Asian "tigers" or the collapse of the Soviet Union, yet virtually everyone today who claims professional competence in such matters can muster half a dozen "fundamental" or "structural" causes why these outcomes had to happen roughly when and how they did.[27] The same phenomenon can be observed every time a bull market in stocks suddenly metamorphoses into a bear market. Looking back, commentators find it hard to resist the inference—given how easy it is now to spot the indicators of egregious overvaluation—that investors back then were a tad dense not to have appreciated where events were heading. And, hearkening back to the 9/11 Commission's warning, cited in the preface to this volume, that "the path of what happened is so brightly lit that it places everything else into shadow," imagine that the nineteen hijackers were somehow apprehended before they could achieve their mission. The terrorist threat posed by Al-Qaeda would have remained, but would there have been near-unanimous support in the United States for bombing Afghanistan just three weeks later? To pose the question is to answer it: "creeping determinism" is the most fundamental obstacle to the time-honored objective of historians to see the world as it appeared to decision makers then, not as it looks now.

It is also an obstacle of more than just academic interest. To illustrate this, consider the origins of the "Troubles" that plagued the Irish province of Ulster in the late twentieth century. In almost every account, four early episodes stand out as turning points.

- In 1969, a radical group of civil rights activists (mainly Catholics) staged a march at Burntollet that Protestant militants savagely disrupted, stimulating attacks by Protestants on Catholics elsewhere, with extensive destruction of property and some loss of life.
- In 1970, a series of arms searches by British security forces in Catholic areas of Belfast led to confrontations and killings, fatally undermining the confidence of most Catholics in the impartiality of the British army.
- In 1971, the "internment" of large numbers of Catholics suspected of subversion by the British security forces, based in part on inaccurate intelligence and carried out with widespread brutality, exacerbated the disillusion, anger, and intransigence of the Catholic population.
- In 1972, the deployment of the British Parachute Regiment to contain an anti-Internment march in the city of Derry resulted in a confrontation on "Bloody Sunday" in which the soldiers shot to death fourteen civilians and injured many more.

In a rare show of unanimity, both Protestants and Catholics normally regard each of these episodes as "inevitable" steps on the path to continuing sectarian violence. Yet the surviving records show that well-placed observers *at the time* vigorously opposed each of these provocative actions. Many civil rights activists argued against the Burntollet march because they predicted (correctly) that it would provoke a disproportionate Protestant backlash, many British politicians feared that arms searches among only one of the embattled religious groups would worsen rather than improve the situation, and senior soldiers opposed both Internment (because they knew they lacked sufficient current intelligence to protect the innocent) and the deployment of the Parachute Regiment against the Derry march (because of its record of aggressive harassment of Catholics in the past). Had any of these "alternative voices" been heeded—or had the London government displaced the pro-Protestant Northern Ireland executive in 1968 or 1969 rather than 1972 (yet another alternative discussed at the time)—the "inevitable" drift of Ulster into three decades of violence might have been averted.

The recognition that the emergence of the "Troubles" was contingent rather than inevitable will not, of course, make the human and material waste of the past any easier to confront or bear; but it should certainly promote an awareness that current and future political choices can (and must) be made from a wide universe of possibilities and not from an overdetermined past that permits only one inevitably divisive response. The world today is plagued by strife-torn societies in which participants use a selective view of their collective past simultaneously to validate their own agenda and invalidate those of their opponents, not only Catholics and Protestants in Northern Ireland but also Israel and Palestine in the Middle East, India and Pakistan in South Asia, North and South Korea, or China and Taiwan in the Far East. The contenders in each conflict not only see their own view of the past as the sole one endowed with validity (and therefore by definition those of their opponents as invalid); more dangerously, for that very reason each also sees a continuation of the conflict as inevitable. Applying counterfactual reasoning to the crucial junctures, to the events perceived as turning points in the early stages of the conflict, reveals repeatedly the existence not only of alternative "roads not taken" but also of advocates who argued strenuously in favor of those alternatives (and often correctly anticipated the deleterious consequences of taking the road actually followed). This is hindsight bias at its most dangerous and pernicious; here, especially, granting contingency its due is essential to the task of understanding and therefore explaining the past.[28]

The most effective cure for the intellectual complacency of hindsight bias turns out to be encouraging people to think counterfactually about history. The experimental literature suggests that if we want to prevent outcome knowledge from distorting our recollections of what we once suspected would transpire we should try to imagine ways in which alternative outcomes could have come about.[29] To be sure, performing such exercises does not come naturally to most participants in experiments, and it probably does not come naturally to most historians and social scientists. But the exercise does have the salutary effect of deflating the "it had to work out that way" attitudes toward the past. Giving freer rein to our imaginations can stop the real world from occluding our vision of possible worlds that may have "almost" come into being at various junctures in history.

Counterfactual Thought Experiments and Their Enemies

What is obvious to us—the unavoidability of counterfactual history and the necessity of learning to do it well—has not been obvious to all historians. Of the many critics, Edward Hallett Carr (1892–1982) stands out as the most uncompromising and influential. His slim volume *What Is History?* (which has sold over 250,000 copies to date, vastly more than any other text on historical method, and remains a staple of all university courses on historiography) made his views plain. "History is," he wrote, "a record of what people did, not of what they failed to do: to this extent it is inevitably a success story." Those who ask "what if?" were therefore for Carr just "bad losers." "In a group or a nation which is riding in the trough, not on the crest, of historical events, theories that stress the role of chance or accident in history will be found to prevail." Best known of all is his declaration: "One can always play a parlour-game with the might-have-beens of history. But they have nothing . . . to do with history."[30]

One could argue that the stridency and intransigence of Carr's views arose because he originally advanced them in the form of lectures drafted in just one month and published almost exactly as they were delivered. But this would be wrong. Carr had been reading widely on the philosophy of history for almost twenty years, and his trenchant statement marked but one exchange in a prolonged debate with other scholars on causation in history. Moreover, for twenty years before that, first at the British Foreign Office and then as assistant editor of the London *Times*, Carr had refined the art of drawing up documents designed to influence policy.[31] He therefore deliberately adopted a polemical tone and scrupulously named his targets (Isaiah Berlin and Karl Popper; Arnold Toynbee and Hugh Trevor-Roper; the members of the Cambridge University History Faculty seated in the lecture hall before him) before skewering them. Two decades later, in his notes for a second edition, Carr remained an unrepentant determinist, dismissing the idea that history might evolve in a random way as "a reflexion of the cultural pessimism of the age. Randomness is an enthronement of ignorance."[32]

Because Carr epitomizes the opponents of counterfactual history, and because so many other scholars have accepted his argument almost without question, a careful reexamination of his argument, its antecedents, and its consequences seems justified. His various objections—recycled in most subsequent critiques—fall under the three principal headings noted earlier: that counterfactual history is hopelessly arbitrary, hopelessly speculative, and hopelessly self-serving. We freely admit that there are many examples of past counterfactual studies to which each indictment fairly applies, but the indictments do not address flaws inherent in the enterprise but rather the flaws inherent in any carelessly executed historical endeavor.[33]

Counterfactual History Is Hopelessly Arbitrary

Carr appreciated that writing any sort of history was devilishly difficult. "From the infinite ocean of facts" the historian must "select those which are significant for his purpose." To simplify this otherwise impossible task, she or he must extract

> from the multiplicity of sequences of cause and effect . . . those, and only those, which are historically significant; and the standard of historical significance is his ability to fit them into his pattern of rational explanation and interpretation. Other sequences of cause and effect have to be rejected as accidental, not because the relation between cause and effect is different, but because the sequence itself is irrelevant. The historian can do nothing with it; it is not amenable to rational interpretation, and has no meaning for either the past or the present.

For Carr "the essence of the historian's job" was "dragging into prominence the forces which have triumphed and thrusting into the background those which they have swallowed up."[34]

This influential passage reveals Carr as an unapologetic proponent of framing historical questions in exclusively factual ways: exploiting all the benefits conferred by hindsight, the historian's chief analytical task is to identify why events had to take the path they did to explain why ex post facto no other path was possible. Counterfactual historians work against this prescriptive grain when they try to resurrect alternative worlds from the graveyard of dead possibilities. Indeed, from Carr's perspective, they risk being overwhelmed by the sheer vastness of the possibilities. We therefore translate his first challenge to counterfactual history into the following challenge: "What criteria—aside from hindsight—can scholars use in choosing which events, forces or agents to place in the narrative foreground and which to relegate to the background?"

Counterfactual History Is Hopelessly Speculative

Carr was also convinced that, even if we could agree on reasonable starting points for what-if speculation, disciplined inquiry would still be impossible for the simple reason that he could see nothing to stop counterfactual history from degenerating into a "parlour game." To make his case, he could point to many examples of such degeneration in the existing what-if literature. Some counterfactual historians write as if they have carte blanche to project whatever they want into their hypothetical worlds—settling old scores; indulging fantasies; amusing themselves and readers with comic coincidences; and above all, titillating those quintessentially counterfactual emotions of regret (over better worlds that almost were) and relief (over worse fates that we barely escaped). Carelessly practiced, counterfactual history quickly becomes a branch of social science fiction.[35]

One of the most famous "lapses into imaginary history" appeared in a collection of what-if historical essays published in 1931: Winston Churchill's "If Lee Had Not Won the Battle of Gettysburg."[36] With characteristic flare, Churchill served up a double-negative counterfactual that was supposedly written from the standpoint of the "real world" in which Lee won, and the later observer correctly guesses the disastrous consequences in the hypothetical world (our world) had Lee been defeated: Reconstruction and carpetbaggers, the Spanish-American War, the ruin of Europe by World War I. Churchill rejoiced that by creating two strong federal republics in North America instead of just one Lee's victory had averted all these mishaps.

Nevertheless, counterfactual musings always require factual checks, and inspection of the key connecting principle that links Churchill's antecedent to the hypothesized consequences reveals that he grounded his counterfactual exercise on an absurd factual premise: that immediately after his victory at Gettysburg Lee issued a "declaration abolishing slavery." This is patently ridiculous. Even a cursory glance at the literature—newspapers, pamphlets, speeches—that appeared in the secessionist states between 1855 and 1864 reveals that slavery formed the bedrock on which the entire cause rested. In the words of Confederate vice president Alexander Stephens, the new republic gloried in the "great truth, that the Negro is not equal to the white man; that slavery—subordination to the superior race—is his natural and normal condition." Admittedly, as a measure of desperation, in the last months of the war the Confederate Congress voted to recruit and arm black troops (albeit without necessarily emancipating them), but even then some white Confederate soldiers deserted rather serve alongside blacks, while others voiced their distaste. Lee, who in any case always vehemently upheld the subordination of military to civilian authority in such matters, would surely have avoided the issue of emancipation as long as his troops held the upper hand.

Carr was right to dismiss "lapses into imaginary history" such as Churchill's; but the carelessness of one practitioner does not automatically discredit the practice. His second challenge to counterfactual history therefore runs: "What criteria can scholars use to winnow out such frivolous scenarios and to stop speculation from running riot?"

Counterfactual History Is Hopelessly Self-Serving

Carr's third objection was that counterfactual arguments, far from being too imaginative, often march in lockstep with the ideological agenda of the investigator. In the absence of strong reality checks, he asserted, historical observers will take advantage of the collapse of traditional barriers to biased scholarship and invent scenarios that justify whatever policy or theoretical claims they desire to promote.[37]

As it happens, other writings by Carr himself provide a perfect demonstration of this danger. They deserve detailed consideration because they epitomize both his methodological inconsistency and the dangers inherent in a careless application of counterfactual arguments. It is now no secret that throughout the 1930s Carr advocated the appeasement of Nazi Germany. First, at the British Foreign Office, as the official largely responsible for Central and Southeastern European affairs, he repeatedly advocated giving Hitler whatever he wanted in order to preserve peace. Thus, in October 1934, while on a tour of Austria, Carr told an American diplomat that he

[d]id not believe that the absorption of Austria by Germany under Hitler will be prevented in the long run by Italy or by any combination of forces and that it was much better, therefore, to permit the Austrian-German union to come to a conclusion. . . . [He] believes that [Hitler] would stop at the border of Hungary and other non-German frontiers. Hitlerism . . . was a purely German invention and would find little sympathy elsewhere in Europe.

Eighteen months later, Carr advised his superiors in the British government that since "Austrian independence continues to exist only to the good pleasure of Germany, [and] the same may be said of the independence of Czechoslovakia," Britain should give its blessing to Germany's annexation of both countries.[38]

When the evils of appeasement had become apparent, however, Carr resorted to historical counterfactuals—albeit only as they are so often used in policy debates: to reduce the cognitive dissonance (and embarrassment) of acknowledging that he had been wrong by arguing that "I was almost right and if only the policy I favored had been properly implemented, things would have worked out so much better." Thus, in the last chapter of *The Twenty Years' Crisis, 1919–1939,* completed a few weeks before the outbreak of World War II, he wrote:

In March 1939 the Prime Minister [Neville Chamberlain] admitted that in all the modifications of the Treaty [of Versailles] down to and including the Munich Agreement, there was "something to be said for the necessity of a change in the existing situation." If, in 1935 and 1936, this "something" had been clearly and decisively said, to the exclusion of scoldings and protests, by the official spokesmen of the status quo Powers, it might not yet have been too late to bring further changes within the framework of peaceful negotiation.[39]

Blinded by such prejudice, the outbreak of war with Germany in September 1939 therefore "came as a shock" to Carr, but he quickly adjusted: "As I became less inclined to appease Hitler," he wrote candidly in a memoir, "I became more inclined to appease Stalin."[40] In 1941, Carr rejoiced when Soviet forces occupied the Baltic states "because only incorporation in some larger unit could restore prosperity to these little countries." Two years later he claimed that:

The sole interest of Russia is to assure herself that her outer defences are in sure hands; and this interest will be best served if the lands between her frontiers and those of Germany are held by governments and peoples friendly to herself. That is the one condition on which Russia must and will insist.[41]

In 1961, having realized that his new appeasement strategy was as misguided as the old, Carr once again resorted to counterfactual speculation. "Under Lenin," he wrote, the passage to a totalitarian regime in Soviet Russia "might not have been altogether smooth, but it would have been nothing like what happened. Lenin would not have tolerated the falsification of the record in which Stalin constantly indulged."[42] As with his justification for seeking to appease Hitler, Carr sought refuge in counterfactual reasoning to explain why events had perversely failed to evolve as he had predicted: to show why appeasing Stalin had not worked (and how easily it might have) and why the Bolshevik Revolution had produced so few benefits (although it had promised so much). Carr's flagrant display of precisely the bad loser mentality that he ridiculed in *What Is History?* highlights both the universality of counterfactual reasoning and, a fortiori, the need to recognize it.[43]

Discovering that even the sharpest critic of the self-serving tendency in counterfactual history himself used counterfactual history in a self-serving manner illustrates in graphic fashion the need to institutionalize checks on the practice. Carr's third challenge thus runs: "What is to stop historians from using counterfactuals simply to 'prop up their prejudices'?"

Procedural Questions in Designing and Conducting Thought Experiments

Answering these three fundamental objections to counterfactual history helped to frame the key questions—procedural and substantive—that this collection of essays would address. Indeed, we crafted three procedural requests for our contributors expressly in order to address (and, we hope, to neutralize) each of them.

Procedural Request 1: Address the "Arbitrariness" Critique

We asked contributors "to be explicit about how they selected, from the vast universe of possibilities, the pivotal junctures at which they believe history could have been redirected." Their answers reveal Carr's "arbitrariness" critique to be wrong. Our contributors chose starting points for their thought experiments in remarkably consistent and disciplined ways. They all respected the minimal-rewrite rule, which excludes what-if scenarios that begin with wild departures from reality (sometimes called "miracle" counterfactuals), and instead launched their inquiries from plausible premises that require tweaking as little of the actual historical record as possible. They ignore fantasies, such as how the Persians might have won at Salamis if only they had had an aircraft carrier, and instead debate how the outcome of the battle might have been altered if a particular human being, the Athenian naval commander Themistocles, had been less intelligent or more risk averse than he was. All contributors to this volume focus on people or things that stand out as "odd," given local historical norms, and that could thus be imagined as easily reverting back to the norm for that time and place. Themistocles is thus doubly fair game: as a human being, subject to all of the frailties of flesh, he passes the minimal-rewrite test (he is easy to delete without altering a lot of other historical facts); and as a human being with unusual talents and opinions, he also passes the "oddball" test.[44]

Procedural Request 2: Address the Objection That Counterfactual History Is Hopelessly Speculative

Perhaps speculation is an appropriate teaching tool in creative writing classes, but it is not appropriate for serious students of history. We therefore asked contributors "to be explicit about the connecting principles they used to draw conclusions about what would have happened if their hypothesized antecedents had taken on other forms." Most contributors adopted three criteria for justifying the connecting principles in their counterfactual scenarios: consistency with well-established historical facts and regularities, consistency with well-established statistical generalizations that transcend what is true at a particular time and place, and consistency with well-established theoretical laws of cause and effect (from the physical, biological, and even social sciences).[45]

The key point is that, whether scholars advance counterfactual scenarios in the service of a deterministic or antideterministic agenda, we need to recognize that as such scenarios grow increasingly elaborate the connecting principles linking antecedents and consequences become increasingly vulnerable to challenge. This is so because logic dictates that the overall probability of a multilinkage argument cannot be greater than, and is almost always less than, the probability of the weakest link in the chain of events. The deeper authors try to see into the futures of their counterfactual worlds the frailer their connecting principles become.[46]

Procedural Request 3: Address the Objection That Counterfactual Thought Experiments Are Hopelessly Self-Serving

We asked all contributors "to be explicit about the distinctive benefits of framing historical questions in counterfactual forms, about which schools of thought are most likely to take umbrage at the conclusions they reached, about what surprised them in working through their thought experiments." Their responses show that counterfactual thought experiments can pack an unexpected intellectual punch because our contributors used their alternative scenarios to probe for gaps and contradictions in a wide range of perspectives on world history.

Skeptics might still object, however, that it is one matter to goad long-standing adversaries and quite another to make "discoveries" in thought experiments that undermine one's own entrenched positions. Indeed, one clever put-down portrays counterfactual exercises as the intellectual equivalent of the marbelator, an invention, Charles Tilly averred, of his uncle. One activates the device by inserting a small marble into the slot at the top, and the ball begins its antic trip through the machine. It clicks and whirs across bridges, down steps, and around corners, sometimes speeding and sometimes dawdling, often veering into the depths of the runways only to shoot out unexpectedly at a lower level. But, after all the commotion, when the marble rolls out of the bottom chute, we still have the same marble.[47]

The what-if premise of a given historical counterfactual—the initial alteration of history—is the marble; the belief system of the historical observer is the elaborate apparatus through which the marble passes. As the counterfactual slowly winds its way through the mind of the observer, it may well trigger a multitude of images and associations that parallel the clicking and whirring of the marbelator: "Well, if x had happened, y might have fallen from power, the discovery of z have been delayed, and such-and-such doctrinal dispute have been resolved differently." In the end, however, the intellectual yield is zero: we discover nothing more than the intellectual prejudices with which we began the inquiry.

For the record, we see the "hopelessly self-serving" challenge as the toughest of all the objections to counterfactual history. Missourian skeptics of a "show-me" bent have a point: if there is no way to check whose claims about "possible worlds" are right or wrong, there is no point in continuing the conversation. How can we surprise ourselves when we ourselves are the source of all the inputs in the experiment? But here the skeptics underestimate humanity in two key respects: our capacity to engage in rigorous self-scrutiny and our capacity to bring alternative worlds to imaginative life.

Counterfactual thought experiments can be, but do not have to be, marbelators. We are capable of uncovering flaws in our thinking, of looking at old facts in new lights, and of infusing imaginative life into lost worlds. And it is in this spirit that we invite readers to explore the chapters in this volume. Each essay offers a distinctively counterfactual perspective on the complex interplay between chance and necessity in shaping world history. Each grapples with the subtle issues that arise in adjudicating conflicting claims about what could or might or would have been but for . . .

NOTES

Andrew Roberts, ed., *What Might Have Been* (London: Weidenfeld, 2004), 3; Stephen J. Gould, *Full House* (New York: Random House, 1996), 164.

1. Strong warnings against wandering down the counterfactual path have come in such prominent British and American scholarly works as Alan J. P. Taylor, *The Struggle for Mastery in Europe, 1848–1918* (Oxford: Clarendon, 1954); Edward Hallett Carr, *What Is History?* (London: Penguin, 1961); David Hackett Fischer, *Historians' Fallacies: Toward a Logic of Historical Thought* (New York: Harper and Row, 1970); and Edward P. Thompson, "The Poverty of Theory," in *The Poverty of Theory and Other Essays* (London: Merlin Press, 1978). The debate for and against counterfactual history has engaged British and American historians notably more than historians from other countries. Even *Historia virtual de España (1870–2004). ¿Qué hubiera pasado si . . . ?* (Madrid: Taurus, 2004), was edited by a British scholar (Nigel Townson) and Britons contributed two of its nine essays!

2. Richard J. Evans, "Telling It Like It Wasn't," *Historically Speaking* 5, no. 4 (2004), http://www.bu.edu/historic/hs/marcho4.htm. See note 11 on the ideological bias.

3. See page 3 above. For equally strong affirmations of both the utility and feasibility of counterfactual history, see Hugh R. Trevor-Roper, "History and Imagination," in *History and Imagination: Essays in Honour of H. R. Trevor-Roper,* ed. Hugh Lloyd-Jones, Valerie Pearl, and Blair Worden (London: Duckworth, 1981); Geoffrey Hawthorn, *Plausible Worlds: Possibility and Understanding in History and the Social Sciences* (Cambridge: Cambridge University Press,

1991); Niall Ferguson, ed., *Virtual History: Alternatives and Counterfactuals* (London: Picador, 1997); Robert Cowley, ed., *What If?: The World's Foremost Military Historians Imagine What Might Have Been* (New York: Putnam, 2000); and Robert Cowley, ed., *What If? 2: Eminent Historians Imagine What Might Have Been* (New York: Putnam, 2001).

4. See Carr, *What Is History?* especially chapter 4. See also pp. 28–34. We feel justified in treating Carr's (1961) objections to counterfactual history as canonical because they appear to have effectively anticipated all the major lines of criticism since then. In his influential critique, for instance, Richard Evans ("Telling It Like It Wasn't") forcefully restates two of Carr's concerns: the power of this seductive genre to trick us into treating imaginative guesswork as a form of reliable knowledge and the susceptibility of the genre to political agendas (especially the "New Right," represented most prominently by Niall Ferguson).

5. Philip E. Tetlock and Aaron Belkin, eds., *Counterfactual Thought Experiments in World Politics* (Princeton, NJ: Princeton University Press, 1996), chapter 1; Roy Sorenson, *Thought Experiments* (New York: Oxford University Press, 1992).

6. Robert Fogel, "The New Economic History: Its Findings and Methods," *Economic History Review*, 2nd ser., 19 (1966): 642–56; *Railways and America's Economic Growth: Essays in Interpretive Econometric History* (Baltimore: Johns Hopkins University Press, 1964).

7. Baruch Fischhoff, "Hindsight Is Not Equal to Foresight: The Effect of Outcome Knowledge on Judgment under Uncertainty," *Journal of Experimental Psychology: Human Perception and Performance* 1 (1975): 288–99. Jack Goldstone, in "The Problem of the 'Early Modern' World," *Journal of the Economic and Social History of the Orient* 41 (1998): 249–84, argues that the term *early modern* is itself a manifestation of hindsight bias inasmuch as it implies a foreordained pathway toward modernity.

8. Our argument here parallels in some respects that recently advanced by Martin Bunzl, in "Counterfactual History: A User's Guide," *American Historical Review* 109 (2004): 435–42. We agree with Bunzl that counterfactual reasoning grounded in factual detail and strong theory is indispensable to causal analysis. But we see less danger, and more value, than Bunzl does in with high-imaginative-content counterfactuals of the sort deployed in the Ferguson and Cowley volumes (and by Eire in this volume). The value does not lie in surface content—in the literal truth status of the claims made—because, as both Bunzl and Evans correctly observe, the authors of high-imaginative-content counterfactuals overtly claim to know more than is humanly possible. The key is to read such tales with the right attitude: maintaining a skeptical distance from the specific claims advanced but still appreciating that ripping what-if yarns provide critical checks to the otherwise pervasive grip of hindsight bias.

9. N. Goodman, *Fact, Fiction, and Forecast* (Cambridge: Harvard University Press, 1983); Sorenson, *Thought Experiments*.

10. Given the recent flurry of accusations that counterfactual history must serve an ideological agenda (Evans, "Telling It Like It Wasn't"), we hasten to add that our arguments for looking at history from a counterfactual perspective are not rooted in an ideological desire to give an unfair cognitive advantage to the

"West was just lucky" camp. To the contrary, we seek only to eliminate what we see as the unfair advantage rooted in the hindsight bias enjoyed by all determinists—not just in the rise of the West debate but in other historical controversies as well.

11. Philip E. Tetlock, "Social Psychology and World Politics," in *Handbook of Social Psychology*, ed. Daniel T. Gilbert, Susan T. Fiske, and Gardner Lindzey (New York: McGraw Hill, 1998), 868–912; Wellington quoted in Roberts, *What Might Have Been*, 7. In this vein, it is useful to clear up the misconception, promoted by recent popular collections of what-if scenarios, that counterfactual history is a plaything reserved for scholars of an antideterministic bent who are convinced that history could have been radically rerouted by tiny changes in carefully targeted background conditions. Although counterfactual history holds special attractions for scholars of this persuasion, the pivotal distinction, we repeat, is not between those who do and do not use counterfactuals: determinists who insist that "if x had not occurred, then the observed outcome, y, would still have occurred" are making every bit as counterfactual a claim as their antideterministic brethren who insist that "if x had not occurred, the observed outcome, y, would not have occurred." The difference lies in the character of the higher-order counterfactual arguments that the competing schools of thought advance.

12. Other excellent examples of such arguments can be found in the chapters in this volume by Carlos M. N. Eire (chaps. 4 and 5), Jack A. Goldstone (chap. 6), and Robin D. S. Yates (chap. 8). On the general issue, see Philip E. Tetlock, "Close-Call Counterfactuals and Belief-System Defense: I Was Not Almost Wrong but I Was Almost Right," *Journal of Personality and Social Psychology* 75 (1998): 639–52; and Philip E. Tetlock, "Theory-Driven Reasoning about Possible Pasts and Probable Futures: Are We Prisoners of Our Preconceptions?" *American Journal of Political Science* 43 (1999): 335–66. "Second-order counterfactuals" are so labeled because they accept and build on initial or first-order counterfactuals of the form "if x had happened, then we would have entered a quite different world, y, rather than the world we inhabit, z." The effect in the first-order counterfactual then becomes the cause in the second-order counterfactual: "if y had happened, then we would have observed events that either take us even farther away from the world we know, z (deviation amplifying), or that cause history to revert back to our familiar z world (reversionary)."

13. Other excellent examples of arguments of this type may be found in the essays by Carla Gardina Pestana (chap. 7) and Holger H. Herwig (chapter 11). We fear that Richard Evans ("Telling It Like It Wasn't") has unfairly caricatured counterfactual history as inherently insensitive to the external constraints operating on the "kings and politicians" who are usually at the center of inquiry. It should be clear from this discussion, and from this volume, that counterfactual historians—like their mainstream brethren—vary widely in their openness to second-order counterfactual arguments that either bring history back on track (by invoking external constraints) or allow history to stray far from the observed path (by poking holes in external constraints).

14. P. Bak and K. Chen, "Self-Organized Criticality," *Scientific American*, January 1991, 46–53; D. McCloskey, "History, Differential Equations, and the Problem of Narration," *History and Theory* 30 (1991): 21–36.

15. Technically, the butterfly effect occurs whenever, in nonlinear systems of differential equations with feedback loops (*A* influences *B* and *B* influences *A*), trivial variations in the starting values of *A* and *B* (say, the initial populations of a predator and its prey in a forest) can have amazingly big effects over time (say, over twenty or thirty generations of interaction). The name was coined when it was observed in a computer simulation of weather patterns that small input errors for air pressure in one location produced unexpectedly different patterns of weather in remote locations several "weeks" later. The analogy is to a butterfly flapping its wings in Beijing triggering a tornado in Iowa several weeks later (for details, see McCloskey, "History").

16. Could have been a contender counterfactuals paraphrase the feelings of the bitter boxer played by Marlon Brando in the film *On the Waterfront*.

17. We do not want to leave the reductionist impression that we believe the stark simplicity of Polya's urn captures the full complexity of history. We claim only that the game is a remarkably concise way of capturing three often over-looked features of historical sequences: initial unpredictability, growing inflexibility with time, and the potential for locking into suboptimal arrangements—be they technological or sociological.

18. Susan Fiske and Shelley Taylor, *Social Cognition* (New York: McGraw-Hill, 1991).

19. The hedge "to some degree" allows us to distance ourselves from extreme relativist positions in the rancorous epistemological controversy over objectivity in history. See Peter Novick, *That Noble Dream: The Objectivity Question and the American Historical Profession* (New York: Cambridge University Press, 1988).

20. Philip E. Tetlock and Richard Ned Lebow, "Poking Counterfactual Holes in Covering Laws: Cognitive Styles and Historical Reasoning," *American Political Science Review* 95 (2001): 829–43.

21. Ibid.

22. Scott A. Hawkins and Reid Hastie, "Hindsight: Biased Judgments of Past Events after the Outcomes Are Known," *Psychological Bulletin* 107 (1990): 311–27.

23. For a delightful fictional exploration of how this might have materialized, see Orson Scott Card, *Pastwatch: The Redemption of Christopher Columbus* (New York: Tom Doherty, 1996). For popular accounts of a couple of brutal episodes that disgraced European expansion, see Adam Hochschild, *King Leopold's Ghost: A Story of Greed, Terror, and Heroism in Colonial Africa* (Boston: Houghton Mifflin, 1998); and, though exaggerated, Mike Davis, *Late Victorian Holocausts: El Niño Famines and the Making of the Third World* (London: Verso, 2001).

24. Empirical support for this postulate can be found in Fischhoff, "Hindsight Is Not Equal to Foresight." See also Hawthorn, *Plausible Worlds;* Tetlock and Belkin, *Counterfactual Thought Experiments;* and Ferguson, *Virtual History.* For parallel arguments in narrative theory, see Michael Bernstein, *Foregone Conclusions: Against Apocalyptic History* (Berkeley: University of California Press, 1994). See also pages 3–4 and 15.

25. Fischhoff, "Hindsight Is Not Equal to Foresight."

26. Hawkins and Hastie, "Hindsight."

27. Fischhoff, "Hindsight Is Not Equal to Foresight."

28. For further details, see the suggestive article by Richard English, "Coming to Terms with the Past: Northern Ireland," *History Today,* July 2004, 24–26. The more general principle at work here may well be a tendency for hard-liners to disparage as soft and naive speculation about missed opportunities for peace in dealing with adversaries who have been "essentialized" as evil (for more examples of how vehemently observers reject close calls that undercut idealized self-images, see Philip E. Tetlock, *Expert Political Judgment: How Good Is It? How Can We Know?* (Princeton: Princeton University Press, 2005), chap. 5.

29. For evidence on the "debiasing" power of "imagine the opposite" manipulations, see Derek Koehler, "Explanation, Imagination, and Confidence in Judgment," *Psychological Bulletin* 110 (1991): 499–519; Hawkins and Hastie, "Hindsight"; and John S. Carroll, "The Effect of Imagining an Event on Expectations for the Event: An Interpretation in Terms of the Availability Heuristic," *Journal of Experimental Social Psychology* 14 (1978): 88–96.

30. Carr, *What Is History?* 167, 132, 127. That this book remains required reading in "historiography seminars" across the English-speaking world more than forty years after its first appearance speaks volumes about the jargon-laden and convoluted works of historical theory published subsequently. Keith Jenkins, in "An English Myth? Rethinking the Contemporary Value of E. H. Carr's *What Is History?*" in *E. H. Carr: A Critical Appraisal,* ed. Michael Cox (New York: Palgrave, 2000), notes this paradox, observing that "even in 1961 Carr's was an old book: old-fashioned and fashioned in old ways" (319). But he fails to grasp that Carr's book survives in part because it remains so much more *readable* than the works of "Foucault, Barthes, Althusser, Derrida, Kristeva, Judith Butler" and the others with which Jenkins wants to numb the minds of aspiring history students. See also the parallel remarks of David Cannadine in *What Is History Now?* ed. David Cannadine (London: Palgrave, 2002), xi—a volume of essays that examines how various aspects of historical studies have evolved since 1961 and assesses how far they reflect the impact of Carr's book.

31. Details on how Carr composed and published his lectures appear in Jonathan Haslam, *The Vices of Integrity: E. H. Carr, 1892–1982* (London: Verso, 1999), 111, 112, 188, 189, 201. See also the thoughtful introduction to a new edition of *What Is History?* ed. Richard J. Evans (London: Palgrave, 2001); and his essay "*What Is History?*—Now," in Cannadine, *What Is History Now?* 1–18.

32. Carr's "proto-political style" is noted by Anders Stephanson in his "The Lessons of *What Is History?*" in Cox, *E. H. Carr,* 285; and by Evans in the 2001 reedition of Carr's book. In his reissue of *What Is History?* (London: Macmillan, 1986), reprinted by Evans in 2001, Robert W. Davies published and discussed Carr's notes for a second edition (quotation from p. xxv).

33. Some readers might ask why we expend so much effort parrying the essentially positivist objections of E. H. Carr and devote so little to exploring connections to other branches of historical theory. We are not philosophers of history, but we do see ourselves as occupying a besieged middle-ground position between the hard-line positivist insistence that history must deal with actual facts, not counterfacts, and the hard-line relativist stand that talking about historical

facts provides good grounds for concluding that one does not know what one is talking about. We find radical relativism as unpalatable as hard-line positivism. We believe that, even though perfect objectivity can never be achieved, it is worth upholding as an ideal and that historians are not—and should not be—free to invent whatever stories they wish about the past. See Novick, *That Noble Dream*.

But, that said, our approach to counterfactual history in certain respects superficially resembles certain postmodern critiques of history. We agree, for instance, with Hayden White, who wrote in *Tropics of Discourse* (Baltimore: John Hopkins University Press, 1978) 126–27, that "every historical discourse contains within it a full-blown, if only implicit, philosophy of history" and that the implicit guiding philosophy of the historian needs to be brought to "the surface of the text." In our view, one excellent way of bringing these implicit philosophies to the surface is by calling on historians to make explicit: (a) their assumptions about the degree to which there are branching points in the narrative at which events could easily have gone dramatically differently, and (b) their assumptions about the degree to which these alternative paths are knowable. Historians who put their counterfactual cards on the table in this manner reveal their implicit ontological assumptions (their acceptance or rejection of deterministic theories that imply either that certain things had to happen or could not possibly have happened) and their implicit epistemological assumptions (their views on the limits of what we can and cannot know about alternative counterfactual worlds).

We also agree with Keith Jenkins, in *Rethinking History* (London: Routledge, 1991), that history is, for a number of reasons, "epistemologically fragile"—that there are often serious limits on our ability to rule out alternative interpretations from the available evidence. It is a mistake to try to sweep under the rug of "objectivist narrative" these fragilities. Good scholarship is, among other things, transparent scholarship, and we see value in encouraging historians to be explicit about the branching points they perceive in their narratives and about the degree to which they think it is possible to make justifiable inferences about what would have happened had events gone down one of the alternative branching points. Finally, we agree with Roland Barthes, in "The Discourse of History," *Comparative Criticism* 3 (1981): 7–20, who maintains that, although the past can be represented in many tropes, some representations are less mystifying than others. The less mystifying ones tend to be more intellectually honest: they self-consciously call attention to their own methods of production and acknowledge the degree to which key components of their narratives and causal arguments are "theoretically constructed" rather than "empirically discovered." Openness about one's counterfactual assumptions is, in this view, a demystifying strategy.

34. Carr, *What Is History?*, 138, 168.

35. For counterfactual histories most aptly characterized as fiction, see most of the essays in J. C. Squire, ed., *If, or History rewritten* (1931), republished as *If It Happened Otherwise: Lapses into Imaginary History* (New York: Viking, 1932); John M. Merriman, ed., *For Want of a Horse: Choice and Chance in History* (Lexington, MA: Stephen Greene Press, 1985); Gregory Benford and Martin H. Greenberg, eds., *Hitler Victorious: Eleven Stories of the German Victory in World War II* (New York: Garden, 1988); and Robert Harris, *Fatherland* (New

York: Random House, 1992). Daniel Snowman, ed., *If I Had Been . . . Ten Historical Fantasies* (Totowa, NJ: Rowman and Littlefield, 1979), provides an honorable exception because he provided each contributor with a procedural agenda, asked them to make clear where their narrative departed from reality, and called for a "retrospective" in which the author assessed the plausibility of the alternative scenario constructed.

In *The World That Hitler Never Made: Alternate History and the Memory of Nazism* (New York: Cambridge University Press, 2005), Gavriel Rosenfeld is so impressed by the weakness of the reality constraints on counterfactual histories of World War II, and by the diverse fictional universes that popular writers routinely spin off from actual history, that he treats counterfactual history as though it were a cultural Rorschach test, revealing much about our contemporary obsessions but not much else. We generally share his view of the material he examines. But counterfactual history comes in many genres—and our focus here is on the power of serious counterfactual historians to deepen our analytic understanding of contingency and causation. Insofar as the cultural or ideological worldviews of analysts distort their analyses, we see all the greater need to establish standards that communities of scholars can apply to check the distortions, recognizing—of course—the impossibility of eliminating all distortions and achieving the chimerical ideal of objectivity.

36. Squire, *If*, 260–84. We thank Mark Grimsley for his help in framing the argument of the following paragraphs.

37. Richard J. Evans has recently made this argument anew; see the references and comments in note 46.

38. National Archives, Washington, DC, Record Series, M1209/4/0195, "Memorandum of Remarks by Mr. Carr of the British Foreign Office regarding Austria," forwarded to Secretary of State Cordell Hull, October 15, 1934; Alexander N. Lassner, " 'Peace at Hitler's Price': Austria, the Great Powers, and the Anschluss, 1932–38" (PhD diss., Ohio State University, 2002), 617, quoting Carr's memorandum of February 1936. We thank Dr Lassner for sharing with us his sensational new materials on the fatally misguided policies pursued by the Great Powers toward Austria during the 1930s.

39. E. H. Carr, *The Twenty Years' Crisis, 1919–1939: An Introduction to the Study of International Relations* (London: Macmillan, 1939), 281–82. Carr silently excised this and other egregious defenses of appeasement from later editions (see, in this case, *The Twenty Years' Crisis*, 2nd ed. [London: Macmillan, 1946], 222).

40. From E. H. Carr, "An Autobiography," written in 1980 and published in Cox, *E. H. Carr*, xix.

41. Charles Jones, *E. H. Carr and International Relations: A Duty to Lie* (Cambridge: Cambridge University Press, 1998), 95, quoting Carr, *The Future of Nations* (1941); Haslam, *The Vices of Integrity*, 102–3, quoting Carr's editorial in the *Times*, March 10, 1943. After the war, Carr the "political realist" (his own term), happy to sacrifice any states that got in the way of their powerful neighbors, effortlessly metamorphosed into Carr the "historical realist" and embarked on a fourteen-volume history that glorified the achievements of the Russian Revolution, in which, according to a perceptive review by Sir Isaiah Berlin, "Mr. Carr

sees history through the eyes of the victors; the losers have for him all but disqualified themselves from bearing witness" (quoted in Haslam, *The Vices of Integrity*, 196). Berlin would form one of Carr's principal targets in *What Is History?* See the telling discussion of the long and bitter debate between Berlin and Carr in Evans's 2001 edition of *What Is History?* xi–xxii.

42. Carr, *What Is History?*, 169–70. Here was a "parlour game" indeed! When Lenin's private papers became available in the 1990s, they showed a brutal, misanthropic, secretive, indecisive tactician who "treated his vast realm like a private estate." See Richard Pipes, ed., *The Unknown Lenin: From the Secret Archive* (New Haven: Yale University Press, 1996).

43. The work of E. H Carr, long the lead critic of alternative histories, contains several examples of this curious double standard: "I can invoke counterfactual arguments, but you can't." So does recent work by the most prominent contemporary critic of counterfactual history, Richard J. Evans. In his impressive new book, *The Coming of the Third Reich* (New York: Penguin, 2003), Evans offers a variety of both implicit and explicit counterfactuals. He believes, for instance, that he knows better than Kaiser Wilhelm II how "precarious and adventurous" was the "route by which Bismarck had achieved unification in 1871." The silly Kaiser saw the whole process as "historically preordained," but Evans knows better (18). Evans may well be right, but the only way to argue his case is by making a host of counterfactual assumptions about how easy or difficult it is to reroute European history in the mid–nineteenth century. Evans becomes even more transparently counterfactual in his assertions about how easily the Nazis might have been thwarted in their bid for power in the end stages of the Weimar Republic. He declares that "had Schleicher been less politically incompetent, he might have established a quasi-military regime, ruling through Hindenburg's power of decree and then, when Hindenburg, who was in his late eighties, eventually died, ruling in his own right," leaving Hitler in charge of a declining and increasingly factionalized Nazi party (442). See other counterfactual ruminations by Evans on page 59 (the German past "did not make the rise and triumph of Nazism inevitable. The shadows cast by Bismarck might eventually have been dispelled"), page 88 (the "more problematical provisions" of the constitution of Weimar Germany "might not have mattered so much had circumstances been different"), page 161 ("Hitler was the product of circumstances as much as anything else. Had things been different, he might never have come to political prominence"), and so on. This all confirms Robert Fogel's dictum that the alternative to open counterfactual history is covert counterfactual history!

44. The combination of the two rules—minimal rewrite with bias toward regularizing the irregular—is deeply consistent with Kahneman and Miller's norm theory account of when people spontaneously think "if-only" thoughts (see Daniel Kahneman and Dale Miller, "Norm Theory: Comparing Reality to Its Alternatives," *Psychological Review* 93 (1986): 156–93). Presented with a story of a traffic accident in which one of the drivers chose, for a change, to take the scenic route home, we are more likely to focus our counterfactual energies on undoing the departure from the norm than on undoing any of the countless normal background details implicit in the story. We are indebted to Alan Megill for pointing out that R. G. Collingwood made a similar observation about causal reasoning in

history long ago, when he noted the tendency to place greatest causal emphasis on those factors that we can most readily imagine could have been different. See Alan Megill, "The New Counterfactualists," *Historically Speaking,* March 2004, 17–18; and R. G. Collingwood, *The Idea of History* (Oxford: Clarendon, 1946).

45. Tetlock and Belkin, in *Counterfactual Thought Experiments,* set out and justified a lengthier list of six criteria for judging thought experiments in history. The three criteria here represent both a simplification of the longer list and an effort to translate rather abstract theoretical arguments into guidelines that could be implemented in actual case work.

46. Richard Evans, in "Telling It Like It Wasn't," observes that "far from liberating history from an imaginary straitjacket of Marxist determinism, alternative, speculative histories confine it in another that is far more constricting. That is because the counterfactual in the sense of an alternative future assumes or posits a whole series of other things that would have inevitably followed." No doubt this critique is on target for some examples of counterfactual history, but there is nothing intrinsic to the logic of our enterprise that is vulnerable to this criticism. We and our authors are acutely sensitive to how rapidly the likelihood of scenarios declines the farther we try to project causation in alternative histories.

47. Charles Tilly, Review of *Revolutions and the Transformation of Societies* by Shmuel N. Eisenstadt, *American Historical Review* 84 (1979): 412.

PART I

Creating the West

A Stillborn West?

THEMISTOCLES AT SALAMIS, 480 BC

Victor Davis Hanson

Ancient and Modern Assessments of the Battle

> The interest of the world's history hung trembling in the balance.
> Oriental despotism, a world united under one lord and sovereign,
> on the one side, and separate states, insignificant in extent and
> resources, but animated by free individuality, on the other side,
> stood front to front in array of battle. Never in history has the
> superiority of spiritual power over material bulk, and that of no
> contemptible amount, been made so gloriously manifest.

So wrote the often apocalyptic German cultural historian and philosopher Georg Hegel of the aftermath of Salamis.[1] If Hegel had in mind
large, impersonal forces that gave the Greeks victory, he was not merely
echoing the assessment of early-nineteenth-century classical scholarship
concerning the significance of that singular September day in 480 BC.
Even contemporary Greeks of the early fifth century would have agreed
with his melodramatic appraisal that the survival of Hellenism and the
West rested on the outcome of a few hours (see map 2). Aeschylus' play
the *Persians* is the only extant Greek tragedy based explicitly on a historical event, that of the singular victory at "Divine Salamis," where the

47

gods had punished the arrogance of the Mede and rewarded the courage of a free Greece. The playwright assumes that his generation of Athenians saved Greece—we know of no similarly entitled tragedy, such as a *Plataea, Mycale,* or even *Marathon,* named after the other key battles of the East-West struggle that could capture the public's fascination over just how close Greece had come to surrendering its freedom.[2] Epigrams after the battle recorded that Themistocles and his sailors had "saved holy Greece" and "prevented it from seeing the day of slavery."[3] Legend had it that on the day of the majestic Athenian-led victory Aeschylus fought with the Athenian fleet, Sophocles danced at the victory festival, and Euripides was born.[4]

The historian Herodotus, who wrote some forty or fifty years after the battle, was equally unequivocal in his assessment of its seminal importance. In the seventh book of his history, he engages in some "what-if" theorizing of his own—the first example to my knowledge of a counterfactual thought experiment in recorded history—to prove that the Athenians alone had kept Greece free at Salamis. He says that *if* the Athenians had not evacuated Attica, and *if* they had not formed a last-ditch naval defense at Salamis, "No one else would have attempted to resist the Persians by sea." He then further surmises that had the Greeks not fought at Salamis with their fleet, a series of inevitable catastrophes would have followed that would have doomed the Greek resistance. Herodotus, who himself had a keen sense of cultural and anthropological determinism—free European men of the polis should fight better than Asiatic subjects of a king—nevertheless felt that a single day had saved Greece. Salamis in his mind was a close-run thing.

The historian says the Spartans would have fallen back to fortify the Isthmus of Corinth—a vain effort at defense because "town after town" subsequently would have been taken by the Persians through unopposed naval landings on the coast of the Peloponnese. That is, without a Greek fleet to resist the Persians, the invaders easily would have landed thousands of troops behind the Spartans' fortifications at the isthmus and forced the Greek states of the Peloponnese to join their cause.

Stripped of their allies, Herodotus goes on to say, the Spartans and their Lacedaemonian kin "would have at last stood alone, and standing alone, would have displayed great valor and died nobly." Then Herodotus adds a final corollary to his contrary-to-fact suppositions: "Either they would have done that [died alone], *or* otherwise, before it came to that extremity, after seeing one Greek state after another embrace the Persian cause, they would have come to an agreement with

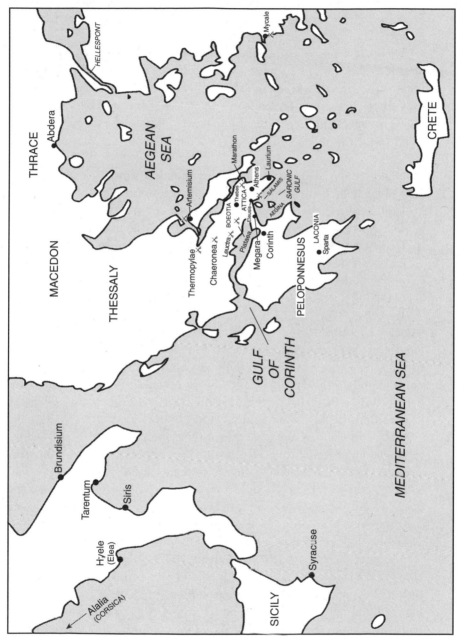

Map 2. The Greek world at the time of Salamis

King Xerxes." Herodotus concludes that either way, "Greece would have been brought under Persian control," a Western Hellenic satrapy similar to the one encompassing the subject Ionian Greeks on the coast of Asia Minor.[5]

The clearest appraisal of Salamis's importance was offered a few years after Herodotus wrote by another historian, Thucydides, who in the first book of his history has some Athenian envoys make the case that their forefathers' bravery at Salamis had once preserved Greece itself. Thucydides' Athenians are quite adamant in arguing that the victory was due solely to their own seamen's efforts, which, he says,

> prevented the Mede from taking the Peloponnesian states in detail, and ravaging them with his fleet, when the multitude of his vessels would have made any combination for self-defense impossible. The best proof of this was furnished by the invader himself. Defeated at sea, he considered his power to be no longer what it had been, and retired as speedily as possible with the greater part of his forces. Such then was the result of the matter, and it clearly proved that it was on the fleet of Hellas that her cause depended.

Thucydides' Athenian envoys add that the victory was hardly a Panhellenic effort but rather was due to the Athenian people, who were willing to evacuate Attica to risk everything at sea; to the Athenian fleet, which made up to two-thirds of the entire Greek armada; and to "the commander Themistocles, through whom chiefly it was that the battle took place in the straits, the acknowledged salvation of our cause."[6]

Thucydides' envoys once more end their argument with a bit of counterfactual supposition: like Herodotus, they argue the what-if supposition that had the Athenians either not fought at Salamis or fought and lost the entire Greek cause would have collapsed—given the fact that the acknowledged inferiority of non-Athenian ships would have made a sea fight impossible, and thus the Persians would have finished the conquest of Greece with an occupation of the Peloponnese.[7]

I suggest that the ancient assessment, for so long echoed by modern classical scholars, was entirely justified and also demonstrable through a series of logical counterfactual corollaries: (a) had not Themistocles planned and led the Athenians' attack, the Greeks would have lost the battle at Salamis; (b) had Athens not led the coalition and chosen to fight at sea off Salamis, the Greeks would have lost the Persian Wars; and (c) had the Greeks not won the Persian Wars, Hellenic civilization would have been absorbed by the Persians and Western culture in turn would have been aborted in its infancy or at least so radically altered as to be nearly unrecognizable.

Consequently, it follows that the efforts of a single individual saved Western civilization in its formative stages. Before examining these three bold suppositions in reverse order, let us first review briefly the main outlines of the battle.[8]

The Battle of Salamis

After the Greek defeat and retreat from the pass at Thermopylae (in the late summer of 480 BC), the Persians eventually occupied all of Greece north of Megara and burned an abandoned Athens (see map 2). The retreating Greek fleet sailed down from the straits of Artemisium opposite Thermopylae, shadowing the Persian advance, and then regrouped in the narrow channel between Attica and the island of Salamis, in full view of Persians who had occupied what was left of Athens. Our ancient sources—the historian Herodotus and the playwright Aeschylus, along with much later accounts of the Roman era by the biographers and historians Plutarch, Nepos, and Diodorus—suggest that the reconstituted Greek fleet was outnumbered by at least two to one and perhaps by as much as three or four to one. We are not sure how many ships were present at the battle on either side—given prior losses at Artemisium and subsequent reinforcements—but there must have been somewhere between 300 and 370 Greek vessels arrayed against a Persian armada of well over 600 warships.[9]

Most ancient observers remark that the Greek fleet was less experienced than the imperial Persian flotilla, which was composed of various veteran contingents from Phoenicia, Egypt, Asia Minor, Cyprus, and Ionian Greece itself. The Panhellenic armada's only hope was to draw the Persian fleet into the narrows between the island and the mainland, where the invaders would not have room to maneuver their ships fully and thus without open seas would lose their numerical advantage and superior nautical skill. Herodotus also speaks of the Greek ships as "heavier," and some scholars suggest that he meant they were either waterlogged, built of unseasoned timber, or simply less elegant—and thus less maneuverable—than the Persians'. Whatever the true case, it was clearly in the Greeks' interest not to go out to sea, where they would be both outnumbered and outmaneuvered.[10]

The Persians, perhaps fooled by a ruse of Themistocles, attacked just before dawn, rowing forward in three lines against the Greeks' two. But very quickly they became disorganized due to Greek ramming and the confusion of having too many ships in confined waters. Themistocles himself led the Greek attack, while Xerxes watched his Persians from afar, purportedly perched on his throne atop nearby Mount Aigaleos on the Attic shore.

The sea battle was fought all day—most likely sometime between September 20 and 30, 480 BC—and by nightfall half the Persian fleet was sunk, the rest scattered, and the morale of the invading sailors was shattered. Although in theory the enemy still outnumbered the Greek fleet, the Persian armada was no longer battle worthy—over one hundred thousand imperial sailors were killed, wounded, missing, or dispersed. Within a few days, Xerxes marched home with some of the survivors to the Hellespont, accompanied by a guard of sixty thousand infantry and leaving behind his surrogate commander, Mardonius, with a still considerable force to continue the struggle on land the next spring and summer. The Greeks immediately declared victory; the Athenians were within a year to reoccupy Attica permanently; and by the next summer Hellenic infantrymen were to stream in from all over Greece to Plataea to finish off the land forces of the Persians, who had retreated northward into Boeotia.[11]

The Persian Wars and the Survival of the West

Before examining the place of Salamis in the Greeks' overall victory against Xerxes, and Themistocles' own prominent role in that sea battle, we must first review the larger question of the status of Greek culture vis-à-vis Persian in 480. Was the early West at this point in its development so vulnerable that it might have perished due to a single invasion from Persia?

First, we must keep in mind the embryonic status of the city-state. The Greek polis as an institution was less than three centuries old when Salamis was fought. From Herodotus we learn that its culture in Mediterranean terms was insular and parochial, without much knowledge of the far older, richer, and more populous empires to the east and south. Herodotus says that before the battle of Marathon (490 BC), the Persian king, Darius, knew very little at all about the Greeks, and in turn the Athenians at Marathon knew even less about the Persians. In a bit of exaggeration, he claims that the Athenians "were the first Greeks known to charge enemy forces at a run, and the first to endure the sight of Persian dress and the men wearing it. Up until then even the word 'Persian' had been a source of fear in Greece."[12]

A decade after Marathon, King Xerxes is made to inquire on the eve of Thermopylae about the nature of the Spartan troops blocking the pass—he apparently has no detailed knowledge of anything Spartan. In short, the Greek world in 480 on the eve of Salamis was not the Greek world a mere year later. On the day before the battle, the entire Greek coast of Asia Minor was under Persian imperial control, as it had been for over a half century despite occasional failed uprisings. Many of the Aegean islands were Persian held. Sicily and the Greek city-states in southern Italy were safe only by virtue of their distance—and they had their own formidable enemies in the Carthaginians to the south, who may have timed their own invasions of the Greek west in 480 to coincide with the Persian assault on the mainland.

When the Athenians on the eve of Salamis threatened to give up the Panhellenic cause and sail to refound their city elsewhere, it was to Italy far to the west that they proposed to emigrate as a likely sanctuary—the one Greek region still remote enough from the Persian fleet. With the expansion of the Persian Empire in the sixth century to consolidate Asia Minor and many of the islands in the Aegean, Hellenic culture in the early fifth century was thus largely confined to the Greek mainland and relatively isolated and unknown by its eastern neighbors. In sum, by the fall of 480, during the first few weeks of Xerxes' invasion, a free Greece was reduced to the Peloponnese and a few square miles of land north of the Isthmus of Corinth. Athens as an autonomous city had ceased to exist.[13]

Athenian democracy in 480 was only a little more than one generation old; the fleet was constructed a mere three years prior to Salamis. The temples on the Acropolis were now burned, along with the major buildings and fortifications of the city itself. Before the Persian invasion, formal dramatic presentation at Athens was but a few years old; Greek history, oratory, or ethical philosophy did not exist as formal disciplines. Greek, much less Athenian, prose writing was not even a recognized genre. The Athenian intellectual renaissance was a postbellum phenomenon, one in large part fueled by the spiritual confidence and material enrichment that followed from the defeat of the Persians.

Western civilization on the mainland during the sixth century BC was largely a nascent local culture of some thousand agrarian city-states, characterized by broad-based landowning oligarchies, small hoplite armies, and a few regional Panhellenic sanctuaries. The locus of much of the early Greek intellectual brilliance—the pre-Socratic philosophers, the lyric and elegiac poets, indeed Homer himself—had been among the wealthier Hellenic cultures to the east, especially among the Aegean islands and in Western Asia. And that area now was mostly under Persian control.[14]

If we can accept that early Western civilization by 480 was both young and fragile—perhaps less than five hundred thousand Greeks in the Peloponnese and on Sicily remained free and autonomous on the eve of Salamis—was there, nevertheless, all that much difference between Hellenic institutions and values and those of Greece's eastern neighbors? In other words, would it have mattered much for the later West if the Greeks had lost or not fought at all at Salamis?

The answer is assuredly yes—for there would not have been a subsequent "West" as we know it. In the age of multiculturalism and "Mediterranean Studies Programs," we often forget just how anti-Mediterranean Greek culture was. The freewheeling Greek tradition of open inquiry and expression, mathematical inquiry, and natural speculation of the seventh and sixth centuries BC, as embodied by thinkers as diverse as Thales, Anaximander, and Heracleitus, was unlike anything found in Egypt or Persia, where royal seers and Magi conducted astrological investigations—only some of them admittedly empirical—under the aegis of state control and subject to religious censure. The words *citizen, constitution,* and *freedom*—the Greek *politês, politeia,* and *eleutheria*—of course were well established in the Hellenic lexicon, but they did not have real counterparts in the Persian vocabulary, reflective of an empire based on a ranked feudal society of tribes and clans governed by a monarch. Greek armies were led by generals elected by vote, or at least subject to civilian oversight; elsewhere in the Mediterranean, the king was usually a quasi divinity as well as an absolute military ruler. Scholars often cite the separation of religion and state as a relatively recent, Western phenomenon, forgetting that throughout Greek literature and philosophy, and indeed within Greek popular culture itself, there was hardly any concept of theocracy. Alexander's institution of divine worship, emulated by the later Roman emperors, was patently propagandistic; most Greeks and Romans were more cynical and understood that there was nothing holy about Alexander or Nero. No wonder the soon to be deified emperor Vespasian quipped as he lay dying, "Dear me! I must be turning into a god."

Greece in some sense was a slave society—there were somewhere between twenty and one hundred thousand unfree persons in fifth-century Athens alone. Yet even the Hellenic approach to servitude was qualitatively different from that of the Persians. In theory, *all* Persians were slaves of the Achaemenid king—not merely peasants and serfs but individual nobles, satraps, and aristocrats as well. Euripides rightly said of the "barbarians"—most likely he meant in this context Egyptians—that "all are slaves but one" (*Helen* 276). And while slavery, ancient and modern, is a reprehensible institution, at least in Greece it coexisted alongside real freedom, and the morality of the institution was the subject of a lively debate among philosophers and sophists from Aristotle to Alcidamas ("God has made no man a slave"). Cognizance that servitude ran counter to classical notions of freedom may have influenced occasional manumissions and explains sometimes unusually close relationships between master and slave. In short, in Greece there was a greater likelihood that slaves might also be tutors, bankers, scribes, and other professionals and craftsmen, and the presence of free men meant the practice would inevitably face scrutiny and criticism unknown in Persia.

The idea of private property—the Greeks' notion of a homestead farm (*klêros*) owned by a free citizen, exempt from taxes and forced exactions, which could be mortgaged or sold—was unknown to most of the millions in the Persian Empire or anywhere else in Asia. Whatever the nature of this peculiar and very young culture in Greece, it was clearly different from both its own Mycenaean past and most other civilizations in the eastern Mediterranean. Unlike the later conquering Romans, the Persians were not impressed by Greek ideas of government, politics, and military practice, but rather felt them dangerous to their own, much older institutions and thus deserving of eradication rather than emulation.[15]

But if Persian culture was different from, even antithetical to, Hellenic values, is there any evidence that Persian imperialists—in the fashion of the Ottoman Turks two millennia later—were usually no-nonsense imperial masters? Modern scholars, after all, stress the forbearance of the Persian satrapies to local subjugated peoples, whether they be Babylonians, Egyptians, Lydians, Jews, or Greeks.

Three points are germane here. First, the Greeks were simply *different* from other conquered peoples of the Persian Empire. The entire core of Greek culture sprang from a prerequisite autonomous and free city-state, the sanctuary from which all ideas of free political, philosophical, literary, and scientific expression arose. Tolerance in the sense of not enslaving a people and allowing them choice in worship was not the same as allowing a polis true autonomy and political freedom. The national religion of Greece was not God or Pharaoh but political freedom and independence.

Thus, while the Persians found it expedient to allow a degree of autonomy and religious liberty to conquered peoples in exchange for obedience, such a policy was impossible with the obdurate Greeks, who alone saw independence as an all-encompassing principle, a conscious prerequisite to their very way of life, and an important abstract virtue as well.

Second, it is clear at least that contemporary Greeks themselves viewed the Persian encroachment into Europe in the late sixth and early fifth centuries as intolerable, spelling an end to their entire Hellenic way of life. Most of the city-states had no intention of surrendering freedom in exchange for limited local autonomy. Thus, for the most part, the Greeks in Asia proved among the most affluent and outspoken—and restive—of the king's imperial subjects.

Third, unlike later Eastern challenges to Western culture—Hannibal's two-decade foray into Italy, the Moorish occupation of southern Spain, and the advance of the Ottomans into the Balkans and Eastern Europe—the Persian conquest of Greece alone promised to be final, inasmuch as Greece in 480 was then synonymous with Western culture itself. There simply were no other westerners to take up the slack and offer succor should all Greek-speaking peoples come under the Persian yoke. Europe west of Greece was tribal, nomadic, theocratic, or monarchical. True, early on Rome had come into contact with the Greek-speaking city-states of southern Italy, but its direct borrowing and absorption of Hellenic culture would not come until its own warring on the Greek mainland during the third to second centuries BC.[16]

Moreover, there is no need for counterfactual thought experiments in the case of a Persian conquest of Greece itself. The example of the defeat of Ionia on the west coast of Asia Minor and its subsequent absorption as the westernmost satrapy of Persia is a matter of historical record. From about 546 BC onward, the Greek-speaking peoples of the western seaboard of Asia Minor and the islands off the Asian coast were incorporated as tributary subjects of the Persian Empire, from which they attempted to revolt, unsuccessfully, from 499 to 494 BC. Unlike their mainland brethren farther west, the eastern Greeks were under the political control of Persian-imposed tyrants, were forced to offer conscripted troops to the king's army, and lacked the sort of unbridled political expression taken for granted to the west or even under previous Lydian strongmen. The Ionian rebels in 499, as Herodotus makes their leader, Aristagoras, claim, were fighting to be free (*eleutheroi*) rather than slaves (*douloi*).[17]

The rather benevolent Persian practice of allowing some executive authority to reside with local aristocrats, and granting rights to religious grandees in the imperial satrapies, did not work well with the subjugated Greeks, who were not so eager to surrender their liberty for the preservation of a national religion. Again, ideas and freedom, not orthodox religious worship or the protection of aristocratic estates, were far more important to citizens of the polis. Under Persian control, eastern Greek traders, artists, and philosophers were only free to the degree that they did not circumvent imperial control; for financial support they often looked for patronage at the imperial court in Sardis—where art served rather than critiqued authority. But perhaps the worst element of Persian rule in Ionia in Greek eyes was its proclivity to empower local aristocrats and tyrants to control and tax their own people—a policy the once-free Ionians resisted bitterly and considered contrary to the egalitarian traditions of the early broad-based timocracies of the city-states, in which all property-owning citizens born to two-citizen parents were in theory equal and in charge of their own local governments.[18]

After the suppression of the revolt, the Persians systematically punished the Ionians—the rebel leader and sometimes turncoat Histiaeus was impaled by Artaphernes and his head pickled. Herodotus says the victorious Persians "trawled" the Ionian islands; that is, they systematically covered entire landscapes by forming a human chain of soldiers with linked arms who rooted out all the inhabitants. Then they lined up the best-looking boys—the lucky ones—castrated them, and sent them to king as eunuch slaves; the most attractive women were sent to Darius's harem. Most males were killed and the general population reduced to serfdom. All sanctuaries and settlements were burned, and most of Ionia ceased to exist as a chain of independent city-states. Contemporary Greeks were appalled at the punishment meted out to the fallen revolutionaries. The Athenian playwright Phrynicus was fined one thousand drachmas for his presentation of *The Capture of Miletus* after the entire Athenian audience burst into tears at his recitation of the fate of conquered Milesians. Oswyn Murray summarizes the end of a free Ionia.

> The failure of the Ionian Revolt marks the end of Ionian history: that group of cities which had dominated the trade of the Mediterranean and the Black Sea from Spain to south Russia, and which had created Greek poetry, philosophy, science and history, did not regain its economic prosperity or cultural eminence until a half millennium later in the very changed conditions of the high Roman empire.[19]

Murray's point should be emphasized. Before the Persian conquest of Ionia, the Greeks on the coast of Asia Minor were more advanced and prosperous than their brethren on the European mainland: pre-Socratic philosophy, epic poetry, and scientific investigation had arisen in Asiatic, not European, Greece in a landscape both materially richer and closer to the wealthier and older empires of the East. But after the conquest of Ionia and the Persian success in putting down the revolt, the sixty-year period of foreign dominance resulted in cultural strangulation and essentially the end of Ionia as a fertile source of Greek ideas. We should imagine the same scenario had Xerxes' incorporated the Greek mainland into his empire—with the understanding that a free Greek mainland at least helped to keep alive hopes of Hellenism in occupied Ionia, but an occupied mainland would have had little or no source of such support elsewhere from autonomous Greeks.

In short, Xerxes' invasion in 480–479 was an attempt to extinguish the free polis, to make mainland Greece into another subjugated Ionia. By September 479, the plan of conquest had almost succeeded. Indeed, Greek territory in the Aegean, in Ionia, and on the mainland itself that was Persian controlled was at least five times greater than that left free in the Peloponnese. Those Greeks who were subject to Persian overlords were probably five times more numerous than the few free Greeks remaining in the Peloponnese and on the islands.[20]

It is true that the Mediterranean-wide Greek colonization movement of the eighth through the sixth centuries BC, the matchless reputation of Greek mercenaries abroad, and the success of Greek maritime traders had proved that the Hellenic approach to the economy, war, government, and science was dynamic and capable of gaining influence out of all proportion to the scant territory and small population of Greece proper. But by the beginning of the fifth century this Hellenic experiment was still evolving, vulnerable, and unfortunately now increasingly bothersome to an empire fifty times larger, with a combined population perhaps seventy times as great.[21]

Salamis and Its Role in the Greek Victory

We can accept, then, that the second phase of the Persian Wars against Xerxes (480–479) saved the unique culture of the Greeks from permanent absorption into the Persian Empire and thereby allowed a nascent West to survive long enough to consolidate and expand its position of influence in the Mediterranean. But did victory at Salamis in singular fashion save the Greeks during the Persian Wars? As we have seen, Hellenic observers of the time at least thought so. The triumph at Marathon ten years earlier had only averted a local punitive incursion of Darius, a single day's battle that saw Athens and Plataea alone of the Greeks take the field. That initial Persian expeditionary force of 490 was not large by later standards: at most thirty thousand invading troops were pitted against a little over ten thousand Greeks. G. B. Grundy rightly questioned why Edward Creasy included Marathon among his famous "fifteen decisive battles of the world," when Salamis, not Marathon, had clearly ended the Persian hopes of conquest.[22]

Thermopylae, fought a decade after Marathon, was a Greek defeat— for all its gallantry, it was perhaps the greatest military setback in the entire history of Panhellenic operations. The nearly simultaneous sea battle at Artemisium was at best a strategic Greek withdrawal. Hence in any analysis of why the Greeks won the Persian wars we are left to consider two pivotal victories: Salamis and the subsequent infantry battle of Plataea. The battle at Mycale, fought at sea off the coast of Ionia at or near the same time as Plataea, inaugurates a period of Greek expansion into the Aegean and Ionia rather than a defense of the Greek mainland per se. And that second victory was made possible only by the previous victory at Salamis.[23]

The battle of Plataea (August 479 BC), fought in a small valley about ten miles south of Thebes almost a year after the Greeks' mastery at Salamis, was a magnificent Greek victory, resulting in the destruction of the remaining Persian infantry in the field and marking the final expulsion of the king's forces from Greece. But that landmark battle—where the Persian general Mardonius was killed and most of the remaining Persians slaughtered or scattered—is understood only in the context of the tactical, strategic, and spiritual triumph of Salamis the September before. The Persians at Plataea fought without their king, for Xerxes, his battered armada, and some of his best infantry had returned to Persian territory nearly a year earlier, after their naval defeat at Salamis. There was to be no supporting Persian fleet for Mardonius' infantry off the coast of eastern Boeotia—it was either on the bottom of the channel of Salamis or long ago dispersed to the east. And while the Greeks had bickered and fought up to the very moments before the battle at Salamis, at Plataea they were unified and confident by reason of their past naval success. Indeed, there may have been more Greeks at Plataea—30,000 to 70,000 hoplites and even more light-armed troops—than would ever marshal in one army again in Greek history. Herodotus says that over 110,000 combined Hellenic troops were present. Thus the Persians fought at Plataea in the summer of 479 as a recently defeated force, without the overwhelming numerical superiority they enjoyed at Salamis and without their king and his enormous fleet. At Plataea the invaders could not be reinforced by sea or land. The Greeks, in contrast, en masse poured into the small Boeotian plain and convinced that their Persian enemies were retreating from Attica, were demoralized due to their defeat at Salamis and abandoned by their political and military leadership.[24]

If the Greeks met a once defeated and now abandoned enemy at Plataea, we still must ask could the Persians have been earlier defeated outright, or at least checked elsewhere, other than at a sea fight at Salamis? That is, if the Greeks had *not* fought in late September 480, were there other strategies that might have dealt the Persians an equally lethal blow, crushed their spirit, and ruined their fleet or infantry forces? The answer is clearly no, for a variety of cultural, strategic, and psychological reasons—all presented explicitly in Herodotus' report of Themistocles' own speeches.

After evacuating its countryside and city, Athens—its fleet of two hundred ships composed almost two-thirds of the Greek contingent—was unwilling to fight one inch farther south. Nearly all the Athenians had been evacuated to Salamis proper, Aegina, and Troizen in the Argolid. Thus by September 480 to sail southward from the Saronic Gulf was to abandon the civilian refugees of Attica to Xerxes' troops—and essentially to end the idea of Athens itself, which, with the loss of Salamis, would now not possess a single inch of native soil. The combined Greek fleet, we must remember, was in retreat of sorts after fighting to a draw at Artemisium in the failed effort to support Greek infantry resistance at Thermopylae.

"If you do not do these things [fight at Salamis]," Themistocles warned his Peloponnesian allies, "then we quite directly shall take up our households and sail over to Siris in Italy, a place which has been ours from ancient times, and at which the oracles inform us that we should plant a colony. And the rest of you, bereft of allies such as ourselves, will have reason to remember my words." In antiquity, most Greeks conceded that the further participation of Athens, the greatest sea power of the Panhellenic alliance, hinged on two prerequisites of time and space: a sea battle had to be fought immediately after the evacuation of Attica, and it had to be fought in a buffer area between the Persians and the Athenians' own vulnerable civilian refugees. A fight off Salamis was thus the only alternative to retain Athenian participation, the foundation of the Greek maritime alliance. We should keep in mind that previously almost all other northern Greeks had not only ceased resistance once their homelands were overwhelmed but actually supplied troops to Xerxes' cause. Thus Athens' threat to embark its population and sail westward was no mere boast.[25]

If fighting immediately after the Persian occupation of Attica was vital to the Greek cause, were there places other than Salamis at which the Greeks might have made a last-ditch stand? On land, no. The Athenians had evacuated Athens because their ten thousand or so hoplites were no match for the Persian horde. After the slaughter at Thermopylae, no Panhellenic hoplite force was eager to marshal on the Attic plain to defend the city against a victorious enemy that was now swelled by the medizing Greeks of Thessaly and Boeotia. The existence of an enormous Persian enemy fleet sailing down from Artemisium meant that any Greek land defense might be outflanked from the rear through naval landings, while the loss of Boeotia had eliminated a pool of some of the best hoplites on the Greek mainland. In Greece's eleventh hour, men and space were getting scarce.

There are no large islands immediately off the Hellenic coast to the south between Salamis and the isthmus or along the northeastern shore of the Argolid peninsula, no narrows and inlets that might have offered the outnumbered and "heavier" Greek fleet a confined channel in which to nullify the numerical advantages of the Persian armada. And even if the Athenians could have been convinced to fight to the south of Salamis, perhaps transporting those refugees on Aegina and Salamis southward to join those already on Troizen, there were only two alternatives of defense: a sea battle in the open waters off the isthmus or a last-ditch land defense behind the fortifications of the isthmus itself. Neither offered hope of victory.

Herodotus reports a speech of Themistocles in which he rejected just such a naval engagement off Corinth: "If you engage the enemy at the isthmus, you will fight in open waters (*en pelagei*), where it is to our worst advantage, inasmuch as our ships are heavier and less in number. In addition, you will forfeit Salamis, Megara, and Aegina even if we should win a victory there." In contrast, Themistocles added that a fight at Salamis would ensure that the Peloponnesians might delay their enemies from approaching the isthmus and thus keep them far distant from their own territory. Thus victory at Salamis might save both Athens and the Peloponnese, whereas even success at the isthmus would come too late for the salvation of Attica. And the key for the Greek defense was to keep its two greatest powers, Athens and Sparta, committed to the spirit of Panhellenic defense.

Mnesiphilus, an Athenian, had also warned Themistocles earlier that should the Greeks not fight at Salamis there was very little chance that the Panhellenic armada would ever again assemble as one fleet, even at the isthmus. "Everyone," Mnesiphilus predicted, "will withdraw to their own city-states, and neither Eurybiades nor any other man will be able to hold them together, but rather the armada will break apart." For that very reason, Herodotus makes Queen Artemesia advise the Persians to avoid Salamis, wait, and then gradually head south by land to the isthmus; she correctly argues that a sea battle at Salamis would be the beleaguered Greeks' only chance to stop the Persian onslaught.

The Peloponnesians in Herodotus' account clung stubbornly to the idea of a land defense and hurriedly fortified the isthmus while their admirals debated at Salamis. But, of course, not only would Athens not have participated in such an effort of the Peloponnesian states—its ships would have been of little value anyway in supporting a land fight behind fortifications—but there is good reason, as Herodotus foresaw, that it would have failed. An intact Persian fleet could easily have landed troops to the rear all along the coast of the Peloponnese. A half century later, even with a fleet only a third the Persians' size, the Athenians practiced with success that strategy of seaborne raiding on the Peloponnese throughout the Archidamian War (431–421 BC).

Furthermore, even without a Persian naval landing to the rear of the Greek defenders, there is no reason to believe the Greeks could have held out. The isthmus is far less defensible than the pass at Thermopylae—the meandering stone wall connecting the Corinthian and Saronic gulfs would probably have been over four miles in extent. Moreover, in later Greek history no defending force was able to keep out invaders from the north by guarding the isthmus through either garrisons or linear fortifications. The Theban general Epaminondas between 370 and 362 BC on four occasions easily brushed aside resistance there, both on his southward and northward passages between Boeotia and the Peloponnese. Herodotus, then, seems correct in asserting that defense behind a wall at the isthmus was no real alternative to a naval engagement off Salamis.

Let us, then, be clear about the role of Salamis. In and of itself, the victory did not destroy outright the Persian fleet, whose remnants limped in disarray home to the Hellespont. Nor did the naval success rid Attica entirely of Persians; the army of occupation returned to burn Athens again under Mardonius ten months after the Greek victory in the late summer 479 on the eve of the battle of Plataea. Rather, Salamis was the critical turning point in the war, which ensured that after the Greek victory the Persians—absent their king, the imperial fleet sunk or in retreat, and their infantry demoralized—could not win the war outright under any conditions. Before Salamis, few thought the Greeks would survive; after Salamis, no one doubted it.[26]

Salamis and Themistocles

As to the third and final counterfactual supposition: did a single man bring the Greeks victory at Salamis, someone without whom Salamis— and hence the Persian Wars and the West itself—would have been lost? First, we can set aside more extraneous speculations that had not Themistocles earlier (in 483 BC) urged the Athenians to build their fleet with the sudden revenues from the silver mines at Laureum there would have been no credible Greek defense in the first place and had he not convinced the Athenians in September 480 BC to evacuate the Attic countryside their hoplite land army would have been wiped out in a glorious Thermopylae-like last stand. In 480 the Athenian phalanx was not to be pitted against thirty thousand Persians but closer to a quarter million infantry, closely aided by a fleet of perhaps seven hundred ships. Most clear-thinking Athenians realized there was no chance of victory in hoplite battle and even less hope in garrisoning an unfortified city: Themistocles was not the only Athenian who saw evacuation as offering the only chance of survival. Similarly, although his singular efforts led to the construction of the Athenian fleet, without whose presence Salamis would have been impossible, we have no real information that such a building program lacked broad support in the democracy and would not have taken place under others' leadership. Both suppositions involve too many extraneous "what-ifs" and second-order counterfactuals to ensure that Themistocles alone was responsible for the presence of the Athenian fleet and the evacuation of the Athenian population. Consequently we need only concentrate on Themistocles' own actions in late September 480 on the eve of the battle, which ensured that the naval engagement at Salamis was fought and that it was won decisively.[27]

Although most Greeks apparently understood Themistocles' logic that fighting at Salamis was in their own interest in providing a forward defense for the Peloponnese, and in keeping the Athenian fleet engaged in the Greek defense, there was still no guarantee that the Peloponnesians would stay given their completion of a massive wall at the isthmus. Thus, two further actions of Themistocles were required to guarantee victory. First, through the use of ruse and deception, he was able to force his wavering allies to fight and to convince the Persians to attack in an unwise and unsound fashion. Second, the deployment of the Greek fleet, the actual tactics of the battle, and the method of attack seem to have been Themistocles' own design.

On the eve of the battle, after two meetings with the representatives of the Panhellenic alliance, Themistocles was outvoted—we should keep in mind that he was probably only half Greek and was often distrusted for his mother's Thracian origins—and there arose a real danger that the Peloponnesians might retreat to the isthmus wall, especially when it was learned that Xerxes' infantry and cavalry were freely roaming in the environs beyond Attica. At the eleventh hour, Herodotus and Aeschylus both mention a secret embassy instigated by Themistocles to the Persian commander in Attica, though they disagree over the contents of his message and its ultimate intent. In Herodotus' account, Themistocles' slave Sicinnus is sent over to the Persians to warn them of a possible Greek withdrawal—a ploy designed to cause the Persians immediately to embark and thereby to force the wavering non-Athenian Greeks to stay and fight. Scholars are divided over the authenticity of the tale, but there is no reason to doubt the general truth of the account, inasmuch as precisely at the point when the alliance was about to break up the news was announced to the Greek admirals that the Persians were at sea and both approaches in the Salamis channel were now blocked; the Greeks discovered that they could not retreat to the isthmus and thus would be immediately forced to fight or surrender.[28]

Because Themistocles all along had urged the resistance at Salamis and had duped the Persians into committing their ships to the narrow channels, it is probable that the actual plan of the Greek deployment was his as well. The secret to the Greek success was to draw the cumbersome enemy fleet farther into the narrows to ensure that it could not utilize its overwhelming numerical advantage. Thus Themistocles had the Greek ships initially withdraw, making the Persians row farther into the channel, on the assumption that the Greeks were in fact trying to flee, as their fifth-column "intelligence" had indicated. In addition, the Persians had sent their Egyptian contingent around the island to block a nonexistent Greek escape through the Bay of Eleusis and the channel opposite Megara. Thus, when the two fleets collided, the Persians, as Themistocles had planned, were dispersed and unable to bring their full strength against the Greek armada. In the confined waters, Xerxes' ships were vulnerable to the ramming of the heavier Greek ships, as Themistocles had also anticipated.

What Themistocles' role was in the actual fighting is unclear; posterity credited the lion's share of the actual fighting to the Athenians, who were under his direct command. In any case, the Persians were lured into the narrows and sent part of their fleet away before the battle through the direct intervention of Themistocles himself, who had forced the hand of both Greeks and Persians to fight a battle that he felt would inevitably result in Greek success.[29]

Miscellaneous Second-Order Counterfactual Suppositions

The idea that a single man can alter larger social and economic currents of history will no doubt disturb many historians. Therefore let us examine the most obvious objections to the notion that Themistocles saved the West, beginning with the role of Themistocles himself at Salamis.

Themistocles at Salamis

Could another Greek or Athenian leader have mobilized resistance at sea? Given the Hellenic reputation for genius and free thinking, might not some other quick-witted and iconoclastic Greek have emerged to buck tradition and urge radically unorthodox plans such as, but not limited to, engaging the Persians in the narrows of Salamis, sending a false message to Xerxes, and in essence being duplicitous with both his friends and his enemies to ensure that both Greeks and Persians fought a decisive naval engagement off Attica? We can quickly dispense with the idea that other non-Athenians were preparing for a sea fight near Salamis or that they offered similarly radical proposals. After the Greek defeat at Thermopylae, the Athenians were aghast to find that the fallback strategy of their compatriots apparently all along had been based on a retreat southward en masse to create a last stand at the Isthmus of Corinth. Eurybiades, the Spartan admiral who commanded the Panhellenic fleet, was not in favor of marshaling off Salamis. No ancient source identifies any other non-Athenian who wished to make a stand north of the Peloponnese after the Persian occupation of Boeotia and Attica. What is remarkable about the account in Herodotus is that Themistocles seemingly had no allies whatsoever, not a single non-Athenian who could be counted on to advance his agenda.[30]

It is true that among the Athenians themselves, very few hoplite con-

servatives were willing to be annihilated in an infantry defense of the
Attic mainland, and so they reluctantly followed the more farsighted,
who saw the need for evacuation by sea and ultimate salvation in the
fleet. Again, a hoplite battle on the plain of Attica would have pitted
roughly ten thousand Athenians against a quarter million Persians. The
invading army of 480 BC was perhaps ten times larger than Darius's force
that had landed at Marathon a decade earlier; thus any idea of hoplite
resistance was predicated not on possible victory but on a sort of suicidal
honor. Even traditionalists such as Aristides saw the futility of a Greek
land defense and so came over to Themistocles' way of thinking and
joined him at Salamis. Only a few diehard reactionaries stayed on the
Acropolis and were annihilated. Later philosophers such as Plato and
Aristotle recognized this Athenian dilemma: salvation lay with Themistocles alone, yet Themistoclean sea power and its accompanying more
radical democracy might be worse for the moral character of the Athenian people than the glorious last-ditch destruction of thousands of
hoplites on the battlefield. No other Greek or Athenian conservative
planned for a massive sea battle off Salamis; we receive the impression
that the veterans of Marathon were dejected that neither courage nor a
wall of spears on this occasion could save Athens.[31]

Of Themistocles' close associates who agreed to fight at Salamis we
hear only of a curious figure, Mnesiphilus, the purported tutor of
Themistocles. Herodotus says that the latter advised Themistocles that he
must at all costs not allow the Panhellenic council to abandon Salamis.
Writing six hundred years after the battle, the Greek biographer Plutarch
objected to Herodotus' inference that Themistocles' strategic insight was
derived in part from Mnesiphilus. Two points are germane about the role
of Mnesiphilus. Plutarch believed that Herodotus had deliberately
magnified his role in advising Themistocles in order to denigrate the
Athenian hero in light of his later controversial career. Most modern
scholars have accepted Plutarch's assessment of the inclusion of the Mnesiphilus story in Herodotus' history and see no real reason to believe that
the strategy and tactics of the Athenians were due to the arguments of an
aged philosopher. Second, even in Herodotus' account it is clear that
Mnesiphilus is an adviser only and is influential only to the degree that
Themistocles can win approval of such ideas in the general Greek council. Thus we have no reason to believe that Mnesiphilus planned the fight
at Salamis and, even if he did, that he had any power to convince the
Greek admirals to plan a defense off Salamis.[32]

Prior to the rise of Themistocles, there had been essentially no Athenian fleet and no Athenian plan to forsake a hoplite battle and fight at sea. Both ideas were revolutionary. Even in the latter fifth century, after nearly three decades of Athenian political leadership that embraced much of Themistocles' anti-Spartan policy and his emphasis on sea power and urban fortification, Pericles only with difficulty during the Peloponnesian War was able to resurrect Themistocles' most radical idea of forced evacuation of the Attic plain. Indeed, a number of modern historians have employed counterfactual suppositions to emphasize just how critical was Themistocles at Salamis. Christian Meier rightly concluded that the Greeks' salvation ultimately came down to the leadership of a single man.

> Only when such a process is determined, either in its totality or at least in its direction and consequences, by a single event, do the particular circumstances that determined this event and its course take on enormous importance of their own. It is hard to imagine that had there been no Themistocles, someone else would have played a similar role. Given the scope of his political and military achievements, Themistocles seems uniquely qualified for the task he was set. Even if the Greeks were in fact superior to the Persians in some ways that were not apparent to the normal thinking of the time, their superiority was not great enough to make their victory certain or even probable. In any case, there had to be someone like Themistocles who could recognize the Persians' superiority as mere appearance and, at the same time, detect the genuine though invisible advantages the Greeks derived from the balance of power.[33]

In short, "there had to be someone like Themistocles" to force a battle off Salamis, someone whose promotion of naval supremacy and evacuation of Attic territory were controversial during and after his lifetime. In the nascent democracy of early-fifth-century Athens, the traditions of hoplite agrarianism—best exemplified in the hallowed memory of sixth-century BC landed government and hoplite excellence at Marathon—were still strong, and there was no guaranteed support for any program of shipbuilding, port and harbor construction, or massive naval deployment. Thus it is hard to propose a series of second-order counterfactual questions about alternate personalities at Salamis: since the Persian occupation of Attica was foreordained after the Greek retreat from Thermopylae, and since Salamis was the last chance to stop the Persian fleet north of the isthmus, the salvation of Attica required an Athenian leader who had a past record of mobilizing sea power and the acumen and skill to force the Greeks to fight when and where they did. As Meier points out, our sources mention no other such individual.

G. B. Grundy years ago likewise summarized the ancient assessment that the Athenian naval strategy in the Persian Wars to force the Greeks to fight north of the Isthmus—even before the battle of Salamis—was the product of one man.

> Themistocles had been most prominent in whatever part of the Greek strategy had been due to Athenian initiative. He had commanded the contingent sent to Thessaly; he had commanded the Athenian fleet at Artemisium. In both cases the adoption of a line of defense so far north of Peloponnesus must have been due to Athenian influence; and it may be regarded as certain that Themistocles was mainly, if not entirely, responsible for the direction in which that influence made itself felt. Indeed, given Themistocles' later sordid career, it is surprising how uniform the ancient tradition is in giving him sole credit for Salamis and the Greek victory there.[34]

Persia's Military Strategy

Granted that no other Greeks could have forced the issue at Salamis, nevertheless was Themistocles' plan possible only because of either Persian stupidity or Persian impotence? That is, was their poor showing at Salamis the result of Xerxes' errors, his poor high command, and the unreliability of his sailors, not the result of Themistocles' brilliance? Might the Persians, then, not have bungled an assault on the isthmus in the same way they did at Salamis? Absent a Themistocles, would not the Greeks have sailed down to the isthmus and capitalized on the poor Persian seamanship, infighting, and tactical blunders that were purportedly present at Salamis? There is some ancient support for the idea that the lapses in Persian strategy and tactics ensured their defeat in Greece between 480 and 479. A half century later, Thucydides, for example, makes the anti-Athenian Corinthians' later claim that the Greek victory was due as much to Persian error as to Greek courage. But even if that were true most of those tactical errors occurred *after* rather than before Salamis (and thus were mostly a consequence of the catastrophic defeat there). The key Persian mistake involved the decision of a panicky Xerxes to abandon Mardonius and his infantry in Greece after the defeat of the fleet. Mardonius' own unwise plan in precipitating infantry battle against Greek hoplites in the plain of Plataea the next year only compounded the prior error of his king.

Yet before the defeat at Salamis it is difficult to cite any Persian lapse in strategy. The pass at Thermopylae was turned within three days. The Greek fleet was sent in retreat southward from Artemisium. Nearly all of Greece north of Attica was pacified and in fact was contributing troops to the Persian effort by the end of September 480. Boeotia was medized. Athens was occupied and burned without much effort.

In short, less than three months after entering Europe Xerxes had conquered all of Greece north of the Peloponnese, had not lost a battle, and had most of his army and navy still intact. Even if Themistocles and the Athenians had been willing to give up Salamis and fight in concert for the isthmus, there is no reason to expect that the outnumbered Greek fleet in open waters would have prevailed. Momentum was on the Persian side, as they were continuously gaining Greek territory and medizing the inhabitants.

On the morning of the battle at Salamis, Xerxes also had good reason to believe Themistocles' emissary, Sicinnus, who warned of an imminent Greek "retreat." Earlier, at Thermopylae, the Greek traitor Ephialtes had similarly offered his services, and through his guidance the pass was turned and the Greeks defeated. It was logical for the Persian high command to assume that there were plenty of desperate and avaricious men on the Greek side who might seek to provide the king with inside information about Hellenic deployments. Furthermore, after the retreat of the Greeks from the north, the Persians' chief worry was their inability to destroy the defeated Greek forces—in two major engagements the latter had withdrawn without being annihilated. The fierce resistance of the three hundred who fell at Thermopylae allowed thousands of Greek hoplites to escape southward, and the fleet that sailed from Artemisium, despite a hard-fought engagement and damaging storms, retreated as a formidable force. Consequently, Xerxes had every reason to believe at Salamis that the vastly outnumbered Greek fleet might escape through the western channel off Megara—and he saw no reason to disbelieve yet another traitor who might apprise him of the Greek plan of retreat.

Few armies in the ancient world could have transported nearly half a million infantry and sailors through Europe and across the Aegean as well as the Persians did and within a little more than a month of fighting inside Greece vanquished the entire mainland north of the Peloponnese with only negligible losses. The Persians did not lose at Salamis; they were defeated by Greek courage, tactics, and the remarkable leadership of Themistocles.

Barry Strauss, in chapter 3 of this volume, suggests that even had the Athenians lost at Salamis they might have sailed to their kindred city, Siris, in Sicily; reestablished there a free, autonomous Athens; and then headed a new Panhellenic alliance that would have defeated the Persian armada sent west to extinguish the last vestiges of Greek freedom. Indeed, in Herodotus' account Themistocles threatened to move the Athenians to Sicily should the Greeks abandon Salamis, but that threat was before, not after, the battle, when he still had a fleet. If the Athenians had lost at Salamis, there would not have been enough ships to transport wholesale the Athenian army and civilian population—and probably an insufficient force to prevent the Persians from storming Salamis and enslaving much of the citizen population in hiding there. Even had Themistocles kept intact his entire fleet of 200 Athenian triremes, he still could scarcely have hauled more than 40,000 adults (the great majority of whom would have had to row) in any given voyage. Yet the population of Attica—adult native-born males—in 480 was about 30,000 to 40,000 in itself. There were probably another 90,000 to 120,000 women and children and perhaps anywhere from 20,000 to 100,000 personal slaves and resident aliens. Several round-trip voyages of sixteen hundred miles would have been necessary to complete the exodus—provided that the evacuated population would have been safe from Persian attack in the absence of the Athenian fleet.

The idea of transporting an entire people under wartime conditions seems improbable—more so when we remember that most of Sicily was largely a Dorian culture, with few close ties to the Ionian Athenians, and itself under assault at the time by Carthage. Athens' later attempt during the Peloponnesian War (415–413) to send forty thousand soldiers there to take Syracuse was an unmitigated disaster that found little support among the city-states of Sicily. In sum, Xerxes in a matter of weeks had ethnically cleansed Attica of all its Greeks in one of the largest transfers of indigenous Hellenic populations in Greek history before the age of Alexander.

Even should the Athenians have transported successfully their population and property to Siris, would not the Persians simply have been content with the Aegean and mainland Greece and thus allowed Sicily to die on the vine? Far more likely a scenario is that the newly transported Athenian refugees would have severely taxed the resources of Sicily and only aggravated the island's normal menu of internal squabbling, not to mention constant warring against Carthaginian expansionism. As we have seen in the Balkans in modern times, one hundred thousand refugees can severely strain their host country; we can imagine what more than twice that number would have done to fifth-century Sicily.

Throughout the early 490s, Athens had been unable to aid the Ionians, who were just across the Aegean, in their efforts to throw off the Persian yoke; thus it is hard to envision under what circumstances Athens might have been able to free Ionia, the Aegean, and all of mainland Greece from Sicily, which was over eight hundred miles away. Rather than having the entire Peloponnese on the Athenians' side, the southern Greeks would have been impressed into the Persian army.[35]

Persian Satrapy

Granted that Themistocles was responsible for the victory at Salamis, and that Salamis saved Greece, are there larger counterfactual questions that must be answered about the fate of Western culture itself? First, in the wake of a Greek defeat, is there any reason to believe that a Persian occupation would have been either long lasting or especially oppressive? Might not the subjugated Greeks have regrouped and revolted at a future date, or, barring that, might not their culture have continued more or less uninterrupted by a benign Persian occupation? In either case, could not Hellenic civilization endured under a Persian satrapy?

Prior to 480, there is no record of a major Persian satrapy successfully revolting from Persepolis. And three decades later (453), when the Athenians were much stronger and the Persians weaker, the revolt in Egypt was put down; the Athenian forces sent there to aid in the liberation of the Egyptians were for the most part annihilated in one of the greatest single defeats in Athenian imperial history. The challenge for the Persian Empire in the sixth and fifth centuries had been conquest, not provincial administration and enforcement, at which they performed quite well.

Until the invasion of Alexander (334 BC), the Persians were remarkably successful in keeping conquered provinces conquered: even the fourth-century rebellious Ionians and Egyptians were eventually to lose their autonomy and were to be restored as Persian dependencies. Alexander the Great attacked an empire that was more or less of the same size and extent as the one that had invaded Greece a century and a half earlier. Recent studies have refuted the old idea of a decadent fourth-century Persia that was imploding from within. Egypt and Cyprus were constant problems, but neither province on its own was able to break wholly free from Persian control. In truth, Alexander succeeded only because he drew on the tactical and cultural legacy of the polis to defeat enormous Persian armies on the field of battle—an intellectual and military tradition (sophisticated phalanx tactics, siegecraft, artillery, elaborate logistics) that would have been impossible after a Persian victory at Salamis and occupation of Greece.

The prior discussion of the sixth-century subjugation of Ionia should dispel any notion that Hellenism would have survived intact or continued to evolve under Persian control of Greece. A free Greek mainland had kept a flame of Hellenism alive in Persian-controlled Ionia—albeit with great difficulty. A distant Hellenic Sicily and southern Italy—supposing that they would have remained free—would not have been able to do much for the Greeks living in a grand Persian satrapy that encompassed all of the mainland and the Aegean. Indeed, the fifteenth-century fall of Byzantium, with its attendant loss of Hellenic territories in Asia Minor, was permanent and irrevocable, and the four centuries of Ottoman rule in Greece itself illustrate how eastern despotism could radically suppress Hellenic culture from the Adriatic to the Black Sea. In both cases, a free Europe could do little to liberate the former territories of the eastern Roman Empire.[36]

But, as Barry Strauss has argued, was the Greek legacy really critical to the later development of Western culture? If almost all of the Greek-speaking lands had become a satrapy of Persia, would the later West still have been any different? Of course, Western civilization is a rich mixture of the Judeo-Christian religious tradition, the Romanization of northern Europe, the feudalism of the Middle Ages, the Protestant Reformation, the French and British Enlightenment, and the Industrial Revolution. The West was formed through the gradual adoption and sometimes dilution of Hellenic ideas, not merely by mimicking Greek culture in all its manifestations through a direct linear inheritance.[37]

That being said, there are very few Western institutions that did not originate in Greece: open markets, consensual government, rationalism, free inquiry, civilian control of the military, and political authority separate from religion are all found in the fifth-century city-state. And all such notions reemerged at various times to embolden Western thinkers during the Middle Ages, the Renaissance, the European Enlightenment, and the creation of the American government. Philosophers, artists, writers, and statesmen as varied as Augustine, Aquinas, Dante, Machiavelli, da Vinci,

Michelangelo, Shakespeare, Locke, Hume, Rousseau, Montesquieu, Hamilton, and Jefferson drew directly on classical antecedents that first arose in an autonomous Greece.

What distinguishes Greece from other fertile areas of Western inspiration is that it is the fountainhead of the West; one can make the argument that in the case of Rome, Christianity, the Renaissance, the European discovery of the Orient and the Americas, the Enlightenment, or the Industrial Revolution there was always some prior general source of Western influence or authoritative texts that sparked these periods of creativity and expansion. But there were no Greeks—or anything like them—before the Greeks.

We must also not make the methodological error of assuming that because these Western ideas are today ubiquitous and proven they were universal notions readily available or easily embraced in the past. And we must not assume that de facto cultural practices—the pedestrian freedom to travel, or to haggle, shout, buy, and sell in the bazaar—are in any way comparable to the abstract notions of liberty and civic rights that are ratified by elected councils, subject to constant political and philosophical scrutiny, and embraced as abstract theoretical notions that can evolve beyond and exist apart from the material circumstances of their creation.

Without a free Greece and its colonies in southern Italy, Roman society would have been markedly different—surely more insular and concerned largely with and influenced by northern tribal European culture; its literature, philosophy, government, law, architecture, and science were all Greek inspired, and it is nearly impossible to see purely Italian roots in many major Roman literary, philosophical, or artistic genres. The freedom found among the tribes of northern Europe, especially in Germany, was a dividend of demography—a relatively small, often nomadic population in a vast geographical area, not unlike the Native American experience. De facto freedom to range widely and be relatively unconcerned with state authority is a far different concept from the Greeks' abstract notion of freedom, a constitutional notion ratified by law that can be extended across time and space under vastly differing demographic and geographical conditions.

One can imagine what German freedom would have amounted to in an urban setting, with an advanced corpus of literature that criticized tribal elders, or with a scientific tradition empirically at odds with the Germanic gods. It is no accident that the Third Reich romanticized the "blood and soil" of the German *Volk* as a pristine sanctuary influenced but not corrupted by the West. Inherent in Nazi philosophy was the idea that Rome had ceased at the Rhine and thus had exempted Germans from the decadent civilizing influence of the West, which weakened the soul of a people through material consumption, too much freedom, and rampant egalitarianism.

Roman literature—in the manner that eighteenth- and nineteenth-century French and English romanticism idealized the aborigines of the Americas—was fascinated with the natural freedom of tribes in Gaul and Germany, but few sober thinkers, ancient or modern, accepted the idea that such nomads and hunters would be anything but murderous when food was short and space limited—or authoritarian and unfree should the population require intensive agriculture, sophisticated trade, and technology to support population densities of the type characteristic in Greece and Rome in classical antiquity. Far more likely, with a growing population and finite land, German freedom without the West would have evolved along Near Eastern lines into a theocracy or palatial autocracy, where elites marshaled labor and capital through a collective and unfree subject state.

In short, without a Hellenized Rome it is difficult to envision Western civilization advancing much in northern Europe or to see the successful spread of Christianity beyond Israel, much less the embrace of the Old Testament outside of the Middle East. Near Eastern cultures were theocratic states, their law codes were imposed without ratification by a consensual body of free citizens, and their written language was essentially employed either as a system of imperial record keeping or as chronology of the deeds of a tiny monarchy or as a repository of sacred religious texts. There really is no Near Eastern literature that is separate from religion or government and no abstract philosophy that deals with questions of ethics and morality in an entirely empirical fashion.[38]

But were Western ideas forever unique to Greece? And even if that were true, was it not possible for Hellenic approaches to culture, government, politics, and the economy to emerge independently and spontaneously at some future date elsewhere in the aftermath of a vanquished Greece? In other words, even if the Greeks had lost at Salamis, would not some culture have emerged elsewhere on its own to provide the world with similar notions of consensual government, free inquiry, capitalism, and rationalism?

We must not confuse cultural interaction and adaptation with core values. Much of early Greek architecture and art was Egyptian inspired.

The alphabet was an ingenious adaptation of a Phoenician script. Greek folktales and some Hellenic religious practices may have had their origins in the Near East. Many types of plants and farming practices, along with everything from triremes to coinage, were imported from Asia Minor. But such cultural interaction has nothing to do with a central heart that embraced consensual government, the role of civilian auditors, the institutionalized notion of free speech and critical inquiry, the chauvinism of an anti-aristocratic, landowning middling class, and a free monetized economy. There is no evidence that such a cargo of politics, military practice, economics, and culture was found in Egypt, the Near East, Persia, northern Europe, or along the western coast of North Africa. The ubiquity of these traditions in the later West should not blind us to the fact they existed nowhere else outside Greece—and are rarely, if ever, found outside Western civilization. As the great cultural historian Jacob Burckhardt concluded, "All subsequent objective perception of the world is only elaboration on the framework the Greeks began. We see with the eyes of the Greeks and use their phrases when we speak."

Although Hellenism offered clear adaptive advantages to any culture that chose to embrace its institutions, its threat to theocratic and despotic rule made it likely that its cultural centerpiece, the polis, would not be emulated elsewhere. Systems that privilege ordinary individuals with freedom and material comfort—and thus threaten the exclusivity of hereditary elites—are not necessarily to be imported therein by local cultures. Both subsequent Greek history and later Western expansion prove that the culture of Western rationalism, capitalism, and freedom is disruptive of indigenous religion and custom and usually is resisted fiercely for that very reason by holy men and tribal leaders alike. The city-state was the product of a slow evolution in the small isolated valleys of central Greece, predicated on the earlier complete collapse of Mycenaean central palatial civilization, itself Near Eastern in inspiration.

Nothing similar to Hellenic society seems to have developed in the similar small valleys and Mediterranean climates of China, northern and southern Africa, and the Americas, suggesting that the early West was not a predictable consequence of natural stimuli. That there were no poleis in similar physical landscapes in Asia, the New World, and Western Europe suggests that the emergence of the free and autonomous city-state was not just a consequence of geography but rather a unique coalescence of terrain, climate, location, and historical circumstance—and in some sense plain luck.[39]

Some Thoughts on Counterfactuality and History

The Spread of Hellenism

In assessing the significance of the victory at Salamis, we must ask at what point did all alternative outcomes to the spread of Hellenism become impossible? Clearly, after the Persian defeat and the rise of the Athenian empire, coupled with the fifth-century Greek Enlightenment, there was little chance that the Persian military would ever overwhelm Greece. The loss of the Athenian expeditionary force in Egypt was the last time Hellenic forces would be defeated by Persians—and such a serious setback still did not endanger the Greek mainland. Otherwise, after Salamis, as a general rule the Greeks always fought the Persians in Persia or its subject states—the ten thousand who marched with the younger Cyrus, Agesilaus and the Spartan attacks in Ionia in the early 390s, and the campaigns of Alexander and the Successors—and never really lost.

Indeed, the growth of Greek economic and military power in the Mediterranean during the fifth and fourth centuries ensured that Hellenism would spread by force eastward into Asia and through emulation and Roman arms westward into Europe. In contrast, before the victory the Greek mainland was vulnerable to foreign invasion by Persia and found itself fragmented and cut off from both Ionia and the Aegean. The defeat of Xerxes humiliated Persia, gave the Greeks an enormous infusion of capital from tribute and booty, sparked a psychological and spiritual renaissance, and left a power vacuum in the Aegean; in that sense, Salamis was in large part responsible for the ensuing cultural renaissance of the next half century. It was fortunate indeed that Xerxes invaded Greece; his catastrophic defeat at Salamis had consequences for Western society that might have been impossible had the Persians simply guarded Ionia and left the mainland alone.

In the age of determinist and universal history, scholars will find it hard to accept the idea that the efforts of a single man could transform the entire political, cultural, and social landscape of Mediterranean civilization with lasting consequences felt to this day. In the modern West, where our national religion has become institutionalized egalitarianism, we find it harder still to confess that one man is not only superior to another but, in fact, greater than any of his age—and at a critical moment responsible for the survival of his entire culture.

The answer to the age-old paradox of whether human agency or larger issues of class, politics, national character, and geography and climate explain history need not be answered with a simple yes or no.

Rather, it seems to me that on very rare occasions in history a few singular individuals are able to alter larger currents of events in a manner not possible either before or after.

In the case of Themistocles, it is clear that Western civilization was perhaps in one of its last stages of vulnerability, after which its sheer resilience and insidious dynamism would make it nearly impossible to eradicate, and so its survival became less dependent on any one man. But when Themistocles, through oratory, threat, and ruse, forced his countrymen to fight at Salamis, the West after a mere three centuries of existence had been reduced to little more than the Peloponnese, an area smaller in size than Sicily and containing less than half a million free Greeks. A single man stood between that last sanctuary and its absorption by an empire of millions, with ideas and values entirely antithetical to Hellenic notions of government, culture, and society. This was an entirely different situation even than Rome's vulnerability after its catastrophic defeat at Cannae, when a Carthaginian capture of Rome would not in the least have affected culture in Greece or a Hellenized East.

No other Greek of his age—Aristagoras, Militiades, Aristides, Eurybiades, or Pausanias—had the desire, intelligence, or vision to realize the full potential and consequences of sea power, much less the necessary practical skills to unite an eroding parochial coalition into a cohesive defense, and still less the brazenness to communicate stealthily on the eve of battle with the Persian king. And no other Greek statesman was willing to put so much confidence in his county's landless and poor citizenry, to such a degree that a polis was to be redefined not as walls, buildings, and land but simply as the collective lives of its citizens of all classes. The odds are greater still that no other Greek of the age would have ignored his city's hoplite army, abandoned its ancestral lands and sanctuaries, and entrusted the defense of its surviving population to the hands of mostly poor and disreputable sailors—all in the hope that they could lead a Panhellenic defense against enormous odds in novel ships that were no more than three or four years old.

In that sense, such counterfactual questions help to restore the role of human agency to history. They inevitably focus on particular key events, often of a few hours' or days' duration, rather than on larger, more insidious currents that do not manifest themselves until decades after the fact. If class, race, culture, technology, geography, and the environment are the fumes of history, then particular individuals serve as the matches that ignite the flames of change. True, the latter in themselves do not create the larger circumstances of combustion, but often without their spark the gas of transformation can easily remain inert. In the case of classical Greek history, itself fairly well recorded by contemporary historians and writers, inscriptions on stone, and a rich archaeological record, the focus on key individuals, particular acts of a day, or accidents of human frailty or chance can bring a much needed humanity back to our discipline, which more recently has sought to explain the course of the Greek experience through much larger fault lines—slave/free, foreigner/Greek, female/male, homosexual/heterosexual, mass/elite, poor/rich.

We in classics have too often forgotten that all of the "others" who appear so frequently in Greek history—whether Sappho, Cyrus the Younger, Aspasia, the rowers of the Athenian fleet and the unnamed ore diggers of the Athenian mines—were first of all people and conducted themselves as such, not always in allegiance to or in cognizance of their gender, ethnic affiliation, race, social status, or economic class. Counterfactuality, then, looks to what people do and assumes that accidents that might happen to a Sappho or Aspasia often do so irrespective of their gender—because in the last analysis they are individuals first, subject, as the Greeks so often remind us, to the same tragic fate that awaits us all.

Counterfactual History

The employment of systematic counterfactual history, however, will probably not capture the attention of most contemporary historians in the university, since it is antithetical to the modern tenets of formal historical inquiry in a variety of ways.

First, counterfactual thought experiments place special emphasis on particular individuals and singular human achievements and thus are at odds with Marxist determinist ideas of class and exploitation and the cherished notion that we humans are all relatively equal in ability and achievement. Surely, another Themistocles—or perhaps a dozen or so such individuals—was present to energize the restless thetic (landless) classes at Athens and so convince the Athenian state that its future lay inevitably with the masses, sea power, and radical democracy. Surely other unrecognized men of Themistocles' caliber were rowing at Salamis, all waiting for the call to serve as figureheads in Greece's fated victory in the great patriotic war against the invader. And followers of Hegel, Spengler, Toynbee, and Braudel might see a Themistocles as unimportant detritus, for a brief second highlighted only by his proximity to the inevitable explosion of colliding racial, cultural, and environmental forces.

Second, many of the essays in this volume concern battle and conquest, illustrating the critical importance of war in world history. Yet military history—especially given the horrors of the twentieth century—is the university's stepchild, often uneasy with the prevailing therapeutic sensibility that believes formal killing is a result of misunderstanding and ignorance, not a struggle of good versus evil, and thus can be better understood through "conflict resolution" and "peace studies." Who is to say that it was a good thing that the Athenians won, since thousands of innocent subjects were killed at Salamis? Might someone have reasoned with the Persians? Most of these poor rowers were simply led to their slaughter by elite leaders—without whose egos, vanity, and ignorance a workable, peaceable solution agreeable to both peoples would have been possible.

Third, counterfactual history ultimately seeks a singular moment in which events are forever altered. Thus it deals in concrete facts and empirical data—quite different from the in-vogue notion that historical reality is socially constructed by a set of arbitrary fictive discourses, themselves a result of the manipulation and exploitation of power along lines of class, race, and gender. In postmodern theory, time itself, much less critical time, holds little meaning, inasmuch as any one day, any one person, or any one event is as important—or as unimportant—as another: to privilege one is of no particular value or interest but simply an illustration of one's own idiosyncratic political or cultural agenda.

Who is to say Themistocles' well-recorded victory is any more significant than an undocumented day in the lives of slaves engaged at the Attic silver mines, who, should they have stopped digging, might have shut down the capital that fueled the construction of Athenian ships? To farmers in the central Greece, did it matter whether their central government was arbitrarily called "democratic" or "tyrannical," Persian or Greek, free or not, since all such entities share the same coercive power relationships with their subjects?

Fourth, conservatives, of course, see counterfactualism as an attack on empiricism and positivism itself, as an entire line of extraneous questioning (which in theory has no end) that ignores the hard work of constructing historical likelihood. Doctrinaire historians have enough trouble finding out what "actually happened" without worrying over the probable or improbable that might have happened if condition A, person B, or event C had been altered. To these traditionalists, counterfactual questions, because they can never be absolutely ruled out, resemble the defense in the O. J. Simpson trial: despite the careful classification of second-order or illegitimate counterfactuals, the possible is still as legitimate and as likely as the probable because it can never be entirely refuted.

Could not the Greeks have fought elsewhere, under a different general, with other allies, a second, third, or fourth time after a defeat? Would they not have continued the war as guerrillas from the Peloponnesian highlands, refugees in Sicily, raiders from free enclaves in southern Italy or Crete? Might not the once conquered Greeks have rebelled anyway by 450, 390, or 350? And who is to say that Western culture was not mostly established by Romans or is properly the legacy of Judeo-Christian religion or the gift of feudal Europe or the product of the Enlightenment, and thus must we not look equally—if to battles—to Cannae, Tours, or Lepanto and—if to great men—to Moses, Jesus, Newton, Darwin, or Freud? Without a Salamis, would not something like the West have emerged on its own in eighth-century Spain, someday in North Dakota, or among the nineteenth-century Japanese?

Fifth, counterfactual history—if it is to explain fundamental and universal questions of the history of civilization—must at some point account for the present dominance of Western culture. Although counterfactual thought experiments may illustrate, not celebrate, the rise of the West, the rise of the West they nevertheless will ultimately illustrate, and in the minds of many contemporary historians that will in itself be termed Western exceptionalism, triumphalism, or chauvinism. Critics will argue that the definition of *influence* is an entirely Western construct; most of the ancient world—peasants in China, nomads in Asia, tribes in Africa, aborigines in Australia and the Americas—were quite unaware of and unconcerned with what happened at Salamis. If their cultures would someday encounter and be changed by the West, it is not so much evidence of Western dynamism as a pathological Western intrusiveness that chooses to project itself in ways other cultures disdain. The "other" is not less able but simply chooses (often in a more "natural," "enlightened," or "moral" way) not to colonize land, exploit people, or desecrate the environment, and thus naturally it is less concerned with material acquisition, state power, and technological advance.

Sixth, and most important, there is something very human and accessible about counterfactual history. People outside of academia engage in what-if conjectures every day in explication of the key events of their own lives and as exegesis of their own (often unhappy) present situations. In that sense, counterfactuality, because it has an obvious resonance and familiarity with the general public, in a way most theoretical history does not, will always be suspect by prominent theorists as a frivolous, parlor-game pursuit, without a properly academic gravitas. Professors in universities who speculate on what might have happened should an ocean liner not have been sunk, should a Hitler have been killed in his twenties, or should a young Mao have been captured will be equated with the less formally educated, who in their golden years brood about their alternative lives, should a job transfer not have been turned down, a suitor not spurned, or a traffic accident avoided.[40]

Quite simply, counterfactual history has no academic cachet.

Conclusion and Postscript

Let us conclude by working in reverse chronological order with the counterfactual suppositions outlined earlier. Imagine that Themistocles had not existed. The Greeks then probably would not have lured the Persians into committing their ships into the narrows at Salamis. Consequently, the Panhellenic armada would not have lingered there and would not have fought in the manner that it did. Thus Themistocles' oratory, ruse, and tactics alone ensured a battle and a Greek victory.

Second, had Themistocles' Salamis not been fought and won, then the Greeks would have been eventually overwhelmed at the isthmus and through subsequent Persian landings in the Peloponnese. No Panhellenic force would have mustered at Plataea the next autumn because even the surviving poleis in the south would have been evacuated, isolated, and dispirited with a Persian occupation now extending from Thessaly to Laconia. Without the fight at Salamis, then, the Greeks would have lost the Persian Wars.

And such a defeat in 480 BC would have ensured essentially the end of Western civilization of the time—Ionia, the islands, and the Greek mainland would have all been occupied under a Western satrapy of Persia. Those few Greeks still surviving in autonomous states in Italy or Sicily would have succumbed to Persian attack or would have remained in inconsequential and eccentric backwaters in an eastern Mediterranean that was essentially a Persian and Carthaginian lake. Without a free Greek mainland the larger tenets of the polis would have been lost and with them the values of Western civilization itself. What allowed Rome later to dominate both Greece and Carthage were its army; its ability to marshal manpower through levies of free citizens; its constitution, under which civilians oversaw military operations; and its dynamic scientific tradition, which produced everything from medicine to catapults, advanced siegecraft, and superb arms and armor. Most of these practices were either directly borrowed from the Greeks or Greek inspired. But by 480 Greece was not culturally prominent in the Mediterranean, and an infant Rome remained relatively unaware of Hellenic civilization.

On the positive side, after Salamis the ancient Greeks would never again fear any other foreign power until they met the Romans, their cultural protégés. No Persian king would ever again set foot in Greece, and for the next two thousand years no easterner would claim Greece as his own until the Ottoman conquest of the Balkans in the fifteenth century— an event that proved that an unchecked Eastern power most certainly would and could occupy and hold a weakened Greece for centuries.

Before Salamis, Athens was a rather eccentric city-state whose experiment with radical democracy was in its infancy and the verdict on its success still pending. After the battle, an imperial democratic culture arose that ruled the Aegean and gave us Aeschylus, Sophocles, the Parthenon, Pericles, and Thucydides. Before the naval fight, there was neither the consensus nor the confidence that Greek arms would protect and enhance Greek interests abroad. After Salamis, for the next three and a half centuries murderous Greek-speaking armies, possessed of superior technology and bankrolled by shrewd financiers, would run wild from southern Italy to the Indus River. The stunning architecture of Greece, from the temple of Zeus at Olympia to the Parthenon at Athens; the great literature of Greece, from Attic tragedy, comedy, and oratory to Greek history itself; the rise of red-figure vase painting and the mastery of realism and idealism in sculpture; and expansion of the idea of democracy— all that proceeded from the Persian Wars, prompting literary and artistic historians properly to mark the Greek victory at Salamis as the fault line between the Archaic and classical ages.[41]

Salamis, then, takes on enormous importance as a critical counterfactual example. First, the battle very easily could have been lost had not the efforts of a single man at a precise moment resulted in a Greek decision to fight off Salamis. Second, Themistocles seems to have been an extraordinary individual: of all the Greek leaders, he alone possessed the vision to commit to a sea battle, the rhetorical and political acumen to win adherents, and the guile and intelligence to force the Persians to commit their fleet to battle in an unfavorable strait. Had the battle of Salamis been the result of a collective decision or the efforts of a typical Greek conservative, rather than a half-Greek, radically democratic, and brilliant iconoclast, it would be logical to imagine a predetermined Greek victory.

Third, Persia and Greece represented antithetical social and political systems; thus, a pivotal victory by either in a war of annihilation presaged a radically different course of history for the entire Mediterranean. Cynoscephalae (197 BC) and Pydna (168 BC) were critical and lasting Greek defeats, but the victors were Roman, and thus the long-term results of the battle ensured the prosperity of republicanism in a manner not terribly different from the Greek legacy of constitutional government itself. History, of course, offers us other key battles, in which the outcome of a few days radically altered the course of civilization—the second Punic War, the Crusades, the fall of Constantinople, the Nazi invasion of Russia—but under all those scenarios the fate of Western civilization itself was not in doubt to the same degree that it was at Salamis, a battle of a few hours only, in a nearly conquered Greece without allies, fought by a democracy less than three decades old.

There is one final postscript about Salamis. The Greek victory saved the West by ensuring that Hellenism would not be extinguished after a mere two centuries of polis culture. But just as important, that triumph was a catalyst for the entire Athenian democratic renaissance, which radically altered the natural evolution of the Greek city-state. As Aristotle saw more than a century and a half later in his *Politics*, what had been a rather ordinary Greek polis, in the midst of a recent experiment of allowing the native-born poor to vote, now suddenly inherited the cultural leadership of Greece.

Because Salamis was a victory of "the naval crowd," in the next century the influence of Athenian landless oarsmen would only increase, as they demanded greater political representation commensurate with their prowess on the all important seas. The newly empowered Athenian naval class refashioned Athenian democracy into a particularly volatile, unpredictable, and aggressive imperial power, one that would soon build the temples on the Acropolis, subsidize the tragedians, and send its triremes throughout the Aegean—and also exterminate the Melians and execute Socrates. Marathon had created the myth of the Athenian infantry; Salamis, the far greater victory, had now superseded it. Imperialists such as Pericles, Cleon, and Alcibiades, not the descendants of the veterans of Marathon, were to be the key players on the horizon.[42]

No wonder the crotchety Plato in his *Laws* argued that while Marathon had started the string of Greek successes and Plataea had finished it Salamis "made the Greeks worse as people." More than a century after the battle, Plato saw Salamis as a critical juncture in the entire evolution of early Western culture. Before Salamis, Greek city-states embraced an entire array of hierarchies—property qualifications to vote, wars fought exclusively by those landowners whose capital and income gave them privilege, and a general absence of taxes, sophisticated navies, and imperialism. Those protocols of the traditional agrarian city-state had defined freedom and equality in terms of a minority of the population who had ample capital, education, or land or all three. Before Salamis, the essence of the polis was not equality for all but the search for moral virtue for all, guided by a consensus of properly qualified and gifted men.[43]

Plato, Aristotle, and most other Greek thinkers from Thucydides to Xenophon, who were wary of what had transpired in the aftermath of Salamis, were not merely elitists. Rather, they saw the inherent dangers in the license and affluence that accrued from radically democratic government, state entitlement, election by lot, subsidies for civic participation, free expression, and market capitalism. Without innate checks and balances, in this more restrictive view, the polis inevitably would turn out to be a highly individualistic but self-absorbed citizen with no interest in communal sacrifices or moral virtue. Better, the conservatives felt, that government should hinge on the majority votes of only those educated and informed citizens with some financial solvency. War—like Marathon and Plataea—should be for the defense of real property, on land, and should require martial courage, not mere technology or numerical superiority. Citizens should own their own farms, provide their own weapons, and be responsible for their own economic security—not seek wage labor, public employment, or government entitlement. The courageous oarsmen of Salamis and their publicly constructed and owned ships changed all that in an afternoon.

With the Aegean wide open after the retreat of the Persian fleet at Salamis and Athens now at the vanguard of the Greek resistance, radical democracy and its refutation of the old polis were at hand. The philosophers may have hated Salamis, but Themistocles' victory had not only saved Greece and the West but irrevocably altered it as well.[44]

NOTES

1. See Georg Wilhelm Friedrich Hegel, *Philosophy of History*, part 2: "The Greek World," sec. 1: "The Elements of the Greek Spirit," in *Great Books of the Western World*, ed. R. M. Hutchins, vol. 46: *Hegel* (Chicago: W. Benton, 1952), 274. Hegel had a propensity for seeing sweeping changes in the aftermath of a single decisive battle; after Napoleon's victory at Jena in 1806, he thought history had essentially "ended" with the rise of the modern liberal state. See F. Fukuyama, *The End of History and the Last Man* (New York: Free Press, 1992), 64–65.

2. Aeschylus, *Persians*, esp. 548–97, 800–42.

3. For example, see Simonides fragments, 2, 3 (Berk).

4. See the discussion in David Kovacs, ed. and trans., *Euripides, Cyclops, Alcestis Medea* (Cambridge: Harvard University Press, 1994), 5–6.

5. See Herodotus' suppositions at 7.139–40. Later, after the victory of Salamis, he has a Tegean tell the Spartans that they must march out to Plataea given the inability of their wall at the isthmus to keep the Persians out (Herodotus 9.9). Counterfactual suppositions are common in all classical Greek prose works, and it should be noted that the Greek language has a formal grammatical construction—the aorist tense in the protasis ("if" clause), followed by the aorist, plus the particle *an*, in the apodosis ("then" clause)—for past contrary-to-fact conditions. Cf. also Hans Delbrück, *Warfare in Antiquity*, vol. 1 of *History of the Art of War* (Westport, CT: Greenwood, 1975), 104–5.

6. Thucydides 1.73–74.1. On direct echoes of Herodotus' assessment of the importance of Themistocles and Salamis in saving Greece in Thucydides' history, see Simon Hornblower, *A Commentary on Thucydides* (Oxford: Clarendon; New York: Cambridge University Press, 1991), 118–20.

7. Thucydides 1.74.2–5.

8. Controversy surrounds the battle, since the fifth-century BC accounts of Herodotus and Aeschylus are at variance on a number of issues. Neither is reconcilable with the much later narratives in Plutarch and Diodorus; the sea level has changed since antiquity; and the identification of a number of key inlets, promontories, and small islands in the channel remains in dispute. For a good overview in English of the problems, see most prominently John Francis Lazenby, *The Defence of Greece. 490–479 B.C.* (Warminister, UK: Aris and Phillips, 1993), 151–97; N. G. L. Hammond, *Studies in Greek History* (Oxford: Clarendon, 1973), 251–310; Peter Green, *The Graeco-Persian Wars*, 2nd ed. (Berkeley: University of California Press, 1996), 153–200; Charles Hignett, *Xerxes' Invasion of Greece* (Oxford: Clarendon, 1963); Walter Wybergh How and Joseph Wells, eds., *A Commentary on Herodotus* (Oxford: Clarendon, 1912), 2:378–87; and Frank J. Frost, *Plutarch's Themistocles: A Historical Commentary* (Princeton: Princeton University Press, 1980). See, most recently, B. Strauss, *The Battle of Salamis* (New York: Simon and Schuster, 2004), 141–208, which reviews in depth the numbers, warfare, and nature of trireme warfare at the battle.

9. For the controversy over the number of ships present, see Lazenby, *Defence of Greece*, 172–75; and Frost, *Plutarch's Themistocles*, 150–53. Aeschylus probably wrote that the Greeks had 310 ships (*Persians* 338–40), Herodotus 380. Of the Persians, Aeschylus says that they had 1,207, and Herodotus confirms that figure; whether the latter drew on the playwright for the figure we are not sure. Modern scholars often put Persian numbers between 600 and 700, but the higher figures may well be correct.

10. For ancient testimony on the "heavier Greek ships" and the importance of fighting in the "narrows" of the Salamis channel, see Herodotus 8.60; cf. Thucydides 1.74.1; and R. Meiggs, *Trees and Timber in the Ancient Mediterranean World* (Oxford: Clarendon, 1982), 126–27. The Greek triremes were more heavily built and lacked the high decks of the Persian vessels, making them vulnerable to boarding from the enemy's larger platforms but also ensuring greater

stability and strength for ramming—which seems to have been the preferred Greek technique of attack.

11. For a discussion of Greek and Persian casualties, see Lazenby, *Defence of Greece*, 170–73.

12. On the Greek unfamiliarity with Persians at Marathon, see Herodotus 6.112. Herodotus suggests that the Persians' relative ignorance of Greek affairs was a reflection of the empire's dismissal of such a strange and impotent state; see 5.105.1; and cf. especially 1.153 and 7.73 for the idea that the Persians knew very little about the Greeks before the fifth century. The only real occasion before Marathon when mainland Greeks and Persians had become familiar was during the Ionian revolt of the prior decade.

13. For Xerxes' ignorance of the nature of his Greek adversaries at Thermopylae, see Herodotus 7.101–5. We should assume that nearly all of the Aegean islands and those off the coast of Asia Minor were under Persian control. Herodotus says that the Persian army after the defeat at Salamis made its way northward and then returned and occupied Athens a second time during the summer of 479. During this second razing of Athens, Mardonius sent his troops to ravage the Megarid, and Herodotus (9.14) comments that this attack on Megara constituted "the most westerly place in Europe which the Persian army reached." Cf. Herodotus for the general perception of contemporary Greeks that the Athenians had essentially become a people without a polis (8.61).

14. On the nature of the rather parochial, sixth-century agrarian city-states, see Victor Davis Hanson, *The Other Greeks: The Family Farm and the Agrarian Roots of Western Civilization* (New York: Free Press, 1995), 181–220. For the intellectual and artistic dominance of Ionia and its relationship with Persia, see Robin Osborne, *Greece in the Making, 1200–479 B.C.* (London and New York: Routledge, 1996), 316–25.

15. See again Hanson, *The Other Greeks*, 127–80. In general for the differences between Hellenic and Achaemenid cultures in the sixth and early fifth centuries, see, for example, John Boardman and David M. Lewis, eds., *The Cambridge Ancient History*, vol. 4: *Persia, Greece, and the Western Mediterranean, c. 525 to 479*, 2nd ed. (New York: Cambridge University Press, 1992), esp. T. C. Young, "The Consolidation of the Empire and Its Limits of Growth under Darius and Xerxes," 53–111. Vespasian is quoted in Suetonius, *Concerning the Lives of Caesars. Vespasian*, 23.

16. On the Greeks' belief that the war was between free men and slaves and was ultimately about the survival of an autonomous Hellenic people, see Aeschylus' stirring words about Salamis in *Persians* 402–5; cf., too, Herodotus 8.60, especially 8.144. For the Persian intent to enslave Greece and make it a satrapy, see Herodotus 7.5.2–3, 7.11–19. The various motivations of Xerxes are discussed in Jack Martin Balcer, "The Persian Wars against Greece: A Reassessment," *Historia* 38 (1989): 127–43.

17. Herodotus 5.49. For Ionia under Persian subjugation, see especially O. Murray, "Ionia and Persia," in Boardman and Lewis, *The Cambridge Ancient History*, vol. 4: *Persia, Greece, and the Western Mediterranean*, 473–80, which covers the wide gulf in the values, politics, the economy, literature, military practice, and religion between the two peoples. See also the classic essay by

A. Momigliano, "Persian Empire and Greek Freedom," in *The Idea of Freedom: Essays in Honor of Isaiah Berlin,* ed. Alan Ryan, 139–51 (Oxford: Oxford University Press, 1979). And cf. the counterfactual speculation of Anthony M. Snodgrass in his *Archaic Greece: The Age of Experiment* (London: Dent, 1980), 202.

18. For Persia's difficulty with the Greeks, who put a much higher value on political rather than religious freedom than did the Jews, see J. L. Myres, "Persia, Greece, and Israel," *Palestine Exploration Quarterly* (1953): 8–22. The Ionian elites, unlike other conquered toadies in the Persian Empire, had enormous difficulty selling their policy of obeisance to a people accustomed to consensual government; cf. Osborne, *Greece in the Making,* 318–22.

19. For Herodotus' description of the aftermath of the failed revolt and the Persian atrocities, see 6.9–33. Cf. Murray, "Ionia and Persia," 490.

20. The population of the Peloponnese in antiquity may have been around a half million people, while in Greece north of the isthmus, the islands, and Ionia there may have resided anywhere from one to three million. Cf. *The Oxford Classical Dictionary,* 2nd ed. (Oxford: Oxford University Press, 1970), *s.v.* "Peloponnesus, Population."

21. For the size of the Persian Empire, see Boardman and Lewis, eds., *The Cambridge Ancient History,* vol. 4, 79–93; and Lazenby, *Defence of Greece,* 17–21.

22. For the importance of Marathon, see Lazenby, *Defence of Greece,* 45–47.

23. For a narrative of the Persian war battles prior to Salamis, see N. G. L. Hammond's essays in J. Boardman et al., *The Cambridge Ancient History,* 491–568.

24. For details on the battle of Plataea, see Lazenby, *Defence of Greece,* 217–47.

25. For Themistocles' threats, see Herodotus 8.62.

26. On Themistocles' arguments, see Herodotus 8.60; on Mnesiphilus' warning, see Herodotus 8.57. Artemisia, commander of Xerxes' Carian contingent, purportedly urged Xerxes not to fight at Salamis, since the Persian objectives had already been met: the destruction of Athens and the disintegration of the Greek alliance. Indeed, in her view, the Greeks would soon enough come to terms with Xerxes individually—the onus was on the Greeks, not the Persians, to fight. See Herodotus 8.68. For Herodotus' point that a planned fight at the isthmus was doomed, see again 8.60, 7.139–40, 9.9. On the later Athenian seaborne raids off the Peloponnese, see H. D. Westlake, "Seaborne Raids in Periclean Strategy," *Classical Quarterly* 39 (1945): 75–84.

27. For the Athenian decision to build a fleet using the revenues of the Laureum silver mines, and the later evacuation of Attica, see Herodotus 7.144, 8.40–42; and R. Meiggs and D. Lewis, eds., *A Selection of Greek Historical Inscriptions* (Oxford: Oxford University Press, 1975), 48–52. On second-order counterfactuals, see p. 38 n. 11.

28. For discussions of Themistocles' secret negotiations with Xerxes, see Herodotus 75; Green, *Graeco-Persian Wars,* 177–81; Lazenby, *Defence of Greece,* 166–69; and Hignett, *Xerxes' Invasion,* 241–43. We should assume that Themistocles may have had all sorts of personal agendas as well, inasmuch he would later claim to have done the Persians a service by warning them of the

Greeks' "intentions." His later exile on charges of treason was probably not entirely the result of envy.

29. On the vital role of Themistocles during the actual fighting, see Hammond, *Studies in Greek History*, 286; cf. Thucydides 1.74.1, 1.138.3. And see especially Plutarch, *Themistocles* 14; cf. Frost, *Plutarch's Themistocles*, 123–66.

30. See Herodotus 8.40 for the Athenian shock and sense of betrayal that the Greeks had no intention of fighting for Boeotia and Attica but apparently all along had envisioned the isthmus as the locus of last resistance should the pass at Thermopylae be turned.

31. On the Athenian alternatives to evacuation and sea fighting, see the discussion in Lazenby, *Defence of Greece*, 256–59. Hignett (*Xerxes' Invasion*, 403–8) has a long discussion of the message from Themistocles to Xerxes but is overly critical in rejecting the authenticity of both Herodotus' and Aeschylus' reports.

32. For controversy over the role of Mnesiphilus, see Frost, *Plutarch's Themistocles*, 21–23, 67–68, 128; and G. B. Grundy, *The Great Persian War and Its Preliminaries* (London: Murray, 1901), 363–66.

33. Christian Meier, *Athens: A Portrait of the City in Its Golden Age*, trans. R. Kimber and R. Kimber (New York: Metropolitan Books and Henry Holt, 1998), 31.

34. See Grundy, *Great Persian War*, 359–60, on Thucydides' famous assessment that Themistocles alone had saved Greece.

35. For the idea that the Persians' blunders helped to cause their own defeat, see Thucydides 1.69.5. See also Lazenby, *Defence of Greece*, 255–56. For the improbability of refounding Athens at Siris, see How and Wells, *Commentary on Herodotus*, 2:255–56; and Green, *Graeco-Persian Wars*, note at 171. For the population of Athens in 480, see Peter Garnsey, *Famine and Food Supply in the Graeco-Roman World: Responses to Risk and Crisis* (Cambridge: Cambridge University Press, 1988), 89–91, which suggests that the families of Athenian citizens may have numbered 150,000, excluding slaves and resident aliens.

36. For the ability of the Persians to put down revolts and the notion that the empire was far more cohesive and stable than is usually thought, cf. Osborne, *Greece in the Making*, 322–25; and S. Hornblower, "Persia," in *The Cambridge Ancient History*, vol. 6: *The Fourth Century B.C.*, ed. D. M. Lewis et al., 2nd. ed., 45–96 (Cambridge: Cambridge University Press, 1994), especially 41: "The extent of satrapal unrest in the fourth century may have been exaggerated by our sources, and in any case some flexibility at the margins can be seen as a sign of Persian strength not weakness."

37. For the nature of the West, see pp. 5–6 above.

38. Many critics of both Hellenism and the West cite the dichotomy of freedom alongside both chattel slavery and the political subordination of women. Three observations must be made. First, the sins of the Greeks are the sins of mankind: women were second-class citizens and people were enslaved in every ancient culture outside of Greece (and in some non-Western cultures today). Second, the freedom of the Greeks was an abstract, evolving idea that began with a small cadre of property owners, spread by the fifth century to poorer citizens under radical democracy, and was still in the process of evolution when it was cut short by Philip and the Macedonians. As Plato worried, once the idea of unlim-

ited freedom and equality was set in motion for some, in theory there was no limit to its extension to others. Third, in an open society, most literature and public discourse are in some sense always antithetical to existing political and cultural protocols; thus tragedies such as Medea, comedies such as *Lysistrata* and *Ecclesiazusiae,* and utopian literature as exemplified by Plato's *Republic* and *Laws* argue for greater equality of women. Aristotle in his *Politics* assumes a hostile body of contemporary critics for his belief in natural slavery, while much of Stoic and Pythagorean philosophy questioned both slavery and the inequality of women.

39. Jacob Burckhardt, *The Greeks and Greek Civilization,* new ed. (New York: St. Martin's, 1998), 12. There have been numerous attempts to suggest that factors such as climate, natural resources, or disease, not culture, explain Western dominance; see, for example, Jared M. Diamond, *Guns, Germs, and Steel: The Fates of Human Societies* (New York: Norton, 1997).

40. For discussion of probable scholarly objections to the use of counterfactual thought experiments, see chapter 1 above.

41. The Persian Wars are usually seen as marking the transition from Archaic to classical Greece; see Snodgrass, *Archaic Greece,* 200–218.

42. For Salamis as the far more influential victory than Marathon, see again Grundy, *Great Persian War,* 406–7.

43. For the effect of the Persian Wars in transforming the evolution of the Greek city-state, see Hanson, *The Other Greeks,* 333–36. On the connection between the Persian victories and the radical transformation of Athenian democracy, see Meier, *Athens,* 207–304.

44. For the pessimistic assessments of Plato and Aristotle of the cultural and political aftermath of Salamis, see Plato, *Laws* 4.707C–E; Plato, *Gorgias* 515C–519A; and Aristotle, *Politics* 2.1274a13–16.

CHAPTER 3

The Resilient West

SALAMIS WITHOUT THEMISTOCLES,
CLASSICAL GREECE WITHOUT SALAMIS,
& THE WEST WITHOUT CLASSICAL GREECE

Barry Strauss

"If Xerxes had won at Salamis, we might still be barbarians."[1] So Voltaire wrote, echoing a judgment shared by most ancient Greeks and modern scholars; at least they agree that the battle of Salamis in 480 BC was a great historical turning point, if not that Xerxes was a barbarian. And so it was, but with a twist, as I argue in my *The Battle of Salamis: The Naval Encounter That Saved Greece—and Western Civilization*.[2] More on the twist later; for now, let us turn to Victor Hanson's splendid chapter in this volume. Hanson not only argues that the Persians could have nipped Western civilization in the bud if they had won at Salamis but also that they could have saved themselves the trouble and attained the same goal more cheaply merely by arranging for the assassination of one man: the Athenian Themistocles. Without his brilliant leadership, the Greek alliance might not have held together and would probably not have fought at Salamis. Without a doubt, Hanson is right. By 480, Themistocles' leadership *was* essential to Greek success.

Had Themistocles been assassinated, say, a week before the battle or even a year before the battle, Athens' elite would have been devastated.

Athens was crucial to the Greek victory at Salamis and Salamis decided the course of the war in 480, and so without Themistocles Greek prospects would have been poor. But that does not tell us very much. Most countries would be devastated by the loss of their war leader in the midst of a crisis because sudden change is destabilizing and great victories usually require great leadership.

Not this question but, rather, three other questions are of greater interest to the student of counterfactual history. First, what if Themistocles had never lived—would that have cost Greece its victory against Persia in 480? Second, if the Greeks had lost the battle of Salamis, could they have bounced back from the Persian conquest of the Peloponnese, which was sure to follow? Third, if the Greeks had not bounced back—if Persia had followed its conquest of Greece with the conquest of Sicily and southern Italy or even of the entire Mediterranean, would the rise of the West have ever taken place?

To answer these questions, I make a complicated counterfactual argument that disputes conventional wisdom, advancing my thesis by means of three separate arguments. The first two arguments are related, as each emphasizes the dynamism, energy, and cunning that characterized the culture of the Greek city-states, in particular, of Athens. These qualities might have been enough to provide Athens with another capable leader had Themistocles never lived, and so the Greeks might have won at Salamis without him. Yet, even granting the first-order counterfactual assertion (i.e., without Themistocles, the Persians would have won at Salamis), we can argue that Persia's victory would have been undone by a later Greek revival. Refugees from mainland Greece would have fled to and regrouped in western Greece or Magna Graecia (as the Romans called the Greek cities of southern Italy and Sicily). They might have turned southern Italy and Sicily into the center of Greek civilization. Within several generations, and perhaps led by the Athenians, they might even have reconquered their homeland from a Sicilian base.

The third argument thinks the unthinkable. What if this second-order counterfactual defense failed? What if neither Athens nor the other Greek city-states recovered from defeat by Persia in 480; what if Persia had gone on to conquer the Greek city-states of western Greece after absorbing the Greek mainland? Would there then have been any Hellenic contribution to Western civilization? Might that contribution have come from some source other than Greece? Would there indeed have been a West?

In a "third-order" counterfactual defense, I argue that in spite of such setbacks there might have been a West, and it might still have risen to global dominance. The loss of Greek freedom would have taken a very heavy toll on Western civilization. Yet it is just possible that by the skin of its teeth the West might have scraped by. Even in a Persian empire, Greek rationalism would have survived. Certainly, a vibrant philosophical culture is possible even under an empire, as it was both during the Roman Empire and during the Muslim caliphate.

That rationalism, combined with the freedom-loving culture of the Germanic peoples, might have allowed something akin to the Italian Renaissance to have emerged from the ruins of a Persian Empire, even without the legacy of a free and independent classical Greece. It is worth noting, in this context, that the Renaissance was no simple return to Greco-Roman antiquity but, rather, a dialogue between late medieval and ancient cultures. Ancient Greece was a singularly important strand in the genesis of the modern West, but it was only one strand.

To be sure, we need not surrender all our long-held ideas. Salamis will rightly remain a "decisive battle" and one at which Themistocles was the architect of victory. The Greeks will maintain their reputation for having made a great contribution to the rise of the West, if not as great as some have held. What will change, however, is the accidental quality of some accounts of the victory at Salamis, the impression that it was a bolt out of the blue or the result solely of one man's genius.

Instead, the victory of Salamis will appear as the culmination of a process by which mainland Greece, a rising regional power, learned and mastered the art of naval warfare pioneered by the Persian Empire. Salamis was less a prod than a lever: It was the moment at which the Greeks translated their potential into reality, but it did not create that potential. If Salamis had never happened, the Greeks might have been able to seize another moment to make the transition.

And if they failed? The cost to the West would have been enormous, but perhaps another people, buoyed by what would have remained of the Greek heritage, would have made the transition later. In short, the West might have risen eventually without Salamis.

Could the Greeks Have Won at Salamis without Themistocles?

The truth is that our ancestors, men of Athens, would not deprive themselves of the credit for any deeds back then. No one would say that the naval battle at Salamis was Themistocles'—it belongs to the Athenians, nor that the battle of Marathon was Miltiades'— it belongs to the *polis*.[3]

Judge of the patriot [Themistocles] by Salamis and the ships, and
thereby shalt thou find him greater than Athens herself.[4]

Was Themistocles indispensable to Athens' victory at Salamis? Was
he indispensable to Athenian resistance to Persian invasion in 480 BC
more generally? As these passages show, the debate was already joined in
antiquity. Indeed, it had already begun in 480. None of the ancient
sources is neutral about Themistocles.[5]

To put the question another way, was Themistocles a product of
Athenian society or was he a unique genius? Would it have been possible
to undo the rise of the West at Salamis had Themistocles never lived?
Themistocles was less a unique genius than a product of his society, so it
would have been difficult to undo the success of the West at Salamis even
had Themistocles never lived.

To demonstrate this conclusion, it is necessary to examine briefly both
the nature of Themistocles' genius and the nature of the society that
would have had to replace him. Let us turn to Thucydides for a capsule
appraisal of the man, and let us focus on the institution that was the
essence of Athenian society in 480: democracy.

Thucydides offers the earliest strong argument for Themistocles'
importance. Note in passing that Herodotus, who offers a far more
detailed account of the Persian Wars, makes much less of Themistocles'
role. Thucydides accords Themistocles rare words of praise.

For Themistocles was a man who exhibited the most indubitable
signs of genius; indeed, in this particular he has a claim on our
admiration quite extraordinary and unparalleled. By his own
native capacity, which was neither shaped by education nor developed by later training, he was at once the best judge in those sudden crises which admit of little or of no deliberation, and the best
prophet of the future, even to its most distant possibilities. An able
theoretical expositor of all that came within the sphere of his practice, he was not without the power of passing an adequate judgment in matters in which he had no experience. He could also
excellently divine the good and evil which lay hidden in the unseen
future. To sum up, whether we consider the extent of his natural
powers, or the slightness of his application, this extraordinary man
must be allowed to have surpassed all others in the faculty of intu-
itively meeting an emergency.[6]

Thucydides thus praises Themistocles' native sagacity, intuition, foresight, judgment, communications skill, in brief, his natural power (*phuseôs . . .dunamis*). Elsewhere he singles out Themistocles' daring (*prôtos etolmêsen*). Themistocles had particular insight into the importance of sea power for Athens, both after the Persian invasion, when he laid the foundations of Athens' sphere of rule, and before, when he foresaw "that the approach by sea was easier for the King's army than that by land."[7]

To turn from the man to the regime, note that when the Persians invaded in 480 Athens had been a democracy for about a generation, ever since the reforms associated with the name of the politician Cleisthenes in 508. Under democracy, Athenian politicians had to submit their proposals to the consideration of the assembly, a participatory body open to all citizens (males only) over the age of twenty. By contrast, under the "tyrants," who had governed Athens for most of the sixth century BC, decisions lay in the hands of the ruling family. Under oligarchy, as in Athens before the tyranny and still in 480 in many other Greek city-states, political power often lay in the hands of various political clubs, which were dominated by a narrow elite of the wealthy or wellborn. Democracy opened Athenian politics to greater competition. Open debate meant that new ideas would be heard and new men would have a chance to advocate them. It may be that Themistocles himself came from outside the charmed circle of the old aristocracy.[8]

The popular audience that sat in judgment of Athens' politicians was less likely to make its decisions on the genteel basis of honor or dignity or glory than on the vulgar considerations of success, power, and profit. That rough-and-ready judge, the people, rewarded ideas that worked and the politicians who pushed them; and they likewise showed the door to failed ideas and leaders. In Athens, beginning in the year 487, that "door" might amount to nothing less than ten years' exile or ostracism for a rejected leader.[9]

Themistocles was a successful politician in Athens not only because he was brilliant and talented but also because he knew how to play the democratic game. But the very rules of that game meant that if Themistocles had not existed the Athenian people would have had to invent him. The people were less interested in famous names than in *results,* that is, in victory against Persian invasion. By arguing persuasively, and correctly, that building a fleet was the best way to beat the enemy, Themistocles won political capital for himself. Let it be added that Themistocles' plan also offered the people *profit* and *power.* Had Athens been saved by its infantry, then victory would have gone to the credit of the middle-class men who alone could afford the suit of armor needed for membership in that body of fighting men (known as the hoplite phalanx). The fleet, by contrast, was open to every able-bodied Athenian, whether rich or poor. Victory would belong to the entire citizenry, and it might end up with the poor leveraging additional political power.

What more vivid symbol of the democratic way of war could there be than the following image of Themistocles' political rival, bowing to the reality of power? Cimon was the leading young politician to represent the aristocrats, which made him skeptical of navies and the unwashed masses who manned them. Yet, as Plutarch writes, on the eve of the Persian invasion of Attica, when the public had to be steeled for the sacrifice ahead:

> Cimon was the first to set a public example, and cheerfully led a procession of his comrades through the Cerameicus up to the Acropolis. He carried in his hands a horse's bridle to offer up to the goddess, in token of the fact that what the city needed at the moment was not knightly valor, but men to fight at sea. With Cimon's gesture, Athens' aristocratic cavalry swallowed its pride and acknowledged the superiority of the sailors, of that group which Thucydides and Aristotle—no doubt speaking for their class—sneered at as "the naval crowd." Such was the "gift" which King Xerxes, no democrat he, had ironically given Athens' upper classes.[10]

It was a boon for Themistocles. It was a boon for shrewdness, for street fighting, for innovation, for risk taking, for political ambition. And these were precisely the qualities that Athens was known for. By the late fifth century, Athenians were famous for their innovation, quickness, intelligence, daring, and industriousness. No doubt these qualities grew stronger after Salamis, in the confidence of victory and in the wake of Athens' naval empire, yet they were already aborning before 480. In the early sixth century BC, Athens had been led by Solon, a name synonymous with wisdom. Herodotus thinks that Athens' reputation in the late fifth century for being first among the Greeks when it comes to wisdom should apply to the sixth century too—at least he finds it hard to understand an example of Athenian foolishness then. Innovation? The establishment of democracy in Athens in 508 was itself innovative, indeed revolutionary. As for boldness, Athens had already displayed it aplenty with its unflinching stand at Marathon in 490. On that occasion, Athens' generals displayed quick wits when, seeing the Persian forces withdraw their cavalry (for a would-be ship-borne attack on the city of Athens), they took advantage of the enemy's sudden disadvantage and attacked—literally *ran* to the attack.[11]

In short, Athens already prized the qualities of a Themistocles before Themistocles displayed them. If it was Themistocles' genius to do the right thing at the right time, we must wonder if he was the only Athenian who could have done so. Yes, Themistocles understood how grave the danger of Persian invasion remained after Marathon, but that he was the *only* Athenian with this foresight, the only man with enough courage to propose building a fleet, as Plutarch says, seems hard to believe. Athenian politicians needed allies; even Plutarch concedes that Themistocles belonged to a political club (*hetaireia*), whose members did everything for each other. Did none of them share Themistocles' anti-Persian conviction?[12]

Yes, Themistocles was intelligent enough to propose that Athens build a fleet with its silver, but he was not the sole intelligent Athenian. That mining profit could be used to finance national defense was not a secret: Thasos had built a fleet and improved its walls in the 490s thanks to its successful gold mines. Xanthippus, son of Ariphron, better known in later years as the father of Pericles, commanded the Athenian fleet at the battle of Mycale in 479. Had he not been ostracized in 485–484, perhaps he too would have supported a shipbuilding program. Many scholars venture the guess that Themistocles supported the ostracism of Xanthippus, as Themistocles did the ostracism of Aristides several years later.[13]

Yes, Themistocles was cunning in the extreme when he tricked Xerxes into fighting in the narrows at Salamis, but Themistocles had no monopoly on craft.[14] Earlier Athenian rulers, including Solon and Pisistratus, inspired anecdotes about their wiliness. Solon, for example, once tricked the enemy into dropping its guard by using Athenian teenage soldiers, whom Solon dressed as women, with daggers under their dresses. When seeking to become tyrant, Pisistratus deliberately wounded himself in the style of Odysseus—the patron saint of Greek guile—in order to talk the people into voting him a bodyguard, which he then turned on his enemies. Cimon, though admittedly too young (at ca. twenty-seven) for a primary leadership position in 480, was, according to Plutarch, as bold as his father Miltiades (hero of the battle of Marathon in 490 BC) and as sagacious as Themistocles.[15]

Yes, Themistocles was decisive, but the rest of the Athenian elite was not weak-kneed. At least, later on, one tradition claimed that, during the crisis as the Persians neared Athens it had been the aristocratic council of the Areopagus and not Themistocles that came up with the money to pay the crew members of the Athenian fleet, who would otherwise have gone hungry. Yes, Themistocles cajoled and threatened the Greek allies into fighting at Salamis, but Themistocles was not the only diplomat in Athens. Herodotus goes so far as to claim that another Athenian, one Mnesiphilus (perhaps Themistocles' near neighbor and mentor, according to Plutarch) gave Themistocles the idea of just what argument to use to persuade the Peloponnesian commanders to stay and fight at Salamis—an allegation that convinced an outraged Plutarch of Herodotus's bias toward Themistocles. But Plutarch had little patience for those who questioned the great man theory of history.[16]

Had Themistocles not existed, then, perhaps some other Athenian would have arisen to take his place. We cannot be sure of that, since democracies do not always turn up victorious leaders. Democratic Athens, after all, *lost* the Peloponnesian War (431–404 BC). But if Athens had not been a democracy, Themistocles' talents might not have availed. Only a regime as open, innovative, energetic, pragmatic, and meritocratic as democracy could have followed the policy that won at Salamis. Doubters need only consider what Athens' prospects would have been like had it been Sparta.

Sparta was an oligarchy or, more accurately, an oligarchy with some monarchic and even democratic features. It might be called a mixed regime, but nonetheless Sparta failed the flexibility test. Sparta did not build a fleet to face Persia in 480. Nor did Sparta build a fleet to use against the Athenian naval empire that followed the Persian Wars. Individual Spartans, to be sure, tried to turn Sparta into a naval power, but to judge their success, consider the fate of the regent Pausanias, would-be admiral of a Spartan grand fleet: circa 471 BC he starved to death on the Spartan acropolis, the victim of a judicial murder sponsored by an elite that had closed ranks against him.[17]

It took sixty-five years and several wars after the founding of the Delian League before Sparta finally took to the sea against Athens with a competitive fleet, and that was only after Athens had all but committed military suicide in its disastrous Sicilian expedition (415–413 BC), weakening itself to the point that Persia—quiescent in the Aegean for three generations—joined the Peloponnesian War on the Spartan side. Indeed, it was Persia that financed and built Sparta's fleet. Finally, Sparta did not construct its fleet until it was so desperate to win that it made an about-face in its whole way of making war. Only then did Sparta's oligarchs allow mavericks to rise to the top, men such as Brasidas, who in 424–422 led an unconventional, overland attack on Athenian allied states in northeastern Greece and Lysander, the master of personal politics who made Sparta's Persian alliance work. Yet once they got to the pinnacle, their position proved unstable.[18] Nor was there any reliable mechanism in Sparta to get rid of military incompetence, as there is in a democracy (ask Lyndon Johnson or Neville Chamberlain). In spite of his string of strategic failures, for example, King Agesilaos stayed in power until the crashing defeat of Sparta at Leuctra (371 BC) and beyond.

This is not to argue that only democracies and no other regimes allow the degree of rivalry and debate that lets the right leader for the right time emerge. As the Spartan case suggests, even the most closed oligarchy may admit new blood and new ideas if pressed hard enough. Neither oligarchy nor monarchy (consider, e.g., a Roman imperial reformer such as Constantine) is completely hostile to innovative, daring, clever leadership, but democracy has far fewer built-in inhibitors of such talent.

Salamis was Themistocles' finest hour, and no one can take that away from him. Yet Themistocles is unimaginable without the Athenian regime—social and cultural as well as political—behind him. Genius he may have been, but had Themistocles died in the mid-480s, or had he never existed, another member of his faction might have replaced him as the advocate of a naval policy and the driving force behind the victory at Salamis. Had Themistocles faltered, it might have been Xanthippus's finest hour or someone else's whose name has not survived. To be sure, had Themistocles died during the Persian invasion but before Salamis, he might have proved irreplaceable. In that case, however, the issue would not have been Themistocles' genius so much as the problem of succession during a crisis.

Before leaving the subject of Themistocles there is one other point to consider. To understand the magnitude of Themistocles' contribution to victory it is necessary to have some sense of the magnitude of the threat that faced him. The more serious the Persian threat and the greater the chasm that yawned between Greek power and the enemy's might, then the more miraculous Greece's victory and the more supernatural seeming Themistocles' achievement.

Yet Greece's military position in 480 was not as dire as it might seem. Beware Monday morning quarterbacks, but open the playbook nonetheless for the big picture. What Persia was trying to do in 480 was inherently difficult. As a joint land-sea operation far from the home base,

Xerxes' invasion of Greece was unprecedented and fragile. The apparently mighty Persian expedition was in fact vulnerable. Without the navy, and the supply ships it protected, Persia's land army could not be maintained. A storm had already destroyed many of Persia's warships before Salamis, and the Greek navy had fought the Persian fleet to a standstill at Artemisium.[19]

All it would take to defeat Persia was a big Greek naval victory. That was within reach as long as the battle could be fought on favorable terms: that is, in a location and under circumstances of the Greeks' choosing. And since the Persians were under pressure to win a quick victory before the eyes of their king, the Greeks might have been able to make that very choice. Furthermore, the knowledge of local nautical conditions is a big advantage, and in ancient warfare the enemy rarely had such information. The Greeks did and used a favoring wind at Salamis. So although they were outnumbered, the Greeks were not without resources.[20]

The number of ships in the battle of Salamis is much debated; in all likelihood, the Greeks had 368 triremes against Persia's approximately 700. In addition to their local knowledge, the Greeks had the advantage of sending out fresh crews against Persian rowers who had been at their oars all night.[21] Themistocles deserves most of the credit for deceiving the enemy at Salamis. He had help, though, both from other Athenians, such as Mnesiphilus and Aristides, and from the Persians—without whose overconfidence his cunning would have failed.[22]

It was Themistocles' genius to play the main role in holding the Greek coalition together and setting the battle up; it was Athens' glory to spearhead the fight. But Greece was no David, and its ships were no slingshot. It was facing a superpower, but as a regional power Greece had a considerable chance of success. Victory would have been harder without Themistocles, but it would have been possible.

To win at Salamis, the Greeks had to be able to count on enemy gullibility, but they did not require enemy incompetence. The Greek commander had to be not a military genius but a man of cunning. Cunning in ancient Greece? Coals to Newcastle, which leads us back to the previous section and the Athenian regime.

Could Athens Have Defeated Persia after Losing at Salamis?

What if victory had eluded the Greeks at Salamis? Could the Greeks still have won the war if their fleet, and not Persia's, lay in ruins that September day? That would have been a tall order, yet historically the Greek city-state proved a buoyant institution, full of dynamism and ready for war. Persia, for example, conquered the Ionian city-states in 546, but they rose in a major rebellion in 499. Although that rebellion ultimately failed, a generation later, after Salamis, an Athenian-led confederacy liberated Ionia. Seventy-five years later, Athens itself bounced back from a major defeat in the Peloponnesian War (431–404 BC) to become a player on the Greek interstate scene in the next century. About seventy-five years after that, Athens rebelled against Macedon (in the Lamian War, 322 BC), which had imposed its hegemony on the Greek city-states at the battle of Chaeronea in 338. Nor did the failure of that rebellion take the fight out of the Athenians, who rebelled again in the Chremonidean War (268–265 BC), their last armed attempt to rid themselves of Macedonian rule— although they continued the struggle through diplomacy. The Peloponnesian War saw mainland Greek states intervene in Sicily, followed by Sicilians intervening in the Aegean. A Greek defeat at Salamis might have generated a large emigration of refugees to Sicily, who would have lobbied for the liberation of the homeland.

The spirit of Greek freedom beat strong even before 480 BC. It had already created democracy, established free enquiry, attacked tyranny, and extolled independence. Greek politicians, soldiers, philosophers, poets, and artists all contributed to a culture of liberty even while the eastern part of the Greek world fell under Persian rule after 546. If the Persians had conquered the Greek mainland in 480 BC, they would not have easily wiped that culture out. Its centers would have migrated westward. There they would have regrouped.

Freedom, it is true, cannot survive without the will and means to defend itself militarily. Failure at Salamis would have shaken the spirit and the flesh of Greek freedom. Yet even had they lost their mainland home as they had lost Ionia, the Greeks would have retained both their resolve and a considerable part of their resources.

Free peoples, after all, have frequently bounced back from defeat. The English, for example, survived the disastrous year of 1940 to celebrate victory in 1945. The Germans lost two world wars in the first half of the twentieth century, the second at an especially devastating cost. Yet sixty years after its defeat, Germany is again the leading power in Europe. Who is to say that a century from now the West will not be led not by the United States of America but by a German-dominated European Union?

Similarly, the resources and energy of western Greece, buoyed after Persia's victory by an influx of refugees from Athens and the Peloponnese, are not to be underestimated. Magna Graecia (the Greek cities of southern Italy and of Sicily) represented by far the wealthiest part of the ancient Greek world. Populous and warlike, Magna Graecia had already absorbed a host of Greek refugees from Ionia. These included several prominent philosophers, who established new schools in the west.

Greek refugees after 480 might have turned Magna Graecia into the powerhouse of Greek freedom. It was Magna Graecia, after all, more than the Greek mainland, that played the historic role of educating Rome and thereby passing on the heritage of Greek civilization. Yet the Roman Republic was in its infancy in 480. In order to teach the Romans, the western Greeks had to survive. What if the Persians challenged their ability?

Would Magna Graecia have been able to absorb the shock of a Persian attack after 480 BC, especially if it were coordinated with a Carthaginian offensive? Similar questions have been asked again and again in history about improbable victories. Would the barbaric Germans have been able to withstand the might of Rome? Would the English have been able to defeat the Spanish Armada? Would the Koreans have managed to drive out a Japanese invasion force in 1598? Would the ragtag Americans have been able to shake off the British Empire in 1776? In each case, the underdog won.

To return to Athens, consider that on the eve of the battle of Salamis, with the Peloponnesian admiral, Eurybiades, threatening to pull out his contingent to make a stand closer to home, at the Isthmus of Corinth, Themistocles countered with this threat.

> The whole war rests on our ships, so listen to me. If you do not do this, we will, just as we are, take our households to Siris in Italy, which has been ours since olden days, and the prophecies say we must found a colony there. You will remember these words when you are without allies like us.[23]

Themistocles won the day, but the threat would not have been easy to carry out had the Peloponnesians forced his hand. Siris was located in southeastern Italy, in today's Matera province of the Basilicata region. Athens had roughly 200 triremes at the time, which could have carried to Italy forty thousand men serving as rowers and marines and in various other professional capacities. Triremes, however, were too small, narrow, and cramped to transfer women and children to Italy or to carry possessions or gold and silver. To move large numbers of people and some property westward, Athens needed merchant ships, and that would have cost money, something that a refugee city would have been short of.

Conditions would only have become worse had the Persians won at Salamis. The Persians are said to have lost more than 200 triremes in the battle of Salamis, nearly one-third of the fleet engaged. Proportional losses, had Athens lost the battle, would have left the Athenians with 140 triremes or so, enough to bring a maximum of twenty-eight thousand men to Italy. And the treasury coffers would have been empty. The Persians would have rounded up as many Athenians on the island of Salamis as they could, and to get the refugees even out of Troezen the Athenians would have had to move quickly.[24]

They could not have counted on their Greek allies to protect them. Had Persia won at Salamis, the alliance would have crumbled. Unprotected by the wall that was being built across the Isthmus of Corinth, Megara would have had no choice but surrender. As for the Peloponnesian city-states beyond the isthmus, how many would have put their faith in a position at the wall that could be turned at will by the Persian fleet? How many would refuse to do the reasonable thing and not give earth and water as tokens of submission to Xerxes? After all, having engorged his lust for revenge in Athens, the Great King would surely treat the other Greeks mildly, wouldn't he? Yes, the Spartans, being Spartans, would have fought to the end, but they might have fought alone, and they would have faced not the reduced Persian force that they met at Plataea in spring 479 but the full Persian levy. In short, had they lost at Salamis, the Greeks would have been outclassed at sea and faced a very serious fight on land, yet it is questionable whether they possessed the political will to hold together long enough to face the test in either sphere.[25]

No, the Athenians could not have counted on safety in Troezen. Nor could they have gone back to Athens, not given the precedent of Miletus, ringleader of the Ionian Revolt against Persia (499–494 BC), whose punishment had been dramatized on the Athenian stage in a play by Phrynichus. When they captured Miletus after a year's siege, the Persians captured whomever they could and murdered the men and enslaved the women and children among them; the latter were eventually resettled on the Persian Gulf. There was a precedent for relocation westward after defeat by the Persians. Large numbers of Phocaeans and Teians had gone west when Ionia was first captured by the Persians in 547 BC, the Teians to Abdera in Thrace, the Phocaeans first to Alalia in Corsica and then to Hyele (later Elea) in southern Italy. Another example is the group of wealthy Samian men, who had supported the Milesians, relocated to Zancle in Sicily in 494. The various refugees did not have an easy time of it; for example, more than half of the Phocaeans gave up and returned home. And the Phocaeans had left in an orderly enough fashion to bring with them "all their movable goods, besides the statues from the temples and everything dedicated in them except bronze or stonework or painting." Athenians would have had no such luxury. So, many of those who could have struck a deal with the Persians would no doubt have stayed in Attica, but the Persians would probably have been in no mood for making deals.[26]

Some doubt whether Athens really did have a foothold at Siris in 480.[27] Nor is it clear that Tarentum, the strongest local power in the region of Siris, would have rolled out the welcome mat. Syracuse in Sicily, the mightiest of the Greek city-states in Magna Graecia as a whole, would probably have had mixed feelings. In the same year that the Persians invaded Greece, the Carthaginians sent a huge amphibious force to Sicily, aimed at conquering Syracuse—maybe even representing a coordinated effort with the Persians, if we can believe the report in Diodorus Siculus. At the battle of Himera in 480, Syracuse inflicted an even greater defeat on Carthage than the Greeks did on Persia. Syracuse might have welcomed the Athenian colonists as potential allies in any renewed war with Carthage. Yet at the same time, they would have recognized Athenians as potential rivals, a power calculation that the ethnic difference—Dorian Syracuse versus Ionian Athens—would only have compounded.[28]

Yet after losing at Salamis, the Athenians might just have managed to plant a colony at Siris and make it thrive in the dog-eat-dog world of Magna Graecia. Or perhaps the Athenian refugees would have succeeded only in scattering to the various southern Italian and Sicilian Greek city-states, there to begin new lives as resident aliens. Nor would the Athenians have been the only mainland Greek refugees in the west; they would have been joined by Corinthians, Aeginetans, Megarians, Spartans, and others. The refugees would have had a leavening effect on western Greek culture and politics, just as Ionian refugees had affected mainland and western Greek culture and politics after 546, and especially after 494 BC Magna Graecia would have become more philosophical, more poetic, and more militarized than it already was. In short, Greek culture would not have been snuffed out by Persian victory in mainland Greece; it would merely have shifted westward.[29]

Whether the Athenians established a colony in western Greece or merely dispersed with other mainland refugees among its cities, they would have represented a powerful force against Persia. As involuntary emigrants, they would have pined for their former homes in old Greece. They or their children or grandchildren might even have had the chance to recapture old Athens. After conquering mainland Greece in 480–479 BC, and after having destroyed and resettled Athens and Sparta, the Persians would have settled down to their customary business of collecting taxes, suppressing democracy, and spying on potential enemies. Eventually, though, they would have grown bored. The ideology of the Persian throne fostered a dynamic of expansion. To put it plainly, every king had to prove he was equal to the traditions of Cyrus the Great by engaging in new conquests.[30] Few fruits could have looked as ripe for the picking as Sicily. The island was as disunited as it was wealthy. Carthage represented a potential anti-Greek ally, whether or not Persia had indeed allied with Carthage in 480. And the survival of pesky Atheno-Sirians free of Persian control gave an added fillip to Persia's westward itch. In short, eventually the satrap of Hellas would have persuaded the Great King to mount a Sicilian expedition.

Perhaps the Persians would have done better in their invasion of Sicily than the Athenians did when they attacked in 415. After all, with its cavalry tradition, Persia is not likely to have repeated Athens' mistake of not bringing along enough horsemen. Carthage represented a far more formidable ally than Segesta and Selinus proved to Athens in 415. Yet sending a huge armada far from its home base was a risky business, as Carthage had learned at Himera. Led by an Atheno-Sirian-Syracusan alliance, the Sicilian Greeks might have smashed the Persian invaders, as they did the Athenians.[31]

The glow of that victory might have sparked an Atheno-Sirian *reconquista*. No doubt many, though not all, mainland Greeks would be eager to revolt against their Persian overlords, just as many, though not all, Ionian Greeks were eager to revolt against the Persians, in 499 BC, after two generations of Persian rule. A dispute over the Persian throne might in turn have given Atheno-Sirian diplomats an opening, just as the dispute between Prince Cyrus and his brother Artaxerxes gave the Spartans an opening in 401 BC to try to reconquer western Anatolia (see Xenophon, *Anabasis*). In return for Greek hoplites—and not just the decadent hoplites of mainland Greece, whose worthlessness had been proven by their defeat in 480, but *real* hoplites from martial Italy—to support his bid for their throne, Prince Cyrus might have tolerated an Atheno-Sirian return to Athens. Of course, such toleration would have been merely a temporary expedient, to be withdrawn after the prince had become Great King. Yet "temporary" might have turned "permanent" when Artaxerxes prevailed.

Artaxerxes' army did not prove strong enough to drive the Spartans out of Anatolia when they invaded between 399 and 395. Only by using bribery to divide Greek from Greek and stir up an anti-Spartan uprising on the mainland (the so-called Corinthian War, 395–387) were the Persians able to force the Spartans back. In alternative history, no doubt Artaxerxes would have tried the same expedient against the restored Athenians. It might not have worked, however, for the simple reason that, much as some of their Greek neighbors would have shuddered at the return of a strong Athens to the Greek mainland, most of them would probably have preferred Athens to the Persian satrap.

Restored in triumph to their homeland, the Athenians would finally have got around to the unfinished business of expanding democracy, a regime that had only survived by the skin of its teeth after the relocation to Siris. (The defeat of the navy at Salamis in 480 would have discredited the lower-class rowers who manned it, but the navy's heroic feat in moving Athenians to Italy would have restored much of their luster.) The Athenian fleet would become the guarantor of the safety of the Aegean. The other Greeks would rally to Athens' banner by joining the so-called Delian League, in which they would accept Athenian hegemony.

Meanwhile, a great era of self-confidence and achievement would have bloomed in Athenian culture. Under the leadership of Pericles, son of the great Pericles, who had shepherded the Atheno-Sirians through many crises, Athens would rebuild the temples on the Acropolis that the Persians had destroyed long before. To this day, the great Parthenon or Temple of Athena the Maiden, remains an icon of Western civilization. Within sight of that temple, on the south slope of the Acropolis, Aeschylus, grandson of that Aeschylus who died in the battle of Salamis in 480 BC, would oversee the production of his immortal tragedy, *The Persians and the Carthaginians,* which celebrated the Atheno-Syracusan naval victory in the Tarentine Gulf (later mercilessly parodied in a comedy by Aristophanes).

It would have taken several generations, but in the end the Greeks would have won the Persian Wars in spite of having lost the battle of Salamis in 480 BC. In retrospect, it would appear that Athens' "Sirian Captivity," though traumatic at the time, served in the long run to strengthen the Athenians. And the best part is that they wouldn't have to face the Peloponnesian War in the future, because Sparta, unlike Athens, would never have bounced back to its former prominence.

To sum up, had Persia won at Salamis it would probably have conquered Greece in 480 BC. It is nonetheless possible to imagine the Greeks regaining their independence within several generations and even creating an Athenian democracy, empire, and golden age culture similar to the ones that followed the Greek victory at Salamis. This counterfactual history sticks closely to the historical record, which documents Greek willingness to relocate in the western Mediterranean after defeat by Persia, the military strength and political ambition of the Sicilian Greeks, the Persian ruling house's ideology of expansion and its penchant for faction, and, above all, the resilience of the Greek city-state. The weakest link in the chain may be getting the Athenian refugees safely to Siris and able to survive there, but doing so does not strain credulity.

Could Western Civilization Have Survived a Persian Defeat of Greece?

Finally, there is the imponderable: if the Persians had conquered Greece at Salamis, would classical Greece ever have made its signal contribution to Western civilization? The negative case is strong. Even without positing a direct line from Plato to NATO, the influence of Greek civilization on Rome and, with its revival in the Renaissance, on early modern Europe was too strong to encourage optimism about where the West would be today without the classical contribution of Plato, Aristotle, Thucydides, Sophocles, et al. Even so, it is just barely possible to imagine Western civilization without the Greek victory at Salamis.

First, to continue the previous line of argument, Greece's intellectual genius, like its military elite, might have been transferred to Sicily and flourished there. Earlier, Greek intellectuals such as Pythagoras and Herodotus had traveled west, and later, in the Hellenistic period, Greek culture would prove portable indeed. Classical Greece might have blossomed in southern Italy and Sicily and then returned to the Greek mainland. Or perhaps it would have stayed centered in the West, rather than the Balkans, and have influenced Rome even earlier and more deeply than it ultimately did.

What, however, if Persia had followed up its conquest of Greece by successfully conquering Sicily and Italy? What if it then turned north and polished off the Romans and the Etruscans? What if Persia then won the inevitable showdown with its erstwhile Carthaginian ally? What, in short, if the Persian Empire had captured the entire Mediterranean, as Rome later would? What if Aramaic and Old Persian rather than Latin and Greek became the lingua francas of the ancient Mediterranean? What if Sardis and, say, Syracuse, rather than Rome and Byzantium, became the great Persian regional capitals, with Persepolis above them both?

Let us admit, at the outset, that this outcome would have been unlikely. True enough, scholars have sometimes underestimated the Persian Empire and its military and political strength.[32] Yet even the most fair-minded historian might question whether Persia had what it would take to repeat Rome's achievement. For example, to conquer the western Mediterranean the Roman army had to defeat ferocious enemy infantry, including the Greek phalanx, the Samnite legions, and the troops of Carthage, the Germans, and the Celts. Yet the Persian infantry found it rough going against the Greek hoplites, to say nothing of the other potential enemies. Repeating Rome's imperial success would have required, on Persia's part, a reform from top to bottom of just about everything having to do with the way the Persians made war. In short, to imagine a Mediterranean-wide Persian Empire is to imagine a different Persia.

For the sake of argument, however, let us do just that: imagine a Persian Empire stretching from Iran to Spain. With that empire in place it becomes harder to imagine Western civilization emerging but perhaps not impossible. In the short run, how different the years 480 BC to AD 476 would have been from the world that actually was. In the long run, the more things changed, the more they might have stayed the same.

To understand how the West might have emerged in spite of a Persian victory at Salamis, one must first ask what the West is. That is, what is meant by Western civilization? More precisely, what is at stake in speaking of the Greek contribution to Western civilization? The term *the West* may usefully be defined in two ways. First, *the West* refers to the Latin Christian civilization that developed in Europe in the Middle Ages, an amalgam of Roman and Germanic civilizations. Second, *the West* refers to that civilization which, beginning in the early modern era, expanded globally from Europe, invented capitalism, and experienced the scientific and industrial revolutions.

In what they were pleased to call the Renaissance, or "rebirth"—that is, the early modern centuries—the European cultural elite incurred much of its debt to Greco-Roman antiquity. Although that debt was not negligible, it must be assessed with a cold eye. If early modern Europe borrowed much from ancient texts, especially newly discovered ones, it also used those texts to justify new developments under the cover of a return. For example, Renaissance polities engaged in a radical separation of church and state, but that development owed less to classical antiquity than to such medieval trends as the investiture contest, constitutionalism, guild associationalism, and—above all—the failure of a centralized imperial-religious authority to emerge. Likewise, Renaissance individualism was foreign to the ethos of the classical world. As for the Western global hegemony that began in the early modern period, the crusading ethos and capitalism, those twin tools of Western expansion, owe little to antiquity.[33]

What then, did antiquity contribute to the West? The Greeks left a trifold legacy of rationalism, republicanism, and the Hellenic contribution to Christianity (a Hellenic-Hebraic-Roman mix). Persian victory in 480 BC would have endangered this legacy, but it need not have destroyed it.

Except, that is, for one peculiarity of Greece's democratic republicanism, the paradox of imperial democracy. After its victory at Salamis, Athens went on to create the world's first empire run by a democracy. This was a shotgun marriage, a fact that was not lost on Athens' thinkers: Athenian philosophers, historians, and poets all asked fundamental questions about the responsibilities of power and the morality of empire, questions that would have been inconceivable outside of a democracy. This debate, alas, would have been lost if the outcome of Salamis had gone the other way.[34]

And yet, even under Persian rule, Greece's cultural genius would not have gone lifeless. Defeat at Salamis would not have spelled the end of Greek philosophy. Had Persia conquered the Mediterranean, Greek rationalism would probably have become less political and turned more toward natural philosophy than it did after the Greek victory of Salamis, but it would not have been snuffed out. Persian imperialism was generally loose and tolerant; as long as their subjects were docile and paid their taxes, the rulers cared little about what they thought. After suppressing the Ionian Revolt in 494 BC, the Persians actually allowed more freedom in the Ionian Greek city-states: in place of their earlier policy of supporting local tyrants, they set up democracies. Under such conditions, Greek rationalism might not have "gone public," as it did under the Sophists and Socrates, but Greek rationalism also flourished in the shade: consider its retreat to private life in the Academy and Lyceum under Plato and Aristotle and to the Garden under Epicurus.[35]

Admittedly, one of the reasons that Greek rationalism survived classical antiquity is that it had been taken up with gusto by the Roman elite. It is not easy to imagine the anti-intellectual Persians, who disparaged the Greeks for talking too much, debating the respective merits of, say, Zeno or Hegesippus. Yet it is not easy to imagine the early Romans doing so either, and they went on to produce thinkers such as Cicero and Marcus Aurelius. If Persia were to become a successful Mediterranean empire on the scale of Rome, then it would have to produce not merely warriors as good as the Romans did but administrators, legislators, and diplomats. Cyrus the Great (r. 559–530 BC), founder of Persia's Achaemenid ruling house, would sooner have run a Greek philosopher through than engage him in dialectic, but not so a Persian such as Tissaphernes, satrap of Ionia in the era of the Peloponnesian War. Able to hold his own against Alicibiades, Tissaphernes might have enjoyed a bout of argument with a Sophist. And a grand Persian Empire would have needed more men like Tissaphernes than like Cyrus.[36]

To turn to Christianity, its emergence and success in late antiquity represents a combination of Greek and Jewish religious and intellectual strands with the administrative universality and security needs of the Roman Empire. Christianity combined the populism and messianism of Pharasaic Judaism and the antinomianism and charisma of Jesus' ministry with the savior cults of the Hellenistic world and the philosophical rigor of Hellenism. The Roman peace helped the gospels spread westward, but let us not forget that they spread eastward too, into Persian realms. Christianity began in Palestine, in the ministry of Jesus of Nazareth, an Aramaic-speaking Jew. It spread westward through the efforts of speakers of Greek and Latin and eastward through the work of Aramaic speakers. Persia's Zoroastrian elite need not have been any more intolerant of Christianity than Rome's pagan elite proved to be; in fact, it might have been more tolerant, since Christianity arguably borrowed both its eschatology and its dualistic strain from Zoroastrianism.

When the Roman emperors adopted Christianity as the state religion in the fourth century AD, they acted through a combination of sincere conversion and raison d'état, reasoning that a fighting faith would unite the empire in the face of military threats from Germans in the north and Persians in the east. Had they too been battered by the Germans, the Persian emperors might similarly have adopted Christianity as a state religion; more likely they would have admitted major elements of Christianity into Zoroastrianism, perhaps adding the Bible to the Zoroastrian *Gathas*. In any case, a universalistic religion teaching ethical monotheism, promising personal salvation, and foreseeing a struggle between good and evil to be resolved in the triumph of good at the end of days and the final resurrection of the dead—such a religion is as likely to have emerged from the pax Persica as it did from the pax Romana.

Finally, what of the third element of the Greek legacy—republicanism? Republicanism refers to the theory and practice of collective self-government requiring a shared commitment to community in order to obtain equality and, above all, liberty.[37] The essence of republicanism is the citizen, who is the most likely casualty if a grand Persian Empire followed the Greek defeat at Salamis. The Roman Empire was not republican, but it had its roots in the centuries-long tradition of the Roman Republic (509–31 BC). Furthermore, the Romans adopted much of the ideology of Greek republicanism to be found in the Greek classics of the fifth and fourth centuries BC, and the emergence of such classics, at least as republican classics, is doubtful had the Greeks lost the Persian Wars. With no republican heritage of their own, the Persians would probably not have preserved the Greek republican tradition, as the Romans did. Had the Persians and not the Romans united the ancient Mediterranean, antiquity's republican heritage is likely to have been considerably attenuated.

That, however, does not mean that there could not have eventually emerged a Europe dedicated to liberal and constitutional government. Perhaps the Germanic peoples, when they eventually broke the pax Persica, as they broke the pax Romana, would have been the ones to give the West those gifts. Let us grant the Persian Empire no more success in conquering Germany than the Roman Empire had. Imagine the Persian Empire being parceled out and conquered, in the long run, by Germans in the north and west and Muslims in the south and east—that is, a similar fate to that of the western and eastern (or Byzantine) Roman empires. The Germanic successor states of the Persian Empire in the West would have been no more autocratic than the Germanic successor states of Rome in our early medieval West were. To be sure, they would have inherited an autocratic tradition and Near Eastern style law codes from the Persians. Yet they would also have been marked by the same ideology of freedom and the same centrifugal forces as Tacitus's Germanic tribes. Unsuccessful at reestablishing a single empire, they would have created a number of independent kingdoms. The kings would have had their hands full carving out a sphere of power among the competing forces of obstreperous mounted warriors, an elite of the Christian-Zoroastrian church, and the middle classes of the slowly growing cities. Unable to establish a strong central government, kings would have to settle for feudal monarchy. In the privileges of the separate orders—knights, clergymen, burgesses—lay the foundations of liberty. Nurtured by the combination of Germanic traditions and the absence of any one center of power, many institutions and notions considered fundamental to Western politics today could have developed without the rich republican legacy of antiquity, for example, English common law, the Magna Carta, parliamentary representation, and the separation of church and state, indeed, arguably the very notion of rights.[38]

Yet if these are the bedrock of liberal and constitutional government, they do not amount to republican government. They would create a government of laws rather than men, a government that respects individual liberty and, by extension, that acknowledges the separation of public and private. They do not, however, explicitly require commitment to the community, civic virtue, or the very idea of the citizen itself. These are republican ideals, which emerged in early modern Europe from a specific link to ancient political thought; Skinner calls them neo-Roman, but their roots go back to Greece.[39] Would these ideas have blossomed in early modern Europe without antiquity's soil to take root in? Perhaps the intense communal life of the Italian city-states would have been enough to nourish them; perhaps pragmatic necessity would have called them into eventual appearance. That is, although in theory even a despot can run a liberal state if he is benevolent, in practice power corrupts, and the only way to have a free society is to populate it with watchdogs, that is, citizens. So republicanism might have emerged willy-nilly. One suspects, though, that without the ancient republican tradition the modern West would be even more liberal and less communitarian than it is today.[40] The result might have spared the world from such upheavals as the French Revolution and from such nightmare regimes as fascism and communism, but it might also have deprived it of more benign visions of community and fraternity.

An alternate Europe might not have been republican, but it is likely to have experienced capitalism, expansionism, and modern science and industry. Not only would it have enjoyed the Greek heritage of rationalism, but it would have experienced those medieval developments that made necessary contributions to these revolutions, to wit, the separation of church and state and the subsequent liberation of materialism, the creation of the joint stock company, and the instrumental attitude toward technology and nature that encouraged the practical application of borrowed technology (e.g., printing). None of these developments owed much to Greek antiquity. By contrast, they did owe much to the wealth generated by overseas conquests, but the European impulse for transoceanic exploration, trade, and conquest was not particularly Greek. Nor was Europe's success, which owed more to new technology (never Greece's forte), the administrative efficiency of the early modern state (which has more in common with Achaemenid Persia than the Greek city-state), and Native Americans' unlucky vulnerability to European germs.[41]

To sum up, had the Persians won the battle of Salamis and gone on to create a pax Persica, a Mediterranean empire that achieved in its day what the Roman Empire achieved in ours, the world today might be surprisingly similar to the world that we know. Both Hellenic rationalism and Christianity, or at least a Christian Zoroastrianism, would have emerged from antiquity. When, in time, imperial Europe would have given way to barbarian invasion, the Germanic kingdoms that took shape would not have been all that different from the Germanic kingdoms that followed the Roman Empire. Divided and warlike, post-Persian Europe might have gone on to create states that display a familiar commitment to constitutionalism and individual liberty. So while the West would have been much harder to win without Salamis, it might have been won nonetheless.

Conclusion

Did Themistocles make a difference in the outcome of the battle of Salamis? Yes. His political, diplomatic, and strategic skills, as well as his cunning and his energy, all played key roles in making the battle possible and making Greek victory its result. Yet the Greeks might well have won without him, at least if he had disappeared early enough for the Athenians to find a replacement. Athenian democracy was sufficiently open to debate, the elite sufficiently open to talent, and Themistoclean skills sufficiently prized as Athenian cultural norms that another individual may well have taken his place.

To argue against a great man theory of history does not mean simply to accept a systems theory instead. Individuals do make a difference in history, but how much depends on several things, beginning with, first, the regime. Democracies, for example, are good at open debate and talent searches, hence they tend to be less dependent on particular individuals than are other, more restrictive regimes. Second, it depends on circumstances such as the nature of the crisis and the timing of an individual's appearance or disappearance from the scene. Third, it depends on the gap between an individual's talents and a society's norms. So, in democratic, cunning Athens, the appearance of a strategist such as Themistocles was not a miracle; had he never existed, it is plausible to think that someone else would have arisen in his stead. To deny, therefore, that Themistocles provides support for the "butterfly effect" thesis is not to resort to historical inevitability. All of this may lead, rather, to a modified systems theory.

If, in spite of expectations, the Greeks had not won at Salamis, could they have defeated the Persian invasion? Probably not in the short term, but they might have recouped their power in the long term, starting from a new base in Sicily. Systemic factors—Greek dynamism, Sicilian Greek military strength and wealth, Persian expansionism, and the odds against a successful Persian invasion of Sicily—all render such an outcome possible.

What, finally, if the Persians had, against expectation, conquered Greek Sicily and then gone on to do what Rome did by winning a pan-Mediterranean empire and keeping it for centuries? Such an outcome is unlikely: the Greek city-state was restive and warlike and likewise the Persian Empire, but neither regime could compare with the Romans when it came to the successful deployment of the *arcana imperii*. Yet, if it had happened nonetheless, would Western civilization exist today in anything like its current form? How great is the ancient Greek contribution to contemporary Western civilization? Would any of that contribution have survived Persian, rather than serial Macedonian and Persian, conquest and in the fifth rather than the fourth century BC?

Greece's enormous contributions to Western civilization are cultural (rationalism, the Hellenic part of the Hellenic-Hebraic mix that is Christianity) and institutional (republicanism). The cultural contributions would probably have survived a pax Persica, the institutional contribution probably would not have. In particular, the democratic debate about power and morality would have been lost. The West borrowed something from the Greeks but not everything. It is just possible that the Renaissance would have gone on to develop republicanism without Greece's post-Salamis achievements, but it is not likely.

In closing, it is worth reflecting on the process of doing counterfactual history. Three points need to be made: the need for caution, the value added by adopting a counterfactual perspective toward ancient history, and the surprises waiting in the course of working through a counterfactual exercise.

Counterfactual history is speculative, and so it requires caution, especially when, as in this essay, an attempt is made to look ahead not only decades but centuries and even millennia. The reader will have noticed that certain of this essay's arguments—the Athenian reconquest of Persian-occupied Greece, for example, or the German origin of the Western notion of freedom—require exceptionally favorable circumstances in order to be plausible. If history is all a matter of getting the right breaks, then perhaps one should abandon the hope of retaining the West if one is to tinker with the results of a battle in 480 BC.

Yet if Salamis is restored to its place as a decisive battle, it must be put in context. As Hanson rightly argues in this volume, Salamis marked a turning point in the Greco-Persian war but it did not, in and of itself, win the war or end the war. One might say that Salamis was a decisive battle in the manner of Gettysburg. To part company with Hanson, however, note that the Greek victory at Salamis depended on Greece's preexisting military vigor and, above all, the presence of democracy in Athens in 480.

Had Athens not become a democracy in 508 BC, then it probably would not have defeated the Persians in 480. For that matter, had Athens not become a democracy, the Athenians would probably never have dared to intervene on the side of the Ionian Greek rebels against Persia in 499. So 508–507 emerges as no less a turning point than 480. Parenthetically, it is worth noting that if Cyrus the Great had not come to power in 559 BC there might have been no Persian Empire to threaten Greece at Salamis in 480. In other words, 480 only ratified a process set in motion earlier.

Second, counterfactual reasoning demonstrates that the Greeks were favored to win in 480. True, they were only a regional power while their enemy was a superpower, but Persia was vulnerable and the Greeks had the tools needed to exploit that vulnerability. They had a fleet and the cunning to use it strategically, which would all but win the war. Again, Salamis is merely the event that brought the probable to fruition.

The counterfactual perspective demonstrates as well that the long-term issues at stake in 480 have sometimes been misunderstood. Had the Persians won at Salamis and had they maintained their hold on Greece, they would not have deprived the West either of Greek rationalism or of Christianity. They would probably have uprooted or at least impoverished two other fundamental Western legacies from Greek antiquity, however: freedom and republicanism (the latter as modified by Rome). Yet, serious as that loss would have been, we may speculate that freedom would have entered the West later via Germanic sources and that the West could have survived the loss of republicanism without losing its essential character.

This Micawberish conclusion—something might have turned up—argues both for the importance of the Greeks to the modern West and for the limits of their influence. As an ancient historian, the author was surprised to encounter those limits as he worked through the exercise, yet he found the conclusion unavoidable. Counterfactual history does tend to lead its practitioners in directions they had not expected to go, because it forces them to focus on essentials. Certain core Western values today have Greek roots, but some of those roots would have survived Persian rule and others just might have reached the West via non-Greek sources.

It is even more surprising to consider how a Persian conquest of Greece might even have strengthened certain Western core values. After all, efficiency is also a Western core value, and the Persian Empire was the most efficient regime seen to date. Monotheism is also a Western value, which Zoroastrian Greece would have done more to foster than did polytheistic Greece. Finally, the West has tended to make the world smaller, first via imperialism and lately via American hegemony, on the one hand, and by economic globalization on the other. With its claims toward universal empire, the Persian Empire might have been more Western than the particularistic, parochial, Greek city-states.

Yet the same forces that made Greece insular also made it individualistic, egalitarian, and sensitive to the abuse of power. Had the Greeks lost at Salamis, the West's greatest lost would have been moral.

NOTES

1. "Si Xerxès eût vaincu à Salamine, nous serions peut-être encore des barbares." "Commentaire sur quelques principales maximes de l'esprit des lois Nr. XLVI, Du climat," in François-Marie Arouet Voltaire, *Oeuvres complètes de Voltaire* (Kehl: Impr. de la Société littéraire-typographique, 1785–89), 35:74 n.

2. Barry Strauss, *The Battle of Salamis: The Naval Encounter That Saved Greece—and Western Civilization* (New York: Simon and Schuster, 2004).

3. Demosthenes 23, *Against Aristocrates*, 198. All ancient sources are cited, after first use, according to the abbreviations in Simon Hornblower and Anthony Spawforth, eds., *The Oxford Classical Dictionary*, 3rd ed. (Oxford: Oxford University Press, 1996).

4. *Anthologia Palatina* 7.235, trans. Paton.

5. For a survey and analysis, see A. Podlecki, *The Life of Themistocles. A Critical Survey of the Literary and Archaeological Evidence* (Montreal: McGill-Queens University Press, 1975).

6. Thucydides, trans., Crawley, rev., and Robert Strassler, ed., *The Landmark Thucydides* (New York: Simon and Schuster 1996), 1.138.3. On Herodotus, see Podlecki, *Life of Themistocles*, 68–71.

7. Thuc. 1.93.4, 7. On Themistocles, see Strauss, *Battle of Salamis*, 11–13, 248–49.

8. See Podlecki, *Life of Themistocles*, 205–7; and Frank Frost, *Plutarch's Themistocles: A Historical Commentary*, rev. ed. (Chicago: Ares, 1998), 54–61.

9. On ostracism, see, for an introduction, Martin Ostwald, "The Reform of the Athenian State by Cleisthenes," in *The Cambridge Ancient History*, ed. John Boardman, N. G. L. Hammond, D. M. Lewis, and M. Ostwald, 2nd ed., vol. 4: *Persia, Greece, and the Western Mediterranean c. 525–479 B.C.* (Cambridge: Cambridge University Press, 1988), 324–46.

10. Cimon: Plutarch, *Cimon* 5.2; cf. Strauss, *Battle of Salamis,* 64–65. "Naval crowd": *nautikos okhlos,* Thuc. 8.72.2; Aristotle *Politics* 1304a22, 1327b7–8; cf. Plato *Laws* 707a–b; Isocrates 12.116. On hostility to sailors by Athenian aristocrats, see Barry S. Strauss, "The Athenian Trireme, School of Democracy," in *DEMOKRATIA: A Conversation on Democracies, Ancient and Modern,* ed. Josiah Ober and Charles Hedrick (Princeton: Princeton University Press, 1996), 313–25.

11. Innovation, etc.: Thuc. 1.70. Sixth century: Herodotus 1.60.3. Marathon: Hdt. 6.112; *Suda* s.v. *hippeis.*

12. The only man: Plut. *Them.* 3–4. Political clubs: Plut. *Aristides* 2.4.

13. Thasos: Hdt. 6.46. Xanthippos: Hdt. 8.131.3; Arist. [*Athenaion Politeia*]. 22.6; cf. Peter Green, *The Greco-Persian Wars* (Berkeley: University of California Press, 1996), 45, 47. Aristides: Plut. *Arist.* 7.1.

14. On "cunning intelligence" as a Greek cultural ideal and practice, see Marcel Detienne and Jean-Pierre Vernant, *Cunning Intelligence in Ancient Greece,* trans. J. Lloyd (Atlantic Highlands, NJ: Humanities Press, 1978).

15. Solon: Polyaenus *Strategemata* 20.2. Pisistratus: Hdt. 1.59.4; Plut. *Solon* 30.1; Polyaenus *Strat.* 21.3; Cimon.

16. Areopagus: Arist. [*Ath.Pol.*] 23.1; Kleidemos ap. Plut. *Them.* 10.6. Mnesiphilus: Hdt. 8.57; Plut. *Them.* 2.4. Bias: Plut. *de malignitate Herodoti* 37 = Plut. *Moralia* 869d–f. Mnesiphilus was prominent enough to be a candidate for ostracism: see D. M. Lewis, "Postscript," in A. R. Burn, *Persia and the Greeks: The Defense of the West, 546–478 B.C.* 2nd ed. (Stanford: Stanford University Press, 1984), 604, 606. On Mnesiphilus, see also Strauss, *Battle of Salamis,* 84–86.

17. Pausanias: Thuc. 1.134.2–3.

18. See Paul Cartledge, *Agesilaos and the Crisis of Sparta* (Ithaca, NY: Cornell University Press,1987), for the workings of the Spartan regime.

19. Artemisium: Hdt. 8.1–23; see also Strauss, *Battle of Salamis,* 14–30.

20. On local knowledge and the role of the wind at Salamis, see Strauss, *Battle of Salamis,* 152–54.

21. For recent discussions of ship numbers and the course of the battle, in addition to Strauss, *Battle of Salamis,* esp. 109–208, see Green, *Greco-Persian Wars,* 60–64, 146–48, 162–63; and J. S. Morrison, J. F. Coates, and N. B. Rankov, *The Athenian Trireme: The History and Reconstruction of an Ancient Greek Warship,* 2nd ed. (Cambridge: Cambridge University Press, 1986), 55–61; and J. F. Lazenby, *The Defence of Greece, 490–479 B.C.* (Warminster: Aris and Phillips, 1993), 151–97, all with reference to earlier scholarship. The scholarship on Salamis is very large. Some other important works in English on the battle of Salamis in recent decades (to say nothing of earlier work or non-English-language scholarship) include Jack Martin Balcer, *The Persian Conquest of the Greeks, 545–450 B.C.* (Xenia 38) (Konstanz: Univ.-Verl. Konstanz, 1995), 257–70; Burn, *Persia and the Greeks,* 450–75; C. W. Fornara, "The Hoplite Achievement at Psytalleia," *Journal of Hellenic Studies* 86 (1966): 51–55; N. G. L. Hammond, "The Battle of Salamis," *Journal of Hellenic Studies* 76 (1956): 32–54; N. G. L. Hammond, "On Salamis," *American Journal of Archaeology* 64 (1960): 367–68; N. G. L. Hammond, "The Expedition of Xerxes," in *The Cambridge Ancient History,* 2nd ed., vol. 4: *Persia, Greece, and the Western Mediterranean, c. 525 to 479 B.C.*

(Cambridge: Cambridge University Press, 1988), 569–88; C. Hignett, *Xerxes' Invasion of Greece* (Oxford: Clarendon, 1963), 193–239; W. K. Pritchett, "Towards a Restudy of the Battle of Salamis," *American Journal of Archaeology* 63 (1959): 251–62; and P. W. Wallace, "Psyttaleia and the Trophies of the Battle of Salamis," *American Journal of Archaeology* 73 (1969): 293–303.

22. Aristides: Hdt. 8.79–82; Morrison, Coates, and Rankov, *Athenian Trireme,* 58; Strauss, *Battle of Salamis,* 119–22.

23. Hdt. 8.62.1–2 (my translation).

24. Persian losses at Salamis: Diodorus Siculus 11.19.3.

25. Wall across the isthmus: Hdt. 8.40, 71, 74; 9.8–10. Megara: Hdt. 8.40, 71, 74; 9.8–10. Peloponnesians: Hdt. 7.139.

26. Miletus: Hdt. 6.21.2. Resettled on Persian Gulf: Hdt 6.18.1–20.1. Phocaeans and Teians: Hdt. 1.164.1–168.2. Samians: Hdt. 6.22.1–6.24.1. Phocaean returnees: Hdt. 1.165.3. "all their movable goods": Hdt. 1.164.3.

27. Jacques Perret, *Siris, recherches critiques sur l'histoire de la Siritide avant 433/2* (Paris: Société d'édition "Les Belles lettres," 1941), 128–30.

28. Coordinated effort: Diod. Sic. 11.1.14. Himera: Hdt. 7.166; Diod. Sic. 11.20–26.

29. See, for example, Oswyn Murray, *Early Greece,* 2nd ed. (Cambridge: Harvard University Press, 1993), 260–61.

30. See Barry S. Strauss and Josiah Ober, *The Anatomy of Error: Ancient Military Disasters and Their Lessons for Modern Strategists* (New York: St. Martin's, 1990), 20–23.

31. Athenian Invasion of Sicily: see Thuc. books 6–7.

32. For a corrective, see Pierre Briant, *From Cyrus to Alexander: A History of the Persian Empire,* trans. Peter B. Daniels (Winona Lake, IN: Eisenbrauns, 2002).

33. For a concise and sage introduction to the Renaissance and its culture, see Alison Brown, *The Renaissance* (New York: Longman, 1988).

34. See Strauss, *Battle of Salamis,* 245–48.

35. More freedom: Hdt. 6.42–43.

36. Talking too much: Hdt. 1.153.2.

37. See Philip Pettit, *Republicanism: A Theory of Freedom and Government* (Oxford: Oxford University Press, 1997).

38. Tacitus: *Germania* 8, 11, 37, 44. English Common Law, etc.: see Brian Tierney, *The Idea of Natural Rights: Studies on Natural Rights, Natural Law, and Church Law, 1150–1625* (Atlanta: Scholars' Press, 1997).

39. Quentin Skinner, *The Foundations of Modern Political Thought* (Cambridge, Cambridge University Press, 1978); *Liberty before Liberalism* (Cambridge: Cambridge University Press, 1998).

40. Skinner, *Liberty before Liberalism;* Stephen Mulhall and Adam Swift, *Liberals and Communitarians* (Oxford: Blackwell, 1996).

41. Separation of church and state: Brian Tierney, *The Crisis of Church and State, 1050–1300* (Englewood Cliffs, NJ: Prentice-Hall, 1964). On the Renaissance context of modern science, see Robert Mandrou, *From Humanism to Science, 1480–1700,* trans., B. Pearce (Atlantic Highlands, NJ: Humanities Press, 1978). On capitalism, see Robert S. Lopez, *The Commercial Revolution of the Middle Ages,*

950–1350 (Englewood Cliffs, NJ: Prentice-Hall, 1971). On military technology, see Geoffrey Parker, *The Military Revolution: Military Innovation and the Rise of the West, 1500–1800,* 2nd ed. (Cambridge: Cambridge University Press, 1996); cf. Jeremy Black, *A Military Revolution? Military Change and European Society, 1550–1800* (Atlantic Highlands, NJ: Humanities Press, 1991). On European conquests, see Mark A. Burkholder and Lyman L. Johnson, *Colonial Latin America,* 4th ed. (New York: Oxford University Press, 2001). On the debate over the impact of the introduction of European diseases among Native Americans post–1492, see John Verano and Douglas Ubelaker, eds., *Disease and Demography in the Americas* (Washington, DC: Smithsonian Institution Press, 1992); and Noble David Cook, *Disease and New World Conquest, 1492–1650* (Cambridge: Cambridge University Press, 1998).

CHAPTER 4

The Quest for a Counterfactual Jesus

IMAGINING THE WEST WITHOUT THE CROSS

Carlos M. N. Eire

One of the most common and most plausible "minimal rewrites" in counterfactual history is that which kills off the protagonist earlier than in real history. Simple enough. But imagine a reverse minimal rewrite: what if instead of killing off a historical figure prematurely you have him survive the incident that cost him his life?

What if you choose someone who is as pivotal for the development of the West as Jesus of Nazareth? What if Pilate had spared Jesus, and the Nazarene had gone on to live a long, long life? Or ten more years? Or even only one more year? What if his person and message had been interpreted differently, as they surely would have under any such circumstances?

All of the gospel accounts tell us this could have happened. Which means that the possibility of an alternative story was more than conceivable: it became an integral part of the Passion narrative as recorded by the earliest Christians. In other words, from early on, the Christian faith depended on having that alternative ending on the horizon as a means of heightening the significance of the Crucifixion event.

Of course, thinking of the plausibility of such a scenario depends on taking the biblical gospels as accurate historical accounts, and one must acknowledge at the outset that these gospels are not impartial documents but highly partisan narratives written for the purpose of instilling and maintaining faith.[1] But building a counterfactual exercise on the gospels does not require any leap of faith. It only requires a leap of common sense: whether or not the gospels are accurate historical narratives is beside the point. They are *the* narratives on which the West built its own history.

All four of the gospels that narrate the story of the trial and Crucifixion of Jesus tell us that the Roman procurator Pontius Pilate was eager to set him free. We are told that the crowd kept calling for crucifixion, but Pilate stalled, unable to pass sentence. At one point in the narrative, Pilate pronounces Jesus innocent, and so does Herod, the local puppet king who ruled over Galilee. He even offers the crowd a choice between freeing Jesus and an outlaw named Barabbas, but much to his chagrin, the crowd chooses the convicted felon instead of the wandering rabbi from Nazareth.[2]

At a critical point in the narrative, according to Matthew's gospel, Pilate receives a message from his wife by means of a servant. Like many Romans, we must assume, Pilate probably placed a lot of faith in dreams, for they were considered messages from the gods. Consequently, one must seriously consider the possibility that Pilate would have been swayed by his wife's dream. As a good Roman might have seen it, there, in godless Judea, where they worshiped a single deity who was very touchy and overly jealous, the gods had spoken to his wife.

"Have nothing to do with that righteous man," the message read, "for today I have suffered much over him in a dream."[3]

But the crowd kept asking for crucifixion, again and again, the gospels tell us. So Pilate orders a severe scourging for Jesus, thinking this would satisfy the crowd's thirst for punishment. Then he orders that Jesus be paraded before the crowd, arrayed in a gorgeous purple cloak—an ironic joke from Herod—with a crown of thorns on his head.

Pilate yells to the crowd, "Behold your King!"[4]

But the crowd shouts out, "Crucify him! Crucify him!"

The gospel accounts tell us that Pilate's own judgment and conscience weighed in heavily against giving in to the crowd. Pilate pronounces sentence: "You brought me this man as one who was perverting the people; and after examining him before you, behold, I didn't find this man guilty of any of your charges against him."

The crowd yells ever more loudly: "Crucify him! Crucify him!"

Pilate pronounces Jesus innocent again. And the crowd grows increasingly hostile. "Crucify, crucify him!" Pilate speaks yet again: "Why? What evil has he done? I have found in him no crime deserving death; I will therefore chastise him and release him."[5]

At this point in the narrative, we are poised on the razor's edge: this is precisely where things could have gone differently. Let us, then, consider an alternative conclusion to the narrative.

The angry mob unnerved Pilate, but his conscience troubled him even more. If he were to release this man, would he have a riot on his hands? What would be the best thing to do here? Spare the life of an innocent man, who posed no threat to the Roman Empire, or sacrifice that life for the sake of peace in Jerusalem?

We must assume that any good procurator would have hated riots and all that property damage, all those corpses, and all those casualties that issued from them. He would have hated losing any of his troops especially. But we also have to assume that a married man might hate the thought of having to tell his wife that he had disregarded her dream. Pilate might have imagined what it would be like to walk on eggshells for the next few weeks, maybe even for months or years or the rest of his life. He could have heard her voice in his own head, speaking clearly and very loudly from the future, any time some misfortune should befall them: "See! See! It's all your fault: I told you not to crucify that man in Jerusalem!" So, the counterfactual historian can say: yes, that was it, that would have clinched it. And then the following plausible narrative can emerge.

Over the roar of the crowd, Pilate shouts at the soldiers: "Release the prisoner. Release him now! Forget any additional punishment. He's suffered enough: release him, and escort him back to Galilee. Now!"

The crowd goes wild, but nothing much happens. A few try to start a riot, but the soldiers take care of that quickly. Roman soldiers knew how to handle such situations. This was an easy crowd to control, compared to others they'd seen. After cracking a few skulls, breaking some bones, and shedding a little bit of blood, the mob disperses. Pilate goes home early and tells his wife about the hard day he's had and how much he appreciated that message she sent him.

And Jesus of Nazareth returns to Galilee under military escort. There, out in the hinterland, he continues to teach and preach, to cure the sick, and to astound the crowds that flock to him like sheep. And the messages they hear and the way they interpret them lead to the development of a different religion from that which we now know as Christianity.

Is any of this plausible? I would like to argue that it is.

All of the gospels point toward the Crucifixion as the supreme moment in Jesus's brief life because they were written decades after the event. In fact, the gospels are narratives specifically constructed to make sense of the Crucifixion as the central redemptive moment. But if one focuses on other parts of the gospels, one can see that some degree of misunderstanding and uncertainty always hung over Jesus and his disciples. For instance, Jesus constantly expresses frustration over the fact that no one seems to comprehend what he tells them, not even his own disciples. Also, though Jesus predicts his own death, he contemplates the possibility of a different turn of events. He prays to the Father as the hour of his Passion approaches: "Father, if you are willing, remove this cup from me; nevertheless not my will, but yours be done."[6] Jesus also predicts the coming of the Kingdom of God and a radical transformation of the world but freely admits that he had no idea when this would happen exactly. He said that only the Father knew the day and hour.[7]

Even more significant for a counterfactual scenario: the gospels themselves tell us that Jesus had no control over how others would interpret what he said, or even over how they responded to it. Some thought he was a prophet or a holy man, others thought he was the reincarnation of Elijah or John the Baptist.[8] Many of the religious elites saw him as a dangerous fraud or as possessed by demons.[9] Some of his neighbors in Nazareth were so enraged by him that they dragged him out of town and tried to throw him from a cliff.[10] Some, including his own relatives, thought he was insane.[11] Everyone, it seemed, had their own Jesus. At one point, he even asks his handpicked disciples, "Who do you say that I am?"[12] Though it is possible to read this question as a test of sorts, it is also possible to interpret it as a sign of exasperation on the part of Jesus—an indication that he was constantly frustrated by the interpretative fog that engulfed his own disciples. There are many such instances recorded in the gospels, such as when he said to them "O men of little faith. . . . Do you not yet perceive?"[13] or scolded them, "Are your hearts hardened?"[14]

And it was not just the fact that every word and gesture of Jesus was open to interpretation and emulation that placed him at the center of an unmanageable situation. Some could even claim to be his disciples without his approval. One of the most revealing incidents in the gospels is that which tells the story of how Jesus' twelve apostles became indignant when they discovered that some man who was not part of their group was casting out demons in the name of Jesus. The apostles try to stop this exorcist, but Jesus rebukes them: "Do not try to stop him . . . for he who is not against us is for us."[15]

Other New Testament texts reveal that there were many rival interpretations of Jesus, his message, and his purpose. The letters of the apostle Paul, written in the 50s and 60s of the Common Era, are filled with references to "false" teachers and prophets. The Acts of the Apostles, which is the sequel to the Gospel of Luke, also tells of dissension among Jesus' followers and of wrangling over questions of faith and behavior. Beyond the Christian New Testament, we have many texts from the second and third centuries that speak of a bewildering array of individuals and groups who had conflicting interpretations of Jesus and his teachings.

Somehow, due to unique and immensely complex circumstances, what we now know as Christianity managed to emerge out of a welter of competing sects. In other words, Christianity defined itself in this interpretative crucible: its message and its institutions developed in the heat of battle among rival claimants to "true" discipleship and in the bloodbath of martyrdom. The emergence of the Christian religion, then, is as inseparable from persecution as it is from the discordant explanations that tried to make sense of the Crucifixion.

Take away the Crucifixion, and you would have the emergence of a different religion. But what kind of religion?

Imagining a different sort of Christianity from the one that came to dominate the West is not difficult for scholars. Not at all. In fact, since the nineteenth century many historians have taken it for granted that the Christian religion accepted by the West was but one version—one that eventually squeezed out all of its rivals. The first great proponent of this view was the German historian Ferdinand Christian Baur. His *Church History of the First Three Centuries* boldly proposed that multiple interpretations of Jesus and his teachings competed with one another, sometimes fiercely, and that many of those sects that vanished had as much of a claim to the historical Jesus as the version that finally triumphed over all others.[16] Since the mid–nineteenth century, holding such a view has become commonplace among historians, especially in light of new evidence such as the ancient Gnostic texts found at Nag Hammadi, Egypt, in the late 1940s. The Jesus revealed in these texts is not always that of the canonical gospels.[17] In fact, in most of the texts he is very different, and so are his teachings. In recent years, these alternative renderings of Jesus and his teachings have reached a wide reading public, becoming perhaps better known in some circles than the traditional orthodox version.[18] A recent work of pulp fiction based on some of these long-lost narratives even managed to become the best-selling book in the United States of America.[19]

For a believing Christian, however, imagining the West without Jesus Christ, the crucified Savior, could turn into an impious exercise, or worse, into blasphemy. Some believers might find this as irreverent as the questions asked by some medieval Christian theologians. Could God have saved the human race by becoming incarnate as a donkey rather than a man? How about if He had become a rock? How about if He had simply forgiven and redeemed everyone, without any incarnation, much less a crucifixion?[20] The answer any traditional Christian theologian would have to give to our impertinent "what-if" question is quite simple: if Jesus hadn't been crucified, there would have been no redemption from sin and death and the entire human race would be headed straight for hell.

One might object that those are theological questions and this is history—counterfactual history at that. But, objections aside, one must think through the implications of doing away with the Crucifixion for the West. Christianity is a religion that depends on historical narrative and specific facts for its belief structure. Consequently, history and theology are inseparable for Christians, and any change in the salvation story means a substantial change in its development and its history.

Some Christians might think that counterfactual speculation about Jesus is blasphemous because the Crucifixion of Jesus is an irrefutable historical fact. This means that if that one fact is changed the Christian religion would not have developed the same way or perhaps even not arisen at all. For these Christians, then, it is not just a theological question that is at stake. No Crucifixion no salvation, no redemption through the cross no Christianity as we know it. Some Christians might find it impossible to accept any speculation that alters the reality of salvation and that their ire over this counterfactual exercise might be similar to that produced by Salman Rushdie's *Satanic Verses* in parts of the Muslim world, though not necessarily of the same death-dealing intensity. When all is said and done, however, these objections by believers are irrelevant, even within the realm of faith. Allow me to explain.

First, counterfactual history does not seek to prove facts wrong but rather to weigh the significance of facts and examine them from different angles: it is not a denial of what happened but another way of analyzing the importance of what did happen. In fact, whatever outrage is evoked by this essay is conclusive proof of the fact that what did happen—in this case the Crucifixion of Jesus under Pilate's orders—made a huge difference for the history of the world and continues to make a difference two millennia later. Not understanding this crucial distinction, or seeing it as specious, could lead to outrage. And when one deals with what is sacred, some believers might see all distinctions as specious.

Second, some believers might also reject any attempt to tinker with historical facts they consider sacred or are key elements of their theology. For some Christians, no historical fact is more sacred than the life and death of Jesus. Incarnational theology—as defined by the great church councils of the fourth through the eighth centuries—proposes that God became a human being, that is, that Jesus was fully divine and fully human. This is the belief that most Western Christians still profess whether they know it or not, a belief centered on history. This is also the sacred belief that some believers do not want to see altered in any way or even approached with any question marks. But to say that Jesus was simultaneously God and a man is an act of faith rather than a statement of historical fact, even though belief in the fact of a God-man is central to the Christian faith. It was not always so among Christians. In the first six centuries of Christian history, there were heated debates and many schisms over the interpretation of Jesus. It is an irrefutable fact that there were Christians who believed Jesus to be God veiled in an unreal human body, others who believed Jesus to have been an ordinary man "adopted" by God as his son, others who believed Jesus to be a lesser divinity than God the Father, and yet others who refused to believe that Jesus could have had a human soul or a human will. To speculate on Jesus living to a ripe old age is not to cast doubt on whatever faith a Christian may place in Jesus as a God-man, as some outraged believers might think, but merely to explore further the significance of that belief for Western history. Rewriting history is not necessarily an attack on core beliefs, even if some may see it as such.

Rewriting history with a different Jesus is nonetheless a daunting enterprise. If you alter the central story of the Christian religion, what might you end up with?

As I argue in chapter 5 of this volume, religion is an unpredictable factor in history, perhaps one of the most unpredictable. Building counterfactual scenarios from the perspective of religious history requires taking into account the elasticity and volatility of belief and the centrality of paradoxical propositions and seemingly irrational behavior.

In this case, one must accept that any fact related to Jesus is embedded in a thick bundle of paradoxes floating on an ocean of interpretation.

Religion is all about interpretation, and a figure such as Jesus of Nazareth is a lightning rod for interpretation. Consequently, to speculate on what might have happened if anything at all had been different in the story of Jesus and his followers is to set sail in a nearly infinite ocean of possibilities.

But within that ocean, one can still ask the question: what if Jesus had lived to a ripe old age? Or to three score and ten? Or even just one year longer than he did? One can also ponder: out of the many possibilities that suggest themselves, which are the most plausible scenarios? And among these is there one outcome that is most plausible?

Given that the Jesus portrayed in the Gospels was wholly dedicated to a very public mission, it is quite likely that after surviving his first brush with the Roman authorities he would have continued teaching, preaching, and healing. Since the gospels record that he traveled to Tyre and Sidon on the Mediterranean coast before being tried by Pilate,[21] it is also likely that he could have expanded his itinerant mission beyond Palestine and the surrounding areas into Syria or Egypt or Asia Minor. Surely he would have continued to attract crowds wherever he went, and not just because of what he said, which was never fully understood. Word of his healing powers and his ability to cast out demons would have made people flock to him. His disciples would have grown in number, and as the number increased so would have the number of ways in which Jesus was interpreted.

It also stands to reason that if Jesus had not been crucified, as he had predicted, many of his followers would have redefined both their messianic hopes and their interpretation of his teachings. Chances are that the confusion that seemed to reign among his followers would have only intensified that controversy would dog Jesus wherever he went, that the religious elites would have continued to threaten his life, and that he would have been subjected to a violent death of some sort. But chances are, too, that if the Romans protected him once they might protect him further, especially because of his teachings, which emphasized submission to earthly authorities. Roman officials might have liked what Jesus had to say, despite all of his talk about a kingdom to come. Well-informed Romans would have known that all of this kingdom talk was very similar to that of the mystery cults that were then flourishing throughout the Mediterranean world, such as that of the followers of Mithras, many of whom were Roman soldiers, or that of the Persian sage Zoroaster, or that of the Egyptian mother-goddess Isis. Romans were eclectic when it came to religion and open to new cults. But imagine the added benefit of a new cult that taught people to turn the other cheek and forgive their enemies: what a wonderful message to preach to a subject people! Anyone who preaches docile submission was worthy of protection, especially if he also encourages people to pay their taxes.

"Render unto Caesar what belongs to Caesar . . ."[22]

Any emperor, even the most deranged, might want to cultivate rather than persecute Jesus and his followers. If only other subject nations could have such a prophet and teacher! So what if these people balk at worshiping Caesar? Better to allow them to teach and practice submission than to insist on worship of the emperor. Any wise Roman should know that Jesus is a gift from the gods—a strange one, since he denied their existence, but a gift all the same.

Nonetheless, any levelheaded historian who takes the unpredictability of religious behavior seriously has to admit, given the controversy he engendered, that Jesus probably would have gone on trial again and ended up on the cross anyway. In such a scenario, the faith that would have emerged might have been virtually indistinguishable from the Christianity that we know. It is fairly safe to assume that the shorter the gap between the first and second trials the greater the similarity. However, if he survived only to die through some other sort of violence, perhaps at the hands of a hired assassin or an enraged listener, then we can assume that what would have emerged would also be less similar to Christianity as we know it.

One thing is fairly certain: if Jesus had lived past the age of thirty-three (the age ascribed to him at the time of his crucifixion, according to tradition), chances are that confusion might have increased among his followers. Certainly, with each year or decade added to his life, the number of followers would have become ever more unwieldy. There would have been so many ways to interpret what Jesus had said and done—especially so many ways to interpret that change he made in the Passover dinner ritual, in which he distributed matzo and wine and said, "Take this and eat; this is my body. Take this and drink; this is my blood. Do this in remembrance of me."[23]

Jesus might have been able to manage his disciples, for the most part, and they, in turn, those who were under their care. But the chain of command, though clear enough, would have stretched too far. And there would have been plenty of fraying and breaking away beyond that tight, narrow chain. Too much. When you are dealing with a religious leader such as the Jesus of the gospels, who eschews violence and strong-arm disciplinary tactics, you are more likely to encounter a proliferation of factions and loose cannons. This is already the situation described in the biblical gospels and epistles.[24] One can only assume that growth in numbers and territorial expansion would have only produced more variety.

At one end, there would be those who still proclaim him to be the Messiah. Among these, there would surely exist a whole spectrum of beliefs. Some would see him as a spiritual savior, some would have no clue as to what he could accomplish but would still worship and revere him, some would see him as a king in the making—a king who would establish a new order on earth. At the other end, there would be those who granted him a special status short of divinity or messiahship. Among these, there would have been almost as many interpretations of who he was as the number of followers. Some would have believed him to be a messenger from the spiritual realm who had come to reveal secret knowledge about the structure of the universe and to expose and defeat the evil that resides in matter. Some of the intellectuals would have approached him as a sage and the founder of a new philosophical school. Some would have believed that he was a great prophet who had come to extend membership in the Chosen People to gentiles. Most would probably be unable to make up their minds as to who he was or what he might accomplish. Most would probably care only for the healing he supposedly imparted to bodies, souls, and minds or the power he had over demons.

Undoubtedly, Jesus' followers would have also developed their own sacred scriptures, all of which explained the meaning and purpose of his life and teachings. But, as happened for real after the Crucifixion, each school of interpretation would have developed its own holy writ, and the number and variety of texts would have been prodigious. Then the interpretation of these holy texts would have given rise to further dissension and splintering.

How could any man control so many followers with so many views? How could anyone control what they think and say? It would be impossible. Jesus could have thought about the numbers that his disciples tossed at him all the time: so many disciples here, so many there, so many that do not agree with one another, so many at each other's throats. Jesus would have prayed for this not to happen, as he did that awful Passover night, when he begged the Father not to take his life, the night before he was tried and tortured by Pontius Pilate.

"Holy Father, keep them in thy name, which thou hast given me, that they may be one, even as we are one."[25] He would have known that all the divisions that already existed would only grow worse without his presence.

We know this for a fact, for this is precisely what happened after Jesus' death by crucifixion. As early as the second century of the Common Era we find individuals such as Irenaeus of Lyons (ca.130–200) writing a treatise, "Against All Heresies, " that is full of information about the bewildering array of teachings that competed with what came to be the orthodox Christian faith. It bears mentioning that Irenaeus claimed to be a disciple of Polycarp of Smyrna (ca. 69–155), who, in turn, had claimed to be a disciple of the apostle John. This means that for Irenaeus all it took was one generation to bridge the gap with the lifetime of Jesus. (Imagine: if Jesus had lived longer, then Polycarp himself might have known Jesus in person and Irenaeus would then have had contact with someone who had touched Jesus himself). And it was not just the teachings of the so-called Gnostics, which Irenaeus took on in his book, that surfaced and proliferated. Jesus *was* interpreted in so many ways: all of the interpretations listed earlier had adherents in the first three centuries of the Common Era and competed with one another for converts. It could be argued that it was only with the advent of Christian emperors who insisted on uniformity that pluriform Christianity began to disappear. And even then, under centralizing emperors, the potential for disagreements and schisms remained high indeed. Rival "heretical" or "schismatic" churches such as those of the Arians, Nestorians, Monophysites, and Donatists flourished in parts of the West and Near East from the fourth century on; some are still thriving.

There is no reason to think that the lack of a crucifixion would have prevented the disciples of Jesus from fanning out to all corners of the earth, in the same way as happened with the Christianity we know. Disciples would have traversed the entire Roman Empire, even as far away as Iberia and Britain. Jesus would also have had disciples beyond the boundaries of the empire: disciples in Ethiopia, Armenia, and Persia, disciples as far away as Scythia, Colchis, and the Indus River valley. Some might have made it all the way to the Middle Kingdom. (We know for a fact that Nestorian Christian missionaries reached China by the seventh century). And, of course, he would have also had disciples in Rome, the seat of power.

And let us not overlook the possibility of disciples among his own people. We know for a fact that the earliest followers of Jesus tried to make inroads among the Jews, who were scattered all over the world: the Jews of the Diaspora. This would have also happened if Jesus had not been crucified. Chances are that among the many opinions and many teachers some would have targeted the Jews of the Diaspora and others would have tried to extend their mission beyond the Jewish people. Jews had been carrying out missionary activity of this sort for some time before Jesus was born, with some measure of success. Most of the gentiles who converted to Judaism, known as "the righteous ones," accepted the monotheistic faith of the Jews but were excused from following all of the law of Moses. This was the model for the missions of the apostle Paul and the key element in the expansion of Christianity. There is no reason to doubt that the mission to the gentiles would have also taken place if Jesus had not been crucified and that this mission would have been successful—perhaps even more successful if Jesus had not been proclaimed the Son of God.

Is there any reason to suspect that an uncontrolled proliferation of competing Jesus sects among the gentiles would have led to extinction within a few centuries? Not necessarily. A lot would depend on social and political circumstances, but we do have plenty of evidence from the first four or five centuries of Christian history that a profusion of sects was not incompatible with growth or survival. One only need cite the astounding growth of Arianism in the fourth century and the complaint of Saint Jerome in 359: "The whole world groaned and marveled to find itself Arian."[26]

However, extrapolating from the history of what actually happened, one would have to conclude that some sects would be stronger than others, socially, politically, and economically, and more likely to survive and thrive, and that the rise to dominance by one group could prove ephemeral. To cite the Arian case again: it might have ruled the day in 359, but by the tenth century Arianism existed only on paper, in those texts that denounced it and told of its demise.

So, in speculating about which Jesus sect might have eventually triumphed in a crucifixionless history, we are left holding a Darwinian set of cards because the speculation leads us to ask why it was that one Christian church alone succeeded in becoming the official religion of the Roman Empire and later of all of Europe. A question such as this invites answers that dwell on factors of strength and adaptability: survival of the fittest, one might say. To proffer a Darwinian argument, which even a believing Christian might be able to accept under another name (that of Divine Providence), one has to define *fitness* loosely, of course—loosely enough to include within it good luck and favorable twists of fate. One also has to take into account not only which organizational patterns would be most likely to ensure success but also which interpretation of Jesus might have made the most sense.

Fully aware of the thinness of the tightrope I am about to walk, and of its distance from the ground, I would like to propose that if Jesus had survived his encounter with Pilate it is most likely that the interpretation of his life and work that would have eventually prevailed would have been that offered by his handpicked disciples and their successors. This is what happened in real history more or less. I would also like to propose that the interpretation of Jesus that would have been most likely to emerge among his disciples if he had not been crucified would have been one that did not see him as a fully divine God-man who was the Messiah but rather as a mere human being or quasi-divine—a great prophet but not fully divine. Such an interpretation, in turn, might have given rise to a Jesus-centered faith that remained much closer to the parent religion of the Jews. In the long run, then, if such a faith had prevailed, the Roman Empire and the West would have become a branch of Judaism. On what grounds can such a scenario be proposed?

First, with regard to the social and political dimension, it stands to reason that one should look for the same kind of organizational structures in the "winning" Jesus sect in a counterfactual scenario as in real history. And who prevailed in real history? It was the group that associated itself most directly with a chain of authority going back to the twelve apostles, physically. It was those who claimed to have been given authority by the laying on of hands in an unbroken chain that could be traced back to Jesus himself and those who claimed that their interpretation could be traced back directly to the apostles. This group proved to be the strongest, most persistent, and most resilient.

Second, with regard to theology, it stands to reason that if Jesus had survived his trial by Pilate, and suffered any other kind of death, the interpretation of his mission would have been different. But why argue that he would have been seen as less than a Messiah or less than fully divine? Couldn't a Jesus who lived to be ninety also be proclaimed the Son of God and the Messiah? The answer to this last question is yes. But keep in mind that the central Christian message of redemption rests entirely on the voluntary sacrificial offering of himself made by Jesus on the cross as a God-man. Not just a man but a God-man, who undoes the damage caused to the human race by Adam and Eve. This was the kernel of the message proclaimed by the apostle Paul, the earliest extant Christian theologian and arguably the most significant interpreter of Jesus among that first generation of followers. Paul's message could be summarized as "no cross, no salvation."[27]

So, without the cross it is more difficult to conceive of Jesus as a Messiah who offers the final propitiatory sacrifice on behalf of a sinful human race. One must keep in mind how central sacrifice was to ancient religions, including Judaism at the time of Jesus. Without sacrifice there could be no cleansing, no redemption. Would a natural death, or death by an assassin make as much sense in sacrificial terms? Possibly, but not as likely as a public crucifixion. And without a crucifixion would there be as much of a logical need to ascribe divinity to Jesus? Especially if he had predicted such an end to his disciples, as the gospels tell us that he did? Yes, it would still be possible, given the unpredictability of religious responses to any event, but it would be less likely to become the dominant interpretation. After all, a would-be Messiah who prophesies inaccurately is less likely to be seen as divine by his followers, or even by himself, after a "certainty" proves false. One must ask: how would the apostles interpret a Jesus who dies of natural causes? How would Jesus interpret himself?

What might have happened if Jesus had lived to a ripe old age, perhaps even beyond the destruction of the temple in Jerusalem in AD 70? Might his aging itself, and his gradual fading away, have been seen as equal in redemptive power to a crucifixion? Imagine Jesus as old and frail. He who once healed the blind can now barely see; he who once made the lame dance can now barely walk; he who once opened the ears of the deaf now can barely hear. He suffers from arthritis, and his mind is somewhere else most of the time. He suffers terribly from a hernia that cannot be repaired and from constant indigestion and a bladder he can no longer control. His hands and feet are so numb sometimes that he cannot feel them at all. He looks as old as he feels, too: thin, white hair, wrinkled, nearly transparent skin, spots all over his body, blue veins snaking all over, too. Incurable fungus on his toenails. No teeth left with which to chew.

This is another kind of crucifixion, dying cell by cell, watching yourself dwindle like the flame on a lamp that is running out of oil, feeling yourself evaporate, like the brackish water in the Dead Sea, drop by drop.

Imagine what interpretations might arise from the fact that he who healed so many does not heal himself. Chances are that any redemptive theology that would develop around any such man would be less likely to proclaim him divine or the Messiah. Chances are that such a man would have been revered as a great prophet. But a prophet of what? Chances are that he might have become much like Mohammed in Islam—a great revelatory teacher, whose basic message proclaims a moral code and the extension of belief in the One God of the Jews to all peoples. Jesus could have been revered in a way similar to that in which Muslims revere Mohammed, but the contours of redemption (soteriology) and that of the world to come (eschatology) would have to be much different from those that evolved in Christianity. Maybe Jesus himself would not have been granted a resurrection and ascension into heaven. It is quite likely that the process of becoming one of the Chosen People would have assumed redemptive qualities and that the soteriology of this religion would have focused on the notion of election and peoplehood rather than on a God-man who is a savior.

Thinking that some form of Jewish universalism might have developed is not too far-fetched. At the time of Jesus, this was already happening.[28] Jewish proselytizers existed. They were there, scattered throughout the Diaspora, seeking to persuade non-Jews (gentiles) to believe in their One God, Yahweh, and to worship him and follow his commandments. Their interpretation of what it meant to be God's elect placed an emphasis on belief and conduct rather than genetic inheritance or specific rites such as circumcision. These "righteous ones," as the converts were known, were usually allowed to consider themselves part of the Chosen People without observing all of the ritual and dietary laws required in the covenant with Moses.[29] Many Jews and non-Jews alike in the ancient world could have believed—as eventually did the apostle Paul and his followers—that Jesus had come to announce a new covenant: one that made all nations children of Abraham.[30] The lack of a cross would make little difference for such a belief.

What if the gentiles of the ancient world had been converted to a monotheism that proclaimed a great prophet and teacher rather than a divine savior? What if that prophet and teacher, so similar to Mohammed, would have been Jesus? The parallels with existing cults would have been close. Many of the religions of the ancient world were centered on great teachers, such as Zoroaster and Mani, who were proclaimed as spiritual messengers rather than divine beings. Philosophical schools such as those of the Stoics, Skeptics, and Epicureans viewed their founders as inspired and could revere them as saviors (*soter*) without divinizing them. Given these parallels, it is highly probable that a religion with a nondivine Jesus could have caught on with great speed, even if it ended up being persecuted. The actual history of Christianity itself proves that persecution can produce more converts rather than fewer if the ideal of martyrdom is promoted in the right way.

And it can also be argued that even if the majority of Jews rejected

Jesus as prophet, the gentile converts would have made all the difference, as they actually did in the history of Christianity, up to the point of vastly outnumbering the Jewish followers of Jesus. Even in the worst possible scenario for the Jews of the first century AD (which actually unfolded), a failed rebellion against Rome and a crushing defeat would have had little negative impact on a new religion centered around Jesus. The destruction of Jerusalem and its temple by the Romans and the dispersal of the Jews from their Promised Land would have probably led to the same triumphalist interpretation among the gentile followers of Jesus as that which arose among gentile Christians: it would have all been interpreted as a testimony of God's vengeance against his Chosen People for having rejected Jesus.

Of course, by now we have entered the realm of higher-order counterfactuals, piling up scenarios on one fictional turn of events. We are left with high probability, or simple probability, which is more than mere plausibility but still a long way from certainty, especially in this case, for when it comes to religion, unpredictability is the rule rather than the exception.

If one dares to remain in this realm of higher-order counterfactuals, and to speculate further about what effect a Jesus-centered Judaism might have had on the Roman Empire and the subsequent history of the West, the tightrope gets even flimsier and higher. But it is still possible to envision a very likely scenario based on what actually did occur.

What might that scenario be? It would still be possible for Constantine, or some other emperor, to adopt this new religion and begin the process of converting the whole West. One must not forget that a form of Christianity that ended up being discarded—Arianism—was actually adopted by some successors of Constantine in the fourth century. What distinguished Arianism was its interpretation of Jesus as a lesser sort of deity, still divine but less so than the Father who had revealed himself to the Jews. Arianism eventually vanished but not without a tough fight.[31] The Arian and Semi-Arian emperors vanished quickly, but Arian missionaries converted the Visigoths to their brand of Christianity, and when these so-called barbarians invaded the empire and finally established their own kingdom in Iberia, they brought their Arianism along, and it was not until the seventh century that they abandoned it for orthodox Christianity.

So, assuming that Constantine came to the imperial throne and converted to a Jesus-centered Jewish faith, what might have ensued?

Fast forward to the early fourth century.[32] Given the success of Jesus' disciples over several generations, and the popularity of his following, the Roman elites enter into the picture. For a couple of centuries, the religion of love and submission has appealed to the vast multitudes of the oppressed in the ancient world, but now it has begun to spread to the upper classes. The ruling class accepts the emerging religion gradually. Some among the elite see the great benefit that could be derived from promoting a common religion focused on a single God and the even greater benefit that could be derived from putting an end to all of the conflicts caused by the many feuding Jesus cults.[33]

The Emperor Constantine is seated on his imperial throne, taking part in the dedication of a new synagogue and shrine to the apostle John, whose body has been brought to Rome. (One must remember that miracle working through physical contact was central to the mission of Jesus and his apostles, and there is a high probability that this would have continued to be a salient characteristic among Jesus' followers.) Constantine is about to make his own conversion official. He is almost ready to undergo baptism, the rite of initiation into the New Covenant. He will become one of the Chosen Ones as soon as Passover rolls around in a couple of months.

This is some synagogue that Constantine has built: the grandest building in all of Rome. Imagine all the pilgrims that will flock to this shrine and all the miracles that will take place there. Imagine all the honor that will spill over to the emperor who built the shrine, brought the body to Rome, and was there at its consecration. Imagine what an exalted place an emperor might hold in any society that believes Jesus to be a mere prophet rather than God Himself. Without a divine Jesus at the apex of society, the emperor could easily slip into a semidivine status as the chief intermediary between heaven and earth.

Constantine has put imperial muscle to work in unifying all of the followers of Jesus. All of those wrangling sects are too untidy for the religion of the state. It is also unseemly for the Chosen People to disagree so much. Calling all of the chief rabbis together at Milan was one of the best ideas Constantine ever had on his own. The rabbis came up with a list of beliefs and defined the Truth for all time: Jesus has been proclaimed a prophet, the greatest prophet of all time. His New Covenant promises to make anyone who is baptized one of the Chosen People. The Messiah will come at some point in the future. What Jesus has accomplished is to pave the way for he who will redeem and transform the earth for good. In the meantime, while the earth awaits the Messiah, there will always be Roman emperors to help prepare the way for his arrival. These New

Covenanters think of themselves as God's Chosen Ones, since they worship Yahweh, but they despise those Jews who don't accept the teachings of Jesus and still follow the law of Moses. They also despise those followers of Jesus who proclaim him to be the Messiah and believe him to have been resurrected. The central rituals of the Chosen Ones are baptism and the celebration of the New Passover meal, which is celebrated weekly on the Sabbath. The council has also approved veneration of the relics of Jesus and those of anyone who has led a holy life. Every synagogue is to have at least one relic enshrined under the pulpit from which the scriptures are read.

The religion that is adopted by the Emperor Constantine likes to think of itself as Judaism. Of course, it's but one branch in a very large tree, and, in essence, it is Jewish only in terms of its ancestry. It will come to be known as the Roman religion. Without a divine savior at its center, this religion is much more open to having a secular ruler as its head. The emperor's position would be more exalted than was the case under Christianity, and it is also quite possible that what we call "church" and "state" could fuse together much more intensely—so much so, in fact, that the emperors could end up as demigods. Without a divine Jesus at the very apex of society, the so-called *caesaropapism* of the Byzantine emperors would look like child's play.

Now that all of the key beliefs have been defined, Constantine's troops can close down the synagogues of all those who reject the Truth as defined at Milan. Now all of his subjects will share the same faith, and be as one, just like the prophet and teacher Jesus and the Father. Now his troops can descend on those few misguided souls who still believe that Jesus was the Messiah and that he rose from the dead. Now his troops can also go after those Jews who refuse to pay any attention at all to Jesus. Now all those who believe falsely can be wiped off the face of the earth for the glory of God and the well-being of the Chosen People and their empire. A little persecution should take care of all those who believe what is wrong.

The whole world has woken up and found itself chosen, or so it seems: Chosen Ones, members of the New Covenant revealed to Jesus by God, according to the Council of Milan. Even those barbarian tribes north of the empire's borders are beginning to accept the new religion from Palestine and Rome, and they are becoming ever more civilized and docile. The old gods are dying fast. The old elite families of Rome continue to cling to the old religion, and the simple people mix the old with the new, but there is no denying the fact that the world has been transformed.

The temples of the old gods are vanishing quickly. Many have been turned over to the worship of the One Jewish God, Yahweh. The sayings of Jesus, and the narratives that tell of his life, are now being given the same attention by learned men as the writings of the greatest philosophers. Gladiators are a thing of the past, as are most of the old, cruel games of the arena. Crucifixions? Nevermore. They've gone the way of wild orgies.

Some are very, very unhappy about the sexual ethics of this new religion. Will anyone ever be able to have fun again?

As Constantine watches the long, intricate consecration ritual, he ponders the reconstruction of the temple in Jerusalem. Should he do it soon? Should he do it at all? This new Synagogue of John the Apostle in Rome is so nice, and it cost so much to build. Isn't this enough for now? Is it not enough that he has also brought to Rome the bed in which Jesus died and the clothes he was wearing that final morning, along with all of his meager surviving wardrobe and those coffers full of his hair and nail clippings? And what about that most precious relic of all, the golden flask containing all the tears that Jesus ever shed, so lovingly collected by the women who followed him around all the time? Isn't all of this enough for now? Should he give in to the nearly endless requests he receives from all around the known world and rebuild the temple?

Constantine imagines what honor would devolve upon him if he were to rebuild the temple. He could go down in history as another Solomon or maybe surpass him in fame. The Temple of Constantine? It sounds so good. Maybe he should also move the capital of the empire from Rome to Jerusalem, instead of to Byzantium, that fishing village near the Bosporus? Or, better yet, why shouldn't the temple be rebuilt at Rome instead of Jerusalem? Rome: the New Jerusalem? Why not? He should ask his advisers. He should ask the chief rabbis, too. And he should check with his wife first. Maybe she's had a dream? Maybe. Just like Pilate's wife.

What difference might all of this have had on the development of the West? Past this point, there is no more counterfactual tightrope but simply a yawning speculative abyss. Up to this point, the scenarios have been built on models of what actually happened. Unlike my other chapter in this volume, this essay has pursued only one line of plausibility, for this is a much larger subject and therefore more complex.[34] (This is not to say that other scenarios could not be considered). And here I dare not venture much beyond Constantine and the Roman religion.[35]

Instead of considering more counterfactual events, then, it might be best to close with some reflections on what Christianity *did* offer to the rise of the West and how its development might have been altered without that one particular religion at its center.

First and foremost, Christianity bequeathed to the West a heritage that was not really its own but rather that of the Jewish people. By adopting the One God of an otherwise insignificant, conquered nation, Constantine set into motion a host of processes whereby the classical culture of the West was gradually buried—along with its many gods and its religious syncretism—beneath the ever-thickening layers of a new culture based on belief in a single jealous God who had revealed himself to only one people and for whom history was linear rather than cyclical. This was no small cultural shift but a massive upheaval, a redefinition of an entire culture. Religion was too tightly woven into the fabric of the ancient world for this cultural revolution not to be anything less than nearly total. Along with a change in myths, rituals, and symbols came a transformation of the whole culture. What emerged as "the West" from the ashes of the old Roman Empire was a Judaized Hellenism, with the law of Moses and the ethics of the Hebrew prophets at its very center— something that Jesus himself proclaimed in the gospels and that his followers took to heart.[36]

But Christianity was *not* Jewish, and that made a huge difference. Paradoxically, Christianity turned the Jews into outsiders at the same time that it proclaimed itself the legitimate heir of the promises made to them by God. Christianity was all about the incarnation of God as one Jewish man, Jesus of Nazareth, who was proclaimed the Son of God, the Messiah, Savior promised in the sacred scriptures of the Jews. This was the defining belief, the epicenter of the seismic upheaval that transformed the Roman Empire.

And Christianity was no simple monotheism either. It would take six centuries after the death of Jesus for Christians to sort themselves out along a spectrum of opinion on how best to define the relations among God the Father, God the Son, and God the Holy Spirit—and how to explain the union between the divine and the human in Jesus. The Christian theology that replaced pagan mythology was as complex as it was uncompromising, and those two traits made it possible for disputes to flourish and impossible for the entire Western world ever to be fully unified under a single church. Witness the fissures that emerged between the churches of Rome and Constantinople and the multiple schisms that dotted the Mediterranean Basin and the Near East with competing churches, each of which was itself riven with subschisms of its own: Arian, Semi-Arian, Donatist, Nestorian, Monophysite, Monothelete.[37] Of course, this fragmentation was never *purely* driven by theology— nothing ever is—but the complex and uncompromising character of Christian theology was such that it deepened rather than lessened the political, cultural, and economic differences of its adherents. It is estimated that when the armies of Mohammed conquered Egypt in the seventh century they found no fewer than eighteen men claiming to be the legitimate Christian patriarch of Alexandria.

What difference would it have made to have only one universally recognized patriarch in Alexandria at that time who was closely connected to the Roman emperor and his army? What if the same had been true throughout all of North Africa and the Near East, all the way to Mesopotamia? Might Mohammed's followers not have hit a solid insurmountable wall rather than a house of cards as they tried to emerge from the Arabian Peninsula? And how might the West have developed without the challenge posed by Islam, with the entire Mediterranean Basin as one world and Jerusalem as its inalienable sacred center?

A religion based on the teachings of Jesus that did not proclaim him to be God *might* have made it easier for Roman emperors to ensure religious unity within the whole empire, and along with this would also follow greater political and military stability and perhaps the capacity to withstand the challenge of Islam (assuming that Islam could even arise in such a world). A caesar who was head of a worldwide religious organization in which no divine human being was worshiped *might* also have had a much freer hand in running the state's religion than did the Christian caesars of Rome and Byzantium. What if Caesar had stood alone before God, without Jesus Christ, the God-man, the Son of God to act as the link between heaven and earth and without a church that was run by men who claimed to be the representatives on earth of the Son of God? What might Caesar have claimed as his due, and what might he have been able to do in the name of God?

Who knows? Maybe such caesars would even have succeeded in reducing or wiping out the Jewish presence in the West through relentless persecution. We have actual historical events that indicate that such an outcome was possible. What if Saint Ambrose, the bishop of Milan, had not condemned Emperor Theodosius I for burning down a Jewish synagogue and ordered him to rebuild it? What if Ambrose had not also excommunicated Theodosius and subjected him to public humiliation in

390 after the emperor ordered a horrendous massacre in Thessalonika?[38] What else might Theodosius and his successors have attempted to get away with?

The liberal Protestant theologian Paul Tillich once argued that by affirming the full divinity of Jesus Christ in 325 the Council of Nicaea made the West politically distinct from the rest of the ancient world and set it on a different path. Tillich did not exactly put it that way: what he said was that having a God-man as a redeemer and intercessor between God and all humans prevented the West from becoming "orientalized."[39] By this he meant that the West avoided political systems in which earthly rulership could be divinized, for all earthly rulers had to remain mere men. Tillich was not quite right about the orientalizing bit, and the way in which he thus attempted to turn the Third Reich into a Western aberration, but I do think he may have been correct about what made the Christian West politically and socially unique. Just think of the long string of conflicts between church and state that form the backbone of Western political history into the nineteenth century. Imagine the West without that.

And that is just the tip of the iceberg, so to speak. What else might have become of the West if it had embraced the prophet Jesus rather than Jesus Christ, the Son of God? What would the West have become without the cross and all it symbolizes?

It boggles the mind.

NOTES

1. Historians have been seeking the "historical Jesus" beyond the gospels since the nineteenth century, with varying results. For the best-known early summary of this search, see Albert Schweitzer, *The Quest of the Historical Jesus,* ed. John Bowden (London: SCM, [1906] 2000). For more recent summaries, see Gregory W. Dawes, ed., *The Historical Jesus Quest: Landmarks in the Search for the Jesus of History* (Louisville: Westminster John Knox Press, 2000); and Raymond Martin, *The Elusive Messiah: A Philosophical Overview of the Quest for the Historical Jesus* (Boulder: Westview, 1999). For one of the most popular recent examples of this genre, see John P. Meier, *A Marginal Jew: Rethinking the Historical Jesus* (New York: Doubleday, 1991).

2. The four gospel accounts are Matthew, 27; Mark 15; Luke, 23; and John, 18–19.

3. Gospel of Matthew, 27.19.

4. Gospel of John, 19.14.

5. Gospel of Luke, 23.13–22.

6. Ibid., 22.42.

7. Gospel of Matthew, 22.36.

8. Gospel of Mark, 6.14–16.

9. Gospel of Mark, 3.22.

10. Gospel of Luke, 4.29.

11. Ibid., 3.21.

12. Gospel of Mark, 8.29

13. Gospel of Matthew, 16.8–9.

14. Gospel of Mark, 8.17.

15. Ibid., 9.38–40.

16. Ferdinand Christian Baur, *Das Christenthum und die christliche Kirche der drei ersten Jahrhunderte* (Tübingen: Fues, 1853).

17. For English translations of these texts, see *The Gnostic Scriptures: A New Translation with Annotations and Introductions,* trans. and ed. Bentley Layton (Garden City, NY: Doubleday, 1987); *The Nag Hammadi Library in English,,* 3rd rev. ed. (San Francisco: Harper and Row, 1988); and the multivolume *Nag Hammadi Codices, English and Coptic,* various editors, (Leiden: E. J. Brill, 1985–).

18. Elaine Pagels is largely responsible for calling attention to this once arcane subject, beginning with the publication of *The Gnostic Gospels* (New York: Random House, 1979). Her readership has continued to expand, and her latest work became a best seller in the United States: *Beyond Belief: The Secret Gospel of Thomas* (New York: Random House, 2003).

19. Dan Brown, *The Da Vinci Code* (New York: Doubleday, 2003).

20. The Franciscan theologian John Duns Scotus (ca. 1265–1308) and his followers liked to defend God's absolute freedom and argued that God did indeed have the power to save without the cross or the church's sacraments. For, as Scotus said, "nothing created must, for reasons intrinsic to it, be accepted by God" (*Nihil creatum formaliter est a deo acceptandum*). Of course, the Scotists defended the necessity of the cross and the sacraments as what God had willed and revealed, but they stressed the point that God had the power to redeem by any means. For more, see Werner Dettloff, *Die Entwicklung der Akzeptations- und Verdienstlehre von Duns Skotus bis Luther* (Münster: Aschendorf, 1963); and Steven Ozment, *The Age of Reform, 1250–1550* (New Haven: Yale University Press, 1980), 33–36.

21. Gospel of Matthew, 15.21.

22. Ibid., 22.21.

23. Ibid., 26.26–27.

24. For one example see the First Letter of John, 2.18–20: "So now many antichrists have come . . . [T]hey went out from us, but they were not of us; for if they had been of us, they would have continued with us; but they went out, that it might be plain that they all are not of us."

25. Gospel of John, 17.11.

26. J. P. Migne, ed., *Patrologiae Cursus Completus; Series Latina* (Paris: Garnier, 1844–1864), 221 vols., vol xxiii, col. 172.

27. For Paul's own summary see 1 Corinthians 15. See also the entire Letter to the Hebrews, which develops this theology much further. Though not authored by Paul (according to widely accepted scholarship), Hebrews was long

believed to have been written by him, and it proved central in the elaboration of orthodox Christology and soteriology.

28. See Louis H. Feldman, *Jew and Gentile in the Ancient World: Attitudes and Interactions from Alexander to Justinian* (Princeton: Princeton University Press, 1993).

29. See Scot McKnight, *A Light among the Gentiles: Jewish Missionary Activity in the Second Temple Period* (Minneapolis: Fortress Press, 1991); and Richard Ralph De Ridder, *The Dispersion of the People of God* (Kampen: J. H. Kok, 1971).

30. Galatians 3.6–29.

31. See Rowan Williams, *Arius: Heresy and Tradition*, 2nd ed. (London: SCM, 2001); Richard E. Rubenstein, *When Jesus Became God: the Epic Fight over Christ's Divinity in the Last Days of Rome* (New York: Harcourt Brace, 1999); and R. P. C. Hanson, *The Search for the Christian Doctrine of God: The Arian Controversy, 318–381* (Edinburgh: T. and T. Clark, 1988).

32. On the history of this period, see Michael Grant, *Constantine the Great: The Man and His Times* (New York: Scribner's, 1994).

33. For an account of the eclipse of paganism, see Ramsay MacMullen, *Christianizing the Roman Empire (A.D. 100–400)* (New Haven, Yale University Press, 1984); and Peter Brown, *Authority and the Sacred: Aspects of the Christianisation of the Roman World* (New York: Cambridge University Press, 1995).

34. See chapter 5.

35. For a version of this essay that allowed for far more speculation, see "Pontius Pilate Spares Jesus: Christianity without the Crucifixion." In *What If?* 2nd ed., ed. Robert Cowley (New York: G. P. Putnam's Sons, 2001), 50–67.

36. Gospel of Matthew, 5.17.

37. For a magisterial account of these theological disputes, see John Meyendorff, *Christ in Eastern Christian Thought* (Washington, DC: Corpus Books, 1969).

38. See N. Q. King, *The Emperor Theodosius and the Establishment of Christianity* (London: SCM, 1961).

39. Paul Tillich, *A History of Christian Thought.* (New York: Harper and Row, 1968).

PART 2

The Rise of the West

CHAPTER 5

Religious Kitsch or Industrial Revolution

WHAT DIFFERENCE WOULD A CATHOLIC ENGLAND MAKE?

Carlos M. N. Eire

Is writing the history of what might have been the same as writing the history of what never was? Not exactly, though it is more a matter of perspective than of fact. What never was edges into the realm of fiction and seems already burdened with finality, laden with nostalgia for the impossible; what might have been has a forward-looking toehold on some truth, aches with potentiality, and brims with possibilities.

Take, for instance, the remains of a blast furnace recently unearthed near the ruins of a Cistercian monastery in North Yorkshire. It appears that the good monks of Rievaulx Abbey had found a way to make pig iron and had already been making it for years when King Henry VIII dissolved the monasteries in 1536, causing their utter ruin. With the monks dispersed, the property confiscated by the crown, and the buildings turned into quarries, the abbey's blast furnace slipped into oblivion, unnoticed, until archaeologists stumbled on it four and a half centuries later.[1]

With hindsight we know, of course, that this was the first step toward the steel mill that never was, a precocious yet stillborn industrial revolution, a dead end if there ever was one. But we are also intrigued by the

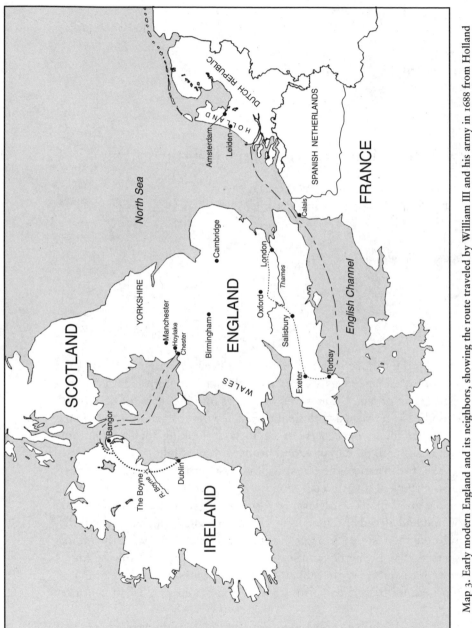

Map 3. Early modern England and its neighbors, showing the route traveled by William III and his army in 1688 from Holland to London and in 1690 from England to Dublin

potential there and tempted, perhaps, to speculate on what might have been. What if instead of "bare ruined choirs where late the sweet birds sang,"[2] William Shakespeare had known vigorous and thriving abbeys, thick smoke belching from their blast furnaces, spiraling toward heaven still, along with the monk's prayers? What might have happened to Western history if Henry VIII had not destroyed Rievaulx Abbey and all the others in his realm? What if England's monarchs had remained faithful Catholics? Where might that turn of events have taken us all?

With an eye on the blasted blast furnace as a point of reference, this essay will attempt to present two contradictory counterfactual histories of Reformation England and its impact on the development of the West. The minimal rewrite will be simple enough: a Catholic monarch remains on the throne in England past 1531. But what might have happened to Western history beyond that seemingly small, and very plausible, change in narrative will be explored along two divergent paths, taking two different approaches to history, each of which leads to a different conclusion. To test the boundaries of counterfactual history, and the thinking processes involved in its writing, this essay will raise the question: is it possible to unmake the West and at the same time also make it even stronger by beginning with the same minimal rewrite of history?

Before plunging into alternative histories of Reformation England, which will require dealing with religion, something needs to be said about religious history and its relation to counterfactual exercises such as this one. Counterfactual history and religion are uneasy partners at best, not easily led to the altar, always at high risk for divorce and troubled, unfortunate issue. To stretch the analogy further, this is a match that cries out for a prenuptial agreement of sorts. Call it a preface in this case.

Religion and Counterfactual History: Some Preliminary Observations

Western religion and counterfactual history have had a long, uneasy relationship. In 413, three years after the sack of Rome by the Vandals, Saint Augustine of Hippo began to write his massive attack on counterfactual history, *The City of God*. The "what-if" question tackled by Augustine in this book was a large one: "What if the Roman Empire had not become Christian?" This was no idle academician's question, however. It was a burning polemical question, related to Christian self-identity at a crucial time in its history. Behind this question lay an accusation leveled by those who favored Rome's ancient religious traditions: Christianity had weakened the Roman Empire so profoundly as to bring it to the point of dissolution. Implicit in this charge was a counterfactual argument: if Rome had not embraced Christianity, Roman hegemony would have remained intact, or at least vigorous enough, to deflect challenges by inferior barbarians. No Christ, no Vandals. It was as simple as that.

Historical determinism might have been as old as Thucydides, but what Augustine did with it had a far greater impact on the consciousness of Western Christendom. Saint Augustine sought to demolish the counterfactual formula of Roman traditionalists with the ultimate determinist argument: human history is not contingent on the wills of humans, the forces of nature, or mere chance. Human history is predetermined by God. Augustine's determinist blast became the reigning historiographical assumption of Western culture for at least a millennium. Some might argue that this determinism lies at the core of Western arrogance still, though stripped of its transcendent claims. Some might also argue that this determinism held sway much longer than just one thousand years and that this very exercise in unmaking the West is, at bottom, an attempt to break free of its hold or at least of its legacy.

It is good to discuss Augustine before getting to Henry VIII not just because of the saint's impact on Western thinking but because his agenda in *The City of God* serves as a convenient heuristic device, a window on the perils of writing a counterfactual history of religion. The basic question here is deceptively simple: where are the "facts" in religion? How one answers this question determines how one goes about writing a counterfactual history of religion or of many significant developments in the history of medieval and early modern Europe such as the spread of monasticism, the launching of the Crusades, the rise of universities, the persecution of heretics, and the Christianization of non-European peoples. But finding "facts" to tweak in religious history is not easy. Even single events that could be considered pivotal, such as the execution of John Hus in 1415 or Martin Luther's defiance of pope and emperor at the Diet of Worms in 1521, do not lend themselves readily to a counterfactual approach. This is because religion necessarily involves beliefs, and beliefs are among the fuzziest of "facts."[3]

Augustine might shed some more light on this problem. The North African bishop and his contemporary opponents had a much different definition of *facts* when it came to religion, a definition no longer accepted by most historians. His argument against the pagan counterfactual polemicists turned on this "fact": the gods who had supposedly protected Rome and brought it to its zenith were not only ontologically inferior to the One True God of the Christians, they were actually evil. The gods of the pagans were no more than fallen angels, that is, demons who had tricked humans into believing that they were divine beings. What we might call "beliefs," then, were facts for Augustine.

In contrast, the only facts that any credible historian of religion has at his or her disposal nowadays are those that pertain to the seen world rather than the unseen. Gods are definitely not facts. It is only belief in divine beings that is a fact. And here is the rub: beliefs are awfully fuzzy facts, for when it comes to beliefs, where is the line between the objective and subjective? Anthropologists and historians of religion tend to agree on one point that is crucial for the definition of *fact* in the realm of belief: religion is an inherently paradoxical dimension of human culture, and therefore also in history, for it seeks to explain the most fundamental facts of human existence by transcending them. What Clifford Geertz has said about ritual also applies to religion in general: it speaks in the subjunctive mood; it speaks of things as they ought to be. Religion interprets facts and seeks to bring order to apparent chaos. Religion is all about interpretation.[4]

This is why Augustine seems a fitting entry point into an exercise in counterfactual religious history. At its very core, and in a paradoxical way, Christianity is a counterfactual worldview: though its beliefs are ostensibly anchored in historical facts, it is the transcendent interpretation of these facts that makes a difference for Christians. It is the *meaning* of all of the facts in the life and death of Jesus that really matters to believers.[5] Paradox is key. In fact, paradox is so central to Christian thinking—especially to the thinking of those Christians who managed to prevail—as to be the measure of orthodoxy.

Because Christians have a predisposition to invest bare historical facts with so much meaning—and with paradoxical meaning at that—predicting the outcome of events in religious history, and Christian history in particular, becomes a very risky enterprise. The number of possible interpretations for any fact, or of the consequences of any event or events, can be well nigh infinite within the context of religious belief. And the most unlikely eventualities are often those that actually materialize, at least from the perspective of the nonbeliever. Who could have predicted in the time of Tiberius Caesar, for instance, that a Jewish troublemaker crucified in Palestine would end up being worshiped by later Roman emperors? Which of the emperors who persecuted the followers of Jesus could have taken seriously Tertullian's absurd boast that "the blood of the martyrs" would actually attract more followers to that bizarre sect?

Looking at Christian beliefs alone as facts is an even riskier business.

Anyone who tries to match up the principles of behavior outlined in the Christian scriptures (the ideal) with the actual record of the history of Christian peoples in the West (the real) will immediately notice a severe dissonance and will often have to strain to find concrete, positive links between Christian beliefs and Christian practice. If we take the so-called Sermon on the Mount at face value, as a guideline for Christian behavior, the ideal and the real will not necessarily match up in Christian history. Principles such as loving and forgiving one's enemies, turning the other cheek, and praising the meek and humble are not exactly those that guided Christian Europe's warrior class for more than a millennium or their colonizing, capitalist descendants for another half a millennium. Beliefs are as malleable as facts sometimes, perhaps even more malleable, for interpretation is the key to practice. Beliefs might predispose cultures in certain directions, but their power over them is never absolute. Beliefs are always open to exceptions, variations, and redefinitions. To claim, as Jack Goldstone does in chapter 6 of this volume, that early modern Catholicism was inherently antithetical to the rise of modern science everywhere, is to assume too much about belief structures and their relation to particular cultures. More on this later.

An unavoidable problem in dealing with "facts" in Christianity, or any religion, is that religion tends to be a fluid and amorphous phenomenon: it clings to cultures at multiple levels and in varying degrees. No two individuals in any given culture can be expected to adhere to the same religion in exactly the same way. This is multiplied by thousands or millions in the case of each culture and more yet in the case of the West as a whole.

With these words of caution behind us, let us now get down to the business of rewriting history.

Catholic England: The Minimal Rewrite

Coming up with a minimal rewrite of England's religious history is fairly easy. Of all of the European states that embraced the Protestant Reformation, England is one of the prime examples of a nation in which religious change was directed largely from above, by the ruling elites. Consequently, envisioning a minimal rewrite often entails no more than suggesting a plausible change in the policies of the state and most often just in the policies of the monarch. Although historians are divided on the question of how much of the religious change that took place in early modern England stemmed from above, as a direct result of royal and parliamentary edicts, and how much stemmed from below, as a result of the individual and collective religious convictions of the crown's subjects, none has seriously challenged or questioned the key role played by monarchs in the religious history of the realm as a whole.[6]

Henry VIII looms larger and more intensely in the minimal rewrite scenario than any of his progeny simply because he was the first English monarch to break with Rome and the first to embark the Church of England on its course toward Protestantism. Rather than taking the easiest path toward the minimal rewrite, which would require coming up with an untimely death for King Henry, perhaps by making him choke to death on a large mouthful of venison at a banquet (always a possibility for eager overeaters such as Henry before the advent of the Heimlich maneuver), let us test the limits of the minimal rewrite rule by considering another plausible scenario. Suppose that Henry VIII, hale and hearty and as lustful as ever, found no reason for his drastic break with Rome. Suppose that Pope Clement VII had granted the king his request for an annulment of his marriage to Catherine of Aragon and that he and Anne Boleyn could have married shortly thereafter. This is not a very farfetched scenario. Henry had as good a legal ground for his annulment as any other powerful monarch: after all, Catherine was his own brother's widow, and canon law forbade such marriages. The papal dispensation that had made such a marriage possible in the first place could be challenged under canon law, and Pope Clement could have found it attractive to court Henry's favor as an ally against the powerful Charles V, whose dynastic inheritance and overseas possessions made him a formidable, threatening presence and whose troops had sacked Rome in 1527. After all, it had not been Clement who gave the dispensation, and Charles was threatening to engulf all of Italy under his dominion. Why not an alliance with England against Charles, forged through an annulment that was utterly defensible?

This is all plausible but not as much of a minimal rewrite as having Henry die. Pope Clement's fear of Charles, and perhaps also his scruples, minimal though they seem to have been, may have exerted far too strong a pull in the opposite direction. Besides, what if Clement had granted the annulment? We know about Henry's sexual appetite, his intrigues at court, and how Anne Boleyn was eventually beheaded for treason. Henry's marriage to Anne would not have been any less troubled if he had not broken with Rome, and the first annulment would not have been the end of the road necessarily. Henry could easily have asked for more annulments and forced similar crises. What then? We have to weigh other factors enticing Henry to break with Rome, such as his desire to appropriate monastic lands. In this case, then, the rewrite does not turn out to be so minimal, for the contingencies pile up deeply and furiously, much like snow in a blizzard.

It seems best, then, to consider the most minimal rewrite, and in this case, as in so many others, it means killing off King Henry. So let him choke to death at a banquet in 1531—that is much less complicated—and let his daughter Mary assume the throne, a girl of fifteen still, under the guidance of a protector and the ever-watchful eyes of her Spanish mother, Catherine; her Spanish and Flemish courtiers; and her Hapsburg relatives abroad. Since she did eventually assume the throne in 1553, under much less favorable circumstances (as a Catholic in a nation well on its way toward Protestantism), it is not too much of a stretch to propose that her succession to the throne could have been accepted in 1531, even though she was female and a teenager. And since her half-brother Edward, the son of Henry and Anne Boleyn (erased from history in this version), did eventually ascend to the throne at the age of nine under the guidance of Protector Somerset, it is not that much of a stretch either to propose the same for Mary. We are now in the realm of a second-order counterfactual, with more contingencies to consider, but it is a fairly solid possibility, as second-order counterfactuals go.

Thus far religion has not entered the scene. This is still political rather than religious history, and the speculation remains much less fuzzy. With Mary on the throne, and her mother Catherine and her nephew Charles V watching closely, it is highly unlikely that England could have become Protestant by government fiat. That much is fairly certain. Here we enter a realm of higher-order counterfactuals. The particulars of how Mary might have ruled and what might have happened during her long monarchy (1531–58) present us with a wide range of highly intriguing possibilities. Let us separate the possibilities into two categories: (a) political and military history and (b) religious history. Of course, these categories intertwine and are never fully separable in the sixteenth century. But let us experiment with a separation to test the boundaries of counterfactual history.

Catholic England: Political and Military Counterfactual History

As far as political and military history is concerned, the counterfactual speculation remains within a relatively stable framework of plausibility. Here follows but one highly plausible scenario, uninterrupted by commentary or analysis. Mary's England remains resolutely Catholic and closely allied to Hapsburg Spain and all its satellite states. This means that the Hapsburg noose around Valois France is tightened considerably and that the French hardly stand a chance on any battlefield against an allied Anglo-Spanish-Burgundian-Flemish-Austrian army that is funded by the gold and silver Charles V receives from America. This also means that the Protestant princes in Germany do not stand much of a chance either. After defeating Francis I decisively in 1536 at the Battle of Noyon, and imposing a humiliating peace treaty that obligates France to supply troops to fight the Protestants, an immense multinational army led by Charles V descends on Germany. It does not take very long for the Protestant Schmalkaldic League to collapse.[7] After a string of defeats, the Protestant league surrenders in December 1538. The leading Protestant princes are all executed, their titles and lands given over to relatives and favorites who will toe the Catholic line along with Charles V. Each and every imperial city is purged of Protestants. Executions abound. Martin Luther is captured and brought to Rome, along with dozens of other leading Protestant clerics, including Philip Melanchthon and Martin Bucer. They are imprisoned at the Castel Sant Angelo and forced to attend daily Mass while Charles V continues to wage war on the remaining Protestant states.

After a brief respite, Charles V's superarmy marches on Switzerland and quickly subdues the Protestant cantons of the north. The Swiss Confederacy is dissolved, the cantons and the cities absorbed into the empire once again. The tiny republic of Geneva caves in without fighting. Following the Castilian model, Charles imposes the equivalent of *corregidores* (*Kaiserskraftsverkörper*) on the Swiss cities. City councils are purged. Executions abound, as in Germany a few months prior. In Basel, the guild of butchers, which had never supported the Protestant takeover of the city, assumes total control of the government. All of the leaders of Reformed Protestantism are killed or captured. In Zurich, Heinrich Bullinger dies while fighting. In Basel, Johann Oecolampadius surrenders without a struggle. John Calvin is identified and captured far from Geneva, in Marseilles, as he boards a ship bound for Cyprus. He and all the Reformed Protestant "heresiarchs" are brought to Rome and imprisoned along with Luther and the other German Protestants. Luther and Calvin are forced to share a tiny cell, where they argue ceaselessly about Eucharistic theology. Upon learning of the Swiss defeat, the Scandinavian monarchs abjure their Lutheranism and promise to restore Catholicism in their lands. They also round up all recalcitrant Lutheran clerics and ship them to Rome.

On October 31, 1539, the twenty-second anniversary of the beginning of Luther's challenge to Rome—and also All Hallows' Eve—in the presence of Pope Paul III, Emperor Charles V and his heir, the future Philip II, King Francis I of France, young Queen Mary of England, her chancellor, Sir Thomas More, and the archbishop of Canterbury, John Fisher, all seated on a grand stage at the ancient site of the Circus Maximus, along with many other rulers and notables from the four corners of Europe, the captured Protestant heresiarchs are led out, one by one, and asked to recant. A handful assent, including Philip Melanchthon, but the vast majority stand firm in their faith. Martin Luther defies the pope and the emperor to the very end, singing hymns loudly. He is eventually gagged. John Calvin is more subdued but equally steadfast. Melanchthon and a handful of repentant former heretics are processed out of the Circus grounds, bound for remote Galicia in northwestern Spain, where they will spend the remainder of their lives doing penance at a Cistercian monastery. Martin Luther, John Calvin, and all the other leading lights of the Protestant faith are summarily burned alive on a colossal pyre, bound by chains in groups of three. Queen Mary of England shields her eyes and holds her nose as smoke begins to billow, swirling furiously in the autumn air. Sir Thomas More fixes his gaze on the swaying pines off in the distance, and stops his ears with his index fingers, to block out the roar of the flames and the screams of the dying. Charles V surveys the spectacle calmly, as does his son Prince Philip. A young Spaniard peering over the heads of others, from the farthest edge of the crowd, takes in the whole scene, transfixed in horror. His name is Miguel Servet, or Servetus, as he prefers to call himself. He will later lead a revolution in medical science and keep his radical theology to himself.

Up in smoke goes the Protestant Reformation.

All of Europe is Catholic once more, united by a single faith, led incontestably by Holy Roman Emperor Charles V. Except for a few pockets of resistance here and there, mostly in remote mountain strongholds, heretics are nowhere to be found. The vast majority of those who do not agree with the new status quo choose to remain quiet, and their secret faith goes with them to their graves. In 1547 Queen Mary of England marries her cousin, King Philip II of Spain. Because this marriage takes place seven years earlier than it did in actual history, our fertile Mary is able to bear two children before dying in 1558. Let's name them Diego and Catherine.

Prince Diego assumes the throne of England as a child of nine, but, of course, this kind of rulership by protector is now quite familiar and widely accepted. He will assume full power in 1567 and reign until 1615. During the reign of King Diego—or Good King Dick'o, as he came to be known—England will enjoy a cultural and economic renaissance unlike any seen before. Granted the right to colonize North America by Philip II in 1574, and to take over the former Portuguese Asian trading posts in 1591, England begins to expand its horizons and its markets. On the stage of the Globe Theater in London, William Shakespeare, or "Sacudelanza," as he prefers to call himself according to the reigning passion for all things Spanish, astounds everyone with his plays. Up in North Yorkshire, around 1590, Cistercian monks, who had recently perfected a steel-making process in their blast furnace, begin to share this technology with some of the local landed gentry. By 1630, England is dotted with small but highly efficient steel mills. Everyone seems to like this metal, and some ingenious monks discover new ways of putting it to use and also of employing coal to make steam and using the steam to power machinery. Before long, machines are being employed to manufacture high-quality textiles cheaply and in massive quantities. By 1680, an industrial revolution is occurring, not just in England but also in North America and colonies of its sister nation, Spain.

Scotland, long a poor cousin to England, cannot avoid the gravitational pull of King Diego. Without the presence of a strong Protestant church on the Continent, Protestantism gains only a weak toehold in Scotland. In 1559, a minor Protestant uprising in Scotland is swiftly and ruthlessly crushed by English and Spanish forces. Its leader, John Knox, is captured and burned alive at Saint Andrews in 1560; the Scottish nobles who supported the rebellion are reprimanded and forced to sign an oath of loyalty to the pope. Those who refuse to do so are executed and their titles and lands redistributed to loyal Catholic relatives. Always keeping an eye on dynastic intertwining, in the inimitable Hapsburg style, a marriage is arranged between James, the son of Queen Mary of Scotland, and King Diego's younger sister, Catherine. Though she is eight years older than James, the pair is married in 1587, when James reaches the age of twenty. Eventually, through further Hapsburg-style inbreeding, the crowns of Scotland and England merge by 1640. Although the two realms retain their own parliaments for another generation or so, eventually they end up sharing a common representative legislature with two houses. Ireland, ever weak, is gradually drawn closer and closer to England's orbit, too, and by 1640 is subsumed into the Anglo-Scottish union.

The seventeenth century also marks the emergence of a mathematical and scientific revolution. Undistracted by costly wars and the inner social turmoil of religious infighting, the rising nation-states of Europe establish royal academies of science much earlier and promote learning by funding new universities and laboratories. Isaac Newton still publishes his *Principia Mathematica* in 1687, since genius cannot be rushed, but instead of devoting the latter part of his life to something as unscientific and inherently Protestant as trying to discover a law of prophecy in the Bible (which Newton actually did) our Catholic Newton continues to make remarkable discoveries in physics, optics, and mathematics up to the very end. He is still knighted by the crown and is also awarded a medal by the papacy.

In the meantime, on other fronts, the Ottoman Turks are gradually driven back from the Balkan Peninsula by Hapsburg armies. The Turks fight fiercely and hold their ground solidly in Anatolia, Armenia, and Syria. But they cannot hold Istanbul. The city once again becomes Constantinople in 1574 and is ruled by a distant relative of the last Byzantine emperor, who, of course, is married to a Hapsburg princess with a prominent jaw. A multinational Catholic navy led by Francis Drake sweeps clean the entire Mediterranean; by 1582 pirates and Turkish warships are no longer a threat to Western shipping. By 1587, Jerusalem falls to an invading Christian force led by Philip II and his son, King Diego I of England. Philip II claims his crown as king of Jerusalem in a lavish ceremony on the old Temple grounds; the title will be inherited by Diego in 1598. This will not be an easy crown to wear, for the Turks prove formidable enemies. Like the crusaders of old, the Europeans in the Holy Land will find themselves constantly at war and often on the edge of defeat. Meanwhile, English and Spanish colonies thrive and expand in America. Trade with the Near East and Asia intensifies along sea routes and overland roads alike. Africa, too, begins to be colonized according to American patterns and also becomes a source of slave labor for European colonies elsewhere, including parts of Asia. By 1700 Western Europe is well on its way to dominating the entire planet.

But wait! Something is wrong with this picture. This scenario does not unmake the West. On the contrary, it makes the West even more formidable at an earlier date. Is there some way to undo this triumphalist counterfactual history of a religiously unified Western Europe? Is there some way of undoing the higher-order counterfactuals and perhaps even the second-order ones? Would it be possible to come up with a Western Europe that is less unified as a result of a Catholic England?

The answer is yes, and the key may lie in religion, the ultimate wild card in premodern European history.

Catholic England: Religious History

Placing Mary Tudor on the throne of England in 1531 might ensure Catholicism for her realm, but it need not necessarily ensure any of the other scenarios outlined above. Two key assumptions made in the preceding exercise need to be questioned.

1. Should one assume that Roman Catholicism would be a sufficient cause for bringing about a Hapsburg-Tudor military alliance or even, if one were formed, that this would ensure a Valois defeat? Further, should one assume that a cowed Valois France would join this alliance and remain a faithful partner? These are highly contingent probabilities, at best, for their key assumption is the "fact" that Catholicism is a strong enough glue to bind these nation-states together, so to speak.

2. Should one assume that even if such a military alliance had become possible, Protestantism could have been eradicated through military campaigns? Should one even assume that the presence of a Catholic monarch on any throne ensures defeat for Protestantism within his or her own realm? These are also highly contingent probabilities, for their key assumption is the "fact" that belief can be coerced or, even worse, that religious behavior is predictable.

Again let us turn to a counterfactual historical narrative, unbroken by commentary or analysis, beginning with the same minimal rewrite: Henry VIII dies in 1531 and is succeeded by his daughter Mary.

Queen Mary I may be resolutely Catholic, but the same does not apply to all of her subjects. Lutheran literature has been streaming into England since the early 1520s. At Oxford, and at Cambridge, especially, there are groups of young intellectuals, many of them from influential families, who favor Luther's way of thinking. Some have even converted to Lutheranism, and are beginning to proselytize. One Cambridge professor, William Tyndale, has fled to the Continent and begun translating Luther's German Bible into English. Tyndale's translation of the New Testament had already reached England by 1526, and the Old Testament translation would be ready by 1536. But attraction to Protestantism is not limited to educated elites: the new evangelical message reaches all corners of the realm and all levels of society. Even at court, there are Protestant sympathizers. Supposing that Queen Mary became "Bloody Mary" even earlier—let's say in 1534—does this in any way guarantee that she would have been able to squelch Protestantism the way Philip II did in Spain?

By no means. Given the indisputable fact that Protestantism had made greater inroads in England than in Spain, and that England also had an older dissenting tradition in the Lollards, whose descendants could be found in pockets throughout the realm, it does not seem wise to assume that Mary could have stamped out Protestantism through vigorous persecution.[8] What can be assumed is that, as in the case of the earliest Christians, and in the case of the French Huguenots, the blood of the martyrs would become the seed of the church—in this case a dissenting church. The allusion to the Huguenots is intentional, for we have in them a parallel case. Despite all of the efforts made by Francis I to eradicate Protestantism in his kingdom, there still developed in France a very sizable and vigorous Protestant minority. It is quite likely, then, that if Queen Mary had begun to persecute Protestants in her realm, England might have had a history similar to that of France in the sixteenth century, that is, one of religiously motivated civil wars.

Moreover, even if we were to assume that a military alliance between Mary and Charles V could have resulted in a victory over the Schmalkaldic League in Germany and the Protestant cantons in Switzerland, should we also assume that this would mark the death of Protestantism on the European continent? Even if all of the civil and ecclesiastical leaders of the Protestant Reformation had vanished in one fell swoop, as proposed in the prior narrative, should it be assumed that their followers would have given up easily? Religion is seldom so predictable. While it is true that some religious dissenters in medieval Europe vanished after intense persecution, such as the Cathars, many others did not. Waldensians and Hussites, for instance, managed to survive in their own strongholds and also secretly among the broader population. The case of the Jewish *conversos* in Iberia for generations also points to the survival of dispersed religious minorities under persecution. The same is true for the Anabaptists, who were persecuted by Catholics and Protestants alike and yet managed to survive.

So even in the case of a massive military defeat, Protestantism might not have been very easily wiped out. Perhaps it might have led to greater unrest and instability. And this is only in the realm of second-order counterfactuals. The minimal rewrite gives us a Catholic on the throne in

England. Beyond this, when the vagaries of religious belief are considered, the possibilities for chaos seem as likely—perhaps even more likely—than the possibilities for the extermination of Protestantism.

Let us first consider one possible chaotic scenario beyond the minimal rewrite: England develops a sizable and vocal religious minority, much like the Huguenots across the channel. If John Calvin were not to survive, it is highly probable that those who became known as Puritans would still emerge. Here, it must be admitted, the question of personal genius enters into the discussion, along with the "great man" theory of history: could anyone else have forged as clear an ideology and as vigorous a religious minority as Calvin? Let us consider it possible that someone else could have done so, even if not in the same way. What would have happened in England under Mary and her Catholic successor with an ever-growing Protestant minority, especially one that included prominent noble families? Chances are that England would have sunk into a long civil war, just as France did between 1562 and 1598. Chances are, too, that under such circumstances no monarch could have rested securely on the throne and that foreign entanglements and military campaigns would have become impossible. Scotland would undoubtedly enter into the fray, possibly as a Protestant state, for the chances of Scotland shaking free of Rome would be high under this scenario.

So much for England as a strong Catholic ally of Spain.

But there could also be greater chaos. Supposing that, as happened with the Huguenots of France, the Anabaptists of Switzerland, and later the Puritans under Charles I, some of the Protestants of England decided to migrate and establish colonies elsewhere—say, in America?[9] Migration is as likely a possibility as civil war. If Mary had begun persecuting Protestants in the 1530s, perhaps some precursors of the Puritans would have sailed to the wilds of North America, far from Spanish settlements, and established colonies across the Atlantic Ocean. Perhaps the site of my own town of Guilford, Connecticut (est. 1639), would have become that of the first settlement by 1575 or even earlier.

Imagine the following scenario, with our old friend King Diego on the throne of England. Protestant colonies begin to proliferate in what is now New England. Unable to stop civil war from raging in England, even with aid from his father, Philip II, king of Spain, King Diego and his father decide that the best short-term policy is to allow the Protestant colonies to flourish for a while as a means of siphoning off Protestants from England. Their long-range plan is to win a decisive victory over the Protestant minority in England and then turn their attention to wiping out the colonies across the ocean. Part of the plan includes establishing some Catholic English colonies in North America to counterbalance the Protestant ones. So, the Atlantic seaboard from Long Island to Cape Hatteras is dotted with Catholic English settlements (south of which lie the settlements of Spanish Florida). Within two generations, the religious and political situation in England is no more stable than before and the American colonies, both Protestant and Catholic have begun to develop distinct cultures. By 1700, religious conflict continues unabated in England, as in France, and it extends to the New World. In 1701, fighting breaks out between the Protestant and Catholic colonies of North America. Prolonged fighting causes these colonies to develop little industry and commerce. Learning takes a backseat to fighting. Even more important, these rival cultures develop such a deep animosity for one another as to become the bitterest of enemies, thwarting the development of anything that might later resemble the United States of America. In fact, by 1800, all of these English colonies in America resemble one giant, feuding West Virginia.

In England itself, the effects of a costly and protracted civil war are profound. Unable to focus on commerce, weakened by the plagues and famines that accompany war, and divided within itself into a patchwork of Protestant and Catholic counties, England fails to develop into a world power. Even the blast furnaces promoted by Cistercian monks around Yorkshire fail to develop into much beyond a curiosity of sorts. England does become Catholic Europe's greatest producer of steel religious kitsch—statuettes, crosses, ex-votos, candelabra, and so on—so durable, and so shiny, but so utterly impractical. Although they produce excellent sheep shears, no one even thinks of turning out cutlery. England cannot produce or trade much else. Even the wool textile industry is damaged beyond repair by the civil war.

As to the rest of Europe, it is not very difficult to imagine the ramifications of England's descent into civil war and chaos. Because of its close ties to Spain, England becomes one of the largest bleeding wounds of the Spanish empire. With one rebellion to stamp out in the Netherlands and one in England, King Philip II and his successors, Philip III and Philip IV, squander even more of the treasure from America, precipitating great crises in Iberia and its empire.[10] By the closing decade of the reign of Philip IV, Spain is but a distant memory. Portugal, Catalonia, Granada, Andalusia, Navarre, and Galicia are all independent kingdoms. The same goes for Spain's European possessions: Burgundy, the Netherlands, and much of Italy. The Spanish colonies in America also achieve independence from Castile by 1701 but fail to develop much in the way of industries or trade. France and Germany, both beleaguered by civil wars similar to England's, also suffer from stunted economies and from a gloomy, pessimistic culture. Once free of the Spanish yoke, the Italian states revert to their late medieval ways. Fighting becomes the order of the day in Italy, as in most of Western Europe. Plague and famine become a constant threat as a result of war and instability. Nearly one-eighth of the European population succumbs to disease and starvation. In some areas, such as England and Central Europe, the toll is even higher.

But that is not all. The Ottoman Turks remain a formidable challenge to Europe in this scenario. Perhaps they could conquer Vienna by 1555? Perhaps they could constantly threaten to expand further, into Austria, Bohemia, Slovakia, Lithuania, and Poland? And what would happen to Venice and its commercial empire in the face of a more vigorous Ottoman Empire? And what about Russia? Instead of consolidating power and expanding east of the Urals, the Russian czars could perhaps find themselves fighting off the Turks for nearly a century on their eastern and southern frontiers. Perhaps only an outbreak of the plague and the sheer physical limits of overextension by the Ottomans could save Europe from Turkish domination?

In addition to all this, the massive witchcraft persecutions of the seventeenth century still take place and on a larger and more devastating scale. The nascent scientific revolution is stifled in the wake of such disasters. Among Catholics, monasticism enjoys a renaissance, and theology once again becomes the queen of the sciences in universities. Among Protestants, anything that cannot be squared with the Bible, as interpreted by the clergy, is deemed anathema. This includes the theories of Copernicus and Galileo, both of whom fade into obscurity. Isaac Newton's stepfather, the Protestant minister Barnabas Smith, forces him to follow in his footsteps, and having no other recourse, Newton complies. The would-be genius spends his long life pastoring simple, drunken souls in his native hamlet of Woolsthorpe and exegeting the books of Daniel, Ezekiel, and Revelation over and over again, seeking to discover the law of prophecy in Holy Writ.

Far away, in China and Japan, those few precious mechanical wonders brought by Europeans when they were at the zenith are beginning to have an impact. And so is the idea of a global empire, brought along with the clocks, telescopes, and Cistercian blast furnaces.

Up in smoke goes Western predominance. Or does it, really?

Examining Two Radically Different Scenarios

It is now time to put to the test both of the opposing scenarios sketched earlier, according to the procedural requests that the editors of this volume have suggested for these counterfactual exercises (chapter 1).

In both scenarios for a legally "Catholic" England, the key choice point is the early sixteenth century. The reasons for singling out this particular time in the history of Europe are the same for each of the exercises. This means that the radically different conclusions reached by each of the scenarios are not the result of different criteria for the choice of the key point; on the contrary, the opposing conclusions are grounded on exactly the same key point for exactly the same reasons. One might ask: why this particular key point?

First, in the sixteenth century Western Europe began its rise as a global power for a variety of reasons, all of which are interdependent: its global extension through voyages of exploration, commerce, and colonization; its technological and scientific advances; its improvements in demographic and economic conditions; and its cultural and intellectual renewal. Second, in the sixteenth century the emerging nation-states of Western Europe began to coalesce into the forms that will allow them to achieve all of the interconnected advantages just listed. The rise of these nation-states in the sixteenth century will also create very peculiar competitive relations among the peoples of Western Europe—a competitive political, military, and economic environment that gives shape to the very evolution of the Western "species," in Darwinian terms, understood literally with regard to the concept of evolution but metaphorically with regard to the concept of a species.

Third, in the sixteenth century Europe underwent a religious crisis of monumental proportions—a crisis that affects virtually every aspect of life in the West in very different ways and in varying proportions. It is not just the fact that this religious crisis causes a major redefinition of Western European civilization, from top to bottom, but also that this rapid and complex process of change also determines in myriad, incalculable ways how the peoples of Western Europe, and their states, relate to one another and the rest of the world. And in each of these three key areas, it must be kept in mind, England plays a crucial role.

An examination of what key assumptions had to be made about antecedents reveals how the assumptions made about counterfactual events depend on the vantage point and the kind of history one is writing.

In the case of political and military history, the key assumptions revolve around the possibility of military cooperation between two Hapsburg monarchies, that of Charles V and Mary I. Assuming such cooperation in the 1530s is no giant leap of the imagination, for this is what actually happened in the 1550s when Philip II married Mary and the English were drawn into war with Spain's longtime enemy, France. Assuming the defeat of the French, and their subsequent cooperation with a united Hapsburg/English force, is no giant leap either, but it does require more speculation. Beyond this, a further key assumption is thinking that an overwhelming military victory over Protestant armies could lead to the end of religious conflict in Europe. This assumption, in turn, rests on a larger one. If religion is considered as an epiphenomenon, that is, as a symptom of deeper underlying social, political, and economic realities, then it seems safe to assume that crushing military victories can stifle and eradicate religious dissent. And there are many historians who view religion precisely in this way.

In the case of religious history, one of the key assumptions listed earlier is reversed. Instead of bringing about the end of religious strife, Hapsburg/Tudor military victories simply lead to prolonged religious wars and greater instability among the rising nation-states of Western Europe. This reversal makes sense if one takes into account the unpredictability and "unreasonableness" of religious belief. Relying on the model of the persecuted Huguenots in France, and extending the paradigm they represent, allows us to consider the assumption as logical and sound. At bottom, the ultimate assumption here is thinking of religion as much more than a thin veneer over "real" political, social, and economic factors. The ultimate assumption is thinking of religious belief as a genuine motivating factor and the source of unpredictable behavior.

The idea of proposing two alternative counterfactual histories that lead to radically different rewrites was not originally part of my plan –it simply evolved as I wrote. And as it evolved it threw into high relief one question put forward by the editors of this volume, who asked all of us to identify the connecting principles that we used in creating our scenarios. It seemed simple enough a question until I reached the point where two very different narratives emerged. Then the question became one about different types of vantage points and logical progressions within a narrative.

In the case of the political and military history, the narrative leads to the creation of an even stronger Western Europe by means of a string of victories that propel a Hapsburg-dominated Europe into a geometric progression of successes. The connecting principles here can be compared to those used by American military experts to come up with their infamous "domino theory" about communist aggression in Asia. In one way or another, the connecting principles in this scenario depend on an almost algebraic equation in which each victory by one side makes it progressively stronger and its opponents or competitors proportionately weaker.

In the case of the religious history, an opposite scenario is created by means of connecting principles that resemble chaos theory more than algebra. Religion is the chaotic factor destabilizing all efforts at control and unification on the part of Catholic monarchs. In the end, a severely weakened Europe is created by a series of interdependent connecting principles very similar to those Michael Crichton borrowed from the physicist Heinz Pagels to develop the plot of *Jurassic Park:* one by one, each minor unraveling of any of the parts of a highly complex system can lead to greater unravelings, in quick, magnifying succession, up even to complete collapse.

The single greatest benefit of framing historical questions counterfactually is the way in which this process makes the value of specific details emerge in high relief. In order to construct plausible outcomes to minimal rewrites, one must weigh the relative impact of specific historical facts on a slightly different turn of events. Even the minimal rewrite itself depends on close scrutiny of specific facts. Take the case of Henry VIII's annulment. The basic question is: could he have received one from Rome? In this essay, the answer was a qualified yes, based on a close examination of several interrelated facts. A secondary question is: what would have happened if Henry's marriage to Catherine had been annulled? Would this alone have prevented England from turning Protestant? In this essay, the answer was not necessarily. And in order to arrive at that answer, many details had to be scrutinized. The same process applies to each and every "turn of events" proposed in a counterfactual history.

The biggest surprise that emerged in the course of developing this counterfactual thought experiment was the emergence of two equally plausible conflicting outcomes, each based on the same minimal rewrite. The idea of proposing two different scenarios emerged naturally in the course of actually constructing plausible rewrites. Although the possibility of achieving this was suggested by the editors', the emergence of the scenarios was a surprising outflow of the process of writing itself. The larger insight gained by proposing that *the rewrite is determined by the kind of history being written* is among the most unexpected surprises ever encountered by this historian.

Various schools of thought are likely to take umbrage at the conclusions reached here, and chief among them, perhaps, is that of counterfactual experimenters! Coming up with two divergent scenarios based on the same minimal rewrite could be seen as a flagrant violation of the counterfactual exercise. Some could object that separating religious history from political and military history is a first-order error. Some could also object to the basic assumptions of either rewrite. Others could object to the proposition that religion *is* more than a thin veneer over deeper social, political, and economic realties or to the proposition that religious behavior is often unpredictable. The ever-dwindling band of Marxists, naturally, would be another group that could take umbrage, since neither rewrite views the class struggle as the single interpretative lens. Finally, Whiggish historians could also be irked, especially at the suggestion that the Catholic religion is not inherently benighted or opposed to rational thought and scientific investigation.[11]

Substantive Questions about Western Predominance

As far as the larger task of undoing the West is concerned, this exercise has attempted to address head-on one of the editors' questions, that of "how easy or difficult is it to rewrite the different kinds of history (military, cultural, religious, economic, etc.) in ways that undo the global ascendancy of Europe?" When all is said and done, coming up with two completely different yet equally plausible scenarios was fairly easy. This is because two specific perspectives were chosen a priori. This exercise shows how plausibility in counterfactual history often depends on vantage points. What historians do when they examine the past through surviving records is to reconstruct and interpret from specific perspectives. *Histoire totale* is at best an unrealistic goal, not a reality. The point I wish to make is this: counterfactual history is embedded in particular vantage points. Because of this, any minimal rewrite can lead to multiple plausible ends—even opposing ones—depending on which set or sets of factors one considers. The more factors one considers, the more complex the rewrite becomes and the harder it is to arrive at plausibility. To put it simply, no historian can ever hope to encompass all factors simultaneously, so every counterfactual rewrite is, at best, a partial rewrite, contingent on the vantage point and the factors considered.

As to the question of when Western dominance became extremely difficult, arguably impossible, to reverse, this essay made it a prime assumption that the sixteenth century was *the* turning point for various reasons—all of which are outlined early in the essay.

Finally, as to the question of whether Western dominance had to take the forms it did, or could have taken more malign or benign forms, this essay points in the direction of various possibilities, depending on the vantage point taken. The simple answer, which is not so simple after all, then, is that a counterfactual historian could make the West go in myriad directions, malign as well as benign, depending on the vantage point.

In the end, the West can be made and unmade with the same minimal rewrite.

NOTES

1. "Breakthroughs—Archaeology," *Discover,* February 1999.

2. William Shakespeare, Sonnet 73.

3. For another counterfactual essay on the Protestant Reformation, see Geoffrey Parker, "Martin Luther Burns at the Stake, 1521," in *What If? 2,* ed. Robert Cowley (New York: Putnam, 2001), 105–19.

4. Clifford Geertz, "Religion as a Cultural System," in *Anthropological Approaches to the Study of Religion,* ed. Michael Banton (London and New York: Tavistock, 1966), 3–29.

5. Quite often it is the *inversion* of meaning that is exalted in such a way as to turn facts into "counterfacts": the birth of Jesus in a stable is *not* a sign of disgrace but rather of exaltation, the crucifixion is *not* a disaster but rather the ultimate triumph over sin and death, and so on. See chapter 4 in this volume.

6. For a sampling of opinions and approaches, see Arthur G. Dickens, *The English Reformation,* 2nd ed. (London: Fontana, 1989); Eamon Duffy, *The Stripping of the Altars* (New Haven: Yale University Press, 1992); Patrick Collinson, *The Birthpangs of Protestant England* (New York: St. Martin's, 1988); and Christopher Haigh, *English Reformations* (Oxford: Oxford University Press, 1993).

7. Two events from real history (a decade later) lend support to such a counterfactual scenario: (1) In 1544 Henry VIII and Charles joined forces to crush Francis I and impose a humiliating treaty on France; and (2) without Francis to distract him, Charles went on to wage war on the German Protestant princes and to defeat them at the Battle of Mühlberg in 1547.

8. There is little agreement on the number of Lollards left by the 1530s, but no one doubts their continued existence. See: A. G. Dickens, *Lollards and Protestants in the Diocese of York, 1509–1558,* 2nd ed. (London: Hambledon Press, 1982); Christopher Hill, "From Lollards to Levellers," in *The Collected Essays of Christopher Hill* (Amherst: University of Massachusetts Press, 1985–86), 2:89–116; Anne Hudson, *The Premature Reformation: Wycliffite Texts and Lollard History* (New York : Oxford University Press, 1988); and John F. Davis, "Lollardy and the Reformation in England," *Archiv für Reformationsgeschichte* 73 (1982): 217–37.

9. The Huguenots actually established colonies in Florida and Brazil in the 1560s (the former wiped out by Philip II of Spain).

10. The Hapsburg dynasty in Spain could remain unaffected in this counter-factual scenario. After the death of Mary Tudor in 1558, Philip would still be able to marry Elizabeth of Valois in 1559 and Ana of Austria in 1570. Cousin Ana could still give birth to the future Philip III. It is also possible for the Spanish succession to remain unaffected by the presence of one of Philip II's sons on the English throne: England could have been left in the hands of one branch of the Hapsburgs, as was done in the case of Austria and the Holy Roman Empire.

11. On this subject, see John William Draper, *History of the Conflict between Religion and Science* (New York : D. Appleton, 1875); Andrew Dickson White, *A History of the Warfare of Science with Theology in Christendom* (New York: D. Appleton, 1896); James J. Walsh, *The Popes and Science* (New York : Fordham University Press, 1911); and John Dillenberger, *Protestant Thought and Natural Science* (Garden City, NY: Doubleday, 1960).

CHAPTER 6

Europe's Peculiar Path

WOULD THE WORLD BE "MODERN" IF
WILLIAM III'S INVASION OF ENGLAND
IN 1688 HAD FAILED?

Jack A. Goldstone

In Paris in 1690, bonfires burned to celebrate the death on the battlefield of William of Orange, recently crowned King William III of England and chief foe of the glorious "Sun King," Louis XIV of France. Although William had succeeded in crossing the channel from Holland, landing a Dutch army in England, and frightening James II into fleeing to France, Ireland had rallied to the cause of James, England's first Catholic king in over a century, against the Dutch usurper. James had returned to Ireland to take command of the Irish army, which, though less experienced, outnumbered the English and Dutch forces that William brought to Ireland to defend his claims in the summer of 1690.

William himself went with a small party to reconnoiter James's position on the river Boyne. However, William was recognized by James's advance scouts. Artillery was quickly set up to shell William's route back to his camp. A shell fragment struck William, tearing his coat and doublet from his shoulder and speckling his linen with blood. News that the leader of England's forces had fallen was quickly sent to James, who posted a message to that effect to Paris. For Louis XIV, control of all of Europe and a Catholic alliance with Great Britain seemed within his grasp.

Except that William was not dead. The bullet had grazed his shoulder but did no real damage. Leading his army on a surprise assault on James's forces, and executing a difficult flanking maneuver, he surrounded James on three sides and routed the Irish and loyalist forces. While pockets of Jacobite resistance remained in Ireland and Scotland, James fled to France once more, leaving William in effective control of Great Britain.[1]

Fate was clearly on William's side. Even contemporaries were struck by the good fortune involved in William's successful transit of the Channel, unopposed landing, and easy victory over James II.[2] Indeed, his success was remarkable, the fortunate outcome of a desperate gamble. In 1688 Europe was girded for war: Louis XIV of France, the most powerful monarch in Europe, was prepared to attack the empire of the Austrian Hapsburgs, who were recovering from war with the Turks to the east. Louis also had designs on the Dutch Netherlands, but these could wait. Louis had been building a secret alliance with James II, so that Britain would not act against France in the coming European conflicts. Although Britain should have been Holland's natural ally—both were Protestant states, and William's wife Mary was James's daughter—James II remained allied with France. James was a devout Catholic and was determined that his newborn son, to be raised Catholic, would succeed him as king, despite the anxiety of the Protestant majority in England and Scotland. Mary, the next adult in line for the British throne, was a Protestant, as was her husband William, and James had no desire to see them glory in a Protestant victory over the Catholic Sun King.

William's position was therefore exceedingly difficult. If France should defeat the Hapsburgs while England remained neutral or supported France, Holland would be completely exposed to the might of Louis's armies. William thus persuaded the Dutch leadership that its only hope of defeating France lay in gaining British support and that this could only be forced by an armed invasion of England. Preparing a propaganda assault claiming that James had abused English rights, threatened the Anglican Church, and passed off a fraudulent infant as his own child, William aimed to defeat James and force him to cede the succession to Mary. William also would demand that James call a free (and clearly Protestant-dominated) parliament that would agree to an Anglo-Dutch alliance. William knew that only by pressing his wife's claims to the throne, and keeping England firmly in the Protestant camp, could he hope to hold out against the power of France.[3]

Taking a great risk by placing the cream of the Dutch army in transports to cross the English Channel, William brought a vast armada to face England. Still, the season was late and the weather treacherous; William's first attempt to cross the Channel was beaten back by fierce storms. He was fortunate to keep his fleet intact for another effort, this time even later in the autumn. To the surprise of everyone, an unseasonably persistent east wind bottled up James II's fleet in its anchorage on the Thames, while the same wind quickly took William's fleet across the Channel along England's southern coast to a favorable landing at Torbay on November 15, 1688 (see map 3 on page 146 above).[4]

With his landing unopposed, a small number of James's opponents in England began to declare their support for William. James II still had a formidable army, which began to march out of London. Yet the defection of some of his prime cavalry units and top military leaders to William's side stunned James and led him to believe he was doomed.[5] To the surprise and consternation of Louis, as well as of James II's supporters, James lost his nerve and simply fled. Anxious to secure a refuge for his wife and child in France, James "left the throne vacant," in the words of the convention that was called to decide the new terms of succession.[6]

This "Glorious Revolution," so swiftly accomplished, created a firm English/Dutch alliance, which was the foundation of Europe's opposition to French power over the next century. It was the revolution that "created a real balance of power in Europe where, before 1688, the continent had been virtually prostrate before the political and military supremacy of France."[7] Even with William's victory, Louis quickly tried to foment a Jacobite rebellion from Scotland and launched a major war against the Netherlands. But in vain—a joint Dutch/English fleet destroyed much of the French navy, while British expeditionary forces in league with Dutch and German forces under the leadership of William turned back the French armies.

William knew full well that he was gambling with the fate of Europe's geopolitics. But he could not have known that he was probably gambling at even higher stakes—with the growth of Western science and the rise of Europe as a technologically superior civilization.

Nations and Powers

Let us first look at geopolitics. Had the wind turned westerly, holding up William's fleet and letting James's powerful navy sail out to intercept them, or had James been as tough-minded as William, rooting out potential Protestant conspirators and willing to fight a desperate battle for control of the throne, under these circumstances James could well have stalled or repelled William's invasion and confirmed his control of Britain.[8] Or had the musket ball that grazed William's shoulder hit eight or ten inches lower, William's life and term as England's king would have been prematurely ended ("It's well it came no nearer" are reputed to be William's first words on realizing he was not severely injured).[9] Either way, William's failure would most likely have been followed by sharp retribution against Protestant leaders who had been in league with William, just as there had been a fierce reaction against the duke of Monmouth's attempted rebellion just three years earlier.[10]

Monmouth had also sailed from Holland, landed a force in the West Country, and called for Protestant support, toleration of Dissenters, and annual parliaments. Yet his military effort was feeble, and after his defeat conservatives rallied behind James II. In addition to the generous revenue for life granted at his accession, Parliament granted James an "over-generous amount of extraordinary supply to suppress" the rebellion, making James financially independent for the rest of his reign.[11] James, for his part, used the provocation to pack the courts with his handpicked judges, who soon decided that the king had the right to dispense with the laws if it so suited him (*Godden v. Hales, 1686*). Commissions of the peace issued for that year replaced over 250 justices of the peace with Catholics. The universities, too, had Catholics imposed on them, and a Catholic army was put in charge of Ireland. These were added to the previous laws adopted to strengthen the restored monarchy of Charles II following the chaos of the Civil War: a Licensing Act (1662), which regulated printing; and a modified Triennial Act (1664); which returned to the crown the initiative in calling parliaments. Charles II had also remodeled corporations and boroughs, increasing the monarchy's influence over elections to Parliament. Even in the American colonies, James II had brought opponents to heel: by 1684 he had impeached the charters of most of the colonies, placing them under more direct and centralized British rule. The separate colonies of New England and New York were reorganized into a single Dominion of New England under a governor with the power to dispense with elected assemblies.[12] Thus in 1685, a few years after the monarchy appeared to be tottering, it had scattered its enemies—the Whigs were broken as a political force—and was on the verge of controlling elections. Parliament, it seemed, might become a "rubber stamp," its membership determined by the crown like that of the French provincial estates.[13] How much more might the king have gained in authority if yet another Dutch invasion was repulsed?

William's goal in invading was to force England to intervene against France. He succeeded magnificently by tying the English throne first to Holland, then to the Hanoverians. The revolution of 1688 put continental concerns at the center of British policy well into the next century.[14] Yet if William had failed, James II, backed by coreligionists in Ireland and Scotland, by Tories in England, and with a cowed Anglican establishment, would have had a free hand in foreign policy and would have delivered the support, or at least the neutrality, that Louis XIV had counted on for his plans to dominate Europe.

With English support instead of opposition, Louis would control the seas, as well as having the largest army in Europe. Without British financing and military leadership, the Netherlands would have found it far more difficult to hold out against Louis's invasion forces. Even if not conquered, the Netherlands would have been intimidated and most likely partitioned. The War of the Spanish Succession, which, despite British and Dutch opposition, put a French Bourbon on the Spanish throne, would have done so with even greater ease. In the eighteenth century, instead of a Europe divided between English/Dutch/Austrian and French/Spanish/Bourbon alliances, Europe would likely have had a simple division along the Rhine between an English/French/Spanish (with an intimidated Netherlands) western sphere and an Austrian/German (and perhaps Russian?) eastern sphere.

Whether this arrangement would have been peaceful or precipitated a yet more massive war is difficult to say, but what seems certain is that the world outside Europe would have been even more powerfully affected. After all, the wars between England and France in the eighteenth century were critical to the fate of Canada and to the English colonies in America. If James II prevails in 1688 and there is no Glorious Revolution, what is the result for the Americas? At the least, there is no English invasion of Canada and taking of Nova Scotia, so Canada remains dominated by French Quebec. In the English colonies, there is no French and Indian War, thus no arena for young George Washington to start his military career. The Catholics in England no doubt would have continued to send Dissenters to the American colonies, and tensions with the mother country would have grown. But with its allies the Stuarts, not the Hanoverians, on the English throne, France has no reason to support the rebellious colonies. Instead, heeding the Stuart call to preserve the power of monarchy against rebellions, France intervenes in the American War of Independence on the British side, helping to choke off American trade and force a settlement in which the colonies remain English possessions.

With France able to take over some of the Netherlands' trade, and relieved of recurrent wars with Britain, its fortunes in the eighteenth century are better. It avoids the financial crisis that brings on the French Revolution and enters the nineteenth century as not only the largest and strongest state in Europe but also still a divine monarchy. Wars with Austria and Germany continue, but they do not overturn thrones, merely shift boundaries. Napoleon becomes a talented officer (though as a commoner not a general) in Louis XVI's armies and follows General Lafayette in triumph into Italy and Austria. Bourbon Spain remains an ally, not an enemy, for nonrevolutionary France, and the independence revolutions in Spanish America simply do not happen, for firm control of the Latin American empire by Spain is an important part of Louis XVI's plans. A slave revolt in Haiti is foiled when both Spain and France send monarchist troops to restore order. By the middle of the nineteenth century, France and its allies control the entire New World and the entire western portion of Europe. They conclude a peace with Austria, Germany, and Russia, so that France can turn its energies to building a global empire in India (in cooperation with Britain), Southeast Asia, and Africa, while Austria and Germany, humbled and turning to the gentler pursuits of philosophy and music in which they still excel, join with Russia to expel the Turks from Europe. By 1900, Europe looks much as it did in 1800, except that Greece and the Balkans are under Austrian control.

Science and Technology

And in the fields of science, technology, and economics? One of James II's first acts after defeating William's invasion is to dismantle the Royal Society, that hotbed of Anglican and anti-Jacobite beliefs and the chief forum for experimental science. Isaac Newton, who had led the opposition to James II's efforts to Catholicize Cambridge University in 1687, is relieved of his professorship, and his followers are persecuted and driven from the universities. The latter's curriculum is given over to Cartesians, whose view of the solar system as a system of vortices prevails for the next century. Advances in mathematics continue but with little practical impact on technology. After all, Descartes had proclaimed that all matter is extension and all force consists of collisions by particles of matter; thus there can be no vacuum (hence no atmospheric or steam engines) and no mysterious forces acting at a distance, such as universal gravity.

France's Huguenots, following the repeal of the Edict of Nantes in 1685, had begun to move to England, Prussia, America, and the Netherlands, bringing with them technical and artisanal skills that were of great importance in improving many crafts; but after James II's triumph, fewer and fewer came to England, reducing its edge in craftsmanship over France. More went to the Netherlands, where the Dutch turned their skills to improving wind-powered manufacturing, or to America, where wood and water to power craft enterprises were freely available.

Encouraged by France's success in ridding itself of its troublesome Protestants, James II and the Anglican hierarchy confer on ways to finally restore religious unity to Britain. A compromise is reached: the Anglican Church will remain independent of Rome but will follow the prayer book of James I and the Catholic calendar. Catholics will have equal rights with Anglicans and freedom of worship. Dissenters will be allowed to practice their religion privately, but under the strongly "High Church" bishops appointed by James II,[15] Anglicanism is enforced as the primary Protestant church. The Anglicans thus trade their continued independence from the pope and a monopoly on Protestant practice for coexistence with Catholicism. A major migration of Dissenters to the Americas ensues.

The British navy, now in alliance with the French navy instead of opposing it, no longer needs to triple in size, as it did under William III and the Hanoverians. Thus there is no huge investment at the Woolwich arsenal, and Henry Cort has no incentive to experiment with improved techniques for puddling and rolling iron, nor John Wilkinson to perfect boring equipment to quickly produce huge numbers of cannons, a process essential to production of cylinders for Watt's steam engines. This matters little, however, for with the disbanding of the Royal Society Boyle's experiments with air pumps and vacuums are not widely publicized and duplicated. Under the impetus of Cartesian physics, experiments with an atmospheric engine (which cooled steam to create a vacuum and thus atmospheric pressure to move a piston) cease. The Lunar Society of Birmingham is unlikely to arise without the example of the Royal Society, so James Watt is not likely to meet the entrepreneur Matthew Boulton who funded his work on steam power. Nor would Watt have spent his apprenticeship repairing Newcomen engines and getting ideas for their improvement. For that matter, as a Calvinist in upbringing, Watt would most likely have left England rather than trying to make his fortune there.

Arkwright develops a spinning machine, complemented by Hargreave's jenny, and cotton production with water-powered mills spreads rapidly and is copied in America and France. But iron for machinery remains scarce and expensive, and once most of the available millstreams have been tapped for factories there is little further capacity for the new mechanized system of manufacturing.

Swift clipper ships ply the oceans linking Britain, France, and the Americas to the west and Europe and Asia to the east. But the clippers can only call at Asian coastal ports and not steam upriver into the interior. Thus China's vast lands are secure against European power.

England continues to burn coal, but no one learns how to put that sooty fuel to any other use than basic heating, and its pollution so fouls London and Edinburgh that by the mid–eighteenth century the Stuarts—sponsoring great reforestation programs to assure adequate supplies of fuelwood—ban the burning of coal within city limits. Eventually, coal use stabilizes at fairly low levels as a bulk-heating fuel with restricted uses, but with the deep coal shafts filling with water, which can only be pumped out as fast as can be done by teams of horses pulling chain pumps, coal supplies grow more expensive and limited.

As we look farther forward from this imaginary world, to circa 1900, it becomes more difficult to be confident about what will happen. Will the study of Newton be revived? Will a new Luther raise followers in England to crack the Anglo-French alliance? Will Huguenot refugees in Silesia develop coal-powered steam engines? None of this can be ruled out. What does seem certain is that if William had failed the progress of democracy, Newtonian science, and British metallurgy and manufacturing would have been set back at least one hundred years.

Does this mean that these streams would have stopped dead or only been delayed by a century? If the latter, then in the great course of things a delay of three generations would not mean a great deal. But history has a way of coming close to major changes and then, if it veers away, not returning to that course. Song China seemed on the verge of a coal-fired industrial revolution in the eleventh century but still had not achieved it by the twentieth century. Rome seemed ready to bequeath a united Europe and Mediterranean to the millennium after Christ, but it was sundered in a few hundred years and was never reunited even after nearly two thousand.

Once discovered, is it truly conceivable that Newtonian science and its implications could have been lost or at least not applied to create a new industrial technology? Actually, Newtonian science could easily have gotten derailed; for example, gravity as an unexplained action at a distance continued to be held in disdain on the Continent for decades after Newton's *Principia* appeared.

The Catholicizing of England's universities, an attack on Newton for treason, and abolition of the Royal Society—could Western science have recovered from such blows?

If Newton's theories had lost support for political reasons and been set aside, it would not by any means have been the first time that valuable insights were discarded. Some of the ancient Greeks taught that the earth rotated and revolved around the sun; so, too, did the prominent eleventh-century Islamic astronomer Abu ibn Ahmad Al-Biruni. The Chinese seem to have lost some of the mathematical insights demonstrated during the Song dynasty of the twelfth century, and mechanical inventions for spinning fibers with water-powered machinery that were made in medieval China were never developed further and fell out of use. Throughout the history of civilization, it is quite common for academic and even technical advances to be lost rather than spreading and transforming the broader culture.

We should recall that even in technically advanced Holland, religion could hinder scientific advance. Margaret Jacob has noted:

> While Calvinism in the seventeenth century may have produced scientific rationalists . . . by the eighteenth century its orthodox clergy had grown fearful of heresy among the laity, and the power of Calvinist orthodoxy in popular culture produced widespread public opposition to aspects of the new science, for example, smallpox inoculation.[16]

Even with William's victory and the emergence of an Anglo-Dutch alliance, the spread of Newton's mechanics was slow. In Holland, study of Newtonian science continued at the University of Leiden but mostly among a small circle of professional academics and mainly through the study of propositions and proofs. It never spread to the broader professional, business, and crafts culture and never inspired experimentation and mechanical innovation. Moreover, as the seventeenth and eighteenth centuries wore on, as the Reformed Church grew more orthodox and less tolerant, the Dutch withdrew from the leading edge of scientific progress.[17] By 1720, the outstanding work of Huygens, van Leeuwenhoek, and others was drawing to a close, as Dutch leadership in science was increasingly curtailed by the conservatism of the Dutch church.[18] As late as the nineteenth century, Holland—once the most advanced commercial, agricultural, and technological nation in Europe—had yet to embark on an industrial revolution.[19]

If the mechanical view of the universe was reined in as atheistic, the Catholic cosmology regained pride of place in Europe, and Newton was vilified and his works banned by censors in England and Holland, as well as France, how confident can we be that Newtonian views would have ever spread beyond a small circle of mathematicians? England would likely have gone the way that Holland did, growing prosperous in agriculture and manufactures but not renovating the world through industrial invention.

The key invention of the steam engine required a rather special confluence of factors—a high demand for coal, which depended on easily reached (meaning water-connected) markets; an understanding of vacuums and pressure to key the idea of an atmospheric engine; a high degree of mechanical and crafts skill for building engines to pump water out of coal mines that were too deep to operate but too lucrative to abandon; and a strata of active entrepreneurs open to risks and ready to challenge orthodox practices while being in close touch with engineers and craftsmen to back innovative ventures. Only eighteenth-century England happened to possess all of these qualities, and they were produced in turn by such unconnected prior chains of events as the immigration of French Huguenots in large numbers, the experiments of Boyle and the Royal Society, and the Act of Toleration of 1689, which granted freedom of worship and property to Dissenters. Silesia's coal fields were not found in a society rife with experimentation or in which entrepreneurs and craftsmen were generally familiar with the new empirical and mechanical philosophy of Boyle and Newton. America had far too much land and forest to make coal-fired power desirable. And with the Dissenters, who had provided so much of the intellectual and financial firepower for the Industrial Revolution, dispersed to far less favorable situations, how likely is it that they would been able to combine to utterly transform a national economy, as happened in Britain between 1760 and 1860?[20]

Jacob notes that even in France, although military engineers learned and applied mechanical knowledge, they had no interest in finding cost-saving measures to reform industry. Products of a hierarchical, aristocratic society and educational system, they kept their distance from mere manufacturers. French military engineers could not evolve into civil engineers because their understanding of their role in the state and their social place prevented such an evolution. Their status and position blocked the emergence of civil engineering on any widespread scale.[21]

Conversely, in an aristocratic society, mere businessmen and manufacturers did not generally gain an advanced technical education. Thus in France:

> many of the very men who had access to capital, cheap labor, water, and even steam power could not have industrialized had they wanted to: they simply could not have understood the mechanical principles necessary to launch a sophisticated assault on the hand manufacturing process.[22]

Democracy Manqué

We have argued that if the Glorious Revolution had failed so, too, would have the American Revolution, while the French Revolution would not have occurred at all. Could a world without any of these revolutions have overthrown monarchy and established popular rule? Monarchies had ruled in China for almost three thousand years, in Islam for over a thousand, and in Europe for almost two thousand in 1789; why should they not continue ever stronger once the two major strongholds of republicanism in Europe—England and the Netherlands—were brought to heel?

Even in England, even with the success of the Glorious Revolution, democracy was slow to arise. Before 1688, Charles II had been remarkably effective in subduing the independence of Parliament, and James II had gained sufficient revenues to reduce his dependence on parliamentary grants. Parliament was revived under William III, who needed it to confirm his title and fund his wars against Louis XIV. Yet William still kept ministerial appointments and foreign policy firmly in his grasp. Parliament only began to take the reins of state power in its hands under the Hanoverians. These German princes, chosen for the British throne in order to preserve a Protestant succession, knew little of English politics or initially, even of the customs or language of the country they came to rule. They depended on parliamentary leaders to shape policy. Even so, Parliament remained far from representative or democratic. The House of Lords provided most leading ministers, and Parliament was elected through a system controlled by the rural gentry. Through the eighteenth century, as J. C. D. Clark has shown,[23] England remained predominantly aristocratic, Anglican, and antidemocratic. Only with the vast expansion of industrial cities, such as Birmingham and Manchester, and the growth of powerful industrialists, leading to the Reform Bill of 1832 and the later Reform Bills into the early twentieth century, did England move to full democratic and representative government.

Yet without William's accession, it seems unlikely that the Dissenters, who did so much to create the Industrial Revolution, would have been able to do so.[24] Without the growth of industrial cities and the expansion of the elite to include industrialists, entrepreneurs, engineers, and successful craftsmen, where would be the push for greater democracy? Urbanization itself provides no such push, or the far more urbanized societies of India, China, and Japan would have moved to democracy long before Europe. Nor can it be argued that England was inherently more democratic than other societies; recall that even to this day Britain is the only country in Europe with the senior half of its legislature consisting entirely of titled individuals who either inherit their positions or are appointed by the crown.

The industrialization that gave democracy a push in England was propelled by self-made men, for the most part, interested in doing things as efficiently as possible—Watt consciously designed his engine to cut costs as much as to create power—and their kind was unlikely to flourish in a hierarchical, rigidly orthodox, Anglican society. Without the assistance of the Huguenots, and the toleration conferred by the settlement of 1689, the technical and entrepreneurial pool of talent in England would have been greatly diminished. Even if Manchester grew on water-powered spinning mills, it might have grown to fifty thousand souls, like the mill towns of New England, but not to hundreds of thousands. Consider Tocqueville's description of Manchester in 1835 as a city of "half-daylight," smothered in black smoke, yet "from this filthy sewer pure gold flows."[25] Or consider Carnot's appraisal: "To take away England's steam engines today would amount to robbing her of her iron and coal, to drying up her sources of wealth, to ruining her means of prosperity."[26]

"No Bishop, no King" James I was fond of saying, as he defended his measures to preserve the episcopacy from claims by Presbyterians and other Dissenters. Yet let us turn this around: no 1689 settlement, no broad toleration for Dissenters, then no spread of Newtonian mechanics and Dissenting entrepreneurs and engineers and no steam engines. No steam engines, then no vast growth of industrial cities in the early nineteenth century; no rapid urbanization, then no Reform Act and no movement toward true democracy. Switzerland might have achieved democracy, and the Dutch provinces might have retained their federal, oligarchical governance, but can one seriously believe that the entire world would seek to model itself on the example of these tiny, militarily minor countries? Without the rise of British sea power and victory over France, without the rise of independent America and the overthrow of absolute monarchy in France, is it conceivable that Latin America or India would have adopted representative democratic institutions? Just as democracy and toleration were key to creating a society in which innovation and entrepreneurship could flourish, so were the technological fruits of that society a powerful means of spreading the apparent virtues of democracy and toleration throughout the world.

But Then Again...

How likely is the notion of a Catholic, or at least Catholic-led, Great Britain after the seventeenth century? And how likely is it that a Catholic-led Britain would have led to the loss of Newtonian science, the Industrial Revolution, and popular democracy in Europe? In other words, how likely is it that this counterfactual could in fact have arrived or that if it somehow took place it would have these consequences?

The idea that England could have been brought back into the Catholic fold, or at least have been politically and intellectually dominated by Catholics, should hardly be surprising in an era in which the richest, most populous, and most powerful states of Europe (Spain, France, Austria) and many of the smaller but still powerful states (Bavaria, the Italian states, Poland) were all firmly Catholic. Viewing England not in isolation but as part of Great Britain, England was joined to one kingdom that was predominantly Catholic (Ireland) and to another that repeatedly rose in Jacobite rebellion to support the claims of Catholic monarchs (Scotland).

Indeed, in the sixteenth century England twice came close to sustained Catholic rule. Mary I sought to overturn the Reformation in England and Catholicize England; had she lived longer and had an heir, England would have become part of the patrimony of the line of Philip II of Spain, her husband. Elizabeth restored the Protestant Church and suppressed Catholicism, but there were many plots to overthrow her in favor of Mary Stuart, the Catholic queen of Scotland and next in line for the English throne. Had these plots succeeded, or had Elizabeth died early in her reign, as had her sister Mary, instead of ruling for forty-five years (a truly rare and astounding event given sixteenth-century life expectancies), the English throne would again have had a Catholic incumbent.

By the seventeenth century, it is likely that Anglicanism was too well established, and popery too feared and reviled, for a forcible Catholicization of England to succeed. But this was neither likely nor what James II intended.[27] James was seeking to fill his army with loyal officers and pack Parliament with loyal and subservient allies who would help him repeal the Test Acts, making it possible for Catholics to hold high offices. If he had succeeded in these aims, there would have been no need to forcibly Catholicize all of England. With a Catholic dynasty assured by the survival of James's son, and with Catholics holding many of the leading civilian and military positions in the three kingdoms, the prestige of the old faith could only have grown. Planting Catholic leaders in the major universities would have ensured a fresh flow of defenders of the old faith and reduced the flow of Protestant leaders. Had William's invasion failed, and those Protestants who assisted him either fled or suffered the penalties for treason, the decapitation of the Protestant leadership would have advanced even further and the prestige and loyalty of Catholics been further enhanced. In a generation or two, the bulk of the population might have remained loyal to the Anglican and Dissenting churches, but the intellectual, political, and military leadership of the three kingdoms would likely have been firmly Catholic.

Furthermore, even if William had somehow negotiated the throne for himself and Mary, but without the Acts of Settlement that permanently banned all Catholics from the throne, the crown would likely have reverted to a Catholic before long. In 1714, on the death of Queen Anne, the closest line of succession ran through Charles I's youngest daughter, Henrietta Anne, whose daughter had married into the Italian House of Savoy. Indeed, mainly through Charles I's descendants, no less than fifty-seven Catholic males in Europe's royal lines had hereditary claims superior to that of Anne's chosen successor, Elector George of Hanover.[28]

What role would a Catholic-dominated England have played in Europe? Certainly it would have opposed the commercial competition of the Dutch, as it did in the series of Anglo-Dutch wars that did in fact fill the latter seventeenth century. As late as 1672, a joint English-French assault pressed Holland to its knees, cutting the Dutch Republic in half and forcing William III back to Amsterdam.[29] Only cutting the dikes, and the naval heroics of de Ruyter, saved the republic. Had William lost the cream of the Dutch military in a botched amphibious assault in 1688, or gotten it bogged down in a stalemate in a series of British campaigns, Holland after 1689 would have been far more vulnerable to the forces of Louis XIV. Given the key role of English forces and leaders in the wars of the League of Augsburg and the Spanish Succession, even English neutrality would likely have been sufficient to assure an outcome more favorable to France and to its prestige and dominance.

The relative prestige of Catholic France versus Protestant England and Holland was of great consequence, as they stood for very different approaches to government, religion, and science.

Holland under William III was a relative bastion of toleration. However, it should be noted that this toleration was very much a product of William's personal belief and intervention and that the long-term tendency of the Dutch Reformed Church was toward orthodoxy and suppression of dissent.[30] Even as things stood, Holland was no marvel of toleration: Descartes and Spinoza were forced to flee for their beliefs, and outside of Amsterdam most Dutch cities banned Jewish settlement and were prone to anti-Catholic riots.[31] Britain under William was even more successful in establishing a kind of ambivalent but institutionalized toleration, allowing public worship by various dissenting groups and considerable latitude to the new experimental philosophy. Most importantly, as a result of William's success, an independent Parliament survived as a partner in rule with the crown.

France, in contrast, was leading the general trend in Europe toward the dissolution and enfeeblement of representative bodies and the firm establishment of state orthodoxy. The revocation of the Edict of Nantes stunned Protestants and marked the growth in power of the absolutist state in matters of conscience as well as political authority. The Jesuits were still strong, and the experimental physics of Boyle and Newton were roundly abused. The teaching of Newton was not part of French schools' normal curriculum in science until after the French Revolution.[32] Without the powerful example of Britain, it is hard to imagine that toleration, representative government, and experimental science would ever have gained a foothold on the continent.

In Spain, Italy, Eastern Europe, and even Holland, the Catholic and Calvinist Churches succeeding in suppressing the early stirrings of empirical, Copernican/Galilean science. England, in contrast, carried the new science to new heights, and France was forced to follow due to its military and commercial defeats at the hands of English competition. Take away that competition and replace it with a conservative, pro-Catholic, and pro-French regime in Britain that joined European monarchs in suppressing the political and scientific heterodoxies of the Royal Society and the independence of its Parliament and it seems unlikely that the steady growth of absolutism across Europe would have been interrupted.

Without steam technology, democracy, and toleration emerging in seventeenth- and eighteenth-century Britain, it is difficult to see how they could have arisen anywhere else. Steam technology was not simply an obvious extension of obvious physical principles. It required first an appreciation of the properties of the vacuum and then an intensive effort to shave costs from a clumsy, expensive apparatus that had use only in special circumstances. The climate of innovation and the innovators and entrepreneurs who applied the new mechanical ideas to revolutionize manufacturing were unique to a relatively tolerant, pluralistic society. Elsewhere in Europe and Asia aristocratic societies sponsoring state-enforced religious orthodoxy stifled innovation and even sought successfully to halt the spread of Newtonian science.

In chapter 10 of this volume, Joel Mokyr points out that many discoveries and technological inventions were made in "multiples," meaning simultaneously by different investigators. If steam engines and cheap steel making were the most powerful and revolutionary of the many inventions that characterized the first Industrial Revolution, couldn't they too have been discovered elsewhere? After all, the understanding and demonstration of atmospheric pressure was a pan-European process, with contributions from Torricelli in Italy, Pascal in France, and von Guericke in Germany, as well as Boyle in England. For that matter, representative bodies were an old and widespread tradition in Europe as well, as most European monarchies around 1500 had some form of estates or national assembly, however oligarchic they were.

Yet Mokyr argues that what multiple discoveries prove is that many individuals, *when working against a common background of knowledge and techniques,* are likely to strike out in similar directions and make multiple findings. It is the common background of knowledge and techniques that is key; we do *not* find multiple discoveries among widely disparate cultures and societies working from different bases of knowledge and technique. Thus Mokyr argues that if the Industrial Revolution had not emerged in the West it is highly unlikely that China or Japan or India would have taken the steps leading to steam engines, electricity, and modern chemical engineering.

The question regarding the pivotal role of England after 1688 then becomes whether Europe as a whole really enjoyed a "common background of knowledge and techniques" in the late seventeenth century.

With regard to political institutions, one can answer in the affirmative, but the common techniques of rule that were becoming standard practice everywhere were absolute monarchy, justified by divine right and buttressed by the revitalization of Roman law and royal bureaucracies, along with support from a powerful religious hierarchy that partnered with the secular state. By the late seventeenth century, Europe had

witnessed the defeat of the *comuneros* in Spain, the defeat of the Fron-
deurs in France, the defeat of Bohemia and the consolidation of the Austro-Hungarian Empire by the Hapsburgs, the rise of the Prussian monarchy in Germany, and the reigns of warrior kings in Sweden and Russia.
The role of the estates was being undermined everywhere. This was also
true in England, where the collapse of the Commonwealth and the efforts
of the Restoration monarchy renewed claims to absolute monarchy.

With regard to science and technology, the common scientific enterprise of the early seventeenth century was being riven by diverging
national patterns of science and the revival of the church. By the late seventeenth century, on the Continent the Counter-Reformation, pietism,
and strict Calvinism had all begun to restore and enforce the authority of
scripture. Partly in response to this revival of church authority and partly
due to the dominance of Cartesian scholars on the Continent, throughout
most of Europe scientific practice became more abstract and mathematical, following the Cartesian approach to deductive, nonexperimental discovery.[33] Only in England did an experimental, Baconian, instrument-
based approach become established as the dominant method of
discovery. It was the widespread diffusion of this approach among
tradesmen, engineers, and factory owners (who systematically experimented to find superior methods of production) that fueled the technological dominance of England in the eighteenth and nineteenth centuries
and led to the perfection and application of steam engines, vastly
improved metallurgy, and a variety of other chemical and mechanical
innovations.

To note just one key difference: in England the Royal Society was a
self-constituted group of amateur experimentalists that welcomed businessmen and undertook public lectures and demonstrations for craftsmen and the general public. By contrast, the Académie Royale des Sciences in France was a professional body, supported by and allied with the
crown, rather more elitist and cut off from men of business and craftsmen.[34] Had an absolutist and Catholic monarchy prevailed in England,
modeling itself on the institutions of the Sun King in France,[35] and abol-
ished the Royal Society or remodeled it on French lines through royal
patronage, the critical links between the proponents of Newtonian
mechanics and practical craftsmen and entrepreneurs that were so crucial
for the development of modern engineering and industry in Britain would
most likely have been fatally ruptured. The distinctively British widespread dispersal of common knowledge and techniques based on Baconian methods and Newtonian mechanics would have been aborted in

favor of continental patterns of deductive and elitist science that nowhere independently produced steam engines or cheap mass-produced steel.

Moreover, without a rapid rise of industry, aristocratic principles of social organization and politics were not likely to be effectively challenged, even in England. Representative democracy is not an obviously desirable and "natural" form of government, quite the reverse. Every major nation on earth, including England and its North American colonies, held to oligarchic, monarchic, or imperial rule into the late eighteenth century. As we have noted, almost all the major representative bodies of Europe had been extinguished or reduced to ineffectiveness during the seventeenth century.

In sum, William's failure would not just have shifted the political map of Europe. It would have shifted, and sharply reduced, its scientific and technological capacity as well.

Europe might have continued to dominate the New World and even to take advantage of Ottoman and Mughal decay to take portions of India and the Middle East, but it would have had no impact on China and little on Japan. Neither widespread representative democracy nor accelerating economic progress would have emerged in the nineteenth century in England. In such a world, conditions in the year 2000 would have been little different than in 1700. And the rise of the West would not even be an idea that occurred for us to debate.

Reflections on the Counterfactual World

It is disturbing, even to this author, to see how swiftly and thoroughly the modern industrial world dissolves away in the absence of a strong Protestant ruler in seventeenth- and eighteenth-century Britain. Or, more accurately, not just a Protestant ruler but one committed to a limited toleration of dissent and opposition to French ambitions. Charles II, though an Anglican, had responded to his father's overthrow by undertaking "the most ambitious scheme of centralization known in England before the nineteenth century. Corporations were reconstituted, the lieutenancy was purged, and the commissions of the peace were rigorously scrutinized."[36] Charles also took subsides from France and actively undertook war against the Dutch. Charles did sponsor the Royal Society, and he issued a declaration of indulgence to tolerate Catholics and Dissenters, so perhaps some progress might have been made in the realm of science, but there is reason to doubt whether Parliament would have ever obtained the upper hand against the Stuarts if not for the succession crisis.

To step back from the details of William's campaign, what we see here is the importance of a large number of trends begun in seventeenth-century England going forward and—far more important—becoming institutionalized in the fabric of society. These include the scientific advances of the Royal Society, both the experimental method of Boyle and the laws of motion and gravity of Newton;[37] the rise of religious pluralism instead of a state-sponsored orthodoxy; and the strengthening of Parliament against the monarchy. What is frightening in hindsight is how truly peculiar each of these trends is in the history of Europe, much less of the world.

The typical trend in science around the globe was for pioneering individuals—such as Aristarchus of Samos and al-Biruni, as well as Galileo—to be criticized for impiety and to have their more radical beliefs impugned and lost. Many societies had political and social crises in the seventeenth century, but the typical outcome was a strengthening of traditional beliefs and central power in reaction to the social disorder. The triumph of the Counter-Reformation in continental Europe after 1650 had its counterparts in the "Circle of Equity" movement in the Ottoman Empire and the "New Evidential" invigoration of Confucianism in China.[38] The outcome of Civil War in England initially moved in precisely this direction under Charles II and James II, as the Restoration regime strongly retrenched the aristocracy and the established church.[39] The "normal" course of events outside of England was for traditional views, supported by the monarchy and the bulk of the aristocracy, to prevail or even to be reinforced by social crises. It was wholly unprecedented for a religious millennial movement—as represented by the Puritans in the Anglican Church, many Dissenters, and later even American revolutionaries—to bind itself to an epistemology (e.g., Newtonian science) that aimed to overthrow classical wisdom. Even Newton may have been dispensable—Leibniz also developed the calculus, and Robert Hooke, Newton's colleague in the Royal Society, was toying with an inverse square force as the basis for holding together planetary orbits. But what was truly indispensable was having the church and state accept and promulgate a radical revision of traditional religious cosmology rather than fight to suppress it.

It was even more unusual for Parliament to gain the upper hand against monarchs. The Fronde led to ending the estates and taming the *parlements* of France; the *cortes* of Spain and the Prussian estates were similarly emasculated. England's Parliament was well on its way to a similar fate under Charles II and James II. While the Dutch Republic remained an oligarchy (*not* a democracy), oligarchies throughout history have shown no tendency to grow into democracies—certainly not in Venice or Holland. In the latter, it took the Patriot revolution of the late eighteenth century to overcome closed oligarchic rule.

Finally, religious toleration was clearly on the way out in Europe. From the 1648 settlement of the Thirty Years' War, which called for rulers to determine the major religion of their territories, through the revocation of the Edict of Nantes, which ended toleration in France, the typical trend was for rulers and state churches to insist on conformity. The Act of Toleration in England was not a well-thought-out policy of religious equality; it was a hastily patched together compromise that still disabled Catholics and Dissenters in political life. In Scotland and Ireland, nonconformity was even more harshly penalized. The restrictions on Catholics were not repealed until almost a century and a half later.

In sum, the particular characteristics we now consider "key" to modern Western societies—(1) an epistemology based on a radical break with traditional and classical knowledge and grounded on experiment and universal physical laws in mathematical form, (2) representative government that gives legislative bodies responsible to the people priority in making laws, and (3) a secular society in which religion is a private choice and pluralism is tolerated without a state-enforced orthodoxy—were actively suppressed everywhere in Europe, except in England, and never emerged autonomously anywhere else in the major civilizations of the world. If not for England having stumbled by chance on a peculiar path that brought all three of these characteristics into institutionalized form from the late seventeenth through the eighteenth centuries, I see no way they would have emerged autonomously anywhere else on earth.

I believe it is precisely this quality that makes this particular counterfactual so powerful and accounts for the rapid "dissolving" of so much of history. In changing England's history to undo the rise of the West we need no great changes in the bulk of world history—*precisely because the bulk of the world was on a different path*. Throughout most of the world, in Europe and beyond, over the centuries from 1200 to 1700 absolutism was increasingly well established, representative institutions were lapsing or being actively suppressed, and national orthodoxies were being defended and radical views of the universe curtailed or suppressed. All that is necessary for the rise of the West to be aborted at this time is for the one area pivotal to that rise to be brought back onto the track of the other major European powers and world civilizations.

This suggests a "rule" for counterfactuals—the most plausible and powerful counterfactuals are those that choose a point at which one group or society departs radically in a different direction from the "normal" or most common paths of development or action elsewhere, and find a counterfactual that simply reverts that exceptional departure to the norm. In such cases, I think it is plausible that equilibrium forces will maintain that "normal" path and the radical departure will be lost—perhaps forever. It seems to me far less persuasive to pick a counterfactual in which the historical course is a normal and common path and to choose a counterfactual that puts a group or nation on a radically different course. In these cases, I think it more plausible that without many additional counterfactual postulates equilibrium will tend to return the group or nation to the "normal" course and the impact of the original counterfactual will be attenuated.

This also provides a guideline for answering another question regarding the rise of the West: at what point in history does it become difficult or implausible by means of counterfactuals to undo that rise? The answer then follows—when for most European or Western nations it has become normal to be well on the way to an industrial, democratic, religiously pluralist society. This point, however, is not reached until after the Atlantic (American, French, Dutch) Revolutions of the late eighteenth century and perhaps not until well into the early nineteenth century. Certainly by this point scientific and technological superiority relative to non-Western societies is so widely dispersed that it would be difficult to put the genie back in the bottle.

This general rule—that the most plausible counterfactuals involve identifying a departure from normal developments and reverting those departures to the norm—in some ways blends several of Tetlock and Belkin's conditions for making counterfactual arguments, namely, a "minimal rewrite," "consistency with well-established theoretical laws," and "consistency with well-established statistical generalizations."[40] Yet these conditions are rather abstract and exist without any identification of "normal" or "common" paths of historical development. Such paths, for example, the suppression of representative institutions throughout most of continental Europe and Asia, are neither "well established theoretical laws" nor "well established statistical generalizations." Rather, they are the most common tendencies in the known set of cases. The ideal that a counterfactual should "restore" or "undo" a deviation from those common tendencies is a far less restrictive condition than consistency with "theoretical laws" or "statistical generalizations," but I believe it is still a useful one.

If these observations on counterfactual history are true, then counter-factual history must rely on some sense of what is a "normal" or histori-cally common path of development for nations and groups, in other words, on some findings of comparative history or social science. Dis-tasteful as this may be for pure historians (who, however, dislike coun-terfactual history in any event), it seems that the plausibility of counter-factual exercises cannot be assessed without some comparative or social science sense of reasonable cause and effect in the context of long-term historical trajectories.

Of course, it would still be excessive to say that all of England's future development could only have been determined by a single event: William of Orange's victory. It is more reasonable to consider a constellation of alternative counterfactuals and ask: how many and how likely are the events that would have put England on its singular path, and how many and how likely are the events that would have restored England to pre-vailing continental patterns? One can imagine many scenarios in which England develops an alliance with Holland, religious pluralism, and industrialization: if Charles II has a male heir who is raised Anglican and decides to reverse his father's anti-Dutch pro-French policy; if James II does not have a son and the succession passes peacefully to Queen Mary, making William king by marriage and their marriage producing a Protes-tant heir; or, for that matter, if the English Revolution leads to a lasting Commonwealth instead of a Stuart restoration. In any of these cases, we can imagine France being contained, Newtonian science spreading, and industrialization coming. The problem is that none of these scenarios is any more likely than not. Moreover, without the crisis of 1688–89, Par-liament may not gain power until much later in these scenarios (even under Cromwell, who derisively dismissed Parliament when it suited him) if at all.

Yet if there are many scenarios that launch England on its peculiar path of Protestant, parliamentary, Newtonian society facing off against a mainly Catholic and absolutist Continent, there are equally many sce-narios in which England is drawn into the continental trajectory. If Bloody Mary has a Catholic heir who, as son to Philip of Spain, takes the English throne; if Elizabeth dies young and leaves the throne to Mary Queen of Scots; if Charles I prevails against Parliament in the English Civil Wars; if Charles II lives longer and continues his centralization of government under the crown; if William's invasion fails and James lives to pass the crown to then James III; in short, at any time over the 150 years from the 1550s to the 1690s, England's movement toward a Protestant crown dependent on Parliament and accepting religious pluralism could have been derailed.

What makes this counterfactual study interesting is not that any one particular trajectory or event was crucial; rather, it is that the role of seventeenth-century England emerges as so pivotal for the trajectory of the entire world. What we routinely associate with "the West" today had in fact little to do with most of the West. Spain and Portugal, Italy and France, Austria and Germany; all were moving more strongly toward absolutism and state-enforced conformity in the seventeenth century, with only England and Holland resisting (and the latter could not do so on its own). If England does not pull free of the continental orbit, with enormous consequences for geopolitics in the Americas and Europe, the West and "the rest" look an awful lot alike. And yet England does not do so because of any long-standing or powerful differences from any other country, in Europe or the world. Chance events that destabilize the monarchy, and lead to a particular set of compromises and half solutions, produce a peculiar path, of no particularly strong probability, that nonetheless changes the world.

This view of course sharply differs from the opinions of many economic and political historians, who see certain Western institutions and characteristics, usually identified as involving the "growth of capitalism," as having made it very likely that Europe would industrialize and dominate other societies. Interestingly, both scholars on the Left, who see the rise of Western economic and technological dominance as malign,[41] and more conventional neoclassical economic historians, who see the rise of Western dominance as praiseworthy,[42] agree in seeing that dominance as a strongly determined outcome grounded in distinctive European qualities and conditions.

Yet I frankly cannot see any way that England prior to 1688 differs so much from other countries, or that Europe as a whole differs from other advanced trading civilizations, as to confirm those views. Private property—a favorite of many legal and economic historians—was hardly respected under the early Stuarts, who remodeled corporations and sold monopolies with abandon. The courts even granted James II the power to dispense with the laws of the realm as he saw fit. By contrast, private property was sufficiently secure in China for merchants to travel with fortunes in silver and for the gentry to amass huge estates. Indeed, even in India, Clive in 1757 remarked regarding Murshidabad, the old capital of Bengal, that "This city is as extensive, populous and rich as the city of London, with this difference: that there were individuals in the former possessing infinitely greater property than in the latter."[43] Much the same could have been said of Lahore, Agra, and Delhi. As Goody notes, "By comparison with some of India's great merchants, the English were by no means rich nor yet remarkable in other ways."[44] Holland, surely, had security of property and legal institutions, which had fueled its golden age, and it had the cheapest capital in all of Europe. Yet Holland was a laggard in industrialization; Belgium and Switzerland industrialized faster.

Whatever the preconditions for advanced capitalist development and international trade, China certainly had them. Whether in agriculture or manufacturing, China's trade in grain, in cotton, in cloth, in ceramics exceeded that of any European nation.[45] Just in regard to pottery, the famous works at Jingdezhen imported vast quantities of refined cobalt oxide (to provide the blue color) from sites six thousand kilometers away in the Middle East, produced customized wares in patterns and shapes for Islamic lands, and shipped boatloads of ceramics to India and the Ottoman Empire. Much of this development was prompted by Muslim merchants, who "probably were responsible for the great investment of capital that transformed the privately owned kilns of Jingdezhen into well-organized industrial complexes controlled by commercial syndicates."[46]

Some scholars have suggested that Japan, like England, was an exception; relatively decentralized, once "feudal," religiously somewhat permissive, and adaptive of inventions in other societies, it may have been able to industrialize on its own.[47]

Yet there is absolutely no evidence to suggest that Japan was moving toward anything like democracy or coal-powered industry before European intervention. Quite the reverse: Japan had largely closed itself off to trade, turned its back on its once advanced musketry, and developed a rigid class system based on the distinction between samurai and commoners, with a military dictator (the shogun) demanding loyalty from local aristocratic lords (daimyo). True, Japan today has adapted elements of European civilization well, but no more so than Taiwan and Singapore (both Chinese) and South Korea.

The European states system is often pointed to as a cause of Western progress; military competition and plural spheres of interest encouraged and permitted change. Yet except for England, this simply was not so. First, Europe was neither the only nor the longest-lived plural states system. China spent almost half of the last four thousand years divided into competing states, including a several-century period between the Han and Tang dynasties, comparable to the Middle Ages in Europe. India was rarely unified and often divided by internecine wars. The Islamic world was divided into multiple states for almost its entire existence, from the multiple caliphates of Spain, North Africa, and Mesopotamia to the opposition between the Ottoman Empire and Persia. Southeast Asia was always a system of competing states, both economically and militarily. For that matter, if military pressure from rivals led to progress, then Austria-Hungary and the Ottomans, who fought almost continuously in the largest and most consequential campaigns in European history from the sixteenth through the eighteenth centuries, should have been in the vanguard of progress. Instead, they were the laggards of the Continent. War and competition are nearly universal in human history; progress of any kind is rarely the result.

Last, some scholars have suggested that China's problems came from a demographic regime inclined to rapid population growth and high population densities, whereas Europe and Japan controlled their family size.[48] This false impression, however, was founded on a misunderstanding of Chinese demography. Chinese families *did* control fertility, although they did so not by restricting marriage in the European style but by restricting fertility *within* marriage. The average twenty-year-old married woman in China had only half the fertility of her counterpart in Europe. Long intervals between marriage and first birth, long parity intervals, prohibitions on widow remarriage, and selective infanticide and child neglect of females meant that women spent much of their fertile lives not bearing children. Until the breakdown of the Confucian moral family regime in the late nineteenth and early twentieth centuries, men did not marry more, and had no more children, in China than in Europe.[49]

The problem in seeking structural conditions for the rise of the West is that the problem is generally one of misplaced explanandums. I have pointed out that certain patterns of events and processes recur frequently in history across varied cultural and geographic regions. Thus in both the seventeenth and nineteenth centuries, agrarian-bureaucratic states in Europe, the Middle East, and China suffered massive political and social dislocations. In nearly every case, one finds a combination of state fiscal problems, inflation, exceptional social mobility, and declining land access and/or real wages behind these events. For so many societies to have such similar crises suggests an underlying structural situation that makes such a pattern of events likely to happen. I have called such recurrent and widespread processes "robust" and suggested that general causes, rather than chance combinations of events, must lie behind them.[50]

In contrast, the rise of industrialization and representative democracy is an extremely rare event in world history. The first is unknown to have occurred independently anywhere outside of the United Kingdom. Almost every element of capitalism can be found elsewhere—massive commercial enterprises, huge production of iron and steel (China in the eleventh century is reputed to have produced as much as England in the eighteenth), large-scale international and domestic trade, urbanization and specialized production for markets, sophisticated finance (our word *check* comes from the Arabic *saak* or "promissory note"). Yet one key item is absent, not even approached, anywhere else—the steam engine. This invention, which makes it possible to turn heat into useful motion, is completely unprecedented; with it, England transforms the world and dominates larger and richer civilizations.

Similarly, although one finds various sorts of oligarchy and urban and village democracy throughout the world, there is no precedent for a large territorial monarchy or empire turning into a representative democracy. The general trend is the reverse—whatever democratic or representative institutions are left over from times of tribal or village practices are increasingly emasculated and tend to atrophy under the assault of centralizing bureaucratic monarchies and empires.

With respect to both coal-powered industrialization and representative democracy, we are trying to explain a rare, exceptional event, not a general process. What is generally the case is that societies last for thousands of years, and can attain great private wealth and great productivity and urbanization, without moving significantly toward industrialization and representative democracy. The robust processes must be ones that tend to maintain cultural orthodoxy, hierarchical elites, and authoritarian states. It is thus very unlikely that industrial development or the institutionalization of representative democracy can be explained by the kind of general laws that underlay robust processes. More likely, this unique, peculiar, one-off trajectory was the result of a unique combination of factors that came together by chance in one location and generally not elsewhere.

We thus are left with a probable explanation for the rise of the West that runs squarely through England and nowhere else. It may resemble "Whig history" in seeing the events of 1689 as pivotal. Yet it is not Whig history in seeing any special virtue or destiny in England's path. Rather, it was clearly something of an accident—other paths were equally if not more likely and were generally taken everywhere else.

Those of us who today enjoy democracy, freedom of conscience, and the wonders of modern scientific and technological progress may give thanks that James's shell came no nearer to William's heart, thus allowing Britain—and ultimately Europe—to find its peculiar path.

NOTES

1. Mark Kishlansky, *A Monarchy Transformed: Britain 1603–1714* (London: Allen Lane and Penguin, 1996), 287–88.

2. Jonathan Clarke, "Providence, Predestination, and Progress; or Did the Enlightenment Fail?" *Albion* 35 (2003): 559–89.

3. John Miller, *James II: A Study in Kingship* (Hove, UK: Wyland, 1977), 285; K. H. D. Haley, "The Dutch, the Invasion of England, and the Alliance of 1689," in *The Revolution of 1688–89: Changing Perspectives,* ed. Lois G. Schwoerer (Cambridge: Cambridge University Press, 1992), 21–34.

4. Jonathan Israel and Geoffrey Parker, "Of Providence and Protestant Winds," in *The Anglo-Dutch Moment,* ed. Jonathan Israel (Cambridge: Cambridge University Press, 1991), 335–63.

5. John Childs, *The Army, James II, and the Glorious Revolution* (Manchester: Manchester University Press, 1980); David Davies, "James II, William of Orange, and the Admirals," in *By Force or Default? The Revolution of 1688–89,* ed. Eveline Cruickshanks (Edinburgh: John Donald, 1989), 82–108.

6. Schwoerer, *The Revolution of 1688–1689.*

7. Jonathan Israel, "General Introduction," in Israel, *The Anglo-Dutch Moment,* 31.

8. J. G. A. Pocock, "The Fourth English Civil War: Dissolution, Desertion, and Alternative Histories in the Glorious Revolution," in Schwoerer, *The Revolution of 1688–1689,* 52–64; Davies, "James II."

9. Kishlansky, *A Monarchy Transformed,* 288.

10. Robin Clifton, *The Last Popular Rebellion: The Western Rising of 1685* (New York: St. Martin's, 1984).

11. J. R. Jones, "James II's Revolution: Royal Policies, 1686–92," in Israel, *The Anglo-Dutch Moment,* 47–71.

12. Richard R. Johnson, "The Revolution of 1688–9 in the American Colonies," in Israel, *The Anglo-Dutch Moment,* 214–40.

13. John Miller, *The Glorious Revolution* (London: Longman, 1983), 3.

14. Jeremy Black, "The Treaty of Rijswijk and the Long-Term Development of Anglo-Continental Relations," in *Der Friede von Rijswijk 1697,* ed. Heinz Duchhardt (Mainz am Rhein: P. von Zabern, 1998), 15–127.

15. Steven Pincus, "The Glorious Revolution," *History Compass,* http://www.history-compass.com.

16. Margaret Jacob, *The Cultural Meaning of the Scientific Revolution* (New York: Knopf, 1988), 189.

17. Mordechai Feingold, "Reversal of Fortunes: The Displacement of Cultural Hegemony from the Netherlands to England in the Seventeenth and Early Eighteenth Centuries," in *The World of William and Mary: Anglo-Dutch Perspectives on the Revolution of 1688–89,* ed. Dale Hoak and Mordechai Feingold, 243–61 (Stanford: Stanford University Press, 1996); Karel Davids, "Shifts of Technological Leadership in Early Modern Europe," in *A Miracle Mirrored: The Dutch Republic in European Perspective,* ed. Karel Davids and Jan Lucassen, 329–65 (Cambridge: Cambridge University Press, 1995).

18. Jonathan Israel, *The Dutch Republic: Its Rise, Greatness, and Fall, 1477–1806* (Oxford: Clarendon, 1995), 895–89.

19. Jan deVries and Ad van der Woude, *The First Modern Economy: Success, Failure, and Perseverance of the Dutch Economy, 1500–1815* (Cambridge: Cambridge University Press, 1997).

20. François Crouzet, *The First Industrialists: The Problem of Origins* (New York: Cambridge University Press, 1985).

21. Jacob, *The Cultural Meaning of the Scientific Revolution,* 185.

22. Ibid., 181.

23. J. C. D. Clark, *Revolution and Rebellion: State and Society in England in the Seventeenth and Eighteenth Centuries* (Cambridge: Cambridge University Press, 1986).

24. Crouzet, *The First Industrialists.*

25. "Cities," *The Economist,* December 31, 1999, 26.

26. Cited in Joel Mokyr, *The Lever of Riches: Technological Creativity and Economic Progress* (Oxford: Oxford University Press, 1990), 90.

27. Miller, *James II;* Dale Hoak, "The Anglo-Dutch Revolution of 1688–89," in Hoak and Feingold, *The World of William and Mary,* 1–29.

28. Hoak, "The Anglo-Dutch Revolution," 7.

29. Israel, *The Dutch Republic,* 796ff.

30. Jonathan Israel, "William III and Toleration," in *From Persecution to Toleration: The Glorious Revolution and Religion in England,* ed. Ole Peter Grell, Jonathan Israel, and Nicholas Tyacke (Oxford: Oxford University Press, 1991), 147–57.

31. Israel, *The Dutch Republic,* 639, 658.

32. Margaret Jacob and Larry Stewart, *Practical Matter: The Impact of Newton's Science from 1687–1851* (Cambridge, MA: Harvard University Press, 2004), 55–57, 85.

33. John Henry, *The Scientific Revolution and the Origins of Modern Science,* 2nd ed. (New York: Palgrave, 2002).

34. Ibid., 46.

35. As Steven Pincus notes, "James II's government, while never under the thumb of Louis XIV, deeply admired his regime, and attempted to mimic his policies" ("The Glorious Revolution").

36. Kishlansky, *A Monarchy Transformed,* 243.

37. Stephen Shapin, *The Scientific Revolution* (Chicago: University of Chicago Press, 1996).

38. Jack A. Goldstone, *Revolution and Rebellion in the Early Modern World* (Berkeley and Los Angeles: University of California Press, 1991), 452–56.

39. Geoffrey S. Holmes, *Politics, Religion, and Society in England, 1679–1742* (London: Hambledon, 1986).

40. Philip Tetlock and Aaron Belkin, "Counterfactual Thought Experiments in World Politics: Logical, Methodological, and Psychological Perspectives," in *Counterfactual Thought Experiments in World Politics,* ed. Philip Tetlock and Aaron Belkin (Princeton: Princeton University Press, 1996), 3–67.

41. Jean Baechler, John A. Hall, and Michael Mann, eds., *Europe and the Rise of Capitalism* (Oxford: Blackwell, 1988); Immanuel Wallerstein, *The Modern World-System,* vols. 1 and 2 (New York: Academic Press, 1974, 1980).

42. David S. Landes, *The Wealth and Poverty of Nations: Why Some Are So Rich and Some So Poor* (New York: Norton, 1998); Douglass C. North and Robert Paul Thomas, *The Rise of the Western World: A New Economic History* (Cambridge: Cambridge University Press, 1973); Nathan Rosenberg and L. E. Birdzell, *How the West Grew Rich: The Economic Transformation of the Industrial World* (New York: Basic Books, 1986).

43. Jack Goody, *The East in the West* (Cambridge: Cambridge University Press, 1996), 13.

44. Ibid.

45. Kenneth Pomeranz, *The Great Divergence: China, Europe, and the Making of the Modern World Economy* (Princeton: Princeton University Press, 2000).

46. Robert Finlay, "The Pilgrim Art: The Culture of Porcelain in World History," *Journal of World History* 9, no. 2 (fall 1998): 155.

47. Alan Macfarlane, *The Savage Wars of Peace: England, Japan, and the Malthusian Trap* (Oxford: Blackwell, 1997); John P. Powelson, *Centuries of Economic Endeavor: Parallel Paths in Japan and Europe and Their Contrast with the Third World* (Ann Arbor: University of Michigan Press, 1994).

48. John Hajnal, "Two Kinds of Pre-industrial Household Formation System," *Population and Development Review* 8, no. 3 (September 1982): 449–94.

49. William Lavely and R. Bin Wong, "Revising the Malthusian Narrative: The Comparative Study of Population Dynamics in Late Imperial China," *Journal of Asian Studies* 57, no. 3 (August 1998): 714–48; James Lee and Wang Feng, *One Quarter of Humanity: Malthusian Mythology and Chinese Realities* (Cambridge: Harvard University Press, 1999).

50. Goldstone, *Revolution and Rebellion.*

CHAPTER 7

Nineteenth-Century British Imperialism Undone with a Single Shell Fragment

A RESPONSE TO JACK GOLDSTONE'S
"EUROPE'S PECULIAR PATH"

Carla Gardina Pestana

What is meant by "the West" as well as by its rise varies over the course of the two millennia ambitiously surveyed in this volume. For Jack Goldstone, the West did not rise until it dominated the Far East, particularly China and Japan. Specifically, Goldstone seeks to obliterate the "Second British Empire" of the nineteenth century. Along with it he aims to annul the technological innovation, democracy, and toleration for Protestant dissent that he sees as both the characteristic features of that empire and its primary causes. At points it would seem that Goldstone really aims to undo the major attributes of the modern world, all of which he says can be traced back to Britain and its impact on the rest of the world. Before examining its specifics, we should pause to admire the boldness and sweep of Goldstone's vision. Killing William III represents an inspired choice. The Glorious Revolution is widely regarded as a, and perhaps the, pivotal event in seventeenth-century English political history. Advocates of its centrality attribute most of the characteristics of modern Britain to the Glorious Revolution. William was the key actor in that drama, without whom it would not have been attempted. The imperial

rivalry between Britain and France that followed the successful installation of William and Mary on the throne of England shaped European
relations for a century. For altering the geopolitics of early modern
Europe in one fell swoop, one would be hard pressed to find a single
event to reverse or a single leader to kill that would serve one's purposes
better.

Goldstone's breathtaking counterfactual history rests on a number of
assumptions. Above all, Goldstone's James II is a remarkably talented
man. At the death of William in 1690, James is able to defeat a large professional army with the mainly inexperienced forces at his disposal at the
Boyne. He handily reconquers England, apparently with the help of the
Irish troops that had emerged victorious after the Boyne, as well as a
French army that Louis XIV sends to assist him. Although Goldstone
does not mention it, James would have also had to put down a handful
of revolutions in his American dominions, where news of the success of
William had been greeted with coups in numerous colonies.[1] Goldstone
further assumes that if the overwhelmingly Protestant and virulently anti-
Catholic English objected to a papist invasion or harbored any hostility
toward a king who would organize such an atrocity, their scruples would
be easily overridden by a triumphant James. James then turns to a massive repression of Parliament (which Goldstone, in the tradition of much
Glorious Revolution historiography, sees as on the verge of subjugation
in 1688 anyway). This is accompanied by a complete purge of university
faculties and, though he does not mention it, of many Anglican pulpits as
well. James drives Protestant Dissenters, heretofore an adaptable and
tenacious minority, completely underground or out of England altogether. Wherever they seek refuge is deemed to be unfit to foster their
unique talents for setting into train changes needed to give birth to the
modern world.

James's own lack of popularity and the offensiveness of his policies to
a substantial majority of his subjects are of little consequence, for James
uses the power of the state to force conformity to his vision of an absolutist and intolerant England. His own oft-repeated goal of toleration of
Catholics alongside other religious groups turns out, in this scenario, to
be at best a charade and at least a suddenly inconvenient position, easily
abandoned. That the state did not have at its disposal the mechanisms for
such large-scale repression does not give Goldstone pause. The sort of
state power that Goldstone expects James to have used developed only
later and largely as a consequence of the changes wrought by a century of
war after 1688. Hence assuming the existence of a state with the power to

obliterate dissent represents another point at which this reconstruction stretches credulity. The cautionary note sounded by Carlos Eire in chapter 5 of this volume about the unpredictability of religious outcomes might be applied to this aspect of Goldstone's scenario: whereas Eire sees "religion [as] the chaotic factor," difficult to control and almost impossible to suppress entirely, Goldstone supposes it to be both predictable and controllable. On the whole, "Europe's Peculiar Path" both minimizes the extent of the opposition to James's policies in England and exaggerates the extent of James's own ability to remake England in the image of France. If much of seventeenth-century English history pivoted on the search for a workable political and religious settlement, as Goldstone at points seems to accept, then it is not at all clear that the political nation could be forced to abandon that goal by an unpopular and not particularly adept James II. Although the earlier revolution, which cost Charles I his head, had taught the elites to avoid political and religious upheaval, they were not as a result willing to accept a settlement so utterly offensive as that which Goldstone imagines James foisting on them. The settlement they were working toward was not in any sense democratic, and we must look elsewhere than to Britain in either the seventeenth or eighteenth century for that feature of the modern world. But many of Britain's leaders remained resistant to what they perceived as creeping popery and the threat of absolutist government, and they supported the Glorious Revolution's outcome as a result of such fears. I cannot therefore follow Goldstone's lead when he declares England easily and permanently remade as a semi-Catholic and absolutist composite monarchy. Whatever follows from that improbable outcome is therefore not convincing either.

Goldstone also believes that England would have willingly become a lesser satellite, revolving around the Sun King along with most of the rest of Europe. English public opinion, heretofore anti-Catholic and suspicious of French power, mounts no effective opposition to this state of affairs for a century. The French monarchs find it less taxing on their treasury to dominate Europe (including paying large subsidies to unpopular British monarchs for an indefinite period) than, in a parallel reality, it would have been to combat British rivals. I find it about as hard to imagine England embracing permanent second-class status as France's junior ally as to imagine it agreeing to the severe diminution of its own commitment to Protestantism, which by 1688 was deeply rooted. In order to grant Goldstone the far-flung result he sees emanating from William's demise, we must accept that James could neutralize various traits of English politics, religion, and culture. I am not persuaded that all that stood between England and the severely altered history that Goldstone describes was William III. The death of William at the Boyne would have had major geopolitical consequences for the United Provinces and France, as well as for Britain. What the long-term effects would have been I find difficult to gauge.

I am uncomfortable with the way in which Goldstone privileges certain kinds of causal explanations in his counterfactual. In response to the mandate from the volume editors to make only small changes, Goldstone has succumbed to a temptation felt by other authors: the temptation to construct his counterfactual scenario by finding someone to kill (or, one might add, not to kill, as in the case of Jesus; see chap. 6 in this volume). This strategy creates a reliance on great men as the causal agents of history. It seems also to predispose this and other of the alternative histories constructed to undo the rise of the West to emphasize geopolitics and military moments over other ways of accounting for historical change. Or is this tendency especially likely in those counterfactual efforts that fall more on the contingent end of the spectrum, as designated in the introduction to this volume? Goldstone of course realizes that the expansive, commercial nature of English culture goes a long way toward explaining its development in the eighteenth century, so he quickly turns from the death of William to James's makeover of England's religion, political and educational institutions, and economy. Doing this requires, however, that he elevate James II to a level of political sagacity rarely reached by any mere mortal, much less any Stuart king.

Goldstone not only kills one great man but also creates another. He makes Isaac Newton carry all responsibility for the science that somewhat misleadingly bears his name. Newton was of course part of a scientific community, building on the work of others, including Galileo (whose own work, far from having been "lost," as Goldstone avers, was identified by Newton as leading him to some of his fundamental insights). Eliminate Newton, by having James II drive him from the university, and Goldstone eliminates the so-called scientific revolution with which he is associated. This strategy puts all the emphasis on the individual and overlooks the more fundamental role of contemporary background knowledge to the making of scientific advances, as discussed by Joel Mokyr in chapter 10. Goldstone uses the new history of science, especially the work of Margaret C. Jacob, to make the point that scientific advances are contingent. Yet another major insight of that scholarship is the realization that science was not the work of isolated geniuses, as early histories of science believed. Goldstone's explanatory devices rely heavily on great men. Do we risk throwing out the dominance of the West only to bring back individual men as the engine running history? What could be more profoundly Western?

A final question could be posed to the daring Goldstone: what became of Mary and Anne, daughters of James? The former provides her spouse, William, with his sole claim to the throne in the first place, and the latter would succeed to the throne and defeat Louis in the War of Spanish Succession. Both disappear from this scenario as if the same shell fragment that killed Mary's husband had also struck them. Mary was the major claimant to the throne and a competent ruler in her own right. During the negotiations between William and the English Parliament in 1688, many preferred that Mary alone be crowned. William and Mary together insisted on the unusual stratagem of a dual monarchy, with various contingencies for succession spelled out in the agreement. That her erstwhile supporters would have utterly abandoned Mary upon the death of her husband seems preposterous. She was the crowned queen, and they had risked much in supporting her along with William in the months prior to summer 1690. The army in Ireland, arrayed against James's generally less experienced and smaller force, would have been suddenly bereft of its leader, and how it would have responded in this situation is a key question. But killing William is not tantamount to defeating his army any more than offing him ensures the collapse of Mary's government. In 1690 and subsequently, she proved an able ruler, governing Britain alone in William's frequent absences. She arguably ruled more ably than her father, whose ability to displace her had the Battle of the Boyne ended in his favor was by no means assured. At the time of William's fictive death in 1690, Mary would have been only twenty-eight. Freed to marry another (and confronting great pressure to do so, just as the previous single, Protestant queen in a hostile Europe had been), Mary might even have gone on to bear a male Protestant heir to the British throne. If not, Anne, who had publicly abandoned her father in 1688, stood next in line for the throne by the terms of Parliament's settlement. Mary and Anne cannot be so easily dismissed. These two women were also major players in this chain of events, and Mary's role would have become all the more important had William died. I would like to end, then, championing not just one but two great women. And I do so without regard for the appearance of their noses.

NOTES

I would like to thank Dr. John Stapleton for his willingness to share his knowledge of William and Mary.

    1. Richard S. Dunn, "The Glorious Revolution and America," in *The Oxford History of the British Empire,* vol. 1: *The Origins of Empire: British Overseas Enterprise to the Close of the Seventeenth Century,* ed. Nicholas Canny (New York: Oxford University Press, 1998), 445–66.

PART 3

The West Undone?

CHAPTER 8

The Song Empire

THE WORLD'S FIRST SUPERPOWER?

Robin D. S. Yates

Could China have had a different history and, if so, could it have pre-vented the rise of the West? Until the irruption of the Western colonial and imperialist powers in the nineteenth century the image of China's timeless immutability and predetermined historical destiny impressed outside observers, such as Western missionaries, as much as it influenced the behavior of the Chinese themselves. Indeed, throughout Chinese his-tory there was a strong tradition that the development of China could not have been otherwise than it actually was, and many American scholars in the 1950s and 1960s argued that China only entered world history in the nineteenth century as a "response to the West."[1] Some scholars continue to employ dyadic concepts, such as "high culture" or "elite culture" as opposed to "popular culture," to essentialize an unchanging China: only recently have they begun to adopt critical insights from feminist and postcolonial theory to restore agency and subjectivity to historical Chi-nese individuals and to emphasize difference, the messiness of contingen-cies and the multiplicity of social practices.[2]

The views about an unchanging China were held as much as a result of ignorance of the particular details of historical contingencies in China's past, although such details were amply recorded by Chinese historians over the centuries, as of a blind acceptance of contemporary ideological, ritual, and/or political imperatives, orientalist or otherwise. It is the force of these imperatives that continues to encourage the notion that China and Chinese culture have existed "for thousands of years," that China was, is, and should forever be a single united state. And that it should be a state presided over by a centralized, bureaucratic administration, albeit one that differs markedly from the ideal legal-rational model conceived by Max Weber and one whose social formations, legal system, attitude toward individual rights, economic structures, and so on were and remain distinctive from those found in the rest of the world.

The power of the ideological code in China is evident from very early times, even though it may have been challenged by marginalized individuals or groups and those whose voices have been lost to history. Before the unification of China in 221 BC by the First Emperor, King Zheng of the state of Qin, most philosophers and statesmen presumed that China had been previously unified under the earlier dynasties, the Xia, Shang, and Zhou (roughly 2000 to 256 BC). So the policies and methods these wandering teachers and statesmen proposed to the various rulers of the contending Warring States were designed to re-create a unification that they thought had been previously achieved in the (idealized) distant past by ancient sage-kings.[3] For them, if not for the rulers they advised, the ultimate unification of the contending states was not only a political necessity but also an inevitable feature of the natural cosmic order. The Son of Heaven harmonized the human realm with the natural world, Heaven and Earth.

Various political concepts were developed to explain the transfer of power from one dynasty to the next. One was the well-known concept of the Mandate of Heaven, in which "Heaven" was thought to bestow on a ruler and his descendants the right to rule provided that they governed according to a strict moral and ritual code. Another was the idea that each dynasty ruled under the aegis of one of the Five Phases (Wuxing) of the natural seasonal cycle and its associated color.[4] Just as the Five Phases followed each other in turn throughout the year—spring/green, summer/red, late summer/yellow, fall/white, winter/black—so would each dynasty follow its predecessor and yield to its successor in harmony with the natural cosmic order. A third was the so-called correct transmission (zhengtong) of dynastic legitimacy. This required the performance of various ritual acts by the emperor who was founding a new dynasty, as well as those performed by his predecessor, the last of the previous dynasty, coupled with success in unifying the geographical territory occupied by peoples who accepted Chinese customs and with behaving in a moral manner.[5]

Chinese historians invented the theory of the "dynastic cycle" to characterize historical change. Perhaps *historical change* does not give quite the right connotation; *historical oscillation* would be a better term with which to describe their views. A period of vigorous youth, flourishing maturity, midlife crisis, temporary renewal, and corruption and decline, and ultimately replacement by a successor, was the typical pattern of every dynasty.[6] This interpretation was written, either explicitly or implicitly, into virtually all of the so-called twenty-four dynastic histories. No one challenged the idea that there could be a different political system without a single emperor at the top, even though in reality China was many times divided between competing imperial contenders and even though for many centuries China was ruled by ethnically non-Chinese imperial dynasties.

In the twentieth century, many Chinese historians adopted Marxist historical analysis, rhetoric, and teleology, anticipating a future communist utopia, yet they too never challenged the validity of the idea that China should always be a united state. In fact, as nationalists they even claimed, and continue to claim, that modern China should inherit and maintain the boundaries that the Manchu Qing empire reached at its greatest geographic extent in the eighteenth century—a belief that has, of course, many political ramifications in the contemporary world. Meanwhile, after World War II their American colleagues, influenced by contemporary social science theories, looked for China to follow the Western formula for advancing into the modern and contemporary world as though no other way was possible.[7]

Yet there are a number of significant moments when possible alternative scenarios could have led to dramatically different results in the trajectory of China's development. In the first part of this essay, I will consider a counterfactual in early Chinese history similar to the possible consequences for the history of the West if there had been a different outcome to the decisive naval battle of Salamis in 480 BC (chaps. 2–3). The second part of the essay will consider a historical counterfactual at a moment when China was quite clearly way ahead in many respects of any of its Western counterparts, during the northern Song dynasty in the eleventh century AD.[8] This alternative scenario would have had a major impact on the later course of Chinese history and could have preempted the rise of Chinggis Khan and aborted the creation of the Mongol empire, which severely disrupted the political and social order of the Islamic world, controlled Russia for two centuries, and had a major influence on the course of Western history. Not only did the savagery of the Mongol assaults on the cities of the Middle East and Europe severely traumatize their peoples and affect their attitudes toward Asians for centuries, down to our own times (the "Yellow Peril"), but the Mongols brought with them advanced technology in the form of gunpowder weapons, which enabled Europeans ultimately to develop the firearms that gave them military superiority over all others.[9] This new technology eventually enabled them to conquer and colonize most parts of the world from the seventeenth and eighteenth centuries on.

China Un-unified

One of the earliest possibilities for altering the trajectory of China's history is at the very beginning of the imperial period. What if King Zheng of the peripheral state of Qin had not defeated every one of his rival states and had failed to found the Chinese empire in 221 BC? If any one of the larger, richer, more technologically advanced states, such as Chu in the Yangzi Valley, the home of Daoist philosophy and shamanic religion, or Yan in the northeast, whose manufacturing capabilities for the production of steel weapons was the most advanced of its day, had been able to resist the advance of the Qin forces, what might have been the consequences?

There are several incidents recorded by Sima Qian in his *Historical Records* (*Shi ji*) during which the founding of the empire could have been aborted.[10] As a young king, Zheng was almost toppled in 237 BC by a coup led by his mother's lover, who had secretly fathered two children by the dowager queen. The plot was discovered, the plotters and their families put to death or exiled, and the king's mother banished to a separate palace away from the court and the center of decision making. Subsequently, even the powerful prime minister, Lü Buwei, formerly a rich merchant, was implicated in the plot and forced into exile and suicide. He had championed the cause of King Zheng's father when he was in exile as a hostage in the state of Zhao and had given the latter his own concubine, the future mother of King Zheng, for his wife. Lü had sponsored the compilation of a text, the *Spring and Autumn Annals of Lü Buwei,* submitted to the throne in 238 BC, that tried to synthesize into one overarching treatise all the philosophies then current as a blueprint for the ideology of a unified empire.[11] Since Lü and his approach were discredited by the attempted coup d'état, the young King Zheng turned more and more to the harsh philosophy of legalism and the prescriptions of Five Phase theorists to guide him in governing the state of Qin.

Then there was the assassination attempt by Qing Ke, who was sent by the prince of Yan to prevent the invasion of his country by the Qin armies after 228 BC. One of King Zheng's former generals living in exile in Yan sacrificed his head so that Qing Ke could package it and carry it west and present it to King Zheng, together with a scroll map of Yan territory that purportedly indicated which lands Yan was prepared to cede to Qin to ensure peace. Qing Ke hid a dagger inside the map, knowing that, according to the strict Qin law, no one except the king himself was allowed to carry a weapon in the inner court. Invited to ascend the steps to present these objects to King Zheng, Qing unrolled the map in front of the unsuspecting and avaricious monarch and grabbed the dagger to stab him, while his courtiers watched in horror in the hall below. The king fled round the pillars in panic, unable to draw his sword or call his guards to his aid. The monarch was only saved by his quick-witted physician, who beat back the would-be assassin with his medical bag. Qing Ke hurled his dagger at the cowering king in one last-ditch attempt to carry out his plan. But the dagger missed its target and buried itself in a pillar. Qing Ke was cut down by the Qin guards but nevertheless achieved immortality through his brave attempt on the life of the tyrant.[12] Even after King Zheng won on the battlefield against his rivals, united China, and proclaimed himself emperor, one of Qing Ke's friends was again almost successful in assassinating him.

A successful assassination of King Zheng in the early 220s would surely have derailed the immediate campaign of unification. It would have permitted Qin's neighbor states to prepare themselves better to face Qin military might and organizational genius, a genius that is becoming more and more evident as archaeologists reveal the secrets of the First Emperor's mausoleum complex near Xi'an in northwestern Shaanxi Province.[13] Within Qin, there would likely have been a serious contest for the throne because Zheng was only about twenty-eight years old at the time and his children would have been very young and easily manipulated by contending factions in the Qin court and bureaucracy. Some of the leading generals might have rebelled against the civilian authorities and been able to establish their own small independent states. The vast region of southwestern China, what is now Sichuan, which had been conquered by the Qin only in the previous seventy years or so, might also have been able to throw off Qin domination and have reverted to its previous cultural and political forms: loose confederacies of tribes.

The Possible Effects

If China had not been united into an empire by the First Emperor of Qin, what might have happened and what might have been the consequences? One might envisage that it would have continued to develop its regional city-state system.[14] In other words, it would then have remained divided into a number of independent states, each occupying a particular ecological niche, exporting its own special products, importing those of its neighbors, and developing its own distinctive cultural traits. The consequences of this scenario might be imagined if we look at the effects of actual unification and at the ways in which the First Emperor and his later Han counterparts attempted to integrate the East Asian subcontinent.

When the First Emperor had conquered all his enemies, he ordered a number of reforms that had long-lasting consequences. First, he ordered that the administrative system of Qin be extended to the whole country. This meant that all areas controlled by Qin were reorganized into a hierarchy starting with a unit of five families at the bottom, through villages, districts, counties or prefectures, and commanderies. Every member of society was responsible for the behavior of family members in the "linked responsibility" system and was obliged to report the crimes and misdemeanors of family members on pain of penalty. In addition, all males were integrated into a system of social status determined by the state that gave each member of society a rank. There were seventeen, rising to twenty, of these ranks, and the state used them to assign military and civil obligations to the population and to award economic incentives, as well as to differentiate the severity of punishments for the same crime. One of the ways in which the Qin, and subsequently the Han, generated a sense of supralocal identity among the indigenous populations was to require them to serve the imperial state either in the military (for the males) or on labor projects (for both males and females) that were far from their homes. Thus the ordinary people learned firsthand about the extent and nature of the empire and were obliged to protect it and build its future with their bare hands, either as convicts or corvée laborers. This experience presumably generated a communal memory that helped develop sense of identity as imperial subjects.[15]

Next the First Emperor ordered the unification of the writing system, so that alternative styles and alternative systems current in the other states were eliminated.[16] Without this unification, the scripts of the various states might well have become mutually unintelligible, reinforcing the dialect differences of the spoken language. Thus the written script would not have been able to act as a unifying force in the way that it did in later Chinese history and would not have been adopted as the lingua franca of East Asia and as the mode of transmission of Chinese culture to other peoples and countries, including Korea, Japan, and Vietnam. The First Emperor also ordered the destruction of all currencies other that of the Qin cash and that roads should have the same width so that carts could have the same axle gauge and be able to travel through the length and breadth of the Qin domain. He insisted on extending the Qin land tenure system throughout the country and proclaimed himself emperor, a term that put himself on a par with certain celestial deities.[17]

The effects of the reform policies were felt in many spheres: the political; the ideological and religious; the social; the cultural; and the economic, technological, and scientific. Thus their failure to be instituted would likewise have had many consequences and would have had a fundamental impact on the course of Chinese history. On the political level, which is usually treated as the fundamental aspect, even by Marxist scholars, the First Emperor established a hierarchical administrative system for local, regional, and central governments staffed by educated functionaries who were appointed on the basis of their skill and competency rather than on their family background or inherited status. Officials were legally bound to report on their activities at regular intervals to the central authorities and were tested, evaluated, graded, and moved, either horizontally to another equivalent position, demoted, or promoted, depending on the results that they had demonstrated. This system required the establishment of complex rules of procedure, generated vast quantities of official documents and correspondence, and was dependent on, and presupposed, widespread literacy.[18]

The structure and organization of the bureaucracy, with the emperor at the top acting as a mediator between Heaven and Earth, was adopted as a model of the entire natural order, including the physical universe and the world of the gods, spirits, and demons, as well as for the human body.[19] Later on, the Han dynasty adopted this basic Qin governmental structure, as well as the legal framework for ordering society, despite the severe reservations harbored by Confucian scholars and theorists about the way in which the Qin had actually applied the systems in practice. It became the model for the later imperial social and bureaucratic order. While many variations on this basic model surfaced during the course of Chinese history, the tension between central control and local or regional autonomy, the right of the center to demand labor and taxes of individual men and women and impose its laws without intervening authorities subverting or denying the center's powers and rights, and the claim of the center to determine social position remained perennial features and problems of the Chinese system. Over the centuries, the power of the center vis-à-vis nodes of power at the local and regional levels or in other networks, such as the Buddhist and Daoist churches and associations based on occupation and birth such as patrilineal lineages, was supported by the ideology and imaginary vision of a morally based centralized state ruling over the "all under heaven" developed by the literate elite. As Mark Edward Lewis has brilliantly argued:

> Writing created a literary double of the actual world, and this invented world became the highest reality. This process was facilitated by the fact that early state administration drew many of its forms and practices, above all its use of writing from the religious sphere, and that political innovations were read back into the spirit world. Thus from its origins the Chinese bureaucratic state was tied to a parallel, imaginary world generated in texts.[20]

With this in mind, one can see that the failure to create an empire in practice that reinforced the textual empire would have prevented the establishment of this imaginary world by the literary elite.[21]

From the ideological perspective, Confucian philosophy might never have become the imperial ideology, as it did under Han Emperor Wudi around 130 BC, a position that it retained essentially until the abolition of the official examination system in 1905 and the collapse of the imperial order in 1911. The position of merchants in Chinese society in traditional times might have been better than it actually was had Confucianism not been adopted as the official ideology. Confucians disparaged the profit motive, and merchants were placed at the bottom of the "four classes" into which Chinese society was traditionally divided. As a consequence, it was always difficult in traditional China to justify political action on the basis of economic advantage. Policies for strengthening the state were often held in suspicion unless they could also be justified on some other, moral grounds, such as fulfilling the aims and policies of previous rulers or reestablishing the Confucian order.[22]

Possibly Mohism might have become the primary ideology with its advanced logical and scientific methods and belief in universal love.[23] Would not then later intellectuals have looked to the future, as the Mohists did, rather than to the idealized past enshrined in the Confucian canons, as the literati actually did? In fact, the Mohists were in the process of developing a rigorous and rational system of propositions that were internally logically consistent and were making significant advances in scientific disciplines that we now gather under the rubrics of physics, mechanics, and optics among others. Their views also suggest that they were moving toward an interest in geometry.[24] But their organized groups were destroyed after, and perhaps as a result of, the unification, and as a consequence their discoveries played no role in the development of later Chinese science.[25] Indeed, the dominant paradigm of the Chinese sciences was based on organic naturalism, correlative thinking, and the idea of resonance and was closely modeled on the structure of the empire.[26] If the empire had not been created, this dominant paradigm might never have been accepted by intellectuals and might never have been the basis of traditional Chinese sciences.[27] What form the Chinese sciences might have taken, and what paradigm shifts they might have experienced, cannot be adequately determined. Clearly significant advances were made using the paradigm of systematic correspondence, yet a number of sciences never adopted the paradigm at all or, if they did, only at a much later stage of their development. For example, pharmacology was only theorized in the Song, from the eleventh century on, but had developed a rich heritage based on empirical knowledge and experiment by that time, even though other of the medical sciences had been deeply influenced by ideas of systematic correspondence for centuries.[28]

Alternative visions of political and social order, such as those of the Daoists in such texts as the *Zhuangzi* and the *Laozi* or *Daode jing* (Canon of the Way and Virtue), where simple autarchy at the local village level in conformity with the natural cosmic order is presented as the ideal form of society, might well have captured the imagination of the educated elite in the various states and formed the basis of society in the East Asian subcontinent. Had this happened, one could not call such a grouping of territorial states "China" because the notion of an inclusive culture sphere and ethnic identity of "Chineseness," in Chinese parlance "Han," is based on the social and political order established by the Qin and Han empires. Another possibility might have been the political and social philosophy called Huang-Lao (Yellow Emperor and Laozi) Daoism, which was popular among members of the imperial elite before the adoption of Confucianism as the basic state ideology.[29] But it is likely that many of the different philosophies that we know existed in Warring States times but were subsequently lost, such as Huang-Lao, would have had the opportunity to flourish and develop in a competitive environment that a multistate system, without one fixed state orthodoxy, would have permitted.[30]

A further consequence in the political sphere of the failure of the Chinese to found an empire is that the Xiongnu peoples of the northern steppe lands might never have united under the khan Mao Dun at the turn of the third and second centuries BC to create a parasitic nomadic empire that only came into being to exploit the riches and stability of the newly established agricultural empire to its south.[31] Barfield argues cogently that the Xiongnu were only able to establish their dominance over other tribal peoples in the vast tracts of central and northern Asia because they were able to extract either by threat of violence or by trade surpluses from the unified Chinese empire. In other words, there was a symbiotic relationship between the two Asian empires. The Xiongnu khans were able to maintain their power by redistributing to their subordinate chiefs the wealth they received from the Chinese either by treaty or by pillage. They created an empire on the steppe parallel to the one in China. So if the Chinese empire had not existed, would it have been possible for the Xiongnu to have created their own? Probably not, and they would have remained divided into numerous small tribes. Thus they might never have initiated the successive waves of migration from the steppe lands toward the settled lands of western Asia. The invasions that severely disrupted the Roman Empire in the fifth century would therefore have been aborted.[32]

On the other hand, this scenario could have removed the incentives for the Chinese states to expand along the trade routes of the northwestern desert, and therefore the failure to create the empire might have jeopardized the establishment of the Silk Road and the first contacts between the Western and Eastern civilizations. Then Roman emperors and members of the aristocratic elite would not have worn Chinese silks and crossbows might not have reached the shores of the Mediterranean, nor even flags. The Chinese, in turn, might not have had the opportunity to adopt West Asian foodstuffs, such as sesame, that are now considered an integral part of their food culture.

Finally, the Chinese popular pantheon is based on the structure of the Chinese imperial bureaucracy.[33] If there had been no imperial bureaucracy, the patterns of religious belief and popular daily practices would have been fundamentally different, perhaps largely influenced by local and regional systems. The failure to establish an imperial system would have had a tremendous impact on the beliefs and values of the Chinese people. Is it likely that we would even recognize them as Chinese?

The suggestion that the East Asian subcontinent had the potential to develop in various alternative ways, some of which are similar to those that the West later followed, calls into question the inevitability of the West's dominance in modern times as springing inevitably from either the institutional arrangements of ancient Greece (the city-state model) or from its intellectual heritage—whether of ideas about freedom and legal rights or its approach to the natural world through its advances in science, technology, and logic.

Instead of exploring these issues further, the latter part of this chapter examines a more recent counterfactual, one that could have happened several centuries before the Mongol conquests under Chinggis Khan and his successors put East and West Asia into permanent contact with each other and brought advanced Chinese technologies, such as gunpowder weapons and printing, to Europe and the Middle East.[34] What if the Song army had been successful in defeating the Tangut Xi Xia state, which was based in the Upper Yellow River valley, in the wars of the late eleventh century AD?[35] If the massive Song army had been able to overcome its logistical problems and defeat the Xi Xia,[36] might it not have managed, in a similar fashion, to defeat Song's other formidable enemy on their northeastern border, the Khitan Liao? By defeating the Liao and taking over its territory before the Jurchen Jin were able to advance from the forests of eastern Manchuria, might not the Song have been able to preempt the Jin attack that lost North China in 1126–27?

At that point, China's scientific and technological achievements could not be matched by any other state anywhere else in the rest of the world. It had invented gunpowder and the cannon.[37] It was vigorously promoting printing and the publishing industry to encourage literacy, disseminate knowledge, and encourage scientific applications to basic economic enterprises.[38] The output of its iron and steel industry was enormous.[39] China's population was the largest in the world, it possessed the highest level of urbanization, and its economy was far more advanced: people used paper as well as metal currency.[40] Yet a failure on the battlefield as a result of poor planning and inadequate logistics in the early 1080s AD profoundly altered the trajectory of Chinese political, intellectual, social, and economic history. By failing to conquer and subdue the Tangut Xi Xia state in the upper reaches of the Yellow River and acquire access to the pasturelands of the northwest for raising good cavalry mounts, Song forces were unable to take back territory in North and Northeast China because the Song cavalry was no match for its adversaries.[41] Subsequently, the Song were unable to hold off a concerted attack on their capital at Kaifeng, Henan Province, by the army of the northeastern Jurchen Jin dynasty, which had destroyed the Liao in a series of campaigns starting in 1114, and lost the whole of the North China Plain in 1126–27.[42]

The campaign cost the Song their legitimate reigning emperor, Huizong, the heir apparent, and many members of the imperial family and court; their control over mines, the sources of iron ore and coal;[43] their access to the saltpeter necessary for the manufacture of gunpowder; their advanced clock, constructed by Su Song,[44] and their access to good cavalry horses. Cavalry mounts were even more inaccessible when the Song were confined to the region south of the Yangzi River by the Jurchen Jin.[45] While the Southern Song dynasty lasted after its defeat in 1127 for another 150 years before the Mongols eventually overwhelmed them,[46] China's ideological, political, economic, social, and religious systems underwent profound transformations that lasted until the twentieth century. China lost its lead over the rest of the world, especially when it was unable to respond to the challenges posed by the new military technologies of the Western imperialist powers in the nineteenth century.[47] If China had not been defeated and had been able to preempt the rise of Chinggis Khan and abort the creation of the Mongol empire, we might then conceive of some quite plausible alternatives for the internal development of China and some significant effects that it might have had on its more distant neighbors.

The Song Dynasty

After the destruction of the Tang dynasty, after three centuries of rule, in 907 and the interregnum of numerous short-lived regional military states known as the Five Dynasties and the Ten Kingdoms (907–60), two military generals, brothers surnamed Zhao, reestablished a central authority in the Chinese heartland under the name of the Song dynasty. But the political, military, and economic situation had profoundly altered from the time when the Tang (AD 618–907) was the most powerful, wealthy, and populous empire in the world. China was now faced on its northern borders with new peoples who had learned how to combine the strengths of pastoral life and organization with the skills of ruling sedentary Chinese agriculturists and other ethnic groups. In addition, they had created written languages for themselves and legitimized their respective states by integrating Buddhist religion and Confucian political ideology. These peoples were the Khitan Liao in the north and northeast,[48] followed by

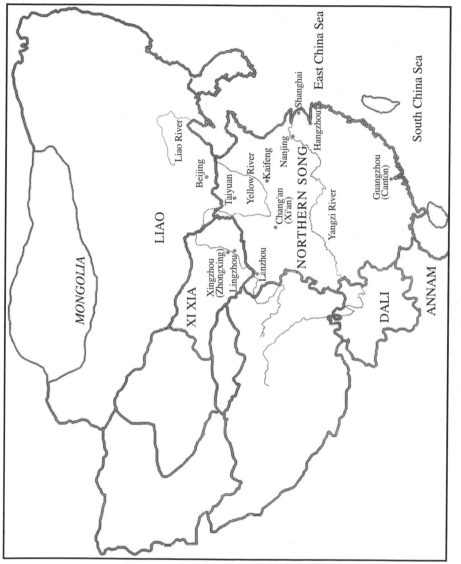

Map 4. Song China and its neighbors circa 1100

the Jurchen Jin farther to the northeast[49] and the Tangut Xi Xia in the northwest in modern Gansu Province astride the Silk Road leading to Central Asia.[50]

Much of the success of the Liao was due to their policy of creating a dual system of administration. They kept the military strictly under the control of the Khitan tribal elite in the north, where they maintained tribal customs and organization.[51] Much of the income necessary to maintain the imperial institutions was, however, derived from the taxation of Chinese sedentary farmers in the south. The latter were governed using a traditional system of Chinese bureaucratic administration staffed by officials, many of whom were of Chinese descent. Thus they were able to look both ways. Out on the steppe, the Liao and Jin were able to keep the numerous tribes disunited by playing one leader off against another, and one tribe off against another, supporting the weaker against the stronger, always assuring that no one gained too much power and authority. They threatened the Chinese of the Song dynasty with their mobile cavalry and exploited their success by demanding huge subsidies as the price of their victories in war and in exchange for the maintenance of peace along the border.

Under these circumstances, could Song China have consolidated its lead over the West in the crucial period of the eleventh to thirteenth centuries? At the beginning of the Song, the dynastic founders were obsessed with recapturing the territory that the Tang dynasty had once occupied. They were successful in conquering the kingdoms in Central and South China, but in the northwest, north, and northeast they were stymied. Although in 979 they were able to capture Taiyuan, modern Shanxi Province, the capital of the Northern Han, the satellite state of the Liao, the buffer region called the Sixteen Prefectures in modern northern Shanxi and Hebei Provinces, previously ceded to the Liao, continued to elude them. F. W. Mote attributes the failure of Taizong to capture Youzhou, the modern Beijing, to the emperor's poor moral character.[52] He desired to prove himself equal to his brother's military genius and simply ignored all advice that warned him not to attack with an exhausted army. When the Liao cavalry reinforcements arrived, they inflicted a crushing defeat on the Song. Taizong ignominiously abandoned the field in a mule cart, leaving his forces to be cut down and abandoning huge quantities of military equipment to the victorious Khitan enemy. All efforts to recover the lost territory failed, and eventually, after several inconclusive campaigns, the Song were obliged to sign the Treaty (or Accord) of Shanyuan in 1004–5.[53] Nap-Yin Lau records the terms as follows.

1. The establishment of friendly relations between the two states
2. Annual payments to the Liao of 100,000 taels of silver and 200,000 bolts of silk
3. The demarcation of borders that would be mutually respected
4. The agreement that both sides would repatriate fugitives from justice
5. The agreement that neither side should disturb the farmland crops of the other
6. The agreement that neither side should construct new fortifications and canals along the border
7. The pledge of a solemn oath with a religious sanction in case of contravention[54]

Shiba Yoshinobu points out that official markets were established on both sides of the border to regulate trade between the two countries and that goods of strategic value were not supposed to be traded. The Song banned the export of "salt, books, maps, and weapons, whereas the Liao forbad the sale of horses." Despite the efforts of government agents on both sides, however, "it was impossible to prohibit the contraband trade that was carried on actively on both sides."[55] Furthermore, even though the Song and Liao treated each other as equals and relatives and formal diplomatic exchanges were the order of the day,[56] competition, espionage, and harassment on both sides continued and the Song sought every sort of way to thwart their powerful adversaries. Later in the century, the Song even used scientific and technological means to prevent incursions of the Liao cavalry, taking advantage of the necessity to control the lower course of the Yellow River in the North China Plain to create an extensive network of hydraulic engineering projects over which they hoped the Liao cavalry could not ride.[57]

As mentioned earlier, in the years after the Treaty of Shanyuan, the Song also found itself confronting the rising power of the Tangut state on their northwest border. The Tanguts skillfully played off the Liao against the Song and eventually their ruler, Yuanhao, proclaimed himself to be the head of a new dynasty, the Da Xia (Great Xia), which the Chinese called Xi Xia, or "Western Xia," in 1038. This arrogation of the trappings of legitimacy in the Chinese style threw down the gauntlet to the Chinese emperor and government in their capital, Kaifeng. Finally, the Chinese felt that they had to meet the challenge after the Xi Xia Weiming emperor sent back the ritual paraphernalia the Song had given him when they formally recognized him as a king.[58] So the Song attacked, but they met with little success against the Tangut positions along the Yellow River and after much haggling over terms a treaty was formalized. The Xi Xia ruler agreed to accept subordinate status vis-à-vis the Song emperor, and the Song in turn agreed to present an annual gift of 153,000 *pi* (bolts) of silk, 30,000 small *jin* (catties) of tea, and 72,000 *liang* (taels) of silver.

A leading figure on the Chinese side in these events was Fan Zhongyan (989–1052), whom the Song tapped to reform the government.[59] Fan tried to reform the bureaucracy by replacing officials he deemed incompetent, by promoting a new young group of Confucian intellectuals, and by attempting to establish schools at the local level funded by the government so that not only the rich and well connected could gain an education and attempt to rise in society through passing the examinations and entering the bureaucracy.[60] However, Fan and his party were quickly condemned by their factional opponents, and it was left to Emperor Shenzong (r. 1068–85) to institute a major reform that attempted to recast the role of the state and the elite in society and the economy.[61]

The Song Counterfactual

Emperor Shenzong considered the recapture of territory that had originally belonged to China to be one of his main objectives and one that would fulfill his obligations as a filial son to his forebears, who had failed in this enterprise.[62] Enthusiastic and dynamic by nature, he wanted immediate action and he did not want to be controlled by chief ministers who wished their emperor to remain behind the scenes while they directed the government.[63] Unfortunately, he inherited serious financial problems from his predecessors, resulting partly from the continued obligation to pay the Liao and the Xi Xia under treaties that had been previously concluded and partly because of the financial malfeasance and incompetence of his officials. His desire, then, was to enrich the state for the ultimate purpose of waging war. He found a chief minister who shared his views about the need for reform in Wang Anshi. But Wang was interested in revitalizing officialdom by reinterpreting the Confucian canons, for he saw the fundamental issue was that members of the literati were suffering from a moral malaise.[64] He was therefore much less willing or interested in taking military risks that could jeopardize the reform effort.[65]

Still, there was sufficient agreement between the two that a series of reforms was promulgated in the management of rural credit, the involvement of the state directly in trade, and the hired service system, which that prepared the state for war by building up state revenues.[66] Even though Wang Anshi retired in 1076 with the new policies under attack from conservative elements, Shenzong pursued his dream of invasion and conquest and kept Wang's group of proreform officials in power at the highest levels.

For the attack on the Xi Xia, large amounts of military matériel were stockpiled near the northwestern border from 1077 on. The excuse that the Song used to launch the war was turmoil at the Xi Xia court in 1081 when Empress Dowager Liang, possibly an ethnic Chinese, imprisoned her son, Emperor Huizong, for showing strong tendencies to draw diplomatically closer to the Song.[67] After much debate, it was decided to divide the 600,000-man Song army into five sections and aim for the Xi Xia capital at Xingzhou from several different directions. The idea was for these far-flung armies to march across hostile territory, where water and supplies were virtually nonexistent, and meet up and launch a concerted attack. However, this plan resulted in a series of blunders that led to the loss of most of the armies, the demotion of most of the responsible generals, and the death of Emperor Shenzong himself at the age thirty-seven in 1085, perhaps as a result of the humiliation his armies had suffered and his distress at losing the opportunity to fulfill his most cherished goal in life. Ultimately it led to the installation of the conservative faction, which worked to dismantle the reform program. Even though Emperor Zhezong (r. 1086–1101) brought reformers back into power after he reached his majority and Emperor Huizong (r. 1101–26) continued the same policies and gained some successes in campaigns against the Qingtang Tibetans,[68] it was too late. Officials were no longer committed to implementing the reforms, the Tanguts were in an impregnable position,[69] the Song army had lost the confidence of the people, and the Liao were crumbling before the onslaught of the Jurchen.

To start with, the campaign began in the summer, leaving only a very few months before the cold weather settled in. Next, the five generals did not see eye to eye on the details of the campaign. Two of them objected to having eunuchs as colleagues at the head of three of the divisions, even though they had all distinguished themselves in battle against the Tibetans and Tanguts in previous campaigns. Then there was the massive logistical problem of transporting huge numbers of men and large amounts of matériel over the desert. Since only a thirty days' food supply was provided, capturing supplies from enemy granaries became crucial.[70]

Nevertheless, the attack produced some initial successes. Lanzhou, now the capital of Gansu Province, was taken, as were several other cities, forts, and granaries. But the armies failed to push quickly toward Xingzhou, and several tactical mistakes were made, including the failure to bring adequate siege equipment to breach the defenses of Lingzhou, quarrels between the commanders, and Wang's refusal to allow his soldiers to cook their food for fear of Tangut attack. This left the men weak and sick. The Tanguts decided not to meet the Chinese head on. Instead, they adopted a strategy of clearing the countryside of food and provisions, a technique that goes back in the Chinese tradition as far as the third and fourth centuries BC. Then they breached the dikes and flooded the Song army besieging Lingzhou. Forced to withdraw, the Song forces fell apart and were decimated by the Tangut cavalry and the deteriorating weather conditions, much as Napoleon's army was in the retreat from Moscow.

The Effects of the Song Victory

Never again were the Song able to mount an assault that had such a potential for victory. If their armies had marched directly toward the Tangut capital and laid siege to it, they might have been able to force a quick surrender. No matter whether they subsequently tried to rule the Tanguts directly or chose to remove the anti-Song faction at court and install a compliant ruler with officials sympathetic to the Song, they certainly could have gained control of the horse-breeding grounds and they could have used the Tangut forces as allies against their mutual enemy, the Liao. Undoubtedly at that point, with the Song the dominant power in the northwest, the Tibetan tribes to the south would have acknowledged their authority and the way would have been open to the Song to reestablish Chinese control of trade over the old Silk Road through the oases in Central Asia to the West.

Let us now consider the possible effects of a Song victory in the Tangut Wars. First of all, let us review the potential geopolitical consequences. While, in historical reality, after the failure in the Tangut Wars, Emperor Shenzong himself succumbed quickly to disease and a broken heart, in the alternative scenario, he would have had no reason to fall into the depressed mental and physical state that led to his untimely demise in 1086 at the age of thirty-seven. He could have enjoyed many more years of vigorous health. With his determination and vision to reestablish Chinese hegemony and with the additional resources of the

Tanguts on the northwest, China might have been able to break the stalemate with the Liao. There could have been two possible long-term courses of action, although it is not clear from the sources what plans the Song had for their armies immediately after they had defeated the Xi Xia. Were they to stay in Tangut territory through the winter, feeding off their enemy's supplies, or were they to leave a garrison there, to ensure that the Tanguts did what the Song wanted, while the bulk of the army returned to Song territory? Or did they intend to launch a strike against the Liao? If the latter, the Chinese could have decided to attack the Liao from two directions in a pincer movement, from the south from the North China Plain and from the west from the Ordos and the great bend of the Yellow River, using their expeditionary forces, no doubt reinforced by cavalry contingents from both the Xi Xia and the Tibetan tribes. This would have required ensuring that the Tanguts remained faithful allies and did not rise up in the rear of the armies that had just been used to defeat them. This would also have required an amount of preparation for an assault from the south equivalent to what had been prepared over several years for the campaign against the Xi Xia. It was not impossible, but there is no evidence of such preparations. Therefore I suspect that an alternative course of action might have been considered as a first step.

This step would have the Song consolidating control over the Xi Xia and then demanding or forcing a renegotiation of the treaty terms with the Liao that had required so many resources to be transferred north, using the threat of invasion as pressure. Undoubtedly in the long-term Shenzong would have also wanted to take back the territories in North China that he considered were rightfully his and he would have used the threat of an attack to try to force the Liao to accede to his demands. In either case, China would have had more resources to support its own efforts at military and bureaucratic reform, and the effects on that polity of a diminution in the subsidy to the Liao would have been serious. Without Chinese resources to redistribute and pay for their military support, the central authorities of the Liao might have lost their legitimacy among their own people and among their subject tribes and might have imploded in the face of determined Song pressure. This would have enabled the Song to seize territory in the northeast that even the Tang and Han had not been able to hold permanently. The Song emperor would then have been preeminent in the whole of East and Central Asia.

At this point in time on the Central Asian steppe, the nomads had been disorganized and fragmented ever since the Kirghiz tribes destroyed the unified empire of the Turks in the mid–ninth century.[71] There was no potential leader or dominant tribe that could have challenged the Song in Central Asia: the Mongols had yet to appear as a distinct ethnic group. Further, we can see the importance of the position and power of the Tangut Xi Xia state by looking at the later history of the region. This requires looking ahead to the late twelfth and early thirteenth centuries, when Temüjin, after bitter struggles, eventually unified the steppe tribes and was proclaimed universal ruler, Chinggis Khan. There were several points during Temüjin's rise to power on the steppe when his career could have been aborted. These include the moment when he was rejected as a child by his family after his father's murder and later, in 1203, when he was almost poisoned and abandoned by all the Mongol clans except for a small contingent of 4,600 warriors after a defeat by the Kereyid confederation. He survived the latter setback by exploiting an opportunity. While the Kereyid were drunk during a feast after their victory, Temüjin retaliated with a surprise attack and after three days of fierce fighting won the field and subsequently executed Ong Khan.[72] The following year Temüjin reorganized his forces into units based on a decimal system of 10, 100, 1,000, and 10,000 men whose leaders were personally loyal to him, rather than purely on tribal affiliation, as had been the case in the past.[73] This is what made the Mongols such a fearsome and successful war machine.

If the Song had been the overlords of the entire Central Asian region during this later period, instead of being confined to the area south of the Yangzi River, they certainly would not have permitted such a free-for-all among the steppe peoples as actually occurred because this would have directly threatened their economic and political interests in Central Asia. Thus Temüjin would never have had a free hand to unite the tribes and reorganize his forces in the way that he did. The Song would have undoubtedly followed their Han and Tang predecessors in employing a divide-and-rule strategy, as well as deploying powerful armies composed of both cavalry and infantry in the field should one leader become too powerful and pose a significant threat to Song overlordship.

But let us turn back to what Temüjin actually did after he gained supremacy among the tribes, reorganized his forces, and was proclaimed Chinggis Khan. First, he knew that he had to challenge the claims of the Jin emperor to supreme overlordship; otherwise his own claims to universal rule would be empty and in time the newly united tribes would become disaffected and would abandon him.[74] He needed an assault on the south so that he could pillage the wealth of the sedentary peoples and redistribute their riches to his followers. This is what the tribes expected of a newly appointed khan. Chinggis realized that a direct attack on the Jin in North China would fail, for they simply had too many military and human resources, had too many well-defended cities integrated into too tight a defensive shield, and had too strong a cavalry for Chinggis' own cavalry forces to be successful in a short campaign. So he threw most of his military strength at forcing the Tangut Xi Xia to recognize his supremacy, and he himself took charge of the attack on the Tangut heartland.

While he probably was obliged to leave a good part of his forces behind to protect against a possible Jin attack in his rear,[75] Chinggis marched south with a powerful army over the Gobi Desert and defeated the initial contingent of 50,000 Xi Xia soldiers outside Wulahai. He then moved on to the fortress of Keyimen, which blocked the only road over the Helan Mountains to the Xi Xia capital of Zhongxing. The Tangut general Weiming Linggong attacked the Mongol forces as soon as they appeared on the plain below the fort with a force of 120,000 men and inflicted a major setback on them. Chinggis chose to wait out the defenders for two months, but they refused to be lured out to battle. Finally, Chinggis decided on a ruse that had served him well in his previous conflicts with the steppe tribes. He pretended to retreat with his main force, leaving only a small rearguard in the field. Weiming took the bait and approached with a small force to challenge the Mongols who had been left behind. Chinggis immediately reappeared with his entire army and crushed the Tanguts, taking Weiming prisoner as well. The Mongols then marched on to besiege the capital.

Once again, the Xi Xia mounted a tremendous defense for two months so that the Mongols could not penetrate the city. As it was by now late autumn, the Yellow River was swollen, so Chinggis decided to flood the city by damming the river and diverting the water into it. This tactic succeeded in inflicting great loss of life and property. The Tanguts appealed for assistance from the Jin emperor, but inexplicably he refused. Finally, in January 1210, the dikes diverting the Yellow River collapsed, flooding the Mongol forces in turn, and they were obliged to pull back to higher ground. Undeterred by this setback, Chinggis sent one of the Tangut generals he had captured as an ambassador to negotiate a peace. The Tangut ruler agreed to the terms, which included marrying one of Chinggis's daughters; handing over large quantities of livestock, especially camels, and native products; and promising allegiance to Chinggis and support in his future campaigns.

There are several points of note relevant to our discussion. First, the

Tangut ruler appealed to the Jin, not the Song emperor, for help against the Mongols. This was because the Song had by that time been pushed too far away from the Yellow River valley to be of any immediate assistance to the threatened monarch. They simply did not have the military resources close enough to the scene of action that would have enabled them to march to Zhongxing in time. On the other hand, the Song had the ability to put up a very effective defense against the Mongols once the latter did decide to attack the south.

The Song defenders held up the flower of the Mongol forces in Sichuan for years by retreating to mountain fortresses, where they were able to harry the Mongol invaders and inflict severe losses on them.[76] They even brought about the death of the Great Khan Möngke, who was leading the campaign in 1259, but whether he was killed by a direct Song shot or disease is still disputed. The Chinese were expert in the defense and attack of cities and fortified strongholds, and that is why Möngke sent Chinese artillerymen to help his younger brother, Hülegü, reduce the Ismaili castles in the west in 1256 and 1257 and then to destroy Baghdad and execute the Abbasid caliph.[77]

Thus it is quite reasonable to conclude that had the Song actually been in charge of the Tangut cities in Northwest China when Chinggis first attacked they would have been able to defeat him and drive him back to the steppe. For Chinggis had at that moment no previous experience in besieging fortified strongholds of sedentary peoples and in fact he made good use of the experience he gathered in his campaign against the Tanguts when he attacked the far more powerful empire of the Jin after neutralizing the Xi Xia. In the light of all these considerations, we can see the potential military significance of a Song victory over the Xi Xia in the 1080s. Chinggis Khan could have been stopped in his tracks by the Song; the Mongol conquests could have been prevented; and the Mongol empire, the largest land empire that the world had seen up to the thirteenth century, could have been aborted. The possible effects of this scenario on the peoples and polities of Europe and the Middle East I leave for others to consider.

Turning to the potential consequences within Song China itself, on the military and economic front the Northern Song capital of Kaifeng on the North China Plain was the center of a vibrant iron and steel industry, as has been mentioned. The reason for this was that Kaifeng was close to the sources of iron ore and coal needed for the casting of the metal. In addition, the Northern Song demand for iron weapons and chain mail armor for their armies was enormous, and that is one of the main reasons why the iron industry expanded to such impressive proportions, as was detailed earlier. When the Jin captured Kaifeng and the whole of the North China Plain in 1126–27, they deprived the Song of the sources of raw materials in addition to totally disrupting the network of foundries and the distribution of iron products. This was disastrous to the Song's ability to mount effective military campaigns later against the northern invaders. Similarly, some historians have suggested that another major consequence of the loss of North China was that the Song no longer had access to the saltpeter-producing regions of China. This was important for the development of gunpowder weapons and cannons, which the Song had invented in the decades preceding the fall of Kaifeng. Since animal husbandry was not well developed among the peoples of South China, the Song probably relied on land that naturally produced an efflorescence of saltpeter for one of the essential ingredients for the gunpowder compound.

> Most of [the saltpeter-producing regions] were conquered by the Chin [Jin] as they pressed south. If, then, there was a shortage of saltpeter in the Southern Sung [Song] domains, that could account for the failure to produce adequate amounts of high-nitrate gunpowder suitable for use with projectile-throwing bombards.[78]

If the Song had never lost the north, their military-industrial complex would never have suffered the collapse that it did, and there is no reason why they would not have maintained, or even enhanced, their military power and resources.

Furthermore, Shiba Yoshinobu has shown that the Chinese interest in maritime trade and overseas migration was beginning to expand.[79] If the threat of attack from the north had been eliminated, it is possible that the Song would have turned their attention to exploring overseas and sought to control the emerging trade in spices and other luxury goods in the South China Sea. At that point in time, it is hard to see that any of the powers in the area, or farther west in the Indian Ocean, would have had the military strength or the backing of such a large and vibrant economy, with its hundred million consumers and producers, to challenge Chinese dominance in this region of the world. Control of trade and taxation by the Chinese government would have inevitably increased its financial strength and could have led to further expansion.

From a social point of view, within China itself, success against the Tanguts might have resulted in Chinese soldiers being highly regarded by the state and society as a whole instead of suffering the radical loss of status they actually did, which was one of the reasons for China's inability to capitalize on its early military technological superiority in the post-1500 period.[80] During the rest of the Southern Song dynasty, the military came to be very much the less prestigious of the two types of officials, civilian and military, and many criminals were obliged to serve out their terms in the army in special units under the supervision of regular forces.[81] Even though the Song army reached an enormous size, up to a million men, its commanders were often men with little battle experience and the civil authorities at the center distrusted the generals and refused to provide adequate supplies or training.

Success in the wars might also have led to the discrediting of the emerging neo-Confucian school of Dao or Li (Principle) (neo-Confucianism). This school encouraged the disparagement of the reformist agenda and laid the blame for the catastrophic loss of North China to the Jurchen Jin in 1127 at the reformists' feet. The radical reforms of Wang Anshi in the educational, economic, and social fields might have had the effect originally intended and not been rescinded by the conservative faction under Sima Guang and his later followers. Although the reforms were partially restored under Zhezong and Huizong, the political atmosphere was poisoned and the leading scholars and members of the elite distrusted the reform faction, considering that those who were supporting the policies were only doing so out of a base profit motive. Thus Chinese intellectuals of the Song could have become primarily oriented toward solving technological and scientific questions, as was the polymath Shen Gua, who played a crucial role in planning the Tangut campaigns,[82] rather than concentrating on becoming introspective philosophers of the ancient Confucian texts.

Finally, let us consider an effect of the potential Song victory that might have had a profound and pervasive influence on the very being and body of Chinese individuals. The school of Dao encouraged Chinese women to play a lesser and lesser public role and conform strictly to the morality and rites outlined in the ancient Confucian canons, instructing them to keep themselves sequestered in the inner quarters. The school's rise to ideological dominance coincided with the increasing popularity of the practice of binding women's feet. Had the rise of the school of Dao been aborted, foot binding, a practice that resulted in women adopting a more passive position in relation to men than had been the case earlier in Chinese history, might also have been discouraged.[83] If the tradition of Dao had not become dominant and if there had been a stronger influence from the culture of the northern pastoral peoples, where women played a much more central role in political and social life, perhaps the way that women, and men, too, embodied themselves in society and viewed themselves as persons would have been quite different than what it was in late imperial China.[84] But exactly how the genders would have constituted themselves in such a different type of society is hard to imagine.

Concluding Remarks

The effects of a Song victory over the Tanguts in the wars of 1081–85 could thus have been very extensive. They could have ranged from changing the balance of power in East Asia to opening up a channel of influence between East and West just at the moment when China was at the height of its technological and scientific lead in the world. As the dominant power on the steppes, China could have thwarted the rise of the Mongols under Chinggis Khan by employing the traditional method of playing one tribe against another. So the Mongol conquests in East, Central, and West Asia, Europe, and India could have been aborted. China could possibly have pushed its power westward, using the tried and tested techniques of combining military advance with administrative consolidation, to make its own first encounter with the states and empires of the Middle East by regaining the lands that had been under its suzerainty in the Han and Tang empires at their greatest extents. In other words, the Chinese could have pushed as far as the Pamirs and Hindu Kush mountains at the western end of the Taklamakan Desert. Since Central Asian peoples were actively involved in trade, they certainly would have come into contact with the Ismaili Assassins, who controlled the trade routes into Afghanistan and Iran. However, it does not seem likely that the Song would have sought to conquer those regions or the ones farther west in the way that the Mongols eventually did. Chinese rulers were never just interested in plunder in the way the Mongols were, nor did the Chinese believe that their emperors should achieve universal rule by force of arms in the way the Mongols did.

With respect to the potential cultural impact of Song dominance in Central Asia, by the late eleventh century Islamic learning had already become quite advanced and the Song themselves were tolerant of different religions. So if the Song had reached the western edges of Central Asia, there does not seem to be a reason why the authorities would have discouraged Western and Middle Eastern merchants, travelers, and religious teachers and intellectuals from coming to China, just as the Tang had done before them. However, it is unlikely that the Chinese would have employed such men as tax farmers and given them significant powers as officials in the way the Mongols later did.[85] What might China have done if it had learned of Euclidean geometry and Aristotelian thought earlier, when it was not committed to the narrow strictures of neo-Confucian dogma, as was the case when the Jesuits brought Western science in the sixteenth and seventeenth centuries? What would have been the effect on the development of European thought and religious practices if Chinese ideas and practices had been introduced by way of the Arabs before the Renaissance and the Reformation? Might not the conception of the deity have changed radically and might not the political, social, and economic history of Europe been profoundly different? How then could Europe have arisen to become the dominant geopolitical force and intellectual power that it did? In such a scenario, profound changes could have been made in the nature of scientific inquiry and philosophical speculation in both West and East. China could have controlled trade in the Indian Ocean and dominated the trade in spices. China might not have "turned inward," in Liu's phrase, in the political, economic, philosophical, and cultural spheres.[86] Rather, it could have been an outward-looking, expansionist superpower. Even the sense of Chinese self and embodiment could have been altered.

If we consider the historical consequences of what I suggest could have happened, either if China had not been unified in 221 BC or if the Song had defeated the Tangut Xi Xia in the early 1080s and preempted the loss of the North China Plain to the Jurchen in 1126, we can see that there could have been many possible outcomes. What is clear is that the nature of the Chinese political system, the traditional political ideology, and the structure of Chinese society and culture could have been altered in such a way that in later times China could have developed along significantly different lines. There was nothing inevitable about the course of Chinese history. In fact, the course of Chinese history has been dependent on rather fragile contingencies. We may therefore suggest in the light of the discussion here that present day China may evolve in dramatically different ways than is sometimes presumed possible by contemporary pundits on the basis of what they claim to be the nature of the Chinese mind; the uniqueness and essential alterity of Chinese cultural practices; or, indeed, the inevitability of the adoption by China of Western-style democracy and human rights. This conclusion may disturb those sinologists who are wedded to a belief in the moral superiority of Chinese civil arts, the efficacy of neo-Confucian thinking (with its liberal tendencies), and the benign role they believe the literati played in later traditional Chinese history, as well as those who are convinced of the long-term viability of the current Chinese political system and those who can conceive of no trajectory for contemporary societies other than the one that has brought North American and European nations to the peak of international power.

On the other hand, China could well have developed a model for the development of civilization in ancient times that did not rely on Greek or Roman precedents. City-states could have evolved without the concepts of citizenship, freedom, and individual property rights. Furthermore, a victory by the Song in the late eleventh century had the potential to make a fundamental interruption in the flow of West Asian and European history. It could have been many more centuries before Europe succeeded in lifting itself out of the backwaters of human historical development. When and how would it have challenged the power of the East? What would have modernization have looked like with Chinese, instead of European, characteristics?

NOTES

I would like to thank my research assistants, Alvin C. W. Chung and Margaret Wee-Siang Ng, for their valuable assistance while I was preparing this chapter. In addition, I am most grateful for the help that the editors of the volume, Philip Tetlock, Ned Lebow, and Geoffrey Parker, gave me. Their suggestions for revision substantially improved the final version, and their patience and understanding are deeply appreciated. I am, however, solely responsible for the opinions expressed. I would also like to express my gratitude to the Killam Foundation and the Canada Council for the Arts, the Social Sciences and Humanities Research Council of Canada, and Fonds pour la Formation des Chercheurs et de l'Aide à la Recherche, Québec, for financial support in the preparation of this essay.

1. Paul A. Cohen, in *Discovering History in China: American Historical Writing on the Recent Chinese Past* (New York: Columbia University Press, 1984), writes: "In the field as a whole . . . the great preponderance of scholarly work during this period [the 1950s and 1960s] was structured either in terms of the Western challenge and how this challenge had been met or in terms of the impact of modernization—Western-carried and Western-defined—on China's traditional culture and society" (2).

2. As Judith B. Farquhar and James L. Hevia have recently argued in "Culture and Postwar American Historiography of China," *positions* 1, no. 2 (1993), "few of the ruling categories of critical European social theory and historiography translate directly to the Chinese situation (511). . . . [W]orks in historical cultural studies . . . prevent us from any longer seeing culture as impersonal and immutable structures which constrain action, or as a product of the work of pre-

constituted individuals. They make it impossible to distinguish 'East' from 'West' along a reason-culture or nature-culture continuum" (516–17).

3. Robin D. S. Yates, "Cosmos, Central Authority, and Communities in the Early Chinese Empire," in *Empires: Perspectives from Archaeology and History,* ed. Susan Alcock, Terrence D'Altroy, Kathleen Morrison, and Carla Sinopoli (Cambridge: Cambridge University Press, 2001), 351–68, 441–44; Mark Edward Lewis, *Writing and Authority in Early China* (Albany: State University of New York Press, 1999).

4. Cf. Nathan Sivin, "The Myth of the Naturalists," in *Medicine, Philosophy, and Religion in Ancient China* (Aldershot: Variorum, 1995), 4, 1–33.

5. Hoklam Chan, *Legitimation in Imperial China: Discussions under the Jurchen-Chin Dynasty (1115–1234)* (Seattle and London: University of Washington Press, 1985).

6. Lien-sheng Yang, "Toward a Study of Dynastic Configurations in Chinese History," in *Studies in Chinese Institutional History* (Cambridge: Harvard University Press, 1961), 1–17.

7. Cohen, *Discovering History in China.*

8. I am deeply indebted to Professor Paul Smith of Haverford College, who permitted me to read two of his important unpublished works, Paul J. Smith, "Shen-tsung's Reign (1068–1085)," in *The Cambridge History of China,* ed. Denis Twitchett, 5A (Cambridge: Cambridge University Press, forthcoming); and "Domestic Politics and the Qingtang Campaigns under Shenzong and His Sons," paper presented at the Workshop on Huizong and the Culture of the Late Northern Song, Seattle, February 1–3, 2001. My knowledge of late Northern Song China has greatly improved thanks to his exceptional generosity and depth of scholarship.

9. Other important Chinese technologies were also transferred to the West, including the magnetic mariner's compass and printing. They profoundly affected the course of Western history. These have been detailed by Joseph Needham and his associates in his *Science and Civilisation in China,* 8 vols. (Cambridge: Cambridge University Press, 1954–).

10. Cf. William H. Nienhauser Jr., ed., *The Grand Scribe's Records,* vol. 1: *The Basic Annals of Pre-Han China,* by Ssu-ma Ch'ien (Taipei: SMC, 1996); Burton Watson, trans., *Records of the Grand Historian: Qin Dynasty* (New York: Columbia University Press 1993); Grant Hardy, *Worlds of Bronze and Bamboo: Sima Qian's Conquest of History* (New York: Columbia University Press, 1999).

11. Cf. John Knoblock, and Jeffrey Riegel, *The Annals of Lü Buwei: A Complete Translation and Study* (Stanford: Stanford University Press, 2000).

12. For the entire story, see Nienhauser, *The Grand Scribe's Records* (Bloomington: Indiana University Press, 1994), 7, "The Assassin—Retainers," Memoir 26, 325–34.

13. It is quite possible that the military formations in the pottery warrior and horse pits were designed by one of Qin's generals, Wei Liao. See Lin Jianming, "*Weiliao zi* yu Qin Shihuang ling bingma yong de yanjiu," in *Qin yongxue yanjiu,* ed. Qin Shihuang bingma yong bowu guan, 465–71 (Xi'an: Shaanxi Renmin jiaoyu chuban she, 1996).

14. Robin D. S. Yates, "The City State in Ancient China," in *The Archaeol-*

ogy of City States: Cross-Cultural Approaches, ed. Deborah L. Nichols and Thomas H. Charlton (Washington, DC: Smithsonian Institution Press, 1997), 71–90; Robin D. S. Yates, "Early China," in *War and Society in the Ancient and Medieval Worlds: Asia, the Mediterranean, Europe, and Mesoamerica,* ed. Kurt Raaflaub and Nathan Rosenstein (Washington, DC: Center for Hellenic Studies, Trustees for Harvard University and Harvard University Press, 1999), 9–46; Mark Edward Lewis, "The City-State in Spring-and-Autumn China," in *A Comparative Study of Thirty City-State Cultures: An Investigation Conducted by the Copenhagen Polis Centre,* ed. Mogens Herman Hansen (Copenhagen: Kongelige Danske Videnskabernes Selskab, 2000), 359–73.

15. See Yates, "Cosmos, Central Authority, and Communities in the Early Chinese Empire." Universal conscription and military service for males were abandoned early in the Eastern Han dynasty (first century AD). After that time, emperors tried to demilitarize the interior and relied on professional mercenary and/or convict armies at the frontiers to guard against external threats. See Mark Edward Lewis, "The Han Abolition of Universal Military Service," in *Warfare in Chinese History,* ed. Hans van de Ven (Leiden: Brill, 2000), 33–75. Yet failure to keep the general population trained in warfare had other consequences. Once the frontiers were penetrated, the central government lacked the skilled human resources necessary to turn back a determined invader, and local policing tended to be put in the hands of undesirable elements in society. Loss of a sense of obligation to the central authorities was also a consequence.

16. For a detailed study of the differences between Qin script and those of the other states and of the effects of the imperial unification on the evolution of Chinese writing, see Qiu Xigui, *Chinese Writing,* trans. Gilbert L. Mattos and Jerry Norman (Berkeley: Society for the Study of Early China and the Institute of East Asian Studies, University of California, 2000), 78–149.

17. These are not all the reforms that the First Emperor proclaimed. For a full list, see Derk Bodde, "The State and Empire of Ch'in," in *The Cambridge History of China,* Vol. 1: *The Ch'in and Han Empires, 221 B.C.–A.D. 220,* ed. Denis Twitchett and Michael Loewe (Cambridge: Cambridge University Press, 1986), 20–102. Cf. Martin Kern, *The Stele Inscriptions of Ch'in Shih-huang: Text and Ritual in Early Chinese Imperial Representation* (New Haven: American Oriental Society, 2000), for a study of the inscriptions on steles that the First Emperor set up at various ritually significant or religiously potent sites around the country.

18. Only a very little of this vast sea of documents has survived, notably those found among the remains of the Han forts in the deserts of the northwest. One site between the towns of Dunhuang and Anxi in Gansu Province has yielded more than thirty-five thousand documents (Hu Pingsheng and Zhang Defang, eds., *Dunhuang Xuanquan Han jian shicui* [Shanghai: Shanghai guji chuban she, 2001]). Some of the Qin laws and statutes were found in the tomb of a Qin local official in Hubei in 1975 (A. F. P. Hulsewé, *Remnants of Ch'in Law: An Annotated Translation of the Ch'in Legal and Administrative Rules of the 3rd Century B.C. Discovered in Yün-meng Prefecture, Hupei Province, in 1975* [Leiden: Brill, 1985]), and early Han laws were found in a tomb at Jiangling, Hubei, (Zhangjiashan 247-hao Hanmu zhujian zhengli xiaozu, *Zhangjiashan Hanmu zhujian (247-hao)* [Beijing: Wenwu chuban she, 2001]).

19. Cf. Aihe Wang, *Cosmology and Political Culture in Early China* (Cambridge: Cambridge University Press, 2000); and Stephan Feuchtwang, *The Imperial Metaphor: Popular Religion in China* (London: Routledge, 1992). "Stressing function over anatomical structure, however, the *Inner Canon* (*The Yellow Emperor's Inner Canon*, the foundational text of the Chinese medical tradition of systematic correspondence) imagined these systems in a political metaphor as a working bureaucracy in which 'somatic posts' are charged like officials with certain duties, each responsible for a sphere of activity" (Charlotte Furth, *A Flourishing Yin: Gender in China's Medical History, 960–1665* [Berkeley: University of California Press, 1999], 23).

20. Lewis, *Writing and Authority in Early China*, 363.

21. Cf. Christopher Leigh Connery, *The Empire of the Text: Writing and Authority in Early Imperial China* (Lanham, MD: Rowman and Littlefield, 1998).

22. Recent research has demonstrated, however, that in the Ming-Qing transition, and up through the eighteenth century when China was able to rebound more quickly than other countries from the worldwide recession, wealthy Chinese merchants had close relationships with eminent literati and senior officials. They competed with the social elite in manipulating their symbolic capital and cultural expertise. See Craig Clunas, *Superfluous Things: Material Culture and Social Status in Early Modern China* (Urbana: University of Illinois Press, 1991); and Ginger Cheng-chi Hsü, *A Bushel of Pearls: Painting for Sale in Eighteenth-Century Yangzhou* (Stanford: Stanford University Press, 2001).

23. A. C. Graham, *Later Mohist Logic, Ethics, and Science* (Hong Kong: Chinese University Press; London: School of Oriental and African Studies, 1978).

24. A. C. Graham and Nathan Sivin, "A Systematic Approach to the Mohist Optics (ca. 300 B.C.)," in *Chinese Science: Explorations of an Ancient Tradition*, ed. Shigeru Nakayama and Nathan Sivin (Cambridge: MIT Press, 1973), 105–52.

25. The imperial state probably could not tolerate a closed group such as the Mohists, who were loyal only to their leaders and only obeyed Mohist law. Within a generation or so of the founding of the Han dynasty the Mohists were known only in association with Confucians (the Ru), even though in preunification times the Mohists were among the most effective opponents of the Confucians.

26. Needham, *Science and Civilisation in China*, 2:287ff.; Robin D. S. Yates, "Body, Space, Time, and Bureaucracy: Boundary Creation and Control Mechanisms in Early China," in *Boundaries in China*, ed. John Hay (London: Reaktion, 1994), 56–80; John B. Henderson, *The Development and Decline of Chinese Cosmology* (New York: Columbia University Press, 1984).

27. Nathan Sivin, "Science and Medicine in Imperial China: The State of the Field," *Journal of Asian Studies* 47 (1988): 41–90; Shigehisa Kuriyama, *The Expressiveness of the Body and the Divergence of Greek and Chinese Medicine* (New York: Zone, 1999); Paul U. Unschuld, *Medicine in China: A History of Ideas* (Berkeley and Los Angeles: University of California Press, 1985). Joseph Needham, in *Science and Civilisation in China*, vol. 2, passim, claimed that a single "feudal-bureaucratic" empire ruled by an autocrat assisted by scholar-officials was one of the main limiting factors preventing the appearance of mod-

ern science in China. Needham's hypothesis does not explain the varying influence of the feudal bureaucratic order on the different sciences.

28. Unschuld, *Medicine in China: A History of Ideas;* Paul U. Unschuld, *Medicine in China: Historical Artifacts and Images* (Munich, London, and New York: Prestel, 2000).

29. Robin D. S. Yates, *Five Lost Classics: Tao, Huang-Lao, and Yin-Yang in Han China* (New York: Ballantine Del Rey Fawcett, 1997). The nature of Huang-Lao philosophy was forgotten for two thousand years until the fortuitous discovery in 1973 of the tomb of a Han aristocrat dated about 168 BC in which silk manuscripts from this tradition, together with many others of unparalleled value, such as two manuscripts of the *Laozi* and early medical texts and maps, were discovered.

30. It is hard to judge as a general rule whether the unified imperial state encouraged or discouraged the development of scientific thinking and the development and dissemination of technology. Astronomy, which was virtually monopolized by the imperial state, made very many significant advances as a result of official sponsorship. Cf. Christopher Cullen, *Astronomy and Mathematics in Ancient China: The* Zhou bi suan jing (Cambridge: Cambridge University Press, 1996); Sun Xiaochun and Jacob Kistemaker, *The Chinese Sky during the Han: Constellating Stars and Society* (Leiden: Brill, 1997); and E. H. Schafer, *Pacing the Void: T'ang Approaches to the Stars* (Berkeley and Los Angeles: University of California Press, 1977). Agricultural innovations were promoted by officials and disseminated to other parts of the country. See Francesca Bray, "Agricultural Technology and Agrarian Change in Han China," *Early China* 5 (1979–80): 3–13; cf. Cho-yun Hsu, "Agricultural Intensification and Market Agrarianism in the Han Dynasty," in *Ancient China: Studies in Early Civilization,* ed. David T. Roy and Tsuin-hsuin Tsien (Hong Kong: Chinese University of Hong Kong Press, 1978), 253–68. However, other sciences were either unaffected by the state or were subject to suppression or attempted rigorous control (e.g., geomancy), so no generalization is valid for all sciences throughout the course of Chinese history.

31. Thomas J. Barfield, *The Perilous Frontier: Nomadic Empires and China* (Cambridge, MA: Blackwell, 1989).

32. The climate in China is believed to have reached its nadir just after the end of the Han dynasty. This may have been one of the influences that propelled the northern peoples into mass migrations into China to the south and across Central Asia toward the west because the steppes may have been unable to support the level of population that they had in more clement times. Under these deteriorating ecological conditions, therefore, it is likely that at least *some* migrations out of Central Asia would have occurred.

33. Feuchtwang, *The Imperial Metaphor.*

34. Thomas Allsen, "The Circulation of Military Technology in the Mongolian Empire," in *Warfare in Inner Asian History (500–1800),* ed. Nicola Di Cosmo (Leiden: Brill, 2002), 265–93.

35. Paul J. Smith, "Shen-tsung's Reign"; Paul C. Forage, "The Sino-Tangut War of 1081–1085," *Journal of Asian History* 25, no. 1 (1991): 1–28; Paul C. For-

age, "Science, Technology, and War in Song China: Reflections on the *Brush Talks from the Dream Creek* by Shen Kuo (1031–1095)," PhD diss., University of Toronto, 1991; Ruth Dunnell, "The Hsi Hsia," in *The Cambridge History of China,* vol. 6: *Alien Regimes and Border States, 907–1368,* ed. Herbert Franke and Denis Twitchett (Cambridge: Cambridge University Press, 1994), 154–214.

36. Liang Gengyao, "Song Shenzong shidai Xibei bian liang de choucuo," in *Song dai shehui jingjishi lunji* (Taibei: Yunchen wenhua shiye gufen youxian gongsi, 1997), 1:41–58; "Bei Song Yuanfeng fa Xia zhanzheng de junliang wenti," in *Song dai shehui jingjishi lunji,* 1: 59–102.

37. Joseph Needham, *Science and Civilisation in China,* vol. 5: *Chemistry and Chemical Technology,* pt. 7: "Military Technology: The Gunpowder Epic" (Cambridge: Cambridge University Press, 1986); Joseph Needham and Robin D. S. Yates, *Science and Civilisation in China,* vol. 5: *Chemistry and Chemical Technology,* pt. 6: "Military Technology: Missiles and Sieges" (Cambridge: Cambridge University Press, 1994); William McNeill, *The Pursuit of Power: Technology, Armed Force, and Society since A.D. 1000* (Oxford: Blackwell, 1982).

38. Mark Elvin, *The Pattern of the Chinese Past* (Stanford: Stanford University Press, 1973); Susan Cherniak, "Book Culture and Textual Transmission in Sung China," *Harvard Journal of Asiatic Studies* 54, no. 1 (1994): 5–125.

39. Robert M. Hartwell, in "A Revolution in the Chinese Iron and Coal Industries during the Northern Song," *Journal of Asian Studies* 21, no. 2 (1962), calculated (34) that the Chinese output of iron production increased from 32,500 short tons in 998 to 90,400 tons in 1064 and 125,000 tons in 1078.

40. Shiba Yoshinobu, *Song dai shangye shi yanjiu (Sōdai shōgyō-shi kenyō),* trans. Zhuang Jinghui (Taibei: Taoxiang chuban she, 1997); Richard von Glahn, *Fountain of Fortune: Money and Monetary Policy in China, 1000–1700* (Berkeley: University of California Press, 1996).

41. Cf. Forage, "The Sino-Tangut War of 1081–1085."

42. For a recent overview of the history of late imperial China, see F. W. Mote, *Imperial China, 900–1800* (Cambridge: Harvard University Press, 1999). For a study of Northern Song's relations with its northern neighbors, see Jingshen Tao, *Two Sons of Heaven: Studies in Sung-Liao Relations* (Tucson: University of Arizona Press, 1988); and for a detailed study of the city of Kaifeng in the Northern Song period, see Zheng Shoupeng, *Song dai Kaifengfu yanjiu* (Taibei: Guoli bianyiguan Zhonghua congshu bianshen Weiyuanhui, 1980). Franke points out that the Jin (Jurchen) were not originally a nomadic people, like the Khitan Liao, but rather forest dwellers and fishermen who developed a mixed economy and relied for their success in defeating first the Liao and then the Northern Song Chinese on a multiethnic force (Herbert Franke, "The Chin Dynasty," in Franke and Twitchett, *The Cambridge History of China,* 6:217). Contemporary scholars of Buddhism are challenging the tenacious notion that the Song "marked the beginning of a long an inexorable decline . . . that extended down through the remainder of the imperial era" (Peter N. Gregory, "The Vitality of Buddhism in the Sung," in *Buddhism in the Sung,* ed. Peter N. Gregory and Daniel A. Getz Jr. [Honolulu: University of Hawaii Press, 1999], 2), 1–20.

43. William H. McNeill, "The Age of Gunpowder Empires, 1450–1800," in

Islamic and European Expansion: The Forging of a Global Order, ed. Michael Adas (Philadelphia: Temple University Press, 1993), 103–39, emphasizes the importance of the availability of sources of metal and advanced mining technology in Europe as one of the factors, together with "property law and political practices," of fundamental importance in enabling the Europeans to outstrip the Chinese in the development of artillery powered by gunpowder.

44. David S. Landes, *Revolution in Time: Clocks and the Making of the Modern World* (Cambridge: Belknap Press of Harvard University Press, 1983); Joseph Needham, Wang Ling, and Derek Price, *Heavenly Clockwork,* 2nd ed. (Cambridge: Cambridge University Press, 1986).

45. Paul J. Smith, *Taxing Heaven's Storehouse: Horses, Bureaucrats, and the Destruction of the Sichuan Tea Industry, 1074–1224* (Cambridge: Council on East Asian Studies, Harvard University, 1991).

46. Although the Song dynasty is usually criticized for its weak military capabilities, in fact the Southern Song held out for a longer period of time and more effectively than most of the countries attacked by the Mongols except Western Europe. See Huang K'uan-chung, "Mountain Fortress Defence: The Experience of the Southern Song and Korea in Resisting the Mongol Invasions," in van de Ven, *Warfare in Chinese History,* 222–51.

47. Cf. McNeill, *The Pursuit of Power.* See chapter 9 of this volume, for alternative possibilities in later imperial times; and Kenneth Pomeranz, *The Great Divergence: China, Europe, and the Making of the Modern World Economy* (Princeton: Princeton University Press, 2000), for comparisons among Chinese, Japanese, and northern European economies in the mid–eighteenth century.

48. Karl A. Wittfogel and Feng Chia-sheng, *History of Chinese Society: Liao* (Philadelphia: American Philosophical Society, 1949); Jing-shen Tao, *Two Sons of Heaven.*

49. Mote, *Imperial China,* 193–248.

50. Ruth W. Dunnell, *The Great State of High and White: Buddhism and State Formation in Eleventh-Century Xia* (Honolulu: University of Hawaii Press, 1996); Dunnell, "The Hsi Hsia."

51. Yang Ruowei, "Junshi zhidu," in *Qidan wangchao zhengzhi junshi zhidu yanjiu* (Taipei: Wenjin chubanshe, 1992), 201–47. Du Chengan, in "Qidan junshi zhidu de jiben kuangjia—Liaochao bingzhi chutan zhi yi," *Fushun shizhuan xuebao: Shehui ban (Liao),* no. 2 (1991): 74–81, points out that all males from the ages of fifteen to fifty were obliged by the Liao to serve in the army regardless of their ethnicity and that there were four main components to the military forces: the central army, local armies, armies of dependent states, and armies of the tribal leaders.

52. Mote, *Imperial China,* 104–9.

53. John Richard Labadie, "Rulers and Soldiers: Perception and Management of the Military in Northern Sung China (960–ca. 1060)," PhD diss., University of Washington, Seattle, 1981, 63–65; David C. Wright, "The Sung-Kitan War of A.D. 1004–1005 and the Treaty of Shan-yüan," *Journal of Asian History* 32, no. 1 (1998): 3–48.

54. Nap-Yin Lau, "Waging War for Peace? The Peace Accord between the Song and the Liao in AD 1005," in Van de Ven, *Warfare in Chinese History,* 213.

55. Shiba Yoshinobu, "Sung Foreign Trade: Its Scope and Organization," in *China among Equals,* ed. Morris Rossabi (Berkeley and Los Angeles: University of California Press, 1983), 98.

56. David C. Wright, "Parity, Pedigree, and Peace: Routine Sung Diplomatic Missives to the Liao," *Journal of Sung-Yuan Studies* 26 (1996): 55–85; Jing-shen Tao, *Two Sons of Heaven.*

57. Christian Lamouroux, "From the Yellow River to the Huai: New Representations of a River Network and the Hydraulic Crisis of 1128," in *Sediments of Time: Environment and Society in Chinese History,* ed. Mark Elvin and Liu Ts'ui-jung (Cambridge: Cambridge University Press, 1998), 545–84.

58. Dunnell, "The Hsi Hsia," 187.

59. James T. C. Liu, "An Early Sung Reformer: Fan Chung-yen," in *Chinese Thought and Institutions,* ed. John K. Fairbank (Chicago: University of Chicago Press, 1957), 105–31.

60. Cf. James T. C. Liu, *Ou-yang Hsiu: An Eleventh-Century Neo-Confucianist* (Stanford: Stanford University Press, 1967), 40–51.

61. H. R. Williamson, *Wang An Shih: A Chinese Statesman and Educationalist of the Sung Dynasty,* vol. 1 (Westport, CT: Hyperion, [1935] 1973); James T. C. Liu, *Reform in Sung China: Wang An-shih (1021–1086) and His New Policies* (Cambridge: Harvard University Press, 1959); Peter K. Bol, "Government, Society, and State: On the Political Visions of Ssu-ma Kuang and Wang An-shih," in *Ordering the World: Approaches to State and Society in Sung Dynasty China,* ed. Robert P. Hymes and Conrad Schirokauer (Berkeley and Los Angeles: University of California Press, 1993), 128–92; Paul J. Smith, "State Power and Economic Activism during the New Policies, 1068–1085: The Tea and Horse Trade and the 'Green Sprouts' Loan Policy," in Hymes and Schirokauer, *Ordering the World,* 76–127; Smith, "Shen-tsung's Reign."

62. Smith, "Shen-tsung's Reign"; Brian E. McKnight, *Law and Order in Sung China* (Cambridge: Cambridge University Press, 1992), 132; Forage, "The Sino-Tangut War of 1081–1085."

63. Smith, "Shen-tsung's Reign."

64. Liu, *Reform in Sung China;* Bol, "Government, Society, and State."

65. Forage, "Sino-Tangut War."

66. Liu, *Reform in Sung China;* Williamson, *Wang An Shih.*

67. My description of the campaign relies heavily on Forage, "Sino-Tangut War"; Smith, "Shen-tsung's Reign"; Wang Tianshun, *Xi Xia zhanshi* (Yinchuan: Ningxia renmin chuban she, 1993); Li Huarui, *Song Xia guanxi shi* (Shijiazhuang: Hebei renmin chuban she, 1998); Dai Xizhang, *Xi Xia ji* (Yinchuan: Ningxia renmin chuban she, 1988), *juan* 15–18, 341–421; and Feng Dongli and Mao Yuanyou, *Bei Song Liao Xia junshi shi (Zhongguo junshi tongshi,* vol. 12) (Beijing: Junshi kexue chuban she, 1998). The Xi Xia emperor Huizong is not the same man as the later Song emperor Huizong.

68. Paul J. Smith, "Domestic Politics and the Qingtang Campaigns under Shenzong and His Sons."

69. See Chen Bingying, *Zhenguan yujingjiang yanjiu* (Yinchuan: Ningxia renmin chuban she, 1995), for an analysis of a military text, written in the Xi Xia lan-

guage and dating from 1102–14, that details many aspects of the Xi Xia military establishment.

70. Forage, "Sino-Tangut War," 13, calculates that 865 metric tons of grain was required per day, but he does not include the amounts consumed by the beasts of burden, primarily donkeys and horses. In at least two of the divisions, Wang's and Gao's, porters outnumbered the fighting men.

71. Barfield, *The Perilous Frontier,* 168.

72. Ibid., 190–91; H. Desmond Martin, *The Rise of Chingis Khan and His Conquest of North China* (Baltimore: The Johns Hopkins Press, 1950), 48–84; J. J. Saunders, *The History of the Mongol Conquests* (London: Routledge and Kegan Paul, 1971), 50–52.

73. David Morgan, *The Mongols* (Oxford: Blackwell, 1986), 88–89; Barfield, *The Perilous Frontier,* 191–92.

74. As Barfield points out in *The Perilous Frontier,* the loyalties of the steppe peoples were notoriously fickle. Even brothers and uncles of Chinggis abandoned him at various points in time when his fortunes were on the wane, and he actually murdered one of his brothers early in his career.

75. In 1208, Yunji, prince of Wei, had gone north as a Jin ambassador to Chinggis's court. He had been treated with little courtesy. This suggests that Chinggis was not interested in remaining a subservient tribute bearer to the Jin emperor. The ambassador reported that it would be advisable to attack Chinggis as soon as possible. However, the Jin emperor died and the plan was put on hold. The prince of Wei was then elevated to the Jin throne, so Chinggis may have expected trouble from him, although he did not think much of the new emperor's abilities. His judgment proved correct.

76. Huang K'uan-chung, "Mountain Fortress Defence."

77. Morris Rossabi, *Khubilai Khan: His Life and Times* (Berkeley: University of California Press, 1988), 20–21; Thomas T. Allsen, *Mongol Imperialism: The Policies of the Grand Khan Möngke in China, Russia, and the Islamic Lands, 1251–1259* (Berkeley: University of California Press, 1987), 194–202; Morgan, *The Mongols,* 91.

78. Lu Gwei-djen, Joseph Needham, and Phan Chi-hsing, "The Oldest Representation of a Bombard," *Technology and Culture* 29, no. 3 (1988): 604.

79. Yoshinobu, "Sung Foreign Trade."

80. McNeill, *The Pursuit of Power.*

81. McKnight, *Law and Order in Sung China,* 218.

82. Nathan Sivin, "Shen Kua," in *Dictionary of Scientific Biography,* ed. Charles Coulston Gillespie (New York: Scribner's, 1975), 12:369–93; Forage, "Science, Technology, and War in Song China."

83. C. Fred Blake, "Foot-Binding in Neo-Confucian China and the Appropriation of Female Labor," *Signs* 19, no. 3 (1994): 676–712. Patricia Buckley Ebrey discusses the various cultural and social reasons for the spread of foot binding in the Song and notes that it was a practice that implicated complex social, psychological, and cultural ideas and negotiations over power. See her *The Inner Quarters: Marriage and the Lives of Chinese Women in the Sung Period* (Berkeley: University of California Press, 1993), 37–44.

84. In Tang times, women rode horses and played polo. The empresses in both the Tangut and the Liao states played important political and military roles.

85. See Allsen, *Mongol Imperialism,* for Mongol fiscal and political policies.

86. James T. C. Liu, *China Turning Inward: Intellectual-Political Changes in the Early Twelfth Century* (Cambridge: Council on East Asian Studies, Harvard University, 1988).

CHAPTER 9

Without Coal? Colonies? Calculus?

COUNTERFACTUALS & INDUSTRIALIZATION
IN EUROPE & CHINA

Kenneth Pomeranz

Background—Europe in a Chinese Mirror

The question of whether China could have had an industrial revolution is largely, but not entirely, independent of one less often asked. Could Europe have had a "Chinese" experience, becoming a society with highly productive agriculture, extensive handicraft industry, and highly sophisticated markets but no breakthrough to a world of vastly expanded energy use and sustained growth in per capita income—so that it eventually faced resource pressures that sharply limited extensive growth as well? Or to put it slightly differently, could the regions of Europe that industrialized in the first two-thirds of the nineteenth century (chiefly, though not exclusively, in Britain) have instead remained "stuck" in a Dutch or Danish configuration, which would have made them much more like China's Yangzi and Pearl River deltas? Although we will need to distinguish these questions carefully, there is enough material that is useful to both—and enough ways in which each sheds light on the other—that it seems to me worth asking them together. I adopted this strategy in *The Great Divergence*, which focused primarily on "could Europe have become China?" a question that, from the point of view of this book, is essentially a "could Europe have 'failed'?" counterfactual. Here I return to the more familiar "could China have industrialized?" question but with my study of the other question very much on my mind. It is both the source of empirical statements about the relative state of X, Y, or Z in Europe and China that I will reuse here and also the source of many of the beliefs that I have been testing by examining the "could China have been a contender?" counterfactual in this essay.[1]

To put things crudely, I argued in the book that China and Europe, and more specifically the Yangzi Delta and England, their most advanced regions, were much more similar as late as 1750 than we have commonly realized. Standards of living appear to have been quite similar. Life expectancy was comparable.[2] Consumption of at least some of the non-grain foods that typically increase in early stages of sustained per capita growth (such as sugar) was also at least comparable, as were levels of production and consumption of textiles, also a common indicator of early growth according to Engel's Law.[3] And while certain aggregate indicators of welfare in China would decline over the 150 years after 1750, I would argue that this did not indicate the "overpopulation" that many scholars claim doomed nineteenth-century China. Indeed, standards of living seem to have continued to inch upward in many Chinese regions, at least until 1850. Any overall decline in per capita consumption before the great catastrophes of the mid-nineteenth century probably reflected in large part greater population growth in the poorer regions of the country, so that the weight of advanced regions in empirewide averages declined rather than a deterioration of economic circumstances within most regions.[4] Institutionally, the eighteenth-century Chinese economy may well have more closely resembled an idealized market economy than did Europe's at the same time (though neither was all that close): certainly it is hard to find in mid-Qing China crucial blockages to the kinds of exchange, development of markets, or accumulation and deployment of resources needed for industrialization. To be sure, the economies of eighteenth-century China and Europe (or the core areas of each) were not identical; but by no means did all the economically relevant differences favor Europe.

To frame the problem slightly differently, one can distinguish a kind of growth that involves successfully exploiting all the opportunities available with given resources and technology, mainly through developing increasingly efficient markets and the division of labor, from growth that shifts the production possibility frontier outward through technological change and/or resource windfalls. During the nineteenth century, the

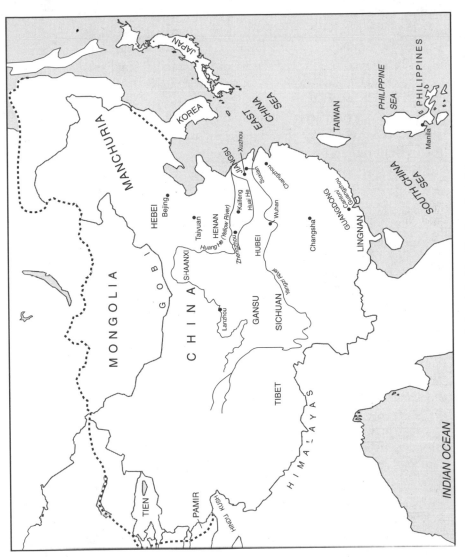

Map 5. Boundaries of the Qing Empire at its height

North Atlantic countries began a staggering burst of this latter kind of growth, which continues to this day; clearly that burst must have had some preconditions, which we can see as European advantages. This does not, however, tell us whether Europe was doing better than China (or perhaps other places) at the first, "Smithian" kind of growth, which had predominated during the previous few centuries. Nor, of course, does success at Smithian growth guarantee success at the other kind of growth. As Joel Mokyr (chapter 10 of this volume) emphasizes, technological change has its own prerequisites, and whatever they may be, they do not simply follow from getting economic institutions "right." I would also argue (here differing from Mokyr) that both technological change and resource windfalls were important to distinguishing the modern European from the Chinese path.

Perhaps most surprisingly, despite very high population densities, China's core regions do not seem to have been doing any worse ecologically than Europe's in the eighteenth century. I have reconstructed nitrogen fluxes from dry-farming areas of North China and England, circa 1800, and they do not show more severe soil depletion in China, and if we added China's paddy rice regions to the comparison,[5] it would get rather lop-sided in China's favor.[6] Even for wood supply and deforestation, there is no clear Western Europe advantage circa 1750, despite its much sparser population. The Chinese used land and fuel more efficiently— thanks to everything from more labor-intensive fuel gathering to more efficient stoves to greater use of crop residues—and they were actually better off in many ways than Europeans.[7] Cores at both ends of Eurasia, I would argue, faced a crucial race in the eighteenth century between mounting ecological pressures and the resources available to counteract these pressures (about which more shortly). These pressures were evident in everything from rising real prices for timber and other land-intensive products to increased erosion (in both China and Europe) to increased flooding and a falling water table (mostly in China) to more frequent sandstorms, erosion, and stagnant per acre agricultural yields (also noted in Europe).[8] All things considered, it is not clear that the problems in China's core were the more serious ones.[9]

Broadly speaking, "development" in core regions meant an accumulation of both more labor and more capital and increased per capita consumption by the growing numbers of people present. But as long as one remained within a world in which Malthus's famous four necessities— food, fiber, fuel and building materials—came from plant growth, having a more or less fixed quantity of land was a potentially serious constraint on such development. Roughly speaking, three kinds of solutions existed. One could trade manufactured products for vegetable products from elsewhere, in effect using plentiful labor and capital to purchase the products of somebody else's land; this, of course, required finding enough trading partners with the right factor endowments and an institutional structure that facilitated this trade (or imposing such a structure through conquest). One could adopt various strategies to maximize the ecologically sustainable yield of one's existing land—though in an age before chemical fertilizers and pesticides, most such strategies were extremely labor intensive. Or one could reduce one's dependence on annual vegetative growth, turning to subterranean stores of building materials and especially energy, which allowed mines with a relatively small surface area to substitute for enormous areas of woodland.

Chinese cores pursued the first option very successfully—so successfully that they were running into rapidly diminishing returns by the late eighteenth century. The same institutions that facilitated vast amounts of long-distance trade, with mostly freehold peasants in the interior trading rice, timber, and so on for cloth, salt, metal tools, and so on, eventually facilitated both enormous population growth and the development of more local handicraft industries on the periphery: both had the effect of reducing the surplus of land-intensive products that those regions had for shipment to core regions. And the political structure that facilitated internal trade did not, for reasons to be discussed shortly, encourage a sufficiently rapid expansion of this trade to overseas areas (such as Southeast Asia), where institutional arrangements favorable to a more rapid expansion of trade would probably have required Chinese conquests. Nor, of course, did China have the geographic and epidemiological luck that helped Europe create a vastly larger hinterland in the New World at relatively low cost to itself.

Chinese cores were also quite successful at exploiting the second palliative for resource constraints: kinds of land management and resource conservation (most of them very labor intensive) that allowed very high yields while slowing (though not completely stopping) environmental degradation. It is important to note that parts of Europe were doing this too: practices such as marling, for instance, raised yields and sustained the soil, but at the cost of significant declines in output per unit of labor.[10] Had other palliatives not succeeded on a huge scale in the late eighteenth and early nineteenth centuries, these areas might have continued still further in a labor-intensive, land-saving direction—in which case Northwest Europe would indeed have looked much more like the Yangzi Delta, the

Lingnan core, or Japanese core areas in the Kanto and Kinai. In Denmark, which may be the part of Europe that went farthest down this road, ecological stabilization was achieved, but industry (even handicrafts) grew very little before 1800, the share of the population living in cities did not increase before 1850, and both wages and per day returns to labor for self-employed farmers declined—all despite well-developed markets and involvement in Western European science.[11]

Moreover, while such strategies were quite useful for sustaining an existing standard of living, this kind of development did not move the society much closer to industrialization and sustainable per capita growth: indeed, if pursued for very long periods of time, they may lead to a balance of factor endowments that potentially inhibit the switch to capital-intensive and energy-intensive technologies.[12] Industrialization required instead a fundamental break with the constraint of production possibilities by the local supply of land—which China did not make but nineteenth-century Europe did, with the help of both fossil fuels and a staggering increase in land-intensive imports. It is probably true, as various scholars have pointed out in response to arguments that profits from the New World were important to European growth, that without the New World the labor and capital that crossed the Atlantic (or at least most of it) could have been profitably deployed nearer home.[13] But if the New World's crucial contribution was not increased financial profits but land-intensive real resources (including much of industrializing England's cotton and later much of its food and timber), it is much less clear that adequate substitutes were available elsewhere.[14]

Based on this sketch, I would argue that the big differences favoring Europe were: (1) advantages in certain, though not all, areas of science and technology; (2) a lucky geographic accident, the location of vast amounts of coal relatively close to the surface in England, where they were close to (a) wealthy areas with very high fuel demands (partly due to especially serious deforestation), (b) good water transport, and (c) a large concentration of artisans who were available to make the crucial improvements on the steam engines that made deeper mining possible and also made it possible to use coal to solve any number of other problems, including the transportation over land of the coal itself; (3) significant unexploited agricultural resources on various parts of the Continent, which could be brought into play to feed growing urban populations and were, ironically, still available in the early nineteenth century in large part because of pre-Napoleonic institutions (especially in Central and Eastern Europe) that had interfered with markets and retarded development (and population growth) far more seriously than any market imperfections in China; and (4) access to the New World, which eventually made available a huge flood of land-intensive products and an outlet for tens of millions of emigrants (who in turn helped bring still more export-producing lands into production).

Probably few people would dispute that at least three of these differences (numbers 1, 2, and 4) mattered, though many would add others; much of *The Great Divergence* is devoted to undermining the case for some of the most commonly cited additions to the list (e.g., differences in property systems) by pointing to China's relative success at exploiting what was possible with its resources and slowly improving technologies and also noting some surprising European shortcomings in getting the most from its existing capital, labor, and especially land. And within this list of four, I put more emphasis than most scholars on the last three points, arguing that, at least for the stages of industrialization down to, say, 1860 (which were the ones that gave Europe its global predominance), science and markets alone could not have provided solutions to some of the resource constraints that faced core regions around the eighteenth-century world without the added benefits of resource bonanzas. Instead, Northwest Europe might well have found itself in a situation not unlike that of the Yangzi Delta or the Kanto and Kinai in Japan, with further gains from trade, specialization, institutional adjustments, and technical advances just barely staying ahead of population growth and even then only with the help of very labor-intensive efforts to maximize agricultural yields while maintaining soil quality, avoiding waste of scarce fuel, and so on.

In such a scenario, any emergent industrial sector would have had to be far smaller, both because of raw material and fuel constraints and because the share of the population that could leave the land would have been smaller: one can imagine fuel-hungry (and strategic) sectors such as iron and steel being particularly affected.[15] Given different factor endowments, technological change might have also taken different directions, saving more land and energy but less labor (and perhaps creating fewer entirely new goods). In all probability, the costs of projecting European power into other parts of the Old World would have been larger and the surplus available to bear those costs much smaller.

This economic scenario would still not rule out the possibility of significant European empires abroad in the nineteenth century. After all, the European forces involved in conquering and holding these empires were relatively small and often not even equipped with the latest weaponry. However, it might well have reduced those empires in scale and duration. Furthermore, Europe's impact on the colonized societies would have been very different had these conquerors—like so many others in the past—brought with them some significant technological advantages concentrated in a few militarily significant sectors (such as iron and steel) rather than a generally transformed economy supporting a much higher standard of living and radically different patterns of work and resting on very large differences in per capita supplies of energy and other primary products.

Could China "Have Been a Contender"?

If European industry—and so its capacity to project military power—had grown much more slowly, East Asia would seem the most likely area to have escaped its gunboats. It was geographically remote, had large and relatively cohesive polities, and had a concept of war more like the West's than that of much of Africa, the Americas, and Southeast Asia (e.g., East Asians, like Europeans and South Asians, generally fought to gain land, not captives, and built large fortifications). Geoffrey Parker has argued quite powerfully that a "military revolution" that did not depend on industrialization nonetheless gave the West decisive advantages over many of its foes (a point I will leave to others to debate),[16] but he agrees that successful assaults on China and Japan required "steamships, steel artillery and sepoys. . . . They did not fall before the military revolution."[17] In such a context, would China have industrialized on its own? (I will omit Japan here for reasons of space, though it may actually have been better situated than China.) Parts of my answer can probably be inferred from the discussion of Europe above; others are laid out below.

It seems to me unlikely, though not impossible, that China circa 1750 was poised to have an industrial revolution anytime soon. This was not, I would argue, because of any of the deficiencies in economic institutions that some scholars have alleged (i.e., an overbearing state, inadequate property rights, a cultural bias against commerce, or a family system that encouraged population growth at the expense of capital accumulation); in all these ways, as I suggested earlier, China was as well-positioned as Europe. But China did face two important handicaps: less favorable resource endowments and less vigorous growth in science and technology. (At least in technology, it should be remembered that this slow growth was off an impressive base of accumulated techniques: this is less clear in at least some branches of science.)

Resource Constraints

Patterns of Growth and the Absence of a "New World"

By the late eighteenth century, the effects of both population growth and
a slowly but steadily rising standard of living (which belies any straightforward "Malthusian crisis") were putting serious pressures on the ecol-
ogy of various parts of China. These pressures were not that different
from those faced by many advanced areas in Europe, but in the absence
of the favorable "resource shocks" discussed earlier (and in the context
of a different political economy), they worked themselves out very differently. Hinterland regions—which had supplied areas such as the Yangzi
Delta with rice, timber, and raw cotton in exchange for manufactures—
boomed, both in population and in their own handicraft manufacturing.[18] This reduced primary products exports to core regions: their
growth essentially stopped, while labor and capital were redeployed out
of manufacturing to manage land and fuel more intensively. After
roughly 1770, population growth in the most advanced region of China
(the Yangzi Delta) virtually ceased, not to permanently surpass the 1770
level until after 1950; other core regions continued to grow but much
more slowly than China as a whole (which roughly doubled in population from 1750 to 1850).

The resulting economic pattern was in many ways "successful" if one
does not judge it by the anachronistic standard of the industrial world:
living standards probably held up fairly well in advanced regions, and
improved in many hinterlands, until the catastrophes of the mid–nineteenth century (which had more to do with a political breakdown, exacerbated by imperialism, than economic failure).[19] Moreover, this pattern
of development, in which best practices were changing fairly slowly but
were diffused effectively across a huge landscape, generally fit the Ming-
Qing notion of what an economy should do: allow as many people as
possible across the huge range of environments in China a reasonably
stable existence as independent producers able to support a family.[20]
However, it did not move China any closer to industrialization; indeed,
its reliance on increasingly labor-intensive kinds of land management to
sustain more people at a comparable standard of living probably biased
innovation in directions that did not make that more likely. By contrast,
it is worth remembering here that the vaunted achievements of the "agricultural revolution" prior to the nineteenth century did not generally
raise the best per acre yields significantly; they enabled roughly constant
yields to be achieved with less labor (and allowed yields on lagging farms

to catch up to more productive ones). That kind of innovation alone could not sustain growth in a situation like that in which China found itself; it only helps if the labor thus liberated can feed itself by trading for primary products from elsewhere.

This resource squeeze did not rule out industrialization, but it biased the direction of innovation in ways that made a rapid wholesale transformation of the Chinese economy—or even the economy of a particular region—much less likely. (It should be remembered here that China is more comparable in size to Europe as a whole than to any European country, and a region such as the Yangzi Delta, with 37 million people in 1770, was larger than any European country other than Russia. Thus, even a breakthrough limited to "only" one such region would have been quite comparable to what happened in the first half of the nineteenth century in Europe, and the industrialization of "Europe" as a whole cannot be said to have happened until after 1945.)

Could China have found a bonanza of "ghost acreage" comparable to what Europeans found in the New World? This seems to me very unlikely without radically altering the world map (so that Fujianese going to trade in Java might have been blown to Acapulco) and/or imagining changes in Chinese politics and society so basic that we would no longer be dealing with "China." Certainly some quite sparsely populated and potentially very fertile land in Southeast Asia lay within easy reach of Chinese ships, and no new technology would have been needed to turn them into "rice bowls" exporting primary products back to the mother country (as happened after 1850 once colonial regimes both enforced property rights in these areas and allowed large numbers of immigrants to come and stake claims to them). But the political conditions for such an initiative were not present in some areas and emerging only slowly in others; and, as the reasons for that were long standing, attempting to remove them would probably not pass the "minimum rewrite" rule.

The costs of conquest, government, and infrastructure development for major Chinese rural settlements in Southeast Asia would have been very large, and there was no clear reason why Chinese merchants should have undertaken those costs without government backing. After all, even in the New World (where the costs of conquest were greatly reduced by the natives' lack of immunity to Old World microbes, while for Chinese going to Southeast Asia the disease gradient ran the other way) these costs were sufficiently large that people would only finance New World colonization if they could find something in the colony to export back home into a market in which high markups were guaranteed. European sovereigns, hungry for tax revenues to support incessant and increasingly expensive warfare, were willing to grant and enforce the necessary monopolies and, as the colonies themselves came to be seen as valuable prizes of war, began to underwrite much of their defense and government directly. And for some of the most lucrative New World exports, geography and climate dictated that an import monopoly was a sales monopoly; sugarcane, for instance, simply would not grow in Europe.[21]

By contrast, although a Chinese merchant/pirate outfit such as the Zheng family empire of the seventeenth century certainly had the capacity to conquer various parts of Southeast Asia (driving the Dutch off Taiwan, capturing and holding various ports all the way to Java for many years, and controlling many of the shipping lanes),[22] it never had access to the sort of protected market back home that would have made it worthwhile to undertake systematic, large-scale settlement. On the contrary, the Zheng flourished only in a dynastic interregnum and never had as firm a grip on any Chinese port as they had on various spots overseas. Even had a less effective Qing military given the short-lived Southern Ming more time to solidify itself, it is far from clear that it would have done so, or that it would have maintained strong ties to the Zheng and their overseas empire.

In more normal times, both the Ming and Qing sometimes supported merchants who traveled abroad (defined as staying away less than three years), but neither dynasty would protect Chinese who settled abroad.[23] The Qing were certainly interested in frontier expansion (acquiring an area roughly half the size of the United States between 1683 and 1759), but this land was in mostly arid and/or mountainous Central Asia and was conquered to create a security zone, not to gain control of economically attractive resources.

For the most part, the Qing did not face the sort of military competition among relative equals that led to innovative fiscal measures and support for mercantilist colonization in the Atlantic world; indeed, since they considered internal discontent the main threat to their rule, the idea of encouraging new, heavily taxed popular "needs" for such things as sugar or tobacco would have made no sense to them.[24] Last, but by no means least, even if the Qing had had a very different attitude toward overseas expansion, almost anything imported from Southeast Asia would have faced substantial domestic competition (Guangdong Province was quite possibly the world's largest sugar producer circa 1750, for instance), which would have limited per unit profit margins on imports.[25] Given all these conditions, the possibility of the Qing providing either the direct or indirect backing that Chinese merchants would have needed to make it worth laying out the huge overhead costs of major agricultural colonies in Southeast Asia seems close to zero.

In the absence of state backing for a Chinese venture, most of these lands remained unexploited until much later. Neither the indigenous kingdoms nor the early European colonial regimes in the islands were willing to grant secure property rights in land to Chinese immigrants; indeed, in some of the more promising areas (near Batavia and Manila), even the lives of members of the large Chinese merchant communities were at substantial risk from recurrent massacres.[26] This situation certainly encouraged these merchants to stay liquid and buy land back home (as many did), if they wanted land, rather than sinking huge amounts of capital into bringing over their countrymen to drain swamps or clear jungles. Meanwhile, none of the rulers of these areas had the capacity to develop these lands as export-oriented rice bowls themselves; they were unwilling (probably because they felt too insecure) to accept a huge flood of Chinese or Indian migrants and (in the case of the colonial regimes) unable to bring in nearly enough Europeans to do this job.[27]

On the mainland, things were somewhat different and perhaps more promising in the long run. Victor Lieberman has suggested more of a trend toward agricultural intensification in mainland Southeast Asia prior to colonialism than we had previously recognized and toward states willing and able to enforce property rights to reclaimed land if this resulted in increased tax revenues. But Lieberman sees this as a cyclical process in which the gradual consolidation of stronger territorial states was punctuated by periodic breakdowns, and in the late eighteenth and early nineteenth centuries all of these states were suffering acute crises.[28] Under these circumstances, the long run was unlikely to arrive soon enough for purposes of a China needing large increases in its supply of basic primary products. In sum, then, while merchants in China's most advanced regions continued to find some new frontiers (such as Southern Manchuria) in which to swap their manufactures for primary products (as old internal frontiers filled up and developed their own handicrafts), they could not find any that were nearly large enough to let them maintain the "small country assumption," and it is hard to find a plausible counterfactual in which they could have done so anytime soon.

Fossil Fuels

The other important positive resource shock that Northwest Europe (at first mostly England) experienced was the turn to fossil fuels; each ton of coal mined provided roughly as much energy as the sustainable harvest from 1.0 to 1.4 acres of prime temperate zone woodland,[29] and coal production soared in the eighteenth and especially nineteenth centuries.[30] Here, too, China had serious disadvantages. It may be easier to imagine these barriers being overcome than the barriers to creating a Chinese New World, but the obstacles were still large enough to make the probability of a fossil fuel breakthrough anytime soon low.

Although China has lots of coal, and had used coal for centuries, there were various, largely accidental reasons why a fundamental shift to fossil fuels like that made by England was relatively unlikely in China's advanced regions. The eighteenth century Lower Yangzi region—China's richest and one of its most deforested—stretched its supplies by trading along riverine and coastal routes for wood and bean cake fertilizer. (The fertilizer allowed people to burn for fuel grasses and crop residues that would otherwise have had to be returned to the soil.)[31] While such trade-based palliatives did not rule out simultaneous experimentation with fossil fuels—the two coexisted elsewhere and might have done so in the Lower Yangzi without leaving many traces in the documents—it was hardly likely that coal in particular would have attracted much attention from the Lower Yangzi's artisans and entrepreneurs: there was little coal either in the region itself or in places easily accessible to its traders. China's nine southern provinces have just 1.8 percent of contemporary China's coal reserves and its eleven eastern provinces 8 percent; by contrast, the northwestern province of Shanxi plus Inner Mongolia have 61.4 percent.[32] Some coal mines did operate in various parts of South China, and within marketing range of Beijing in the north,[33] but they were mostly small, poorly positioned to take advantage of China's richest and most fuel-hungry market, and, especially in Ming times, intermittently hampered by inconsistent government policies.[34] By far the largest deposits, which theoretically might have justified major investments in production and transportation improvements, were those in the distant and landlocked northwest; since the price of coal in this area doubled with every twenty-five miles it moved over land,[35] such improvements would have had to be very dramatic to make coal an affordable solution for the fuel-hungry Yangzi Valley. (Transport costs were also the key to whether particular concentrations of potential fuel—whether timber, peat, or coal—were worth exploiting in preindustrial Europe.)[36]

While the returns to linking China's northwestern coal deposits with the Yangzi Delta seem so huge in retrospect that it is tempting to imagine some people making an enormous effort to do so, it is not clear how they could have done it, and most of the returns to such a project that we can now imagine were invisible ex ante. Indeed the Yangzi Delta in particular is so poor in power sources—it has no coal or peat, never had much forest, is essentially flat (making its water useless for power), and is even poorly positioned for wind power—and in ores of all kinds—that one scholar has spoken of it following a "super light industrial path" in which energy-intensive production was simply absent from the region and its products were either acquired through trade or used very sparingly. Woks, for instance, used little iron and stir-frying in them economized on fuel.[37] If he is right, developers of northwestern coal not only would have had to imagine that they could extract huge amounts of coal and crack a seemingly insuperable transport problem but that suddenly cheap power would lead the Lower Yangzi to undertake various kinds of production in which it had not previously engaged. Meanwhile, northwestern coal miners, operating in a generally infertile, inaccessible, and backward region, were not particularly likely to learn of technical developments elsewhere that they might have been able to apply to their problems and had little chance of encountering artisans who had learned precise workmanship in specialized luxury crafts such as clock making. Such artisans did exist, and their skills, if not their numbers, seem to have been not far behind their Western counterparts—but they were almost all in the Yangzi Delta or along the southeast coast, where there was a veritable craze for clocks and mechanical toys with elaborate jack work.[38] And even if northwestern mine operators had seen how to improve their mining techniques, they had no reason to think that extracting more coal would allow them to capture a vastly expanded market: seemingly insuperable transport problems would still have separated their mines from the rich but ecologically needy fuel users of China's major cities.[39]

Finally, the biggest technical problem faced by northwestern Chinese coal miners was fundamentally different from that in England. English mines tended to fill with water, so a strong pump was needed to remove that water. But in the northwestern Chinese coal mines the water problem was secondary: instead they were often so arid that spontaneous combustion was a constant threat. It was this problem—one that required ventilation rather than powerful pumps—that preoccupied the compiler of the most important technical manual of the period, and while the problem was never fully solved, at least one contemporary historian of mining has pronounced the approaches described in that manual quite sophisticated for their time.[40] Even if better ventilation had ameliorated this problem—or if people wanted coal badly enough to pay for this high level of danger—solving it would not have also helped solve the problem of transporting coal (and things in general), as the steam engines that pumped out Britain's mines did. It is important to remember in this context that early steam engines—prototypes of which had been developed in various times and places but not pursued—were so cumbersome, dangerous, and fuel hungry that initially they were seldom worth deploying anywhere except at the pithead of a coal mine, where fuel was virtually free.[41] Thus, the steam engine made the coal bonanza possible, and having coal mines that needed draining but were well worth exploiting and close enough to numerous artisans to facilitate improvements helped make steam engines worth tinkering with and perfecting. Overall, then, while general skill, resources, and economic conditions in "China," taken as an abstract whole, may not have been much less conducive to a coal/steam revolution than those in Europe as a whole—and were probably adequate to make such a breakthrough possible if they had come into combination—the distribution of those endowments made the chances of such a revolution much dimmer than in Europe.

There were a few coal mines that were closer to Jiangnan's market and artisans but not many. The mines in Xuzhou and Suxian in northern Jiangsu, not too far from the Grand Canal, would have been the best positioned among the few mines potentially within reach of the Yangzi Delta, but even there the cost of coal in Qing times doubled by the time it reached the county seat, which was also the canal port.[42] Like their counterparts farther north, these mines had been part of a heavy industrial complex (particularly focused on iron and salt production) in Song times and seem never to have fully recovered from a series of disasters (including huge shifts in the Yellow and Huai rivers and Mongol removal of most of the area's iron workers) in the twelfth through the fourteenth centuries that made the surrounding region poor. In the eighteenth century, when the government decided to encourage coal production in this area with the explicit goal of alleviating the Yangzi Delta's fuel shortage, it also chose to give the mining licenses to poor and unemployed people, who mostly dug small, shallow mines.[43] (The mines near Beijing were also generally small and not heavily capitalized, in part because the state preferred to avoid creating large concentrations of potentially rowdy miners.)[44] While it seems unlikely that even better capitalized mines would have achieved the major breakthroughs needed to transform China's energy, transport, and metals sectors, having such small opera tors in charge at the few sites in China where coal was within relatively easy reach of both large markets and concentrations of skilled artisans certainly did not improve the odds.

Still, this part of China's resource squeeze is much easier to imagine being reversed in a single, relatively uncomplicated counterfactual than the lack of a New World type of land bonanza—we could simply imagine that the northern Jiangsu mines had been closer to the size of the huge mines of the northwest. Under those circumstances, it is fairly easy to imagine another canal being dug to link this coal to the Grand Canal; much longer canals had been dug to move coal to iron smelters and other fuel-using industries near the capital (Kaifeng) during the pre-1200 coal boom. Thus one can imagine, without too much strain, one part of Europe's three-part resource bonanza being duplicated in China; and so it does not strain the minimum-rewrite rule to imagine the window for industrialization, which I have argued was closed by resource constraints, being kept open a while longer. And Chinese science and technology were probably up to the task of creating an economical steam engine and many of the other technologies of the First Industrial Revolution (as we shall see). Certainly one can imagine a large increase in coal mining had the resources been more accessible and in the production of various fuel-intensive goods (iron and glass, for instance) with potentially significant implications for the economy, military capacities, and perhaps also for further experimentation and technical progress. But to see what the chances were that China would have been able to create sustained per capita growth, we need to turn to an important disadvantage, which I discussed only briefly in *The Great Divergence:* the state of Chinese science and technology circa 1600–1850.

Science and Technology: Limits and Possibilities of a China "Left Alone" Longer

Chinese science and technology, though not (as some have charged) completely stagnant in the Ming and Qing, were less well poised to create a sustained run of technological breakthroughs than in Northwestern Europe. Technological change continued in the seventeenth and eighteenth centuries but at a slower rate than in the tenth to fourteenth centuries and with a bias toward land-saving rather than either labor- or capital-saving technologies. Chinese science, some branches of which went through what might be described as stagnation or even regression from the fourteenth through the early seventeenth centuries, had begun to move back onto what seems, in retrospect, a more promising track in the seventeenth and eighteenth centuries. Lost mathematical knowledge was recovered,[45] philosophy moved in a more materialistic direction, European mathematical and scientific ideas (as filtered through Christian missionaries) were intensively studied, and lots of new empirical work was done in a variety of areas. (Some of the more active areas, such as optics and especially acoustics, were not very rich in immediate economic applications but represented new developments in physical science nonetheless.) A huge boom in the publishing of popular medical and agronomic texts indicates a fairly wide interest in at least practical "science,"[46] and far more literati than we had previously suspected were interested in more abstract developments in the physical sciences.[47]

Perhaps equally important, in the long run, the early Qing seems to have been marked by important developments in the way in which knowledge was produced and shared. In an essay on the Ming thinker Xie Zhaozhe (1567–1624), Mark Elvin notes that he showed at least some signs of all but one of what Alastair Crombie has identified as the characteristic styles of thought of Western science.[48] The one exception was the "postulational": a deficit that, even if it was societywide in Xie's time, was significantly reduced as various Chinese learned Euclidean geometry in the seventeenth century. (Initially, Euclid's work did not excite much interest, but as it proved to be extremely valuable for astronomical work, which people did care about, it came to be more widely studied.)

However, Elvin also notes an important puzzle with broad implications. Although Xie was a strongly empirical thinker who believed hypotheses had to be validated or invalidated on the basis of observed facts, he had no systematic method for weeding out falsehoods in the written statements of others: Elvin notes that Xie repeatedly reasoned logically about some natural phenomenon but made the wrong decision about which of various printed "facts" were actually true. Xie was diligent about searching the copious printed sources available to him—and the range of such sources would grow exponentially in the sixteenth through the eighteenth centuries—but institutions did not apparently exist to expose particular factual claims to continuing public scrutiny and report the results of reevaluation in easily accessible and verifiable ways.[49] Even more striking, Elvin adds that, though Xie had a wide network of correspondents across the Chinese empire, it never seems to have occurred to him to enlist these people in a search for data relevant to his hypotheses, nor did they use him in this way. Thus, while Xie had numerous theories about geology, epidemiology, nutrition, and zoology that could have been confirmed or overturned by systematic observation in other parts of China, he never attempted to organize anything of the sort. As Elvin puts it, what was missing was the idea of a shared "'program,' a plan of collective systematic work" of a kind that seems to have emerged in sixteenth- and seventeenth-century Europe.[50] In chapter 10 of this volume, Joel Mokyr places considerable emphasis on this shared knowledge base and a network of people who were collaboratively and competitively expanding it as a crucial precondition for sustained technological development, and he argues that nothing very close to it existed outside the West.

But in the later seventeenth and eighteenth centuries, we see exactly this kind of network emerging in China as part of the so-called empirical research movement. Benjamin Elman notes a number of crucial developments among the increasingly dominant *kao zheng* (evidential research) scholars of the seventeenth and eighteenth centuries.[51] Notation books that recorded the new data a scholar found replaced the records of dialogues and spiritual progress common in the fifteenth and sixteenth centuries and were increasingly exchanged among scholars. Mathematics and mathematical astronomy were increasingly used to verify dates in ancient texts and expose impossible claims to have witnessed certain events; textual scholars were expected either to have the requisite mathematical skills or to consult (and credit) people who did. Collaboration among scholars with various specialties was increasingly common and was expected to produce improvements on ancient texts, not just recovery of them. In addition, increasing numbers of publications described themselves as follow-up studies to earlier works (whether or not the author had any personal connection with the earlier one), aiming to extend or adjust earlier findings in the light of specific new evidence.[52] Scholars working on the reconstruction of ancient tools, musical instruments, and other artifacts not only emphasized the need for mathematics but built actual models, published the plans they had followed, and encouraged others to try to reproduce their results and check them against archaeological finds.[53] Though no scholarly periodicals existed, letters about scholarly matters were considered public documents and were widely copied and circulated. Precise citation of sources became expected, and a new emphasis on making an original scholarly contribution emerged. In part because of this new emphasis on originality and progress, debates about scholarly priority became common (and sometimes heated); this also indicates that research methodologies and data were being widely exchanged, making such determinations difficult while testifying to precisely the sort of common research program that Elvin finds absent in the sixteenth century.[54] More and more branches of learning were affected by strategies of inquiry and standards of proof heavily influenced by mathematics on the one hand and experimentation on the other and by an expectation of progress.[55] Also interesting are the frequent references to scientific and mathematical techniques introduced by the Jesuits (and to the use of the Roman alphabet as a convenient device for recording phonological research)—particularly because the court had generally kept the missionaries at court in Beijing, hundreds of miles from the scholarly centers in the Lower Yangzi region (and later in Changsha and Canton), where we find people discussing their findings.[56] There was no close analogue to the European scientific revolution in late imperial China and no sign of significant progress in some fields that would eventually prove crucial to Europe's Second Industrial Revolution (e.g., electricity), but the climate may have been more conducive to such developments in the future than Mokyr suggests.

Still, it requires some very strong (and probably unjustified) assumptions to say that these trends would necessarily have continued if left undisturbed or that had they continued they would have produced effects comparable to those of Europe's scientific and technological breakthroughs. In the crucial matter of sharing and verifying information as part of a research "program," the patterns described by Elman had barely penetrated many of the lines of inquiry we would call the natural sciences.

Consider, for instance, the study of environmental change. China's "long eighteenth century" is full of important observations and hypotheses, some of them occurring in advance of the same points being established in Europe. The Kangxi emperor, looking back on many years of receiving reports on weather throughout the empire, made some important and largely accurate guesses about climatic change; the local official Niu Yunzhu, among others, gathered information about the effects of deforestation on future erosion, the ability of the soil to hold water, and perhaps even the extent of future precipitation itself; the early nineteenth century scholar Dong Bi'nan, looking at the long written record of everything from what crops were grown in his area to the frequency of tiger attacks on villages, made several shrewd observations about human activities, habitat change, and extinction; and scholars worried about environmental problems in the Lower Yangzi region figured out fairly subtle and difficult-to-observe ecological relationships, such as how changes in ground cover were lowering the water table.[57] At least some of their insights were ahead of what Europeans had figured out at the same time.[58] But this knowledge was not systematically reported to anyone outside the localities involved (where it had policy implications). Thus when Niu, for instance, wanted to know how deforestation was affecting snowmelt, runoff, and soil moisture in his new jurisdiction, his approach was to summon an elderly and respected farmer from the area. Though a learned man, he apparently did not consult accounts of what had happened in other jurisdictions, and his conclusions were placed in a policy memorial that, as far as I know, did not circulate more widely until it was published in a collection of writings on statecraft eighty years later. The contrast to late-eighteenth-century Europe—in which a half century of odd weather (the so-called European monsoon) and related changes gave birth to systematic efforts to collect and share daily rainfall and temperature data from numerous locations, both in Europe and its colonial dependencies[59]—is striking, though just a few decades before China (where the state was already gathering monthly rainfall records for every prefecture in the empire)[60] would have compared quite favorably to Europe in the gathering of meteorological data. By the early nineteenth century we find more signs of a systematic program of research on these matters: scholar-landlords and scholar-officials in the lowlands of the Yangzi Delta seem to have been fairly well informed about changes in land use in highland areas well upstream of them and to have made use of local histories and anecdotal reports from those places to test hypotheses and scrutinize the predictions of people advocating particular state policies. But even at this fairly late date, it is hard to tell how systematic and organized a research program existed, even in the presence of hotly contested issues affecting direct material interests, which hinged in part on an understanding of the workings of nature.[61] Certainly the discussion was less scientifically sophisticated than the eighteenth-century English arguments about the building of water mills and their effects on factories downstream cited by Margaret Jacob as evidence of a spreading "scientific culture."[62] And it is also significant that as far as we know artisans were largely outside even such networks of "scientific correspondence" as were developing in seventeenth- and eighteenth-century China.

The development of correspondence, systematic citation practices, meetings, and so on to systematically share data on geology, epigraphy, historical phonology, and other fields is nonetheless quite significant. Among other things, it establishes that many of the villains often asserted to have made a scientific community devoted to cumulative empirically based progress impossible in China (a "despotic" state; an "established" Confucianism, with its supposed lack of interest in the material world, belief that everything important was already known, and/or tendency to sweep all talented young men into the study of a sterile exam curriculum; the lack of universities or academies with secure corporate legal identities and privileges; and the absence of Western-style jurisprudence as a model for both the establishment of "facts" and the application of invariant rules)[63] were less of a barrier than has been claimed. Thus, China might have been in the process of creating such a culture of shared scientific inquiry—with all that implies for speeding up the rate at which new discoveries are made and slowing the loss of old knowledge—by its own path not too far behind early modern Europe. But the best we can say is that something of this sort was not foreclosed and its emergence might have been no more surprising than Europe's scientific revolution appears looking forward from the early Renaissance. And even had it emerged, a more recognizably "modern" Chinese science might well have applied itself to problems different from those of its European counterpart.

It would certainly be a huge stretch to say that, if left alone, China would have developed the technologies of the Second Industrial Revolution (based on electricity and systematic chemistry) anytime soon. Thus the assumption of various Marxist and Chinese nationalist scholars that had China developed "capitalism" sustained industrial growth would have followed seems quite unwarranted.[64] Here I should also note one way in which I was surprised as I worked through this counterfactual. While I never shared the position that industrialization was bound to follow from any particular set of economic arrangements, I was inclined to minimize the importance of science in the early stages of the process, while emphasizing "tinkering." But if one assumes that "sustained" growth would have eventually required exploiting electricity and the chemical processes that allowed coal and petroleum by-products to be turned into substitutes for so many vegetable and mineral products, the importance of science becomes undeniable. In fact, if one pushes it far enough, a belief in the sufficiency of tinkering for the First Industrial Revolution, and in the indefinite sustainability of that breakthrough without the further advances that occurred in the late 1800s, would threaten to reinstate something close to the position I was criticizing—namely, the belief that capitalism was bound to lead to industrial capitalism—having added only the proviso that resource shortages cannot be too severe. But one could make a stronger case for a more modest but still very significant claim: that given a different resource situation China's markets, skills, and other endowments could have pulled off a long period of sustained growth and industrial development based on First Industrial

Revolution technologies that were accessible without modern science. Such growth might not have lasted indefinitely, as Western technological growth has so far, but it might well have lasted several decades and given us a world with a strikingly different, less Western-dominated, political and military history.

Joel Mokyr (in chapter 10 of this volume) suggests that the possibility of a Chinese steam engine (and thus, presumably, a concomitant evolution in fossil fuel use, iron and steel use, and transportation) was considerably lower than suggested here. While acknowledging that the Chinese had the crucial bits of scientific knowledge and artisanal skill (e.g., in metallurgy), he nonetheless finds it "telling" that the relevant knowledge dates back close to two millennia in China without steam engines ever having been developed for regular use prior to their importation from the West, while in Europe working models appeared within roughly fifty years of the demonstration of atmospheric pressure. While this is an interesting contrast, I am not sure how telling it really is. The argument hinges on an implicit assumption that the epistemic environment in China was not changing much, so that the failure to convert prototypes into working machines in the past has predictive value for what would have happened in an undisturbed nineteenth-century China. Given the changes in intellectual climate during the late Ming and early Qing discussed earlier, this assumption seems shaky. After all, an advanced Martian surveying European history down to 1600 might have said the same thing, since steam-powered temple doors were known in Egypt shortly before the Roman conquest, but nothing further happened in the next eighteen hundred years. I am thus inclined to stick to my more sanguine view of the possibilities for a Chinese steam engine and to my claim that some of the principal obstacles had to do with accidents of geography, supplies of fuel and other resources, and perhaps government mining policies rather than with technological or scientific problems per se.

Many of the key technologies of the First Industrial Revolution—particularly the steam engine and its applications to transport and factory production—do seem to have been potentially solvable with existing Chinese science and would have been more likely to be solved if different factor endowments had encouraged work in those particular directions as much as they did in England. The Chinese had long understood atmospheric pressure and had the basics for a steam engine. Indeed, Needham argues that the common Chinese box bellows, which used rotary motion to produce a blast of hot air, was essentially a steam engine backward and the gear work needed to convert rotary to linear motion had been available for centuries. A small toy boat powered by a steam engine had been demonstrated by a Jesuit priest at court in the eighteenth century, and Needham, at least, thinks he was working from both Chinese and European models.[65] And while Chinese mines of all kinds tended to be small scale, not very well capitalized, and surprisingly backward technologically, given the sophisticated use of (for instance) water pumps in other settings, it seems quite possible that once they had been in operation a bit longer (and so had depleted the deposits closest to the surface) those few mines that were well positioned with respect to the Yangzi Delta core might have found the means to adopt much better technologies (such as steam-powered pumps) had they been known. One could then imagine a gradually improving steam engine finding more and more uses, as occurred in Europe. But the odds of this happening before, say, 1900 without the machines being introduced from Europe were probably below 50 percent.

Moreover, even if we imagine a Chinese breakthrough in the related areas of coal, steam, iron, and steel, it seems much less likely that this would have turned into the sort of string of subsequent innovations and (so far) sustained growth that has occurred in the West; as far as I can tell, Chinese science would not soon have been up to the task of making major breakthroughs in (for instance) electricity and organic chemistry. And I would certainly agree with Mokyr that, despite a large number of skilled artisans, the odds against making most of the inventions central to these later stages of the Industrial Revolution by tinkering are too high to make this plausible. (This conclusion should certainly offend partisans of the Marxist and Chinese nationalist schools and, perhaps, in a different way, hard-core followers of Douglass North, for whom the rate of invention seems to be mostly a function of property rights in ideas.)

A Different Counterfactual: With Sino-Western Contact but No Opium War

What might have made the odds for a Chinese breakthrough better, however, would have been a situation in which one still had European expansion but in a weaker form.[66] If we imagine a Europe (as suggested earlier) with a much smaller industrial sector, because of more severe resource pressures, but with many of the same inventions, one might also imagine a rather different relationship between Europe and East Asia, one in which, unable to insist on an open market for opium, Europeans might have instead sold China more Indian cotton (as they did for a while before opium took off),[67] more clocks, toys with elaborate gears, eye-glasses, and telescopes (for which there was a real craze among the elite in coastal Fujian Province and which Chinese artisans reproduced quite successfully),[68] and various other such goods, and in which the science and mathematics introduced by missionaries (which did find a receptive audience among some seventeenth- and eighteenth-century literati)[69] might have had a better chance of taking hold before a catastrophic political breakdown like the one that occurred when domestic problems and foreign pressures intersected in the mid-nineteenth century. (In another context, R. Bin Wong has suggested that under slightly different circumstances Europeans might have paid for some of their tea by selling arms;[70] had that trade taken off before China began to fragment politically, it might have solidified the Qing hold rather than undermined it further.) If one thus imagines China granted a few more decades of peace—not because the West did not show up at all but because it showed up differently—it becomes easier to imagine a major economic breakthrough than if China had simply been "left alone." At least parts of coastal China might have followed an economic path more similar to that of Meiji Japan. (The two were probably not far apart economically in the first half of the nineteenth century, and, except for having a somewhat larger window on the West, Japan's science was very similar to China's.) Under such a scenario, the extension of Western knowledge and trade might have done much to block the further extension of its political hegemony. One might still also need a major relaxation of Chinese resource constraints, which would hardly be certain but cannot be ruled out. Even in reality, parts of China benefited considerably from growing imports of rice from Southeast Asian deltas in the late nineteenth century, wood from various parts of the Pacific Rim, and so on, mostly paid for with light industrial exports, services, and remittances from overseas Chinese. With a more competitive manufacturing sector, and without the huge balance of payments problems created by opium imports and indemnities for lost wars, these imports could presumably have been much larger. And, as discussed earlier, a steam engine placed on ship or on rails could have delivered massive amounts of fuel to the Yangzi Delta, even if we do not imagine that coal being differently located. Of course, the combined probability of all these events is not large, even if individually they seem fairly likely, and even taken together they would not guarantee two centuries of sustained Chinese per capita growth without a steady stream of further technological change. So the combined probability of China being as thoroughly transformed as Europe, Japan, South Korea, and

Taiwan have been over the last two centuries would remain remote, even without damage from Western imperialism. But a significantly better nineteenth and twentieth century for China—both economically and politically—does not seem so unlikely had the West been in contact with East Asia but lacked the industrial edge that allowed them to inflict devastating military blows fairly cheaply. And imagining such a scenario has its uses for discussing explanations of what did happen—to which I now turn.

Lessons of the Exercise—for Others and for Me

Whom should this last counterfactual—of a more beneficent East-West encounter leading to more rapid Chinese development—offend? How has working through it affected me?

In addition to the groups already mentioned, it seems to me this could offend a wide variety of people—from "modernization theorists" to strong believers in "moral economy" to many Marxists (or former Marxists turned geographically deterministic anti-Marxists, such as Wittfogel). All of these schools share a belief that China was a "traditional society" (or "feudal" or "oriental" or "Confucian" society, depending on the particular writer) that, for better or worse, could only have become modern by being blasted out of its entrenched way of doing things and being forced to adopt alien ways under threat of permanent subjugation.[71] If, on the contrary, a more limited and consensual set of contacts might have resulted in enough Western science and technology being grafted onto China's existing ways of doing things to result in substantial industrialization (especially if it was also accompanied by more accessible coal and/or a surge in raw materials imports), then a whole series of binary oppositions that have been common in history and social science do not hold water; modernity becomes (as much work on both early modern and more recent East Asian growth has also suggested)[72] much less of an indivisible "take it or leave it" whole that must transform an entire culture for sustained economic growth to occur.

Indeed, it was largely my unhappiness with such stark and all-encompassing contrasts between "the West and the rest" that led me into this research. If there had been significant similarities between the Chinese and European economies as late as the 1700s, then it seemed unlikely that they were as fundamentally dissimilar in their potential for sustained per capita growth as much of the literature suggested; the more I looked, the greater the similarities circa 1750 seemed. Moreover, it seemed to me that many of the theories that posited some essential European cultural characteristic that made a breakthrough uniquely likely (e.g., Landes's "enterprise,"[73] which lumps together scientific curiosity, entrepreneurial drive and the freedom to pursue it, and geographic exploration and expansionism into a single phenomenon) or some basic Chinese failure (e.g., "despotism" or "traditionalism," said to inhibit all of these) were so broad that they could not possibly help us specify what differences really mattered, much less help us see the relationships among various differences and similarities. Thus counterfactuals that were at least in part beyond culture, such as the location of coal deposits or even continents, were attractive; so were counterfactuals that reversed only events a relatively short time before the nineteenth century. (Although changing geology or geography does, in one sense, involve going way back in time, it need not involve changing any human events relevant to our story before the relatively recent point at which the resource or place in question begins to matter for Chinese or European growth.)

Sometimes seeing what might have happened if we change these antecedent conditions helped me identify other factors that were more firmly embedded in Chinese culture and society, while simultaneously defining them more narrowly and precisely than most earlier comparisons did. Thus, for instance, the Chinese empire was not generally "xenophobic" and hostile to foreign trade, as is sometimes claimed—and Chinese society in general was still less so—but the regime did have an enduring set of priorities, rooted in their orientation toward reproducing empire, that made them indifferent or even hostile to overseas colonization and mercantilism. Similarly, Confucian paternalism and preferences for stability did not make the regime hostile to commerce, or to technical innovation in general, but they did make it suspicious of miners (who tended to form large, often migratory groups of males not firmly embedded in families) and prone to encouraging mining only when it met state needs (e.g., southwestern copper mines that provided specie) or helped succor the poor (the small-scale coal mining in northern Jiangsu discussed earlier).[74] While I would not say that a "minimal rewrite" of history would suffice to make independent Chinese industrialization very likely, I think it makes it plausible, and that slightly less minimal but still reasonable rewrites make big changes in results possible until roughly 1800. As I argued earlier, slowing European growth (without wholly stopping it), even as late as the late-eighteenth century, seems to me quite a bit easier than jump-starting Chinese growth in a world without foreign science; if many conditions need to be met for industrialization, it stands to reason that it can be at least partially derailed within the minimal-rewrite rule.

For me, though, the main payoff of the counterfactual exercise comes from the joint result of considering both the Chinese and the European counterfactuals. That payoff comes not from imagining an industrialized China and a nonindustrialized Europe, since the joint probability of those two changes seems to me fairly small and the consequences so large as to be almost unfathomable. What strikes me as important about combining the two is that it changes the exercise we are engaged in. Asking "could China have 'succeeded'?" or "could Europe have 'failed'?" alone leads us back toward taking one path (usually Europe's) as normative and expected and asking why the other did not take it and therefore did not succeed or fail. Putting the two counterfactuals together, I think, is more useful for imagining whether there were other paths to similar results, and allowing that a different destination was possible along either path forces us toward more nuanced hypotheses of why what did actually happen was at least likely—hypotheses in which some differences may not have mattered or may have even weighed in the opposite direction from the difference in outcomes. Thus, a combination of counterfactuals seems to me to help us see the changing nature and direction of various China/Europe differences at various moments and to see how certain differences that might have seemed quite salient at one moment might later be unimportant or even related to the emergence of differences in the opposite direction. An example of such a difference would be Europe's relatively low per acre yields in the early modern period, which one might have predicted would be a major brake on growth but turned out to matter very little in the age of soaring trans-Atlantic trade and rising off-farm contributions to farm production such as petrochemical fertilizers. Since there are crucial relationships about which we still know very little—we do not know much, for instance, about likely demographic responses to changing resource constraints in either China or Europe, which makes estimates of how altering those constraints would have changed per capita growth very speculative—the value of the exercise seems to me less in trying to go far forward into any particular counterfactual world than in using a variety of them to challenge conventional ideas of "inevitable" trajectories and to eliminate or narrow hopelessly broad explanatory factors.

What surprises me most, however, is something different, which did not emerge from imagining either a radically different China or a radically different Europe in isolation but imagining an interaction of a

China and Europe that had both been more modestly altered (in line, I think, with the minimal-rewrite rule in each case, though perhaps not once we consider joint probabilities). This was the robustness of at least the First Industrial Revolution somewhere as an outcome of movements in various parts of the early modern world. In *The Great Divergence,* I emphasized that I thought Europe needed several favorable circumstances—some self-generated, some largely happenstance or conjunctural—to industrialize as it did and that we needed to take seriously the historical possibility that perhaps nobody would have industrialized; I did not think the most likely alternative was that if Europe did not somebody else clearly would have. I would still argue that with different global conjunctures European scientific and technological advances could have produced much more limited growth, which would have been neither self-sustaining nor sufficient to give Europe a truly global political hegemony. But once one grants that something new was happening in European science, and grants the importance of the same global conjunctures that I pointed to in my book (the "discovery" and depopulation of the New World, Chinese silver demand, European navigational advances, the marketization of various large economies around the world, missionaries who were also bearers of European math and science, and so on), it becomes easier than I would have imagined to picture industrialization, including the fossil fuel revolution, sprouting in at least a couple of places. And while fossil fuels and steam power alone would hardly have given us contemporary "first-world" living standards, they would probably have sufficed to change the material world more than anything else in the preceding few millennia: shattering Braudel's "biological old regime" by relaxing the food versus fuel tradeoff, allowing unprecedented speed and volume in transport and travel (and thus creating enormous changes in the division of labor and comparative advantage), making unprecedented amounts of iron and steel available, allowing enormous quantities of earth and rock to be removed or displaced, and so on.

Thus, even if less favorable resource endowments made industrialization in Europe slower and more halting, this new wave of growth was still unlikely to peter out completely like various earlier rounds of intensive growth (in which technological change was less based on applied science and new developments had been less rapidly communicated across vast spaces). So if still not persuaded that the rise of the West to global dominance was bound to happen, I am now increasingly prone to think that the emergence of sustained economic growth—one of its most salient features—was not quite as dependent on coincidence as I had implied. Perhaps, then, the emergence of economic "modernity" somewhere (with Western scientific advances playing a key role) is more robust than the rise of the West as a geographic and political condition

NOTES

1. Readers familiar with Kenneth Pomeranz, *The Great Divergence: China, Europe, and the Making of the Modern World Economy* (Princeton: Princeton University Press, 2000) may find much of the first half of this chapter familiar; from p. 248 onward, the proportion of new material gets much larger.

2. Ibid., 36–40.

3. Ibid., 31–43, 116–52, app. F. My claims about standards of living (and various other things) were challenged in Philip Huang, "Development or Involution in Eighteenth Century Britain and China," *Journal of Asian Studies* 61, no. 2 (May 2002): 501–38, with a response from me in the same issue ("Beyond the East-West Binary: Resituating Development Paths in the Eighteenth Century World," *Journal of Asian Studies* 61, no. 2 [May 2002]: 539–90), and in a further exchange between us in the February 2003 issue 62, no. 1 (157–81). Standard of living issues are particularly emphasized in my response (175–79). A series of essays by Robert Allen comparing the Yangzi Delta and England so far also suggests comparable living standards and real wages into the late eighteenth century. See his "Agricultural Productivity and Rural Incomes in England and the Yangzi Delta c. 1620–1820," "Real Wages in Europe and Asia: A First Look at the Long-Term Patterns," and "Mr Lockyer Meets the Index Number Problem: The Standard of Living in Canton and London in 1704," all accessed on August 23, 2004, at http://www.economics.ox.ac.uk/Members/robert.allen/default.htm

4. Pomeranz, *The Great Divergence*, 124, 288.

5. This would be more appropriate in that it would allow us to compare the richest and most densely populated parts of China and Europe to each other, but I have eschewed it in order to make comparisons between areas growing similar crops and to bias the comparisons as much as possible in favor of Europe. A fuller discussion appears in ibid., chap. 5.

6. Ibid., 215–27, 303–6.

7. Ibid., 228–42, 307–12. Based on evidence I have seen more recently, I might now make these claims a bit more equivocally, but I think their basic outlines stand.

8. See generally ibid., 215–42. On timber prices, see Ernest Labrousse, *Esquisse du mouvement des prix et des revenus en France au XVIIIème siècle* (1933; reprint, Paris: Librairie Dalloz, 1984), 343, 346–47; and Li Bozhong, "Ming Qing shiqi Jiangnan de mucai wenti (The Timber Problem in Ming-Qing Jiangnan)," *Zhongguo shehui jingji shi yanjiu* 1 (1994): 86–89, 93–94. On deforestation, see Michael Williams, "Forests," in B. L. Turner et al., *The Earth as Transformed by Human Action* (Cambridge: Cambridge University Press, 1990), 181; H. C. Darby, "The Clearing of the Woodland in Europe" in *Man's Role in Changing*

the Face of the Earth, ed. B. L. Thomas (Chicago: University of Chicago Press, 1956), 203–4; and Ling Daxie, "Wo guo senlin ziyuan de bianqian (Changes in China's Forest Resources)," *Zhongguo nongshi* 3, no. 2 (1983): 34–35. On flooding, see Peter Perdue, *Exhausting the Earth: State and Peasant in Hunan, 1500–1850* (Cambridge: Harvard University Press, 1987), 196, 202, 219–33; and Anne Osborne, "The Local Politics of Land Reclamation in the Lower Yangzi Highlands," *Late Imperial China* 15, no. 1 (June 1994): 1–46. On gullying, soil degradation, and stagnant yields, see Piers Blaikie and Harold Brookfield, *Land Degradation and Society* (London and New York: Methuen, 1987), 129–140; and Mauro Ambrosoli, *The Wild and the Sown* (Cambridge: Cambridge University Press, 1997). On erosion, sandstorms, and so on, see Thorkild Kjaergaard, *The Danish Revolution, 1500–1800* (Cambridge: Cambridge University Press, 1994), 18–22.

9. For discussions of many of these problems (though with little on England), see Blaikie and Brookfield, *Land Degradation and Society,* 129–40; and Kjaergaard, *The Danish Revolution* (which, despite its title, has some good examples from beyond Denmark). For some English examples (though without any quantification), see Ambrosoli, *The Wild and the Sown,* 367, 374, 392–95, 412.

10. See, for instance, Kjaergaard, *The Danish Revolution,* 151, 158, 160.

11. Ibid., 55–56, 151–60.

12. See Kaoru Sugihara, "The European Miracle and the East Asian Miracle: Towards a New Global Economic History," *Sangyō to Keizai* 11, no. 2 (1996): 27–48; and "Agriculture and Industrialization: The Japanese Experience," in *Agriculture and Economic Growth,* ed. Peter Mathias and John Davis (Oxford: Blackwell, 1997), 148–66. For a somewhat different argument about how "premodern economic growth" as a way of dealing with ecological constraints can become self-perpetuating and make industrialization less likely, see Mark Elvin, "Blood and Statistics: Reconstructing the Population Dynamics of Late Imperial China from the Biographies of Virtuous Women in Local Gazetteers," in *Chinese Women in the Imperial Past: New Perspectives,* ed. Harriet Zurndorfer (Leiden: Brill, 1999), 135–222.

13. See, for instance, Jan DeVries, *The Economy of Europe in an Age of Crisis, 1600–1750* (New York: Cambridge University Press, 1976), 213; and Patrick K. O'Brien, "European Economic Development: The Contribution of the Periphery," *Economic History Review* 35, no. 1 (February 1982): 17.

14. See generally Pomeranz, *The Great Divergence,* 274–97, 313–15. On the specific possibility of comparable amounts of cotton coming from somewhere else or alternate fibers being used, see pages 275–78, 315.

15. It is worth noting here that it was virtually impossible to ship charcoal over long distances and still have sufficiently large chunks of it in suitable condition for iron making. See John R. Harris, *The British Iron Industry, 1700–1850* (London and New York: Macmillan, 1988), 26; and M. W. Flinn, "The Growth of the English Iron Industry, 1660–1760," *Economic History Review,* 2nd ser., 11, no. 2 (1958):150. Thus even if enough "fuel" in the abstract had still been available for a surge in iron output (thanks perhaps to economizing on other uses as the price rose), it is not clear that it could have been mobilized for this purpose.

16. Geoffrey Parker, *The Military Revolution: Military Innovation and the*

Rise of the West, 1500–1800, 2nd ed. (Cambridge: Cambridge University Press, 1996), 115–45. For arguments that the conquest of India—the first large and lasting victory of European arms on the Asian mainland and a condition for many that followed—was a closer call than Parker suggests, see C. A. Bayly, *Imperial Meridian: The British Empire and the World, 1780–1830* (London: Longman's, 1989). For the Americas and Siberia, the organizational, technical, and conceptual differences Parker notes are indeed striking, but whether they would have proved decisive without the epidemiological factors that inhibited "native" recovery from initial defeats is less clear. For the Southeast Asian islands and parts of the African coast, where disease did not favor the Europeans, Parker's explanation of their victories seems to me very solid, but we should remember that their mastery did not go far beyond the coast; even the interior of larger islands such as Java were often not subdued until the nineteenth century, while Mindanao held out even longer and the Dutch settlement on Taiwan fell to Chinese invaders.

17. Parker, *The Military Revolution*, 117, 145.

18. Li Bozhong, *Agricultural Development in Jiangnan, 1620–1850* (New York: St. Martin's, 1998), 108; Perdue, *Exhausting the Earth*, 56–57, 129, 132; Yamamoto Susumu, "Shindai Shikawa no chi-iki keizai (Regional Development in Qing Dynasty Sichuan)," *Shigaku Zasshi* 100, no.12 (December 1991): 7–8, 10–11, 15. For a general survey, see Pomeranz, *The Great Divergence*, 242–51.

19. I discuss the interaction among political failure, economic change, and environmental stress in Kenneth Pomeranz, "Re-thinking the Late Imperial Chinese Economy: Development, Disaggregation and Decline, circa 1730–1930," *Itinerario* 24, nos. 3–4 (December, 2000): 49–66.

20. For a more detailed version of this argument, see R. Bin Wong, *China Transformed: Historical Change and the Limits of European Experience* (Ithaca: Cornell University Press, 1997); and "The Political Economy of Agrarian China and Its Modern Legacy," in *China and Capitalism: Geneaologies of Sinological Knowledge*, ed. Timothy Brook and Gregory Blue (Cambridge: Cambridge University Press, 1999), 210–45.

21. For a fuller discussion, see Kenneth Pomeranz, "Two Worlds of Trade, Two Worlds of Empire: European State-Making and Industrialization in a Chinese Mirror," in *States and Sovereignty in the Global Economy*, ed. David Smith, Dorothy Solinger and Steven Topik (London: Routledge, 1999), 87–94; and Pomeranz, *The Great Divergence*, 189–206.

22. For quick surveys of the rise and fall of the Zheng family in historical context, see John E. Wills, "Maritime China from Wang Chih to Shih Lang: Themes in Peripheral History," in *From Ming to Ch'ing*, ed. Jonathan Spence and John Wills, 223–28 (New Haven: Yale University Press, 1979), 201–238; and John E. Wills, *Mountain of Fame: Portraits in Chinese History* (Princeton: Princeton University Press, 1994).

23. Jennifer Cushman, "Duke Ch'ing-fu Deliberates: A Mid-Eighteenth-Century Reassessment of Sino-Nanyang Commercial Relations," *Papers on Far Eastern History* 17 (March 1978): 137–56; Wang Gungwu, "Merchants without Empire," in *The Rise of Merchant Empires*, ed. James Tracy (Cambridge: Cambridge University Press, 1990), 400–421.

24. For relevant accounts of the logic of imperial Chinese political economy

see Wong, *China Transformed,* 105–51; and "The Political Economy of Agrarian China and Its Modern Legacy."

25. Pomeranz, *The Great Divergence,* 120–122, 204–5.

26. Leonard Blussé, "Batavia, 1619–1740: The Rise and Fall of a Chinese Colonial Town," *Journal of Southeast Asian Studies* 12, no. 1 (March 1981): 159–78; Wang Gungwu, "Merchants without Empire"; Rafael Bernal, "The Chinese Colony in Manila, 1570–1770," in *The Chinese in the Philippines, 1570–1770,* ed. Alfonso Felix (Manila: Solidaridad, 1966), 40–66.

27. Blussé, "Batavia"; and Leonard Blussé, *Strange Company: Chinese Settlers, Mestizo Women, and the Dutch in VOC Batavia* (Dordrecht: Foris, 1986).

28. Victor Lieberman, *Strange Parallels: Southeast Asia in a Global Context, c. 800–1830,* vol. 1: *Integration on the Mainland* (Cambridge: Cambridge University Press, 2003), esp. 31–37, 44, 54.

29. Vaclav Smil, *Biomass Energies* (New York: Plenum, 1983), 36; E. Anthony Wrigley, *Continuity, Chance, and Change: The Character of the Industrial Revolution in England* (Cambridge: Cambridge University Press, 1988), 54–55.

30. M. W. Flinn, *The History of The British Coal Industry,* vol. 2: *1700–1830: The Industrial Revolution* (Oxford: Clarendon, 1984), 26, 121–28; B. R. Mitchell, *British Historical Statistics* (New York: Cambridge University Press, 1988), 247.

31. Li, "Ming Qing Jiangnan de mucai wenti," 86–89, 93–94; Li Bozhong, *Agricultural Development,* 4, 200, n. 23; Pomeranz, *The Great Divergence,* 225–29. See also William Rowe, *Hankow: Commerce and Society in a Chinese City, 1796–1889* (Stanford: Stanford University Press, 1984), 58–59, 61, 269–73, on the enormous timber trade passing through Hankou, much of it on its way to the Lower Yangzi.

32. Sun Jingzhi, *Economic Geography of China* (New York: Oxford University Press, 1988), 93.

33. See, for instance, Huang Qichen, *Zhongguo gangtie shengchan shi, shisi—shiqi shiji* (A History of Chinese Iron and Steel Production, Fourteenth to Seventeenth Centuries) (Zhengzhou: Zhongzhou guji chubanshe, 1989), 70–72, for a seventeenth-century list.

34. Ibid.,109–40.

35. G. William Skinner, "Regional Urbanization in Nineteenth Century China," in *The City in Late Imperial China,* ed. G. William Skinner, 211–49 (Stanford: Stanford University Press, 1977), 217.

36. Jan DeVries and Ad van der Woude, *The First Modern Economy: Success, Failure, and Perseverance of the Dutch Economy, 1500–1815* (Cambridge: Cambridge University Press, 1997), 37.

37. Li Bozhong, *Jiangnan de zaoqi gongyehua* [Proto-industrialization in Jiangnan] (Beijing: Shehui kexue chubanshe, 2000).

38. See Joseph Needham (with assistance from Wang Ling), "Physics and Physical Technology," vol. 4, pt. 2 (sec. 27 overall) of Joseph Needham et. al., *Science and Civilization in China* (Cambridge: Cambridge University Press, 1965), 513–15, 522, 525–28, 531 (mentioning seventeenth-century clocks an inch across, which required very fine work and clock makers who could copy the finest of

Western imports); see also pages 285 and 296 on odometers with differential gears as early as the eleventh century.

39. See Skinner, "Regional Urbanization," 217, on transport costs. See also Tim Wright, *Coal Mining in China's Economy and Society, 1895–1937* (Cambridge: Cambridge University Press, 1984), 9, citing a quintupling of the price of coal in northwest China between the mine and the riverbank fifty kilometers away. Cf. also DeVries and Van der Woude, *The First Modern Economy*, 37, on Europe: "Historically, the exploitation of energy deposits has depended more on the costs of transportation than on the costs of gathering the resource itself."

40. Sun Yingxing, *Tian Kong Kai Wu* (1637) juan 11, cited in Yu Mingxia, *Xuzhou Meikuang shi* (A History of the Xuzhou Coal Mines) (Nanjing: Jiangsu guji chubanshe, 1991), 23. Water appears to have been a lesser problem, even at the Xuzhou mines, which were in a much wetter area than Northwest China (27).

41. On steam engines elsewhere, see Needham, "Physics and Physical Technology," 255. On fuel consumption, costs, and the distribution of steam engines in England circa 1800, see Joel Mokyr, *The Lever of Riches: Technological Creativity and Economic Progress* (New York: Oxford University Press, 1990), 88, 90. I make this argument at greater length in Pomeranz, *The Great Divergence*, 59–60, 67–68.

42. Yu, *Xuzhou Meikuang shi*, 27.

43. Ibid., 21.

44. See Xu Dixin and Wu Chengming, *The Development of Capitalism in China, 1522–1840* (New York: St. Martin's, 2000), 289–307.

45. At least that is the standard view; a work in progress by Roger Hart questions whether the knowledge in question, mostly having to do with how to solve systems of equations, including higher-order polynomials, was ever really lost.

46. Ellen Widmer, "The Huanduzhai of Hangzhou and Suzhou: A Study in Seventeenth Century Publishing," *Harvard Journal of Asiatic Studies* 56, no. 1 (1996): 95–115; Xiong Pingzhen, *Yuyu: Chuantong Zhongguo de qiangpao zhidao* (Caring for the Young: The Newborn's Way in Traditional China) (Taibei: Lianjing, 1995); Paul Unschuld, *Medicine in China: A History of Pharmaceutics* (Berkeley: University of California Press, 1986), 183–97.

47. Benjamin Elman, *From Philosophy to Philology: Intellectual and Social Aspects of Change in Late Imperial China* (Cambridge: Harvard University Press, 1990), 79–85; John Henderson, *The Development and Decline of Chinese Cosmology* (New York: Columbia University Press, 1984), 153–68; Kawata Tei'ichi, "Shindai gakujutsu no ichi sokumin (Sidelights on Scholarship in the Qing Period)," *Tōhōgaku* 57 (1979): 84–105.

48. Mark Elvin, "The Man Who Saw Dragons: Science and Styles of Thinking in Xie Zhaozhe's *Fivefold Miscellany*," *Journal of the Oriental Society of Australia* 25–26 (1994): 40.

49. Elvin (ibid., 21–22) compares this to the emergence of such a network in seventeenth-century Europe, relying on the work of Barbara Shapiro.

50. Ibid., 22, citing Alastair Crombie.

51. Elman, *From Philosophy to Philology*, 174–75.

52. Ibid., 199, 204–5.

53. Ibid., 181–84.

54. Ibid., 221–22.

55. Ibid., 216–29.

56. See, for instance, ibid., 216, 228–29.

57. Cited in Helen Dunstan, "Official Thinking on Environmental Issues and the State's Environmental Roles in Eighteenth Century China," in, *Sediments of Time: Environment and Society in Chinese History*, ed. Mark Elvin and Liu Ts'ui-jung (Cambridge: Cambridge University Press, 1997), 606–8. See also Robert Marks, "It Never Used to Snow: Climatic Variability and Harvest Yields in Late-Imperial South China, 1650–1850," in Elvin and Liu, *Sediments of Time*, 411–12, on Kangxi; Robert Marks, *Tigers, Rice, Silk, and Silt: Environment and Economy in Late Imperial South China* (Cambridge University Press, 1997), 331–32, 343, 345, on Deng Bi'nan; and Anne Osborne, "The Local Politics of Land Reclamation."

58. Cf. Richard Grove, *Green Imperialism: Colonial Expansion, Tropical Island Edens, and the Origins of Environmentalism, 1600–1800* (Cambridge: Cambridge University Press, 1995), 153–67, 264–428.

59. Ibid., 309–79; H. H. Lamb, *Climate, History, and the Modern World* (London and New York: Methuen, 1982), 235–36.

60. See the discussion of these memorials in James Lee, Cameron Campbell, and Guofu Tan, "Infanticide and Family Planning in Late Imperial China: The Price and Population History of Rural Liaoning, 1774–1873," in *Chinese History in Economic Perspective*, ed. Lillian Li and Thomas Rawski (Berkeley: University of California Press, 1992), 159–63.

61. For an overview of the situation, see Osborne, "The Local Politics of Land Reclamation," 14–36.

62. Margaret Jacob, *The Cultural Meaning of the Scientific Revolution* (New York: Knopf, 1988), 239–43.

63. See, for instance, Toby E. Huff, *The Rise of Early Modern Science: Islam, China, and the West* (Cambridge: Cambridge University Press, 1993), 237–320, which relies heavily on the work of Derk Bodde, particularly with respect to the role of Chinese law. But Bodde's last formulation of at least part of this relationship (*Chinese Thought, Science, and Society* [Honolulu: University of Hawaii Press, 1991], 332–45) seems to me more ambivalent than it is in Huff's reading. See also Joseph Needham, "History of Scientific Thought," in Joseph Needham, et. al., *Science and Civilization in China*, vol. 2 (Cambridge: Cambridge University Press, 1956), 518–83.

64. There is also a parallel set of arguments with regard to India.

65. Needham, "Physics and Physical Technology," 135–36, 225–26, 285, 296, 369–70, 387.

66. In imagining this scenario, it should be noted, I am no longer asking questions that invite comparison with Mokyr's analysis in chapter 10 of this volume. He treats the rise of the West as an all or nothing phenomenon and asks whether, in the absence of the scientific and technological achievements made in Europe after 1550, any other place is likely to have duplicated this trajectory. In part because the late sixteenth century was a period of relatively strong Sino-Western contact and in part because I do not think the West had clearly overtaken China economically until at least the late eighteenth century, I am here imagining sce-

narios in which the Western economic trajectory stalled circa 1750 or proceeded, though more slowly—and with a sufficiently smaller and later growth of heavy industry to diminish Europe's military and political predominance during the nineteenth century, at least vis—vis East Asia—to see what might have happened to East Asia's own development in such a situation.

67. Michael Greenberg, *British Trade and the Opening of China* (Oxford University Press, 1951), 89–92; Robert Marks, "Maritime Trade and the Agro-Ecology of South China," in *Pacific Centuries: Pacific and Pacific Rim History since the Sixteenth Century,* ed. Dennis O. Flynn, Lionel Frost, and A. J. H. Latham (London: Routledge, 1999), 94–97.

68. Wilt Idema, "Cannons, Clocks, and Clever Monkeys: Europeana, Europeans, and Europe in Some Early Ch'ing Novels," in *The Development and Decline of Fukien Province in the 17th and 18th Centuries,* ed. Eduard Vermeer, 467–69 (Leiden: Brill, 1990); Needham, "Physics and Physical Technology," 513–15, 522, 525–28, 531.

69. Nathan Sivin, "Science and Medicine in Chinese History," in *Heritage of China,* ed. Paul Ropp (Berkeley: University of California Press, 1990), 192–93; Joanna Waley-Cohen, *The Sextants of Beijing: Global Currents in Chinese History* (New York: Norton, 1999), 107–12.

70. R. Bin Wong, "The Search for European Differences and Domination in the Early Modern World," *American Historical Review* 107, no. 2 (April 2002): 459–61. On Chinese interest in Western weapons before the Opium War, see Waley-Cohen, *The Sextants of Beijing,* 118–22.

71. Robert Dernberger, "The Role of the Foreigner in China's Economic Development, 1840–1949," in *China's Modern Economy in Historical Perspective,* ed. Dwight Perkins (Stanford: Stanford University Press, 1975), 19–47; and John K. Fairbank, "Introduction: the Old Order," in *The Cambridge History of China,* vol. 10, pt. 1: *Late Ch'ing, 1800–1911,* ed. John K. Fairbank, 1–34 (Cambridge: Cambridge University Press, 1978), 5–6, 19, are examples of this position in respected mainstream Western scholarship. Joseph Esherick, "Harvard on China: The Apologetics of Imperialism," *Bulletin of Concerned Asian Scholars* 4, no. 4 (1972): 9–16, is a scathing critique of this position, tracing its roots back to apologists for the Opium War itself. Hou Wailu, *Zhongguo fengjian shehui shi lun* (Essays on the History of Chinese Feudal Society) (Beijing: Renmin chubanshe, 1979), is a classic example of Chinese Marxist scholarship that (ironically) leads to a similar conclusion about the necessity of an outside force to destroy "feudalism" in China. Paul Smith, "Introduction: Problematizing the Song-Yuan-Ming Transition," in *The Song-Yuan-Ming Transition,* ed. Paul Smith and Richard Von Glahn (Cambridge: Harvard University Press, 2003), 1–34, esp. 2–7, provides a very helpful survey of the entire idea of an "early modernity" in Song China followed by stagnation, tracing it through Chinese, Japanese, and Western variants.

72. See, for some of the many examples, Kawakatsu Heita, *Nihon bunmei to kindai seiyō: "Sakoku" saikō* (Japanese Civilization and the Modern West: "Sakoku" Reconsidered) (Tokyo: Nippon Hōsō Shuppan Kōykai, 1991); Sugihara, "The European Miracle and the East Asian Miracle"; Sugihara, "Agriculture and Industrialization"; Hayami Akira, "Kinsei Nihon no keizai hatten to

Industrious Revolution (Modern Japanese Economic Development and the Industrious Revolution)," in *Tokugawa shakai kara no tenbo: Hatten, kozo, kokusia kankei* (A View from Tokugawa Society: Development, Structure, and International Relations), ed. Hayami Akira, Saito Osamu, and Sugiyama Chuya (Tokyo: Dobunkan, 1989), 19–32; Wong, *China Transformed;* Yu Yingshi, "Rujia sixiang yu jingji fazhan: Zhongguo jinshi zongjiao lunli yu shangren jing-shen (Confucian Thought and Economic Development: Modern Chinese Religious Ethics and the Merchant Spirit)," *The Chinese Intellectual* 6 (winter 1985): 3–45; Pomeranz, *The Great Divergence.* P. Steven Sangren, in his *History and Magical Power in a Chinese Community* (Stanford: Stanford University Press, 1987), has a particularly interesting section on attitudes toward money and economic growth in Taiwan, which are very "traditional" yet perfectly compatible with rational investment and capital accumulation.

73. David Landes, *The Wealth and Poverty of Nations* (New York: Norton, 1998), 31.

74. See Xu and Wu, *Chinese Capitalism,* 249–307.

King Kong and Cold Fusion

COUNTERFACTUAL ANALYSIS &
THE HISTORY OF TECHNOLOGY

Joel Mokyr

What do we mean by *historical contingency?* At the most intuitive level it means that the things that really happened in history did not have to happen, that something else *could* have happened. Counterfactual analysis then looks at that "something else" and wonders what it could have been and what antecedent it would require. For an economist, contingency can be formulated in terms of the uniqueness and stability of steady states or historical trajectories. The issue of contingency revolves around how many dynamic equilibria there are. In the limiting case there is a unique and stable equilibrium path, to which the economy always returns, even if accidents cause temporary derailments. But if the system has more than one such steady state, as is likely, small events and shocks might determine whether the system ends up in one or another. If the system is at an unstable equilibrium, a minor perturbation might throw it off course and it may never return to its original path. For a historian, the issue seems altogether more obvious: of course, different outcomes must have been possible since so many times accident and serendipity can be shown to be of importance. How *much* different the outcome would have been, even had some initial conditions differed, is much more controversial, as the essays in this volume attest.

How "contingent," then, is *economic* history? There appears to be a consensus that it is the least contingent kind of history. *Karl Marx*'s inexorable forces of historical materialism literally left little to chance. Few opportunities were left to luck, accident, or even individual action in a world governed au fond by class struggle and the forces of production. In an 1894 letter, the aging *Friedrich Engels* wrote:

> Men make history themselves, but not as yet with a collective will according to a collective plan . . . [T]heir aspirations clash and for that very reason all such societies are governed by *necessity,* the complement and form of appearance of which is *accident.* The necessity which here asserts itself athwart all accident is again ultimately economic necessity.[1]

On the ideological right, *mutatis mutandis,* the same kind of arguments can be heard. The powerful, impersonal forces of free, competitive, and efficient markets mean that if a single individual, no matter how influential and successful, were missing, he or she would have been replaced by the spontaneous action of large social and economic factors.[2] Even a middle of the road, level-headed economic historian such as *David Landes* insists that major events in economic history must have deep causes rooted in the foundational structure of a society. In other words, major trends in economic history are not contingent.[3]

At a basic level this statement must be incorrect. After all, economic history is profoundly affected by political history. *Ned Lebow* has recently argued that World War I was a highly contingent event. Many of the critical developments in the economic history of Europe in the subsequent decades may have been equally adventitious.[4] The war heavily flavored the two decades that immediately followed it. The European economies that had been cruising at a steady rate toward more integration and technological sophistication, and had enjoyed rising incomes and living standards, were blown off course in a matter of days and took three decades—and arguably far longer in Eastern Europe—to resume their paths. For decades, the economic history of the continent was dominated by financial instability, fiscal chaos, inflation, unemployment, and balance of payments difficulties—none of which had been anticipated, let alone experienced at a remotely comparable scale, before the fateful shots fired by Gavrilo Princip. Nature can inject economic history with an element of chance as well: equally "contingent" was the accidental transport of a few spores of *Phytoph-tora infectans* in a ship from the United States to Flanders in 1845 and from there by an unknown route to Ireland. The resulting potato blight dramatically changed the course of Irish economic history, and its lingering effects were still evident in Ireland in 1950. It also had long-run ramifications on the demographic makeup of both the United Kingdom and the United States, to say nothing of a century of Anglo-Irish relations and British politics.

It appears to be more difficult to make a strong argument for contingency and accident in the development of *technology*. Technological factors were an important element in economic growth in the West; in fact, the Industrial Revolution was the period in which technology elevated itself from a relatively minor contributor to growth to an important—though never the *sole*—factor behind the economic miracle we refer to as "the rise of the West." Any story that concerns the inevitability of the rise of the West will need to concern itself with the differences in the technological history between the West and the rest. While these differences were not the only ones that explain the meteoric material and political success of Western Europe in the nineteenth century, they constitute the most obvious and visible contrast. This dimension of global history has been brilliantly depicted by Daniel Headrick.[5] It would be rash to attribute Europe's dominant position *entirely* to technology: institutions, geography, culture, and attitudes broadly defined obviously played a role as well. But technological gaps were concrete, palpable, and stark. There was no arguing with the advantages of steam-driven gunboats, telegraphy, steel, chemicals, electricity, internal combustion engines, and the economic and political edge they implied.

Things had not always been that way. Europe's technological advantage over the rest of the world in the sixteenth century was at best tentative: half a century before the great discoveries, Chinese seafaring junks easily rivaled the best European ships, and in terms of military technology, metalworking, and textiles Europe was as much an imitator as a model to be imitated. The First Industrial Revolution changed all that, and, while in the longer term Europe's ability to exploit its technological advantages for purposes of political domination were to be ephemeral, there can be little doubt that in terms of technology it became the leader that non-Europeans emulated. That raises the hard question of whether the technological advances that catapulted Western civilization to the dominant position it held in 1914 (and, in many ways, still held in 2005) were themselves inevitable or contingent. Technology is knowledge, and if we are to make sense of its evolution over time we have to deal with it in those terms.

A standard argument in the canonical history of knowledge, associated above all with the work of sociologists of science such as S. C. Gilfillan and Robert K. Merton, is that progress in knowledge, whether scientific, technological, or other, is largely deterministic. That is, the growth of science and technology developed by means of a rational dynamic that made discoveries and inventions inevitable.[6] This dynamic consists of "external forces" such as the sociopolitical environment, relative prices, institutions, and so on, and "internal forces" in which knowledge moves by means of an evolutionary momentum of continuous development along historically contingent trajectories. While these internal forces may seem indeterminate to some extent, in effect they are often portrayed as deterministic. The main supporting evidence for determination is the phenomenon of apparent independent duplication, which demonstrates ostensibly that if one individual had not discovered a particular idea or made a given invention somebody else would have.[7] In this view the "impersonal" (deep underlying social and economic) forces of history determined the course of technological progress. Had James Watt and Richard Trevithick never been born, by this account, the history of steam power and the Industrial Revolution would have been only marginally different. Had Henry Ford never lived, the cheap mass-produced car would still have been produced. History is stronger than people, or, as Robert P. Thomas put it, it was the play that mattered, not the actors.[8] Counterfactual analysis in such a setup would confirm that the path of technology is inexorable and the equilibrium steady state is unique and stable. There would still have been cheap steel without Bessemer and in all likelihood aspirin without Felix Hoffman.

That the long list of multiple "independent" inventions and discoveries implies an "inevitability" of technological progress is an overly simplistic inference, and it answers the wrong question. To turn Thomas's metaphor around, the actors may not have mattered, but there would be no *Macbeth* without the Bard. Every discovery and invention is made by an individual conditional on a certain background knowledge. Elsewhere I have referred to this knowledge as the epistemic base of a technique.[9] It is not the individual who is necessarily indispensable but the background knowledge to which he or she has access.

We tend to think of the inventors as "accidental" given that society possesses the knowledge necessary to formulate the question and find the answer. Is this the correct approach? How inevitable is the emergence of this knowledge? To phrase it differently, the question should not be "had Edison never lived, would we have had an incandescent lightbulb?" but rather "had the Western world never discovered electricity, would non-Western cultures eventually have developed the incandescent lightbulb"? My answer to this question is basically negative. Western knowledge of nature was neither "better" nor "deeper" than the beliefs of the Chinese, Africans, or Aztecs. It just happened to be the kind of knowledge that led to the emergence of lightbulbs. The propositional knowledge it created was *different* to the point that had the West never existed humanity would probably never have seen digital computers, antibiotics, or nuclear reactors.

A counterfactual of "what would the world have looked like without the Industrial Revolution in the West?" would not preclude economic growth. Growth can emerge from the establishment and gains of trade; from better government and institutions; from the gains due to improved allocation, mobility, and economic freedom; and from the accumulation of capital. Yet it is hard to believe that without the technological breakthroughs of the past two centuries economic growth could have been sustained. The twentieth century was not the first in which growth of any kind occurred, but degree is everything here, and, as many scholars have emphasized, the rates of growth in the twentieth century differed enormously from those in the more remote past.[10] Without the Industrial Revolution and subsequent events, the world would have settled into an economic trajectory in which trade and good government might lead to periods of feeble (by our standards) growth, to be undone by wars or Malthusian pressures. Technological change would not have come to dominate income levels.

Phrasing the question as an explicitly counterfactual statement is, at some level, a purely rhetorical device—but an effective one. We do not have to imagine the counterfactual world: some parts of our actual world are a fair approximation.[11] My argument is that what made the West is neither efficient institutions nor capitalism (other economies had them) but its tendency to understand, control, and exploit natural phenomena and regularities in a specific way. As Cowan and Foray put it, the persuasiveness of a counterfactual lies in our ability to infer the consequent from the antecedent by establishing a relationship between the two.[12] In much of the counterfactual analysis in economic history, classical price theory provided the theory that allowed us to do this.[13] A "theory of useful knowledge" is not nearly as well developed, but in important historical questions we have to make do with what there is.

To make things a bit more precise we may distinguish between *prescriptive knowledge* or *techniques* (which I shall call λ-knowledge) and their epistemic basis in *propositional knowledge* (Ω-knowledge).[14]

Techniques are instructions (codified or tacit) on how to go about manipulating natural phenomena and regularities for the material benefit of people, much like instructions in computer programs, cookbooks, and how-to manuals. Propositional knowledge consists of the awareness of natural phenomena and regularities that underlie the instructions that constitute a technique. It is far larger than what we normally include in "science"—it includes basic understanding of mechanics and energy of the principles of engineering practice such as fulcrum and levers, winches, and pulleys, as well as of the behavior of plants and animals, geography, the properties of materials, old wives' tales, and similar pieces of knowledge. Techniques thus depend on *some* prior knowledge of nature, which I will call their *epistemic base*. Without such a base, a technique could exist no more than a particular protein could be expressed without a gene.[15] While epistemic bases are never complete (in the sense that the natural phenomenon is never *wholly* understood), their size tends to be one of the determinants of the likelihood of the invention occurring. In the limit, a base can be so narrow that it consists of only one element. I have termed such techniques "singleton techniques" because their domain is a singleton. These techniques are normally discovered by serendipity or trial and error, and while their impact can at times be significant, further refinements and adaptations tend to be limited and soon run into diminishing returns. This is a commonplace observation: the better we understand a particular natural phenomenon, the easier it is to search in some specific and purposeful way for an improvement or an adaptation to changing circumstances, and the more plausible it is that technological change becomes sustained and self-reinforcing.

To comprehend the ex ante indeterminacy of technological history, we need to face three separate sources of contingency. First, how inevitable is it that propositional knowledge itself emerges? Second, how inevitable is it that such knowledge, once it exists, will be mapped into new techniques? Third, given the existence of a menu of techniques, how likely is it for a given technique to be selected? To come to grips with that triplet of questions, we need to formulate, however superficially, some theoretical framework that allows us to understand the manner in which useful knowledge evolves over time. An evolutionary framework of some kind, which is by construction nondeterminist and selectionist, seems appropriate to a historical understanding of technological knowledge.[16]

Cowan and Foray correctly point out that precisely because evolutionary theory is rich enough to realize that history can produce many different outcomes, its predictions are not very tight and counterfactual analysis runs the risk of not being very compelling. Insofar as we are trying to explain a minor technological feature, this is perhaps true. But in the larger picture, evolutionary counterfactuals seem to make sense even in a highly indeterminate world, provided we are not too specific. For instance, Stephen Jay Gould famously asked if we rewound and replayed life's tape would the history of life look the same, and he answered in a resounding negative.[17] Others have not been so sure, but the phrasing of the question clearly suggests the obvious attractive rhetoric of the counterfactual in evolutionary tales. In Cowan and Foray's terminology, what Gould is suggesting is a "weak" counterfactual, one that identifies important events that foreclosed certain options. If history is a branching process, consisting of a huge number of bifurcations, then the present has been produced by an endless set of decisions on paths not taken. By identifying the branching points, as Cowan and Foray note, we can show "why the economy followed the route it did." In the final analysis the counterfactual tale serves not as a means of prediction or a normative assessment of where we are relative to where we could have been, but as a pedagogical tool to understand why the world is the way it is.[18] Its weaknesses are that we cannot be very specific about the alternative paths that could have been taken. All we know is that the actual world was not the only possible one, and speculate about the points in history at which other branches would have clearly led to very different outcomes.

An Evolutionary View of the History of Technology

The concept of looking at human ideas and knowledge in a Darwinian setup is quite natural and has occurred to many scholars. The innovation that Charles Darwin proposed was not just to show that species had descended from other species, but more basically that historical processes could be described through a mechanism of random mutation and nonrandom selection. In the words of ultra-Darwinists, it was this notion that constituted "Darwin's dangerous idea."[19] Philosophers of science, following the pathbreaking work of Donald Campbell, have been refining notions of evolutionary epistemology and its implications for the history of science.[20] The basic idea is simple: new technological ideas, like mutations, are highly stochastic. In a world in which inventions are based on very narrow epistemic bases, and in which serendipity played a predominant role, selection would be the main force that provided directionality to this process. In a world in which inventions are based on a deeper understanding of nature, new technology would be the result of a deliberate, purposeful search for new forms (a search that never occurs in nature). Yet even then, unless such knowledge could become so deep that it infallibly yields the desired results, there will be a randomness (or, better put, a blindness) in the process that generates innovation, which requires post-invention selection.

The advantages of an evolutionary approach to the "history of knowledge" have been widely discussed and need not be restated here.[21] Two points are worth noting, however. The hard questions of contingency versus destiny come up with *both* Ω-knowledge and λ-knowledge. The issue can be well illustrated by the following example: the discovery of America by Europeans was one of the greatest additions to the Ω-set of the West in history. Conditional on the technological advances in shipbuilding and navigation in the fifteenth century, as well as on European greed and curiosity, it is reasonable to think that the discovery itself—as opposed to its precise timing—was inevitable: had Columbus not made the journey (or decided to sail east like Vasco da Gama), sooner or later someone else would have made the journey and America would still have been there in exactly the same location. Had the Europeans by 1490 not advanced their maritime skills relative to the ancient Greeks, the discovery seems less probable (if not impossible).[22] Yet, even had they *never* found the route, America would still be there.

Is the same true, say, for the laws of physics and chemistry, for our understanding of infectious disease, indeed for the theory of evolution itself? Are most natural laws and regularities "facts" that await our discovery, that sooner or later will become part of Ω simply because they are "true"? Or are they, as many modern scholars in the humanities assert, social constructs much like the American Constitution or the rules of basketball? Would another society have discovered a very different way of looking at nature, one that would not have led to relativity and quantum theory and microbiology but to something entirely different, unimaginable but possibly equally able to explain the observable world around us and map this knowledge into widely used techniques? This is one of the trickiest questions in the philosophy of science, and I am not going to solve it here. Cohen and Stewart are persuaded that propositional knowledge is really "there" and not what they call a "brain pun" because our knowledge of nature maps into techniques that work visibly: chemistry works—it makes nylon tights and polyethylene sheets.[23] Physics works—airplanes fly and pressure cookers cook rice. Every time. To be sure, the fact that a technique "works" is not proof that the propositional knowledge contained in its epistemic base is in some sense "true"—in many cases techniques that were effective were based on knowledge that subsequent research has rejected.

The second point about evolutionary theory as a historical tool is that it explains the form of creatures not in terms of their "DNA" but in terms of their historical development within a changing environment. A Newtonian explanation of why "an entity" is what it is is time independent. In one witty formulation, God gave the easy problems to the physicists.[24] Open, time-variant systems such as evolution do not lend themselves to precise formulations that predict accurately, given only sufficient boundary conditions. Moreover, as John Ziman has pointed out, whereas closed systems such as physics tend to be statistical in that they reflect *expected* values, evolutionary systems tend to amplify *rare* events (such as successful mutations or brilliant ideas).[25] Because these rare events are themselves not inexorable, and because it is unknown *which* of them will actually be amplified, as opposed to being rejected, by the selection process for one reason or another, they infuse an irrepressible element of indeterminacy into the system. Changes in the environment will induce adaptation in some species and lead to extinction in others, but there seems to be no foolproof rule that indicates when one or the other outcome will prevail. A counterfactual analysis can then proceed under the assumption that a "rare event" that did in fact occur in history did not happen. What it cannot do with any persuasion is replace it with another rare event that did *not* happen, since we cannot really pick one from another one just as (un)likely.

Thus far, most scholars working in this area have tended to apply evolutionary epistemology more to science than to technology.[26] A strict Darwinian analogy is partial at best and misleading at worst.[27] Above all, "natural selection" through some kind of fitness criterion is only a *metaphor* in evolutionary biology. Nobody, of course, does any real selecting. This is not the case in evolutionary epistemology: there is conscious selecting. The "choice" of technique is a reality for every engineer, every farmer, every artisan, every homemaker. Choosing a technique is costly in that at the very least it involves an opportunity cost, and indeed often real resources.[28]

In any event, this setup places the central issue of technological history in sharper focus. An evolutionary theory cannot predict with any accuracy what knowledge will appear any more than a biologist can predict what mutations will appear. It can, however, rule out the emergence of techniques that require an epistemic base that does not exist at that time, and it predicts that when techniques emerge as singleton or narrow-based techniques, they are likely to become dead ends rather than the basis for a technological trajectory. It also implies that the emergence of a potential knowledge base for a set of techniques is never *sufficient* for technological advances to emerge, since there is nothing to guarantee that this knowledge will be actually used for anything. In short, an evolutionary approach suggests leaving the tight and neat world of sufficient or necessary conditions and takes us into the messy world of Darwinian thinking, full of contingency and chance.

The question I take on with this approach is whether every technique that existed had to be and whether techniques that are not observed could not have been. In any Darwinian system, either in a world of living creatures or one of technological options, selection can take place only if the *raw materials* on which the choices occur exist. The Weismannian orthodoxy states that mutations are uncorrelated with the environment and that hence we cannot predict what kind of mutation will occur in nature and cannot fully understand why some traits develop and others do not. Understanding what we observe begins with asking why there are things we do not observe, and this is of course the way to approach counterfactual history. The answer to the question posed earlier begins with the fundamental distinction between species that are not observed because they were selected against, those that are not observed because the mutations that would have brought them along never came about, and those that could never exist except in our imagination because they violate some law of physics.[29] Thus current biologists distinguish, with some inevitable gray areas and ambiguity, five existing "kingdoms" of living beings, and about sixteen important phyla of the Kingdom Animalia or Metazoa. But some phyla that *could* have existed today because they did at some point in the past are no longer there.[30] Given the important role of chance and catastrophes in the extinction of species, this in and of itself suffices to drive home the point that accidents play a major role in any kind of evolutionary tale of the past.

To illustrate this logic, I follow Daniel Dennett, who distinguishes various levels of "could have been" compared to the actual. Dennett points out the difference between the logically impossible and the physically impossible.[31] Similarly, certain life forms are physically impossible, such as insects the size of elephants. Beyond that, there are life forms that are physically possible but biologically impossible in the sense that there is no evidence that anything even remotely similar ever emerged, such as flying horses (Dennett's example). At a further level there are life forms that were biologically possible but apparently never emerged, such as flying marsupials or legged snails. Finally, there are forms of life that existed much like the species in the Burgess Shale but were "selected against" and are today extinct. As Dennett recognizes, there are pitfalls in these distinctions (the differences between physically and biologically impossible are fuzzy, and extinction could have many causes besides having been negatively selected), but for our purposes such a hierarchy of the possible will be useful to study the difference between actual and possible techniques.

Consider the universe of techniques illustrated in figure 1. First, because we are dealing with human knowledge, most definitions are true only for a specific point in time. The largest metaset, which is timeless (but also therefore rather meaningless), is that of *imaginable* techniques. This set includes all techniques that could conceivably be concocted by the human mind. Its dimensions are huge, but in the final analysis it is constrained by the limitations of the human mind. Smaller and wholly contained in this set is the set of techniques ever *imagined* until time t. This is an expanding set, since new science fiction novels and starry-eyed engineering students dream up new techniques every day. Another subset of the imaginable techniques is the set of *imaginable and possible* techniques, that is, those that are not contradicted by the laws of nature as we understand them today.[32] In principle, the set of possible techniques is fixed, but because human knowledge is imperfect, in practice we define *possible* as "believed to be possible at our time (t)." We cannot be certain that the two are identical—in fact, we can be fairly sure they are not—but it is by definition the best we can do right now.

A subset of the set of techniques possible to the best of *our* knowledge is the set of *potential* techniques at time t. This is the set that was within the technological capabilities of that age. Roman society could not possibly build X-ray machines, but there was no reason they could not have made spectacles or navigated at sea using instruments. A subset of that set is the set of *feasible* techniques, that is, the intersection of the set of potential techniques at t with the "imagined" at t set, techniques that are

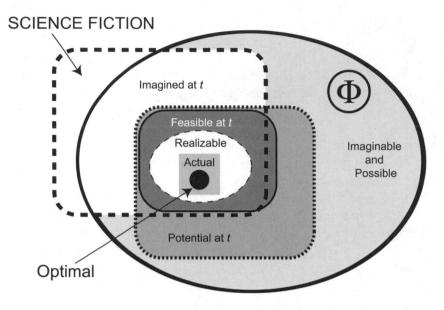

Fig. 1. Metasets of techniques

not only possible at all *and* within the technological capabilities of the time but were also imagined by someone.[33] Feasible techniques have the minimum epistemic base necessary to write out the instructions fully. Within the feasible set lies the *realizable* set. Feasible techniques may not be realizable because even though the minimum epistemic base to write out the instructions that comprise the technique existed there was too little complementary knowledge to carry it out on a significant scale.[34] Another reason for which a technique could be feasible but not realizable would be some blocking element such as the physical absence of a crucial ingredient (say, a society may know how to make atom bombs but cannot lay its hands on enriched plutonium). More commonly, feasible techniques are not realized because of social prejudice, superstition, resistance of vested interests, or because the idea somehow does not "catch on," for instance, when the full benefits of the technique are underestimated.

Selection occurs at this level. The set of feasible techniques constitutes the "menu" from which selection occurs. The set of *actual* techniques in use, those that are actually selected, is a subset of the realizable set. Another subset of realizable techniques is the set of *rational* techniques.

These techniques dominate other techniques in their ability to satisfy whatever objective function we impose, equivalent to the lowest unit iso-quant in economics. Finally, there is a set of *optimal* techniques (a subset of rational techniques), which is that segment of the rational set that is best suited to any given environment, although this requires a precise definition of what *best suited* means. Note that figure 1 also includes a set of techniques that are possible and imaginable but never occurred to any-one, perhaps because the kind of societies that were able to produce them did not have a chance to get to that point. I shall return to this idea at the end of this essay.

The history of technology is largely about how we get from potential techniques to feasible techniques (i.e., which of the techniques possible to a society actually occurred to anyone); the transformation of a number of feasible techniques to realizable ones; and the emergence of the actual historical techniques that were selected, put into use, and are observed by economic historians. There should, however, be a fair amount of interest in techniques that could have emerged but did not or in techniques that could have emerged much earlier than they did. Counterfactual history here is handicapped by hindsight bias: that is, we know which techniques occurred historically, and for that reason they seem more plausible than others.[35] Techniques that were imagined but did not occur are written off as science fiction. Even techniques that were tried briefly but were then selected against are normally dismissed as obviously inferior to those techniques that were eventually selected. The dirigible and the electric car, to pick two obvious examples, are frequently dismissed not only as "never were" but also as "never could have been," though such infer-ences are often unwarranted.

We can picture the evolution of techniques as the result of the coevo-lution of two separate but interactive Darwinian systems. One is the growth of the propositional knowledge base Ω itself, in terms of discov-eries in science, geography, the gradual accumulation of applied engi-neering and farming knowledge in terms of what works where, and the thousands of little anonymous pieces of experience and artisanal knowl-edge ("microinventions") that together make production more efficient over time even in the absence of scientific breakthroughs. The other is the growth of the techniques implied by that knowledge. These two systems interact in multiple and often subtle ways. In some ways its development over time resembles the evolution of systems of living beings: phenotypes, much like techniques, depend on changes in the genotype to develop rad-ically new forms. Much evolutionary change also occurs through "adaptation," that is, the activation of hitherto inert genetic material activated because of changes in the environment. Unlike biological systems, however, knowledge systems allow feedback from the system of "doing" to the system of "knowing."[36] Substantial advances are made in knowledge when new tools (i.e., techniques) permit the accumulation of more knowledge. Thus the shipping and navigation technology of the fifteenth century made the geographical discoveries of the sixteenth possible, just as the improved microscope (discussed shortly) prepared the ground for the discoveries of Louis Pasteur and Robert Koch.

If the argument I have made here is correct, the counterfactual to the "rise of the West" is that if it had not happened in the West, it probably would not have happened anywhere, at least not in any form remotely resembling the industrial development of the West (and eventually the world) as it took place. What is striking about the economic history of the modern era is not just the great advances in steam, iron, textiles, and engineering in the closing third of the eighteenth century, but the *continuation* of the inventive activity after 1815 or 1820, when the Sturm und Drang of the first Industrial Revolution had apparently spent itself.[37] Such sustainability would not and could not have been attained without a continuously widening epistemic base.

The Epistemic Bases of Techniques

Apart from their entertainment value, imaginable but infeasible entities such as King Kong or cold fusion seem to serve little purpose. They illustrate, however, that the set of feasible techniques is a function of time. For instance, directed human flight in heavier-than-air machines must be considered in the "imaginable, possible, but infeasible" set until 1903. Yet when techniques are being imagined, do the imaginers rule them out as fun but impossible or do they attach some nonzero probability to the event ever becoming a reality? Much of modern science fiction literature must in its heart of hearts realize that many of the techniques imagined, such as traveling at speeds exceeding the speed of light and thus venturing far outside the solar system, are simply impossible *with today's knowledge.* Cold fusion is a somewhat different matter: while the claim was received with great scepticism, it was admitted that experimental methods were needed to confirm it since our knowledge was inadequate to rule it out a priori. In this sense it is different from perpetuum mobile machines. Yet such categories are all time variant and depend on consensus knowledge at a specific point. The idea of the "fountain of youth" would probably have been in the impossible category half a century ago, but now it seems to have shifted categories with research on the "aging genes."

A large number of techniques that eventually arise are first imagined, then understood to be possible, and finally realized. Many others remain dreams and never penetrate to the inner circles of figure 1 either because they are impossible (e.g., the philosopher's stone) or just not feasible at that particular time (human flight). Roger Bacon (1220–92), to cite the most famous example, described gunpowder and spectacles, both of which became feasible in his own age. He also insisted on the possibility of mechanically propelled carriages and ships, and hot-air balloons. Technological dreams inspire, at some subtle level, technological creativity. Informed technological speculation has always been and remains an inspiration to actual progress. While precise linkages cannot be demonstrated, Bertrand Gille concluded in his survey of Renaissance technology that "the growth of mechanization also appears to have been in large measure the result of a speculative type of thinking . . . before their practical applications were discovered, machines were created for their intellectual amusement."[38] Many of the great Renaissance *compendia* (theaters) of machines were lavishly illustrated "imaginative excursions" into what might be.[39] Eugene Ferguson argues that such imagination contained the "seeds of the explosive expansion of technology in the West."[40]

All the same, the fact that a machine or any kind of device can be *imagined* is only one small part of technological history. What are the boundaries between a technique that is *imagined and possible* (by our standards); one that is *feasible,* that is, within the technological capability of a society to build; and one that is *realizable,* that is, can be activated in production? Realizability requires an epistemic base sufficient to write out the instructions fully and the ability (i.e., human capital) to carry them out and make them an *economic* reality so that they can be made at an affordable price.

As noted earlier, *any* technique in use requires an epistemic base, that is, sufficient relevant knowledge about the underlying exploitable regularities of nature. Even an ancient farmer with no knowledge whatsoever of soil chemistry, plant genetics, pests, hydraulics, and so forth needed to know certain basic regularities about the weather, water control, seeds, soil manipulation, and so on if he or she was to produce a crop. Through most of recorded history people produced chemicals without chemistry, smelted and refined iron without metallurgy, and bred animals and plants without genetics. Techniques differ in the width of the epistemic base they required to become feasible. Steel could be manufactured by medieval blacksmiths in Damascus and Toledo centuries before three French academicians showed in 1786 that its physical properties are determined by the quantity of carbon it contains. However, an age that did not understand electricity at all could not build generators, let alone transistors.

Yet, while the knowledge bases in the more remote past were thus very narrow, they still existed. It was recognized that pig iron mixed with wrought iron in some fashion produced, after much toil, an intermediate product of superior quality called steel. Animal refuse hauled to arable fields tended to improve crop yields. Breeding unusually big horses with other unusually big horses begat a line of large horses. Patients with contagious diseases were understood to infect other people through close contact and were isolated. Even if their causes were not known, the regularities of high and low tides could be observed and exploited for navigation and tidal mills. If natural patterns and regularities could be discerned, whatever the metaphysical interpretation people gave to them, they lent themselves to exploitation.

Three inferences can be drawn from this setup. The first and most obvious is that if the necessary minimum Ω-knowledge was lacking altogether certain techniques would simply not develop. The second is that techniques that were created on a very narrow epistemic base would not be used as well as they could be and could not form the base of sustainable and continuous technological development.[41] The third is that when the epistemic base was very narrow, a great deal of research was carried out that may have led to blind alleys or even to techniques that proved ineffective, such as mesmerism. The widening of epistemic bases increases the component of purposeful search and reduces the randomness of technological advances a little: knowing *why* something works prevents spending too much effort on dead-end projects that do not work.[42] For sustained technological progress to take place, the λ-set needs to have a large and growing knowledge base to support it. This is not only true for creating new technologies but also for improving and extending existing technologies that had existed earlier on a narrow base.

Compare, for instance, the advances in power technology in the eighteenth century. As is often pointed out, the knowledge base of the steam engine did not include the principles of thermodynamics that predict its energy efficiency. The early engine makers, however, relied on two important additions to useful knowledge that preceded it: the understanding of atmospheric pressure, discovered by continental scientists such as Evangelista Torricelli and Otto von Guericke; and the mid-seventeenth-century notion that steam was evaporated water and its condensation created a vacuum. Between those two insights, the idea of an *engine* took shape. The gradual growth in the understanding of thermodynamics in the nineteenth century made the improvement of combustion engines of all kinds easier and allowed techniques to move in novel directions through the work of men such as William Rankine.[43] At the same time, however, experimental and theoretical hydraulics advanced continuously, and consequently much of the "action" in eighteenth-century power technology took place in the remarkable improvement in the age-old technology of water power, culminating in John Smeaton's breast wheel and Benoît Fourneyron's water turbine.

The emergence of an epistemic base is never a *sufficient* condition for technological change to occur. Many societies might investigate nature for its own sake, without the Baconian notion that the main purpose of that knowledge is to improve our material welfare through the control of natural forces. It is this part that makes counterfactual history in this area so perplexing. We can be reasonably certain that in an age that did not have microscopes, the germ theory of disease would not have occurred to anyone. But even given microscopes, was the germ theory inevitable the way America was inevitable? Furthermore, given that the germ theory was accepted, were the techniques it mapped into, including antibiotics, therefore also inevitable?

Counterfactual Technology

How likely was it for the techniques that we actually observe to have emerged, and can we place probabilities on techniques we can imagine but did not emerge? Defining such ex ante probabilities of events that actually occur is sensible if we know something about the entire distribution, even if only one event has materialized.[44] Using something like a probability gets around the endless confusion of a sufficient condition (which sets a probability at unity if a condition is fulfilled) or a necessary condition (which sets a probability at zero if the condition is not met). But for most observers there are few necessary or sufficient conditions in economic history as there are few factors that have no substitutes or need no complements. Moving in the continuum between "very likely" and "very unlikely" without categorically ruling anything in or out seems prima facie a more satisfying way to think about the likelihood of the emergence of new techniques.

Historians have criticized attempts to try to explain why something did *not* happen.[45] But a statement such as "the ex ante probability of this event happening was low," while little more than a rephrasing, drives home the fact that, at least for some historical issues, some events did not happen because they had low ex ante probability. This does not mean they could not have ever happened given enough time. But if they did not, there was not enough time. The question "why not?" is not entirely out of place, especially if an event very similar to the event in question happened elsewhere.[46] It remains to be seen if such probabilities are in any sense a useful tool in the history of technology.

But all such probabilities need to be made conditional on something. It makes almost no sense to speak of unconditional probabilities because the emergence of techniques depends on the epistemic base underlying them. Yet, as I noted earlier, the probability of a singleton technique emerging is not always zero, and it is also possible for a knowledge base to exist without the implied technique ever emerging.[47]

Clearly, there is an important difference between the unconditional probability of a technique i being invented $P(\lambda_i)$ and the probability conditional on knowledge; existing $P(\lambda_i | \Omega_j)$. For example, Ptolemaic astronomy and fifteenth-century Euclidian-based geometry may have been quite unlikely to emerge (the Chinese never developed Euclidian geometry or Hipparchian trigonometry). But conditional on the fact that those pieces of knowledge had emerged, it was much more likely for a set of navigational tools to be developed and the road to the New World to be discovered even if the unconditional probability was low; that is, it would have been unlikely to observe these techniques *without* knowing that Hellenistic mathematics and astronomy existed.[48] If the conditional probability was sufficiently high, we would observe multiple inventions if different inventors had access to more or less the same knowledge base Ω_j. Such multiple inventions would demonstrate not that inventions were inevitable but only that they were highly probable *given the state of knowledge*. Even given a state of knowledge, however, the evolution of certain techniques is never inexorable, though we will shortly see what boundaries can be placed on the process. Much like homoplasy in nature, certain techniques might evolve from very different types of Ω-knowledge and yet look quite similar.[49]

What, then, determines the state of propositional knowledge? In part, knowledge itself depends on technology: our ability to observe and process what we observe into exploitable regularities is in part determined by technology. Without instruments, we would not be able to see the moons of Jupiter or Tubercle bacilli.[50] Technology also determined how accessible the existing knowledge is to those who do not have it since it sets the costs of the physical dissemination of useful knowledge, either in codified form (e.g., through printed matter) or in tacit form through the movement of people. Finally, technology sets concrete challenges and puzzles to scientists and natural philosophers that focus their minds on specific problems. Beyond its interaction with λ, however, the growth of Ω has an internal dynamic logic that makes it conditional on some prior state. The past strongly constrains the present by limiting the choices.[51]

For instance, between 1880 and 1900, bacteriologists discovered a new pathogenic germ about every two years because the Koch postulates and the new experimental methodology they implied made it relatively obvious.[52] The farther removed in the evolutionary chain the piece of propositional knowledge on which we condition is, the less likely it appears. The invention of the internal combustion engine by F. A. Otto in 1876 seems plausible given the new thermodynamics of the mid-nineteenth century, but how "probable" was it given only the work of Christiaan Huygens in the seventeenth century or given only the writings of medieval scientists such as Roger Bacon?

To understand why some techniques are observed in history and why other potential and even realizable techniques are not, we need to know more about the development of Ω. Here we find ourselves in the position of the biologists. There is an observable world of contemporary and past forms of life that actually existed or exists. In addition, there is a set of "feasible" or "realizable" life forms that never emerged. Watching the famous tavern scene in the first *Star Wars* movie provides some idea of the life forms we can imagine, even though few of those fantastic creatures actually are realizable, at least under terrestrial conditions (which, of course, is the point). All the same, some imaginable and possibly viable life forms never emerged because the mutations that would have created the genotypes for them never occurred, although there is no a priori reason why they could not have. To be sure, an examination of the actual—albeit often in "niche" conditions—shows how rich and surprising the realizable set of life is.[53]

There are equivalents of these life forms in human beliefs about nature. It is easy to point to a variety of contemporary "weird" beliefs in the "flat earth tradition," from astrology, extrasensory perception, recovered memory syndrome, megavitamin diets, dianetics, and Reiki to millenarian doomsday prophesies that are still held and at times form the basis of human technological action.[54] Looking into the past does nothing to reassure the historian that selection processes guarantee the survival of rational ideas and forms of knowledge that produced techniques that worked "best." It might seem that today, more than in any other age, we choose techniques primarily on the basis of results and costs rather than superstition or conformism, but there are too many exceptions to this rule to feel very smug about this.[55]

Is it then conceivable that forms of knowledge could have developed, consistent with the laws of physics and chemistry as we understand them, that would have created technological societies quite different from our own? Some historical experiments can be pointed to in which useful knowledge developed independent of Western societies: the pre-Columbian societies in America and to a lesser extent Africa and East Asia (which always had *some* contact with the West). Much like the marsupials of Australia, which, unconnected to the placental-dominated Eurasia, differed from life forms on the Eurasian continent while solving similar problems, non-European societies developed different forms of knowledge that underlay their agriculture, medicine, energy use, materials, construction, textiles, and so on. It is hard to know whether the differences between pre-Columbian American or Chinese forms of Ω-knowledge and the West were due to accident or to the fact that they operated in different physical environments. To a large extent, however, the Chinese dualistic approach to universal truth known as yin and yang as well as its medical applications must be seen as representing an alternative path to the challenges of human health and disease rather than as an adaptation to a specific Chinese environment.[56]

The course of the evolution of useful knowledge is hard to understand and impossible to predict. It is externalist in that the agenda of research and the resources dedicated to it interact in complex ways with its environment: institutions, values, relative prices, income, religious beliefs, and the physical parameters of a region. The environment, economics teaches us, sets the selection criteria by means of which techniques are chosen, but it does not directly determine the menu of technological options. It is internalist in that people are inherently curious and ambitious men and women who will expand the horizons of knowledge to satisfy their own and others' curiosity. Between them, greed, ambition, curiosity, and altruism go a long way in explaining why propositional knowledge grows, but in and of itself this does not help us understand the forms it ends up taking. In some ways, then, the biological analogy is helpful to counterfactual analysis. We can point to environmental factors (e.g., radiation) that increase the *frequency* of mutations, but there is no known way of predicting with any precision *what* mutations will occur. Similarly, we can point to *economic* environments that are conducive in some ways to the emergence of new useful knowledge, and we can point to the institutions that encourage and aid enterprising and resourceful individuals to apply this knowledge to production. The question of why *a specific kind* of knowledge or another emerged however, is hard to understand even in hindsight. Much in the development of knowledge in the past depended on the choice of "legitimate" topics of investigation and the rhetoric of scientific discourse (i.e., what determines whether something is widely believed), and hence on the conventions of authority and expertise and in general on the sociology of knowledge. The scientific revolution in the West formulated a conception of a rational and mechanistic universe that behaves according to certain rules and regularities, natural laws that can be exploited. But this rationalistic approach was not the only way to approach the natural world and itself was anything but an inevitable historical development.

Propositional knowledge thus retains an irreducible element of contingency and indeterminacy. It is this aspect of it, more than anything else, that makes it so irresistibly similar to biological evolution despite the obvious differences. Some viable life forms were wiped out because of the accident that they were invaded by a mutant or alien species that was more adapted to their particular environment or had sufficient flexibility to adapt more quickly. Similarly, non-Western techniques might have evolved very differently and produced novel forms had they not been invaded by Western ones and had their evolutionary lives not been cut short. One historian of China, A. C. Graham, raises an interesting counterfactual question when he asks what would have happened to the scientific revolution in Europe had seventeenth-century Europe been invaded by a culture that had plastics, electronics, and napalm. Had Western science not arrived in the way it did, it seems unlikely that something *similar* would have arisen in China or the Middle East and taken the rest of the world by storm.[57] As matters turned out, Chinese natural knowledge and medicine followed a very different path, a path that was terminated when for all intents and purposes oriental science surrendered upon exposure to European science, much like the way indigenous flora and fauna were overwhelmed when exposed to European species after Europeans arrived in America and Australia.[58]

Morcover, contingency is compounded by the indeterminacy of the selection mechanisms that retain new techniques for survival. In this respect, the analogy with evolutionary biology fails us badly. In living beings *fitness* has a precise meaning, and in principle we can observe traits and assess whether they contribute to the likelihood of survival and reproduction. In the selection of techniques, the criteria for selection are to a large extent socially and culturally determined. In a "pure" economic world, to be sure, contribution to profits might be the only selection criterion. But very few economies ever operated that way. Techniques were selected or rejected for a variety of reasons, which themselves were contingent. Similar considerations hold for selection at the level of Ω. Modern Western science and engineering eventually drove out many—if by no means all—of the useful knowledge underlying African and Asian production. To what extent this selection followed some kind of optimizing rule or was imposed by political and military means remains a matter of dispute.[59] At times, techniques from one society could clash with the values and prejudices of another. Resistance to modern useful knowledge, from Copernican astronomy to the theory of evolution and modern genetics, is legend and has to be taken into account in any list of the selection criteria.[60]

But even in historical situations in which market forces were allowed to determine the selection of the techniques to be used, there was often an indeterminacy as to which techniques would actually prevail. This was particularly true in the early stages of the emergence of a new technology; frequency dependence, meaning that fitness depended not only on the intrinsic features of a specimen but also on the number of others around, was a widespread phenomenon. In such environments, almost trivial reasons can lead to the domination of one technique over another.[61] Consider the example of radio: by the end of World War I, three feasible technologies for transmitting continuous waves had emerged: the oscillating arc; the radio-frequency alternator; and the vacuum tube, perfected by De Forest, which eventually became the standard technique of the industry. There is no obvious technical reason why radio technology could not have been constructed on the basis of the arc or the alternator any more than there is a good reason why the perfected steam car produced by the Stanley company in the 1930s disappeared or why the VHS format beat out Beta in videotape recorders in the 1970s.

Above all, as I argued earlier, technology is contingent because the useful knowledge conditioning it is contingent. The scientific revolution as it evolved in Western Europe between 1550 and 1700 turned out to be of central importance to the evolution of modern technology, but we have no clear-cut idea of how probable it was in and of itself. Given that $P(\lambda)$ always depends on $P(\Omega)$, the likelihood of modern useful knowledge emerging needs to be discussed. By *modern useful knowledge* I mean much more than just the developments in mechanics, energy, chemistry, optics, biological sciences, and so on. "Modern science" was part of a larger package that arose in the postmedieval periods from Greek and medieval seeds. The scientific revolution, in addition to increasing the *size* of Ω, involved three important changes in its social background and attributes: (1) a scientific *method* of observation, experimentation, and testing, including a convention of *open science* in which discoveries in Ω were placed in the public sphere rather than kept secret, with notions of authority, proof, and evidence that were very different than anything seen elsewhere; (2) a scientific *mentality* that assumed a rational, mechanistic, orderly universe with laws that are universal and understandable and that eschewed mysticism, magic, and supernatural phenomena, an approach that implied the logical (but not inevitable) step of analyzing natural phenomena by means of mathematical tools whenever possible; and (3) a *scientific culture* that was anthropocentric and materialist, that regarded the purpose of useful knowledge as driven by material needs, and that was devoid of qualms about the relentless manipulation of natural phenomena for the benefit of mankind.[62]

There was nothing inevitable about these social norms *themselves*. Indeed little is known about why and how such social norms emerge. Given that they emerged, however, the likelihood that modern Ω-knowledge (scientific and other) and the techniques that derived from it would occur the way they did is enhanced. Yet they were far from certain even then. These characteristics of European thinking coalesced during the scientific revolution and the Enlightenment and played a substantial role in the Industrial Revolution. They conditioned the growth of Ω, which itself conditioned the growth of new technology. They appeared in the West, but were they fluke or destiny? Did they relate to the religious traditions of the West, as argued by Lynn White, to the heritage of Greek and Hellenistic cultures, or were they a function of Europe's political fragmentation?

It is fair to say that simplistic notions that predict inevitability such as "necessity is the mother of invention" are unsatisfactory and little more than empty boxes.[63] Just as there was nothing inevitable about a kangaroo or a cockroach, there was nothing inevitable about the specific forms of John Dalton's atomic theory or James Clerk Maxwell's electromagnetic theory. Even conditional on the emergence of "modern Western science," the precise forms that modern technology took seem less than wholly determinate. In energy, materials, communications, farming, and medical technology, to pick some areas at random, alternative scenarios can easily be imagined. Some, like semaphore telegraphs, funicular railroads, lighter-than-air flying machines, wind and water power on a large scale, direct current, and analog computers were experimented with and then rejected because other techniques were selected. There is nothing predetermined about a Windows 98 operating system, french fries, the dashboard of a Toyota Camry, or the zipper.[64] If we could push the "rewind" button of technological history and replay the tape, we might get a quite different story.

Exactly *how* different depends not only on how far back the rewinding goes but also on the level of knowledge we are examining, that is to say, what facts we are conditioning the probability on. The essence of the argument made earlier is that if we *only* rewind the tape of λ but keep Ω the same the λ tape would look different in detail but not in essence. It may well be, as argued by the technological equivalent of "ultra-Darwinists" such as Liebowitz and Margolis,[65] that in most cases the market (or whatever other selection agency was operative) chose the "best" outcome. But such optimality is always conditional on what is known at that time Ω_t. Had the techniques that were eventually selected never appeared on the technological menu, the technological "species" we call modern technology would still have been *modern* (i.e., of our time) but may have functioned and looked quite different.

Western versus Oriental Technology: Chance or Fate?

We are now in a better position to return to the question of the rise of Western technology. The specific forms and manifestations that Western technology took were certainly contingent, but these may not have mattered. Had the West "selected" lighter-than-air instead of fixed-wing aircraft or funicular instead of locomotive-pulled railroads, its economic success and political domination would have been little changed. If the selection rules by which new techniques are chosen were changed, the same would have been true. The religious strictures that prevented Islam from adopting the printing press for centuries and the politics of insulation and the ban on firearms practiced in Tokugawa Japan should remind us that such selection rules may still have a profound influence even when the underlying Ω-knowledge has become available. A fortiori, if the propositional knowledge on which Western techniques were based was allowed to change, and if the metarules by which intellectual resources were allocated, research topics chosen, and hypotheses formulated and tested were allowed to be different, the technological face of society would have ended up very different indeed.

Can we picture what Western technology would have looked like in the absence of certain epistemic bases? For instance, the growth in the understanding of electricity in the eighteenth century was slow and halting. Many scientists, such as the great eighteenth-century French physicist Charles-Augustin de Coulomb, believed that magnetism and electricity were unrelated. But in 1819 a Danish physicist, Hans Oersted, brought a compass needle near a wire through which a current was passing. It forced the needle to point at a right angle to the current. It turned out that electricity and magnetism were related after all. From this point on, the knowledge basis started to increase quickly, and what happened subsequently may well be considered close to inevitable. Electromagnetism, once discovered, was turned into a legitimate field of inquiry by the work of William Sturgeon, Michael Faraday, and above all Joseph Henry, who advised both the Englishman Charles Wheatstone and the American Samuel Morse, who built the first practical electromagnetic telegraph systems.

The early nineteenth century was a period in which "demand" for rapid communications was increasing, in part because the French Revolution and the pursuant wars increased the need for rapid long-distance communications, but also because of the integration of capital markets and the development of railroads. Was the electromagnetic telegraph "inevitable"? It seems to depend on whether we think that advances in the understanding of electromagnetic phenomena, above all Oersted's discovery, were inevitable. It is inconceivable that Oersted would have been able to conduct his famous experiment without the voltaic battery invented twenty years earlier. But we can be more precise than that. In this particular case, it is fairly straightforward to speculate that in the presence of electricity, but without Oersted, electrochemical telegraphs were a viable alternative, though they too depended on voltaic piles.[66] Until deep into the 1840s, inventors experimented with electrochemical telegraphy. It never did attain practical success, but it could have had it not been for the greater effectiveness of electromagnetic techniques.

In the absence of voltaic piles or similar devices relying on a growing understanding of how to generate a weak electrical current—which would have thwarted all electrical telegraphy—something quite different would have emerged. Claude Chappe's semaphore system, a mechanical telegraph based on a much simpler knowledge base, was used quite widely in the first decades of the century and might conceivably have become the "norm" for long-distance communications, albeit in forms modified beyond anything we can imagine.[67] It might have been less "efficient" than what actually emerged, but nobody would have known the difference, just as we cannot know of possible techniques that were within our reach but just never occurred to anyone.

On a larger scale, then, I am arguing that from the point of view of AD 1000, the events in the West were rather improbable, even if from the point of view of 1700 they were not. By the time of the Glorious Revolution—and here I differ from Jack Goldstone (in chap. 6 of this volume)—the culture that created the growth of the epistemic bases of technology that led to the Industrial Revolution was in place and would have required more than a minimal rewrite to dislodge. It did not depend on Britain as much as some (British) economic historians would have us believe. The European continent was perfectly capable of rapid technological progress, even if a Continent-led Industrial Revolution would have been somewhat different in emphasis and timing from the one that actually took place.

Now suppose these intellectual developments had not happened in Western Europe, for example, because the Colombian voyages inflicted on Europe a catastrophic epidemic comparable to the one the Europeans inflicted on the destination areas. Would some other area in the world have followed a somewhat similar pattern? Would, for example, Africans have eventually invented a steam engine if left alone by Europeans? The critical question is not whether there is coal in Africa (there is) or whether some Africans had the ironworking skills (they did), but whether the underlying knowledge of atmospheric pressure would *ever* have occurred in an African cultural setting. It is always difficult to test a counterfactual argument, but we are not completely in the dark. The best test case we have to compare the rise of Western science and technology to is China. China developed a large and substantial body of knowledge of nature largely independent of the West, cataloged in great detail in the volumes put together by Joseph Needham and his collaborators (*Science and Civilization in China*). The question "if some invention had not been made in the West, would it have been made anywhere else?" may be unanswerable. But the least we can do is ask whether there is a high probability that it would have been made in China. Needham, whose work on Chinese science and technology led him to view the great divergence between East and West as the central historiographical issue of our time, viewed science and technology as "inseparable."[68]

The nature and characteristics of Ω-knowledge as it developed in China were not "less" or "worse" than what transpired in the West, but its ability to serve as an epistemic base for Chinese technology clearly did not work as well if our criterion is "ability to generate economic growth."[69] Chinese technology, no matter how sophisticated and advanced, remained grounded on a narrow epistemic base. Needham cites with approval the verdict of a ninth-century Arab author that "the curious thing is that the Greeks are interested in theory but do not bother about practice, whereas the Chinese are very interested in practice and do not bother much about the theory."[70] As a general statement about scientific knowledge in China, this is not entirely accurate. In medicine, theory and practice were never separated. But medicine was the exception.[71] In engineering, mechanics, chemistry, mining, and agriculture, the savants and the fabricants in China were as far as or farther apart from one another as they ever were in Europe.[72] It is perhaps telling that while a considerable number of Chinese *techniques* in one form or another found their way to the West there are few instances of Chinese propositional knowledge (not to mention science proper) being adopted by the West.

To return to the previous example, would the Chinese have invented electrical telegraphy if the West had not? As is well known, the Chinese in the Song period had discovered magnetism and developed a floating needle that served as a compass. They had figured out some fairly advanced properties of magnetism, such as magnetic declination (the error term in the compass due to the difference between the magnetic North Pole and the geographical north of the planet), known as early as the ninth century AD, and magnetic remanence (acquisition of magnetic properties due to cooling), known in the eleventh century. Yet the understanding of electricity, let alone the connection between electricity and magnetism, seems to have eluded them.[73] Given their understanding of the properties of magnetized needles, the Chinese expanded this knowledge in obvious directions (above all the compass), but they failed to make the less probable leaps made by Oersted and Henry. In the absence of Western influence, China would probably not have gone in that direction in historical times.

The issue of steam power is more complex. Kenneth Pomeranz (chap.

9 in this volume) feels that the Chinese had the "basics" for the steam engine. Knowledge of the atmosphere, and the understanding of water condensation can surely be found, and if *all* that was required to make a steam engine was the knowledge of physics of, say, a James Watt or a John Smeaton, it is indeed likely that in the absence of the West the Chinese would have stumbled on something like it. But it is telling that the earliest reference to the epistemic base of steam power in China dates from the Han period and may well predate Thomas Newcomen by almost two millennia. Yet nothing happened in China that we know of with certainty.[74] In the West, by contrast, models of a working steam engine appeared half a century after Evangelista Torricelli's demonstration of atmospheric pressure. Furthermore, the mechanical bellows described by Wang-Chên in 1313 had the structure of a reciprocating steam engine "in reverse." Watt's idea of double-acting cylinders and his famous sun-and-planets gear, which led to the transformation of Newcomen's pump to a source of industrial power, may well have had oriental antecedents. But the essence of the engine was the deeper problem that Papin and Newcomen solved: the conversion of heat into work. Needham concedes that in this regard Europe did something that the Orient did not.[75] All the same, early steam engines in Europe were constructed on a narrow epistemic base, and in that regard it is hard to disagree with Pomeranz that the Chinese *could* have invented it. But the likelihood is small.

One can find other examples in which Chinese society did not come up with Ω-knowledge that would have led them in all likelihood to techniques that would have been of use to them. Consider optics. For understandable reasons, there seems to have been a universal interest in the topic.[76] Optics is not an exactly delineated area of useful knowledge since it involves physical and physiological phenomena (the nature of light and the process by which it is received and processed by the human body). Optics was born in classical civilization but remained essentially unapplied, the myth about Archimedes constructing concave mirrors that burned Roman ships notwithstanding. The greatest advances before Johannes Kepler's celebrated essay, *Expounding the Optical Part of Astronomy* (1604), were made by Alhazen (Al-Haytam, early eleventh century), who studied curved mirrors and lenses and first established that light travels from the source to the eye and not vice versa. Yet from a technological point of view, the first successful application was the emergence of eyeglasses in the 1280s.[77] Without some underlying Ω, the probability of this technique emerging was low indeed.[78] Given, however, that this knowledge emerged, the eventual occurrence of even better spectacles (correcting for myopia in addition to presbyopia), telescopes, and microscopes was more likely. Yet how probable was the development of useful optics? As Needham has demonstrated, the Chinese tried.[79] It is true that glass, though known in China, was not in wide use, in part the result of supply considerations (expensive fuel), and possibly in part due to lack of demand (tea was drunk in porcelain cups). But knowledge must have played a main role: not having access to the Hellenistic geometry that served not only Ptolemy and Alhazen but also the sixteenth-century Italians such as Francesco Maurolico (1494–1575), who studied the characteristics of lenses, made the development of optics difficult. The probability of a microscope being invented by someone who does not have access to geometry is very low, though it cannot be ruled out that a different kind of mathematics, not imagined by us, could have achieved the same results.[80] Had China been the world, or had the West never had Western science, optical devices similar to the ones we have would in all likelihood never have been developed.[81] And yet, as the steam engine example demonstrates, the presence or absence of an epistemic base does not always by itself determine the likelihood that a technique will be invented. A technique has to be "imagined," that is, it has to occur to someone, who can then map from Ω to produce a new technique in λ. There is nothing automatic or self-evident about this process. A lot depends on the connections between the intellectuals with the time and education to give free rein to their imaginations and the people slaving away in fields and workshops.[82]

The complexity of the question is demonstrated with a later invention, anesthetics. Much like eyeglasses, the "demand" for or necessity of anesthetics were hardly time or society specific, although the willingness and ability to tolerate and inflict pain are of course to some extent culturally determined. For hundreds of years, Europeans suffered unspeakably from operations conducted without anesthesia. Discovering that a number of substances could knock a patient unconscious without long-term damage must have increased the total consumer surplus (if not necessarily the gross domestic product) by a considerable amount. Yet the discovery seems to have been not just accidental, but made almost in an absentminded fashion, underlining both the lack of inevitability in invention and the absence of a need to fully understand the natural processes underlying the technique (let alone the science). Ether was first synthesized in 1540 and known as "sweet vitriol"—why did it take three centuries for its properties to be fully recognized?[83] It could have happened a century earlier, alleviating unspeakable agony for hundreds of thousands of "patients" of the surgeons of the time.

Could anesthesia have been invented in China? Unlike optics, in this case there was no need for some breakthrough in the underlying knowledge base since little of that took place in the West either. Nobody in the mid–nineteenth century had any idea *how* precisely ether, chloroform, or other substances knocked out the patient. The Chinese embarked on another route toward pain relief: instead of chemical intervention, their path led to physical means through acupuncture. Yet much of Chinese medicine was based on the use of herbal medicine, and the prevalence of opium in the nineteenth century indicates that chemical intervention in sensatory bodily processes was by no means alien to them. Perhaps more plausible is the explanation that surgery itself was rare in China.[84] Conditional on that premise, perhaps the Chinese should not have been interested in anesthesia. But this argument does not seem wholly satisfactory, even disregarding the obvious questions of the discomforts of childbirth. Was there anything in Chinese culture that made surgery less acceptable? To maintain simply that Chinese medicine was "different" from Western medicine and therefore failed to develop surgery, anesthesia, aseptic methods, and so on strikes me as a simplification. As noted earlier, there was not one, but many types of Chinese medicine, just as there were different approaches to other parts of natural science. Yet none of them resulted in the adoption of surgery as a widely practiced form of medicine outside of cataract surgery.[85] It must be concluded, therefore, that Western medicine itself was not "inevitable." Even given that it existed, the discovery of anesthesia was not inevitable, it did *not* occur just when the time was "ripe," and its story provides a powerful illustration of the historical contingency of techniques even when their social usefulness is unassailable and they can be made without a wide epistemic base.

The history of useful knowledge and science in China, then, is a good example of an "alternative" route that knowledge can take in different settings. It is easy and indeed tempting to attribute the differences between the growth of Ω in China and in Europe entirely to different institutional settings and social environments, or even the differences in geographic endowments.[86] But this ignores the evolutionary and sequential nature of Ω. The evolution of useful knowledge is a stochastic branching process: each step is conditioned by the state of knowledge at that time, and the direction of movement has a contingent element. By allowing for the possibility that at any point the evolution of knowledge could have gone on to a different branch than it actually did, we are implicitly allowing for a world that "knows" nature in a different manner than we do, and thus exploits it in very different way. This, perhaps, is an appropriate way to think of how knowledge might have developed in China or pre-Colombian America without the West.

Even in similar institutional environments, the trajectory of useful knowledge may end up much different because a crucial ingredient was absent or present by accident, or some decision that could easily have gone one way ended up going another. To visualize the contingent nature of what actually emerged, we should carry out the following thought experiment: think of a hypothetical society that would regard the "modern" and "progressive" West in the same way that Western historians such as Toby Huff and Derk Bodde have thought about Islamic and Chinese science: admirable in some ways but ultimately unsuccessful by the standards of another economy. Such a society might have spawned technologies we can only guess at. The only alternative is to take an arch-Whiggish view and argue that Western science is the only "true" knowledge and that there are objective truths out there to be discovered by the right people the way America was in 1492. This line of thought would have it that Europeans got it "right" and the Chinese (and everyone else) did not. Given that in this view there is only one objective truth, the question is then whether given enough time the Chinese or someone else would have found a road to electromagnetism, the germ theory, and quantum mechanics. But if there is more than one scientific "truth," just as there is more than one "true religion," then that likelihood must be viewed as vanishingly small.

Such are the philosophical issues involved in the counterfactual analysis of technology. What is not in dispute is the effectiveness of Western technology in the battlefield, the factory, the mine, the hospital, and the research laboratory. No single element can entirely explain it by itself: an anthropocentric outlook that became the hallmark of medieval occidental Christianity, the appearance of autonomous institutions such as independent universities, the heritage of Greek and Hellenistic science, the role of medieval monks in bridging the chasm between savants and fabricants, the technology of information itself (which defined the characteristics of the Ω set such as the invention of movable-type printing), or the emergence of standards of open science and a pan-European "community" of scholars sharing norms and ideas. Nothing of the sort developed elsewhere, a condition that has bothered the greatest historical minds of our century, including Max Weber, Lynn White, Eric Jones, Joseph Needham, Nathan Sivin, and David Landes, to name just a few.

It would be as pretentious as it would be pointless to survey or add to this debate in this essay. But the evolutionary framework I proposed before may help to place one or two issues in sharper perspective. The argument I am making is *not* that for most of human history the epistemic base of technology in Europe was broader than in the Orient. As late as the middle of the seventeenth century, the differences between the epistemic bases on which technology rested in the West and China was not large, as far as such matters can be assessed.[87] The great divergence between the two worlds must be associated, rather, with the culture of useful knowledge in Europe and the institutions that supported it, which over time developed characteristics that allowed the epistemic bases of technology to eventually become ever wider in a host of different areas. Over time, this created a self-reinforcing virtuous cycle that created the gap between West and East in technology over a relatively short time in the late eighteenth and early nineteenth centuries.[88] By the end of that period, the unhappy events of the Opium Wars epitomized that gap. The questions of when and how the gap emerged and whether it was inevitable are thus entirely dependent on the conditioning of the probability. Conditional on the scientific revolution, as defined earlier, the emergence of the steam-powered gunboats that humiliated China in 1840 looks possible, but anything but inevitable. In between, however, came a movement I have termed "the industrial enlightenment"—that segment of the European Enlightenment that directed the agenda of research into pragmatic questions and sought to disseminate useful knowledge to those who could best use it in production.[89] But how inevitable were the scientific revolution and the industrial enlightenment and how likely was it that the propositional knowledge that Europeans created would be mapped into the new elements of prescriptive knowledge that eventually created sustained economic growth? Above all, what mattered here was the institutional environment in which knowledge was created and distributed and the incentives that the economy provided to take advantage of the opportunities created by new knowledge. The institutional environment in Europe that created the intellectual origins of the Industrial Revolution was based on the opportunities for rebels and heretics to propose new ideas challenging conventional wisdom and getting away with their lives. It was also responding to the commercialization of life and the growing sense, best articulated by Francis Bacon, that the purpose of knowledge was to enhance material welfare and power over the environment. But had a Catholic Counter-Reformation under Habsburg leadership been successful in subjugating Protestant Europe, this movement may well have been extinguished.

Beyond that, it is important to realize that not only the social context of knowledge differed. In the West, the selection environment of useful knowledge was more stringent than elsewhere. The physical world, in the Western view, was *orderly,* that is, the same causes would lead to the same effects and one could separate the logical and comprehensible sphere of the natural world from the theological issues of Creation. These views have clear medieval roots and hark back to Plato's *Timaeus.* But it is hard to see why such interpretations would be inevitable.[90]

There is selection on Ω as well in the sense that people accept some views of the world and reject others. But the stringency of the selective pressures could vary. In a low-pressure intellectual environment, many "species" of Ω-knowledge could coexist even if by some logical standard they were mutually inconsistent. People might believe that there are natural regularities to which there are exceptions (such as magic). The selection criteria in Ω are culturally contingent, and it is easy to envisage a cultural climate in which the question "but is it true?" can be routinely answered by "sometimes" or "maybe" or "if God wills it."[91] Furthermore, the selection criterion "is it true?" might have to compete with such criteria as "is it beautiful?" or "is it morally improving?" or "is it consistent with the wisdom of our tradition?" In the West, selecting knowledge often involved the question "does the implied technique work in practice?" and a more stringent and pragmatic selection mechanism had important implications for the shape of technology.[92]

It is quite possible, then, to imagine societies in which the structure of Ω is such that inconsistent pieces of knowledge coexisted side by side and were accepted as the basis for techniques in the same communities at the same time.[93] The idea that two natural laws that negate each other could not both be true seems to be primarily a Western one. This notion is close to the absence of a definitive concept in Chinese thinking of the idea of a rigorous demonstration or "proof," as Sivin has pointed out.[94] To be sure, even in the West the precision tools of testing one paradigm against another (with the exception of astronomy) were lacking until the nineteenth century, but once they emerged, the beliefs in phlogiston and caloric disappeared, cellular interpretations of human pathology prevailed, and so on. The Copernican and the Ptolemaic views of the world and the germ and miasma theories of disease were recognized by both sides to be mutually exclusive (they could not coexist), so one of them had to go. But such a stringent selection environment *itself* is not preordained.[95]

Indeed, Chinese thinking about useful knowledge has had difficulty with the idea of "laws of nature," as Needham has pointed out. All the same, the statement that they completely replaced Western laws of nature by "an organic world of two primary forces and five phases . . . [and that] the explanation of the patterns of existence is not to be sought in a set of laws of mechanical processes, but in the structure of the organic unity of the whole" seems too strong.[96] The idea that there are regularities in nature that are predictable and exploitable is too obvious to be completely cast aside by any culture.[97] Translation becomes a key here, as the Chinese employ such words as *thien fa* (laws of heaven). Yet, as Needham insisted, these are laws without a lawgiver. In that sense, of course, the Chinese may have been closer to a twentieth-century way of thinking about nature than to the thinking of Kepler and Newton. For the ancient Chinese, the world looked more like a "vast organism, with all parts cooperating in a mutual service which is perfect freedom."[98] Needham compares this to an endocrine system in which causality is hard to pin down, and notes that modern science cannot do without it. Others have found different ways in which Western and oriental knowledge diverged. Sivin has stressed the lack of unity and coherence in Chinese science caused by the absence of an overarching philosophical view of nature. In his words, China had sciences but no "Science."[99]

In any event, given that useful knowledge as it emerged in China was profoundly different from that of the West, technological history would have taken a very different course without Western "modern science." There is thus no reason to believe that a world without the West would have come upon the internal combustion engine, the microprocessor, or stereotactic surgery. The Chinese might have, however, quite likely stumbled on the smallpox vaccination, semaphore telegraph, hot-air ballooning, Bessemer steel, aspirin, or other inventions requiring narrow epistemic bases. However, the mutually reinforcing interaction between science and industry that created modern metallurgy, chemical engineering, biological technology, and such were unlikely to have emerged.

This is not to say that without the rise of the West, the Orient would forever have been as inward looking and stagnant as it was in 1850. Asians might once again have built a grand fleet and explored the world. A Japanese-Korean-Chinese collaborative effort, under the right set of circumstances, might have created a dynamic not unlike the North Atlantic semicompetitive research program that produced the Second

Industrial Revolution. Material wealth and even a degree of technological sophistication can be and were created with narrow-based techniques. At some point, however, the gains from further technological experimentation would have started to level off without the mutual reinforcement of Ω-knowledge and λ-knowledge.

And yet at the end of the day, it is hard to know precisely whether oriental science, had it been left alone long enough by the West, would not have developed into something so radically different from what we are used to that we cannot even imagine it. That takes us back to figure 1: an evolutionary view of the world suggests that there are possible states of the world that, while not imagined, *might* have occurred given the opportunity and sufficient time. The problem is that such opportunities, too, depend on historical contingency. This kind of area is precisely what the region ϕ denotes. We can, by definition, have no idea what ϕ may contain or how large it may be. Just as a lot of indigenous flora and fauna in isolated demes have their evolutionary path cut short or altered irreversibly by a catastrophic event or the invasion of a fitter species, technological evolution can be affected by the invasion of a "fitter technology." There is no way of knowing whether pre-Columbian Peru or Maori New Zealand would ever have developed forms of technology that would astound us the way Marco Polo was astounded by China and the way New Guinea natives were astounded by Western technology. We can be pretty sure, however, that unless they somehow managed, against all odds, to produce an Ω set similar to that produced by Galileo, Lavoisier, or Maxwell, the technology in use in these areas would have looked very different from what it looks like now.

NOTES

I am indebted to the excellent research assistance of Steven Nafzinger and Amit Goyal. Yoav Kislev, Peter Meyer, Deirdre McCloskey, Wolfgang Latsch, and the editors have made very helpful comments on an earlier version.

1. Cited in Robert Tucker, ed., *The Marx-Engels Reader*, 2nd ed. (New York: Norton, 1978), 767.

2. Robert Paul Thomas, "The Automobile Industry and Its Tycoons," *Explorations in Entrepreneurial History* 6, no. 2 (winter 1969): 139–57.

3. David. S. Landes, "What Room for Accident in History? Explaining Big Changes by Small Events," *Economic History Review* 47 (1994): 637–56.

4. Richard Ned Lebow, "Contingency, Catalysts, and International System Change," *Political Science Quarterly* 115, no. 4 (winter 2000–2001): 591–616.

5. Daniel Headrick, *The Tools of Empire* (New York: Oxford University

Press,1981); *The Tentacles of Progress* (New York: Oxford University Press,1988).

6. See Robert K. Merton, "Singletons and Multiples in Scientific Discovery," *Proceedings of the American Philosophical Society*, 105 (1961): 470–86; and S. C. Gilfillan, *The Sociology of Invention* (Cambridge: MIT Press, 1935). The dated but still excellent literature survey in A. E. Musson, "Editor's Introduction," in *Science, Technology, and Economic Growth in the Eighteenth Century*, ed. A. E. Musson (London: Methuen, 1972), 1–68, remains a good place to start examining this literature.

7. The seminal sociological essay making this point was W. F. Ogburn and D. Thomas, "Are Inventions Inevitable? A Note on Social Evolution," *Political Science Quarterly* 37 (1922): 83–98, although the phenomenon had been discerned much earlier. See Merton, "Singletons and Multiples in Scientific Discovery."

8. Thomas, "The Automobile Industry and Its Tycoons," 140.

9. See Joel Mokyr, *The Gifts of Athena: Historical Origins of the Knowledge Economy* (Princeton: Princeton University Press, 2002).

10. For a recent restatement, see J. Bradford DeLong, "Cornucopia: The Pace of Economic Growth in the Twentieth Century," NBER Working Papers, no. 7602, 2000.

11. Areas that have rejected Western influences, such as Afghanistan, North Korea, or Burma, or areas that have for one reason or another not been able to absorb much of it (say, in Papua New Guinea), have perhaps been fortunate in terms of preserving what they regard as their unique culture. But they have done so at a staggering price in terms of material well-being. These countries illustrate in vivid color what the entire world might have looked like had the "West never risen." I should add the obvious caveats that such regions are selected and thus not representative of what, say, Japan or Taiwan would have looked like, and that even in those countries that have avoided Western influence the impact of the West and the negative reaction to it obviously contaminate the experiment.

12. Robin Cowan and Dominique Foray, " Evolutionary Economics and the Counterfactual Threat," unpublished paper, MERIT, University of Maastricht; and IMRI. Université Dauphine, 1999.

13. The most famous example is Robert Fogel, *Railroads and American Economic Growth* (Baltimore: Johns Hopkins University Press,1964).

14. The term *useful knowledge*—first proposed by Kuznets—is elaborated in some measure shortly. For a more detailed discussion, see Joel Mokyr, "Science, Technology, and Knowledge: What Historians Can Learn from an Evolutionary Approach," Max Planck Institute on Evolutionary Economics, Working Papers, no. 9803, 1998; and "Knowledge, Technology, and Economic Growth during the Industrial Revolution." in *Productivity, Technology, and Economic Growth*, ed. Bart Van Ark, Simon K. Kuipers, and Gerard Kuper (The Hague: Kluwert Academic Press, 2000), 253–92.

15. Formally, this is not quite accurate; beavers may build dams and bees hives, although, as far as we can tell, there is no "knowledge" underlying these techniques.

16. Joel Mokyr, "Useful Knowledge as an Evolving System: The View from Economic History," in *The Economy as an Evolving Complex System, III: Cur-*

rent Perspectives and Future Directions, ed. Lawrence E. Blume and Steven N. Durlauf (Oxford: Oxford University Press, 2006), 307–37.

17. Stephen Jay Gould, *Wonderful Life: The Burgess Shale and the Nature of History* (New York: Norton, 1989), 48.

18. Cowan and Foray, "Evolutionary Economics and the Counterfactual Threat," 16.

19. Daniel Dennett, *Darwin's Dangerous Idea: Evolution and the Meanings of Life* (New York: Simon and Schuster, 1995).

20. Donald T. Campbell, "Blind Variation and Selective Retention in Creative Thought as in Other Knowledge Processes," in *Evolutionary Epistemology, Rationality, and the Sociology of Knowledge,* ed. Gerard Radnitzky and W. W. Bartley, III, 91–114 (1960; reprint, La Salle, IL: Open Court, 1987); Michael Bradie, "Assessing Evolutionary Epistemology," *Biology and Philosophy* 1, no. 4 (1986): 401–59; Franz Wuketits, *Evolutionary Epistemology and Its Implications for Humankind* (Albany: State University of New York Press, 1990); Kai Hahlweg and C. A. Hooker, eds., *Issues in Evolutionary Epistemology* (Albany: State University of New York Press, 1989).

21. Richard Nelson, "Recent Evolutionary Theorizing about Economic Change," *Journal of Economic Literature* 33 (March 1995): 48–90; John Ziman, "Selectionism and Complexity," in *Technological Innovation as an Evolutionary Process,* ed. John Ziman (Cambridge: Cambridge University Press, 2000), 41–51.

22. Hindsight bias is perhaps at play here: we know that the Greeks and Romans did not discover America, and while Vikings and probably Basques reached the North American coast, this knowledge did not become accessible to many others. Hence the most acceptable assessment would be that had the technology not advanced, the discovery might still have occurred, but with lower likelihood.

23. Jack Cohen and Ian Stewart, *The Collapse of Chaos: Discovering Simplicity in a Complex World* (Harmondsworth: Penguin,1994), 54.

24. Richard N. Lebow, Janice Gross Stein, Steven Weber, and Steven Bernstein, "God Gave Physics the Easy Problems: Adapting Social Science to an Unpredictable World," *European Journal of International Relations* 6, no. 1 (2000): 43–76.

25. Ziman, "Selectionism and Complexity."

26. For some exceptions, see Edward Constant, *The Origins of the Turbojet Revolution* (Baltimore: Johns Hopkins University Press, 1980); Walter Vincenti, *What Engineers Know and How They Know It* (Baltimore: Johns Hopkins University Press, 1990); and the essays in Ziman, *Technological Innovation as an Evolutionary Process.*

27. See Mokyr, "Science, Technology, and Knowledge"; "Evolutionary Biology, Technological Change, and Economic History," *Bulletin of Economic Research* 43, no. 2 (April 1991): 127–49. "Evolution and Technological Change: A New Metaphor for Economic History?" in *Technological Change,* ed. Robert Fox (London: Harwood, 1996), 63–83.

28. The underlying Ω-knowledge is also subject to selection, but here the concept is less sharp. Selection may be viewed as the process in which some people choose to believe certain theories and regularities about natural phenomena and reject others. This is the way evolutionary epistemology thinks of it. Alterna-

tively, we may think of knowledge being stored in people's minds and storage devices, but some knowledge is being discarded because of positive storage costs. Those two types of selection do not wholly coincide. Historians of science preserve knowledge of discredited theories, while some knowledge is believed to be "true" but sufficiently trivial to be discarded.

29. Mark Ridley, *The Problem of Evolution* (Oxford: Oxford University Press, 1985), 55–56.

30. A glance at the phyla that did at some point exist was provided by the celebrated Burgess Shale. Gould, in his *Wonderful Life,* has maintained that fifteen or twenty extinct organisms unearthed there "deserve" by the distinctness of their anatomy alone the rank of a separate phylum. Regardless of what other biologists think of this claim, given the unusual circumstances of the Burgess Shale, one has to concede that the diversity of actual life on earth may exceed anything we deem possible.

31. Dennett, *Darwin's Dangerous Idea,* chap. 5. In Dennett's words, Superman, who flies faster than the speed of light, is logically possible but physically impossible; Duperman, who flies faster than the speed of light and stays in the same place, is even logically impossible.

32. This set is not quite identical to the set believed to be possible at any time t. Today $(t = T)$ we believe that travel at speeds exceeding the speed of light, transforming lead into gold by chemical means, creating a perfect perpetuum mobile, and the passing of acquired characteristics through animal breeding are not possible, yet people at various times in the past believed such techniques to be possible and spent resources trying to develop them.

33. Note that the "imagined and possible" set includes a large component that could not be achieved by the technological means of the time and hence is not in the feasible set. Roger Bacon, Guy de Vigevano, Francesco di Giorgio Martini, and for that matter Jules Verne all imagined techniques that were beyond the reach of their times, so that they were in the potential but not the feasible sets. Bertrand Gille points out that mechanization was in part the result of a "speculative type of thinking; Da Vinci was not the least of its representatives." See Bertrand Gille, "The Fifteenth and Sixteenth Centuries in the Western World," in *A History of Technology and Invention,* ed. Maurice Daumas (New York: Crown, 1969), 42. At the same time we can think of many examples of techniques that were quite within the technical potential of certain societies but simply never occurred to anyone before. Once seen, they were embraced with enthusiasm. One thinks of wheelbarrows and spectacles (invented in the Middle Ages) or barbed wire and anesthesia (invented in the mid-nineteenth century).

34. While the Dutch inventor Cornelis Drebbel actually succeeded in building a prototype of a submarine in 1620, there was no chance of it ever becoming a reality before the advent of electrical power and the invention of the internal combustion engine. Blaise Pascal and Gottfried Leibniz imagined and designed calculating machines, but the engineers of their time were simply unable to construct the parts to make such machines within reach. They were feasible but not realizable.

35. See chapter 1.

36. See Mokyr, *The Gifts of Athena,* 95–104.

37. For details, see Joel Mokyr, "Long-Term Economic Growth and the History of Technology," in *Handbook of Economic Growth*, ed. Philippe Aghion and Steven Durlauf (Amsterdam: Elsevier, 2005), 1113–80.

38. Gille, "The Fifteenth and Sixteenth Centuries in the Western World," 42.

39. In 1588, for instance, Agostino Ramelli published *Le Diverse et Artifiose Machine*, which is full of lavish pictures of cranes, sawmills, hurling engines, and other devices nobody had ever seen. Yet Ramelli clearly described what he thought was possible.

40. Eugene Ferguson, *Engineering and the Mind's Eye* (Cambridge: MIT Press, 1992), 115, 120. It is not precisely clear what effect the writings of someone like Jules Verne had on the actual development of technology, but the notion that his *20,000 Leagues under the Sea* inspired some developments in submarine construction is attested by the fact that in 1886, Andrew Campbell and James Ash of England built a submarine driven by electric motors and powered by a storage battery, and named it *Nautilus;* the idea of running it by an internal combustion engine while on the surface and electric motors while submerged became the standard for the industry.

41. Thus in the eighteenth century, it was discovered that cinchona bark was an effective remedy against malaria without the slightest notion about the etiology of the disease or why and how cinchona bark and its active ingredient, quinine, worked. Yet it was known that it did, and thus the technique was used. In this case the entire knowledge on which the technique was based that "it worked." Cinchona use never led to an effective cure, let alone prevention of malaria, and its widespread use against other fevers remained, without any beneficial effects. The canning of food was discovered by Nicolas Appert in 1795, but because the underlying bacteriological principle was unknown, the food was prepared at superoptimal temperatures and was therefore unappetizing and unpopular until the Pasteur revolution of the last third of the nineteenth century.

42. Leonardo da Vinci, in a famous drawing, showed the impossibility of perpetual motion by building a device that consisted of sticks with weights attached to them and then pointing out that "no matter how much weight is attached to the wheel which weight causes the motion, doubtlessly the center of such a weight will stop at the pole and no instrument that human genius can invent can avoid such an effect," followed by, "Oh, followers of continuous motion, how many varied geniuses you have created in such research. You belong to the same fold as those who seek gold (alchemists)." Cited in Marco Cianchi, *Leonardo's Machines* (Milan: Becocci Editore, 1984), 82.

43. Donald Cardwell, *From Watt to Clausius: The Rise of Thermodynamics in the Early Industrial Age* (Ithaca: Cornell University Press, 1971), 186–238; David F. Channell, "The Harmony of Theory and Practice: The Engineering Science of W. J. M. Rankine," *Technology and Culture* 23, no. 1 (January 1982): 39–52.

44. If I win the Illinois lottery, I might say that the ex ante probability of this event was negligible, even if it actually occurred, and it is hard to say that it was inevitable. The event "it will snow in Chicago at least one day in January" may not be regarded as inevitable, but it is surely a high-probability event. Finally, if I predict that tomorrow the sun will rise in the east at some time I pick from astro-

nomical tables, the probability of that event was in fact indistinguishable from unity, and counterfactual analysis makes no sense.

45. Nathan Sivin, "Why the Scientific Revolution Did Not Take Place in China—or Didn't It?" in *Transformation and Tradition in the Sciences,* ed. Everett Mendelsohn (Cambridge: Cambridge University Press), 531–54; Lynn White, review essay on Joseph Needham's *Science and Civilization in China,"Isis* 75, no. 276 (1984): 172–79.

46. To ask why any historical event that seems a priori feasible (because it did happen elsewhere) did *not* take place is useful analytically. Why did Canada not have slavery? Why did the United States not have a successful socialist movement? Why did the Soviet Union fail to develop the microprocessor? These seem useful questions precisely because the event *did* take place in comparable situations.

47. We may write the probability of technique λ_i emerging conditional on its knowledge base Ω_i as $P(\lambda_i|\Omega_i)$. One problem is that they have to be defined over some unit of time to be meaningful: clearly, if $t \to 0$, $P(\lambda) \to 0$, and if $t \to \infty$, $P(\lambda) \to P^*$. In what follows, I shall ignore this complication.

48. In his letters trying to persuade Queen Isabella of Castile to bankroll his expedition, Columbus quoted a statement by the thirteenth-century English monk Roger Bacon to the effect that because the earth is round one could circumnavigate it.

49. Without geometry and Ptolemaic astronomy the Chinese navigators were still able to find latitude at sea, although it is unclear which instruments they used. See Joseph Needham, *Science and Civilization in China,* vol. 4, pt. 3: "Civil Engineering and Nautics" (Cambridge: Cambridge University Press, 1971), 567.

50. Derek Price has argued that rather "adventitious" changes in research technology were actually crucial in determining the speed and direction of scientific progress. See Derek J. de Solla Price, "Notes towards a Philosophy of the Science/Technology Interaction," in *The Nature of Knowledge: Are Models of Scientific Change Relevant?* ed. Rachel Laudan (Dordrecht: Kluwer 1984), 112.

51. Formally this means simply that if Ω follows a stochastic process $\Omega_{t+1} = \Omega_t + \varepsilon_t$, the term ε_t is bound away from large values so that evolution cannot change too much at one time. "Inevitability" might be a statement about a high value of $P[(\Omega_{t+1})|\Omega_t]$ or it might be a statement about $P[(\lambda_i)|\Omega_i]$. The former is a statement about the evolutionary path of propositional knowledge and the pace and direction of discovery. The latter is a statement about mapping probability, that is, the likelihood that a given piece of propositional knowledge will be applied.

52. In point of fact, the crucial event in all likelihood was the invention of the modern microscope by Joseph J. Lister (father of the surgeon), an amateur optician, whose revolutionary method of grinding lenses (around 1830) greatly improved image resolution by eliminating certain chromatic and spherical aberrations. Lister's method of combining the lenses of compound microscopes on the basis of theoretical reasoning rather than trial and error reduced average image distortion by a huge proportion, from 19 to 3 percent. Cf. Stanley Joel Reiser, *Medicine and the Reign of Technology* (Cambridge: Cambridge University Press, 1978), 76. It provides a good example of the complementary and mutual reinforcement of Ω-knowledge and "practices" (i.e., techniques).

53. Any of a hundred descriptions of "weird life forms" will do. Consider the reproductive behavior of *Hippocampus Erectus* (the common sea horse) in which—contrary to almost all other life forms—the *males* carry the fertilized eggs in a brood pouch and then lay them much like all other species. A tropical frog, *Dendrobates*, observes the following division of labor. The mother lays her eggs and covers them. The father visits the site from time to time and urinates on the eggs to keep them moist. The mother then returns to carry the young tadpoles on her back, one by one, depositing them in the branches of a tree and visiting them from time to time. If they survive, she lays a few infertile eggs for their nutrition. See Robert Wesson, *Beyond Natural Selection* (Cambridge: MIT Press, 1991), 76. It is hard to imagine that this kind of trait is "inexorable" by any definition.

54. Michael Shermer, *Why People Believe Weird Things: Pseudoscience, Superstition, and Other Confusions of Our Time* (New York: Freeman, 1997); Martin Gardner, *Science: Good, Bad, and Bogus* (Buffalo: Prometheus, 1981).

55. A striking example of this is the polygraph ("lie detector" machine), which is widely used by investigative agencies despite its very dubious credentials and inadmissibility in courts of law. See Kenneth Alder, "To Tell the Truth: The Polygraph Exam and the Marketing of American Expertise," *Historical Reflections* 24 (1998): 487–525.

56. Of course, it is also possible, as Cohen and Stewart (*The Collapse of Chaos,* 55) point out, that there is a truly alien science whose knowledge is completely orthogonal to ours and that knows things that never occurred to us, and vice versa. Or, more disturbing, perhaps all of *our* physics has been led down the wrong path and some other civilization could have done it better, or just differently, and achieved better results. Given the ability of the knowledge underlying Western science today to map into techniques that actually work, such a view is unlikely to gain much acceptance today. All the same, we cannot dismiss the possibility that some future scientists will look at the science of the late twentieth century with the same disdain we reserve today for phlogistic chemistry.

57. A. C. Graham, "China, Europe, and the Origins of Modern Science: Needham's *The Grand Titration,* in *Chinese Science: Explorations of an Ancient Tradition,* ed. Shigeru Nakayama and Nathan Sivin (Cambridge: MIT Press, 1973), 68.

58. Alfred Crosby, *Ecological Imperialism: The Biological Expansion of Europe, 900–1900* (Cambridge: Cambridge University Press, 1986). See also chapter 9 in this volume.

59. Modern science is now recognized as the one and only basis of pharmaceutical knowledge by the People's Republic of China, leading to a reassessment of the Chinese materia medica by its criteria. Cf. Paul Unschuld, *Medicine in China: A History of Pharmaceutics* (Berkeley: University of California Press, 1986), 285.

60. Mokyr, *The Gifts of Athena,* chap. 6.

61. Brian W. Arthur, *Increasing Returns and Path Dependence in the Economy* (Ann Arbor: University of Michigan Press, 1994).

62. Ibid., chap. 2.

63. Thorstein Veblen heaped scorn on the aphorism as a "fragment of uncritical rationalism" and insisted sarcastically (with considerable exaggeration) that

invention was "always and everywhere" the mother of necessity. See Thorstein Veblen, *The Instinct of Workmanship* (New York: Macmillan, 1914), 314–17. Similarly, Carlo Cipolla states that "necessity explains nothing; the crucial question is why some groups respond in a particular way to needs or wants which in some other group remain unfulfilled." See Carlo Cipolla, *Before the Industrial Revolution,* 2nd ed. (New York: Norton, 1980), 181. Lynn White points out that this fallacious aphorism can be traced to the twelfth century and cites numerous counterexamples. See Lynn White, *Medieval Religion and Technology* (Berkeley: University of California Press, 1978), 222.

64. The highly contingent story of the zipper is retold in Henry Petroski, *The Evolution of Useful Things* (New York: Knopf, 1993).

65. S. J. Liebowitz and S. E. Margolis, "Path Dependence, Lock-in, and History," *Journal of Law, Economics, and Organization* 11, no. 1 (April 1995): 205–26.

66. The idea of using the chemical effects of electricity as a means of long-distance communication was proposed as early as 1795 by the Catalan scientist Francisco Salvá and was worked out in some detail by the Bavarian S. T. Von Soemmering in 1809.

67. The Chappe semaphore telegraph, operating throughout France, as well as in other parts of Western Europe, was quite successful: it could transmit under optimal conditions a bit of information from Paris to Toulon in twelve minutes, in contrast to the two full days it would take a messenger on horseback. A hundred-signal telegram from Paris to Bordeaux in 1820 took ninety-five minutes, and in 1840 half that. Given that a "signal" was picked from a code book with tens of thousands of options, this was a huge amount of information. The optical telegraph at its peak covered five thousand miles and included 530 relay stations. The Chappe system was a government monopoly and did not serve as a means of transmission of private information, yet in the absence of the electrical telegraph there is no reason why it could not have played a much larger role. Another widely used visual telegraph was developed in 1795 by George Murray in England. This system rapidly caught on in England and the United States, where a number of sites bearing the name Telegraph Hill or Signal Hill can still be found, particularly in coastal regions. Cf. Alexander J. Field, "French Optical Telegraphy, 1793–1855: Hardware, Software, Administration," *Technology and Culture* 35 (1994): 315–48; and Daniel Headrick, *When Information Came of Age: Technologies of Knowledge in the Age of Reason and Revolution, 1700–1850* (New York: Oxford University Press, 2000).

68. Nathan Sivin,"Science and Medicine in Imperial China: The State of the Field." *Journal of Asian Studies* 47, no. 1 (February 1988): 47.

69. We should not turn the story into what Nathan Sivin has called "a saga of Europe's success and everyone else's failure" ("Why the Scientific Revolution Did Not Take Place in China," 542). Yet he himself notes a few pages earlier (537) that "the privileged position of the West comes . . . from a head start in the technological exploitation of nature." It is unreasonable to explain such a head start without admitting that something that westerners learned about nature was different from what was learned in China.

70. Joseph Needham, *Clerks and Craftsmen in China and the West* (Cambridge: Cambridge University Press, 1970), 39.

71. Sivin, "Science and Medicine in Imperial China"; Toby Huff, *The Rise of Early Modern Science* (Cambridge: Cambridge University Press, 1993).

72. Needham points out that the Greek distinction between theory and practice, the former suitable for a gentleman and the latter not, has a precise equivalent in the Chinese distinction between *hsüeh* and *shu*. Cf. Joseph Needham, *The Grand Titration* (Toronto: University of Toronto Press,1969),142.

73. Joseph Needham, *Science and Civilization in China,* vol. 4, pt. 1: "Physics" (Cambridge: Cambridge University Press, 1962), 238.

74. In his famous essay on the topic, Joseph Needham, "The Pre-natal History of the Steam Engine" (published in his *Clerks and Craftsmen in China and the West,* 145) tells of a document from the second century BC in which a Chinese author explains that "to make a sound like thunder, put boiling water in a vessel and sink it into a well. It will make a noise that can be heard several dozen miles away," an experiment that anticipated Magdeburgian effects. More recently Kenneth Deng has argued that Chinese propositional knowledge was such that the steam engine was highly unlikely. See Kenneth Deng, "Why the Chinese Failed to Develop a Steam Engine," *History of Technology* 25 (2004): 151–71.

75. Needham points out that "Newcomen . . . appears more original, and also at the same time more European, than [was previously realized and] . . . he stands out as a typical figure of that modern science and technology *which grew up in Europe only*" (*Clerks and Craftsmen in China and the West,* 136, 202, emphasis added).

76. A. C. Graham and Nathan Sivin produce an interesting early beginning of Chinese Mohist studies (fourth century BC) in certain areas of optics, but the insights of these writings led nowhere, presumably because they were incompatible with the mainstream of Chinese natural philosophy. Cf. A. C. Graham, and Nathan Sivin, "A Systematic Approach to the Mohist Optics," in Nakayama and Sivin, *Chinese Science,* 105–52. Whether they would have led to applied optics if Mohism had become mainstream in China is hard to know, but Graham and Sivin (107) note that the optical propositions have no direct connection with technology. Other scientific sections of the Mohist canon, however, do have such applied interest, and perhaps Mohist thinking is an example of a technological equivalent of an extinct Burgess Shale "could have been."

77. It can hardly be a coincidence that Alhazen's *Optics* was translated into Latin in 1269, about a decade and a half earlier.

78. G. N. Cantor, "Physical Optics," in *Companion to the History of Modern Science,* ed. R. C. Olby et al., 627–38 (London: Routledge, 1990).

79. Thus, in the *Hua Shu* (Book of Transformations), dated to the middle of the tenth century, there is clear-cut reference to four types of lenses that enlarge, reduce, upright, and invert. The author points out that when he looked at people he realized that there was no such thing as largeness or smallness, beauty or ugliness (Needham, "Physics," 117).

80. In a recent essay, David Pingree surveys some of the achievements of Indian mathematics, known as *jyotisa,* which achievements he judges to be supe-

rior to those of any culture prior to the advent of printing. In his view, these brilliant minds remained largely isolated due to the "social, economic, and intellectual milieux in which they worked." See David Pingree, "The Logic of Non-Western Science: Mathematical Discoveries in Medieval India," *Daedalus* (fall 2003): 45–53.

81. It is telling that when Western applied optics arrived in China through Jesuit travelers in the seventeenth century, Chinese artisans such as Po Yü and Sun Yün-Chhiu soon constructed microscopes, searchlights, and magnifying glasses. Needham himself concedes that the view that regards spectacles to have been a Chinese invention is a myth. Subsequent to their invention in the West, they found their way to China rather quickly. One must conclude that the Chinese were not indifferent to applied optics, but were simply unable—given their Ω-knowledge—to create the techniques. See Colin Ronan and Joseph Needham, *The Shorter Science and Civilization in China,* vol. 1 (Cambridge: Cambridge University Press, 1978), 257; and Needham, "Physics," 118–19.

82. Needham points out that Chinese artisans were remarkably good at carrying out empirical procedures of which they had no scientific understanding. The real work in engineering was "always done by illiterate or semi-literate artisans and master craftsmen who could never rise across that sharp gap which separated them from the 'white collar literati'" (*The Grand Titration,* 27). In chapter 9 of this volume, Kenneth Pomeranz points out that networks diffusing certain types of scientific knowledge clearly existed in China, but artisans were largely outside them.

83. Nitrous oxide (laughing gas) was discovered by Joseph Priestley in 1772. No less an authority than the great Humphrey Davy suggested in 1799 that as it "appears capable of destroying physical pain, it may be possibly be used during surgical operation." Ether had also been manufactured since the eighteenth century for use as a solvent but, although its anesthetic properties were known in the early nineteenth century and mentioned in an anonymous note in the *Quarterly Journal of Science and the Arts* in 1818, they were not applied to surgery until 1842. In that year, Crawford Long in Jefferson, Georgia, removed the diseased toe of a slave boy under anesthesia. The technique was publicized widely in 1846 by an American dentist, W. T. G. Morton, who extracted a tooth using ether. Two years earlier, Horace Wells had used laughing gas for similar purposes. The celebrated Scottish gynecologist James Simpson discovered at about the same time (1847) the properties of another chemical solvent, chloroform. Within a few years the idea "caught on," and surgery went through its greatest revolution ever. See Ulrich Tröhler,. "Surgery (Modern)," in *Companion Encyclopedia of the History of Medicine,* ed. W. F. Bynum and Roy Porter, vol. 2 (London: Routledge, 1993); Arthur W. Slater, "Fine Chemicals," in *A History of Technology,* ed. Charles Singer et al., vol. 5 (Oxford: Oxford University Press, 1958); and Sherwin B. Nuland, *Doctors: The Biography of Medicine* (New York: Knopf, 1988).

84. Paul Unschuld, *Medicine in China: A History of Ideas* (Berkeley: University of California Press, 1985), 150–52.

85. Although the Chinese are known to have experimented with cataract surgery, influenced by Indian medicine, in the ninth and tenth centuries, the initiatives did not take off. When an American medical missionary, Peter Parker,

opened a clinic in Canton in 1835, cataract patients flocked to him by the thousands. Chloroform anesthesia was reportedly used in China in 1848, within two years of its use in the West. See Unschuld, *Medicine in China: A History of Ideas,* 152; and S. Yung, "History of Modern Anesthesia in China," in *Anaesthesia: Essays on Its History,* ed. Joseph Rupreht et al. (Berlin: Springer Verlag, 1985).

86. Huff, *The Rise of Early Modern Science,* chaps. 7–8; Kenneth Pomeranz, *The Great Divergence: China, Europe, and the Making of the Modern World Economy* (Princeton: Princeton University Press, 2000).

87. Derk Bodde makes this point very strongly when he claims that by 1668 "the traditional technologies of Europe and China alike were both based more on practice than on theory and had both reached approximately the highest point possible for such technologies before the advent of modern science." Theory, however, was not really the issue. By 1700, Europeans had already vastly expanded the dimensions of Ω, in geography, hydraulics, optics, the manipulation of domesticated animals, graphical representation, astronomy, scientific instruments, crop rotations, and so on. Like Needham, Bodde seems too closely wedded to the linear connection between "scientific knowledge" and technical progress. His notion that "in 1687 Newton's *Principia* was published . . . [and] less than a century after, steam was beginning to turn the wheels of Britain" implies a simplistic causal connection that cannot be defended. See Derk Bodde, *Chinese Thought, Society, and Science* (Honolulu: University of Hawaii Press, 1991), 235.

88. Bodde (ibid., 362) provides a list of Chinese inventions, such as the astronomical clock, mathematical navigation, and the seismograph, that became "magnificent dead ends" (to use David Landes's term) and were not further developed. Bodde ascribes this to a Chinese lack of interest in theory. In my view, they all represent examples of singleton inventions or at least inventions with very narrow epistemic bases.

89. See Joel Mokyr, "Presidential Address: The Intellectual Origins of Modern Economic Growth," *Journal of Economic History* 65, no. 2 (June 2005): 285–351.

90. The twelfth-century mini-Renaissance, which included such writers as Peter Abelard, William of Conches, Hugh of St. Victor, Adelard of Bath, and others, might be thought of as "neo-Platonist" in this regard, as it laid down the foundations of a rational and mechanistic view of the universe that itself became the foundation of seventeenth-century natural philosophy. Huff (*The Rise of Early Modern Science,* 105) notes that twelfth-century Islamic writers developed philosophical views that were Platonist enough to be offensive to the Islamic religious elite but that did not elaborate the rationalistic and mechanistic worldview that Western Europeans built on Plato's edifice.

91. An example is the Jain belief of *syadvada,* which can be summarized as saying that "the world of appearances may or may not be real, or both may and may not be real, or may be indescribable, or may be real and indescribable, or unreal and indescribable, or in the end may be real *and* unreal *and* indescribable." Cited by Robert Kaplan, *The Nothing That Is* (Oxford: Oxford University Press, 1999), 45, emphasis added.

92. Bodde (*Chinese Thought,* 97–103) points, for instance, to "correlative

thinking" as the metaparadigm of Chinese thinking: the organic harmony of the natural world depended on that of the social world, the two were closely intertwined, and one could look at one to explain the other. This meant, for instance, that natural disasters could be caused by the misconduct of the emperor. Such correlative thinking is found everywhere. Johannes Kepler tried to correlate the three laws of motion with the Holy Trinity, and William Harvey's discovery of the circulation of blood was correlated with the meteorological circulation of water. In the view of Huff (*The Rise of Early Modern Science,* 252), who follows Bodde's lead on this, "China never outgrew this way of thinking and thus did not embark on the path of causal thinking as did the West."

93. Unschuld (*Medicine in China: History of Ideas,* 4–15) points out that in 3,500 years, Chinese medicine adopted demonic medicine, Buddhist medicine, religious healing, Western medicine, and other foreign systems, but not in some kind of linear succession in which one system is replaced by another. Instead, often the new and the old continued to exist side by side more or less peacefully. It is interesting to note here Lynn White's remark ("Review Essay," 177) that in China one could be a Confucianist, a Taoist, and a Buddhist all at the same time.

94. Cited in Graham, "China, Europe, and the Origins of Modern Science," 62.

95. Huff (*The Rise of Early Modern Science,* 105) maintains that in Islamic society, many interpretations of nature were occasionalist, quite typical of later Islamic (Ash'arite) worldviews. Such interpretations assume that natural phenomena are not necessarily subject to immutable and observable causal laws, but only to the omniscient and omnipotent will of God.

96. Ibid., 251.

97. Needham (*The Grand Titration,* 322) cites Wang Pi, a Chinese writer from AD 240, as stating: "We do not see Heaven command the four seasons and yet they do not swerve from their course, so we also do not see the sage ordering the people about, and yet they obey and spontaneously serve him." The thought, he adds, is extremely Chinese. Yet the regularity of the seasons can be interpreted as a "law" even if it is unclear who legislated it. Other texts confirm the recognition of regularities (*Ch'ang*) such as the one described in Bodde (*Chinese Thought,* 332–43). Bodde, however, stresses that such texts do not invalidate Needham's belief in the absence of a Chinese equivalent of natural laws because such views were in the minority and could not have survived the rise of neo-Confucian thinking from the eleventh century on.

98. Ronan and Needham, *The Shorter Science and Civilization in China,* 1:167.

99. Sivin, "Why the Scientific Revolution Did Not Take Place in China," 533.

Hitler Wins in the East but Germany Still Loses World War II

Holger H. Herwig

Counterfactual thought experiments are troubling. At heart, they raise the question of whether they can force the historian into new modes of thinking, into probing the past in terms of paths not taken, into considering possible alternative histories (often derided as "mythistory"). At best, they can eliminate so-called hindsight bias and question long-held assumptions (in other words, steer us toward true revisionist scholarship). They can reveal the gravity of decisions taken, or not taken, and of potentially abiding consequences. As Robert Cowley has eloquently put it, "If nothing else, the divergent tracks in the undergrowth of history celebrate the infinity of human options. The road not taken belongs on the map."[1] Hence, it is at least reasonable to assume that counterfactual thought experiments can tease out further assumptions on which historical interpretations rest.

As a newcomer to counterfactual thought experimentation, I set out to avoid extremes. To this end, I eschewed the "miracle" counterfactual, the descent into what has been derisively called "social science fiction." That would have been too easy, with little relation to known historical reality. Such recourse to frivolous counterfactuals would only have fed the skeptics and denigrated the experiment. It serves little purpose, for example, to have students in an American war college speculate on what might have happened had Hannibal possessed a hydrogen bomb or had Napoleon possessed stealth bombers.[2]

Thus, in the essay at hand, I did not have Adolf Hitler assassinated early in June 1941, before the invasion of the Soviet Union on June 22, and did not have a Nazi leadership struggle to cancel that operation—with the result that Europe today might well be a German condominium. Nor did I have Hitler suddenly abandon his radicalism and become the leader of a benign "European community" or have German scientists score an early breakthrough on nuclear fission and thus allow Hitler gleefully to "eradicate" Paris and London, Leningrad and Moscow. Rather, I sought to follow Max Weber's advice to attempt only "minimal" or "plausible" rewrites of history,[3] to pursue counterfactuals that were embedded in reality: that is, ones that were supported by reasonable evidence. Most important, I accepted the basic premise of this volume—that the counterfactual framing of historical questions can tweak out the wider spectrum offered by choice and that in the process it can provide a much-needed antidote to the "certainty of hindsight analysis." Put differently, I believe in coterie, in decision making by human beings. I believe in choice, in paths both taken and not taken, and not in determinism.

Indeed, the historian would do well to take to heart the comments of a very young Winston S. Churchill on the eve of the Boer War—namely, that "antiquated War Offices, weak, incompetent or arrogant commanders, untrustworthy allies, hostile neutrals, malignant Fortune, ugly surprises, [and] awful miscalculations" are omnipresent on the "morrow of a declaration of war."[4] Political as well as military leaders are always confronted with choice. The historian judges them—with the 20/20 vision of hindsight—on the basis of whether they were right or wrong, moral or immoral. Finally, to avoid the stinging criticism that all counterfactual thought experiments are, eo ipso, hopelessly subjective, I strove to keep the "experiment" as close as possible to what we know about Hitler's foreign and racial policies, his eastern settlement and building programs, and his apocalyptic vision of "total" war. To that end, I relied on contemporary evidence—war diaries, speeches, informal discussions, formal agency briefs, and the like—provided by key decision makers to buttress my counterfactual propositions. Put simply, I adhered to the test of reasonable evidence. Last but not least, I tried to keep in mind the three major protocols of counterfactual thought experiments laid out in chapter 1 in this volume: to be explicit about how "the pivotal junctures" at which history could have been "redirected" were selected; about the "connecting principles" used "to draw conclusions about what would have happened" if "hypothesized antecedents had taken on other forms"; and about "the distinctive benefits of framing historical questions in counterfactual forms," as well as about what was most surprising in working through thought experiments. In my concluding remarks, I will assess how far I have adhered to these protocols.

The New Order in the Germanic East

To appreciate the nature of a future Germanic East, it is necessary briefly to sketch out Hitler's pre-1941 invasion views on the future of European Russia. The historical record on this is rich. Three days after coming to power, Hitler convened his military chiefs and laid out before them the main tenets of his "program": authoritarian rule at home, rapid rearmament, radical revision of the Treaty of Versailles (1919), and "the conquest of *Lebensraum* in the East and its ruthless germanisation."[5] The Nazi party (NSDAP) would secure the inner front—that is, "neutralize" potential enemies such as socialists, communists, and Jews—so that the army could concentrate on a policy of aggressive expansion. Hitler found no opposition that February 3, 1933. General Walther von Reichenau, a future commander of Sixth Army during the campaign against the Soviet Union, summed up the feelings of many officers: "We are National Socialists without party cards . . . the best and most serious."[6]

Four years later, on November 5, 1937, Hitler repeated his expansionist aspirations to Germany's military and diplomatic leaders. The Führer asked his military adjutant, Colonel Friedrich Hossbach, to take careful notes, as Hitler regarded his comments as a sort of "political testament." For our purposes, it suffices to note that Hitler proposed that Germany seize Austria and Czechoslovakia as the necessary prerequisite for the main *Drang nach Osten* (drive to the east): a war to the bitter end against Soviet Russia, to be completed at the latest by 1943–45. Neither War Minister Werner von Blomberg nor Commander in Chief of the Army Werner von Fritsch, nor Commander in Chief of the Navy Erich Raeder objected to the planned destruction of Austria and Czechoslovakia or to the extension of the war into the Soviet Union. They limited their "critique" to suggestions that Hitler might not be correct in arguing that Britain and France would stay out of a general European war.[7]

The shared mentality between Hitler and his generals about the nature of the campaign waged in the east beginning in June 1941 is also well documented. From day one of his political career, Hitler stressed the twin doctrines of race and space. The Führer nurtured a virulent, vulgarized version of social Darwinism. The rise and fall of civilizations, he argued, were directly related to their success or failure in maintaining racial purity. Human beings, like plants and insects, either survived or perished. This was a fundamental law of nature, one that had nothing to do with morality and everything to do with the will to fight (*Kampf*). In the case of Russia, Hitler from the start envisaged a cataclysmic war between two irreconcilable ideologies.

Space, to Hitler, translated not only into the radical annexationism of Generals Paul von Hindenburg and Erich Ludendorff of World War I but also into the heartland notions of geopoliticians such as Halford Mackinder and of Karl Haushofer: control of the Eurasian land mass stretching from the Rhine River to the Ural Mountains. Under the slogan "blood and soil" (*Blut und Boden*), Hitler sought nothing less than the conquest of Soviet Russia and the eradication of what he called the "Jewish-Bolshevik bacilli" that ruled the land. Conquest of *Lebensraum* in the east went hand in hand with the biological extermination of "lesser" races. Hitler desired to establish a new order by destroying the enemy in the east. For him, borrowing the words of General Friedrich von Bernhardi (1912), it was all or nothing: *Weltmacht oder Niedergang,* world power or demise. If there was a "rational" calculus behind the Führer's vision, it ran roughly as follows: the "logic of escalatory war" combined with the "terrorist logic of national regeneration" would allow a "purified" German society to establish its hegemony over continental Europe.[8]

The steps toward the barbarization of war in the east are well known. On February 10, 1939—that is, two years before the attack on the Soviet Union—Hitler informed his field commanders that the coming struggle would be "purely a war of *Weltanschauungen,* that is, totally a people's war, a racial war." He asked the Wehrmacht's leadership elite to pledge unconditional loyalty to him as their ideological Führer.[9] No objections were recorded. Hitler repeatedly referred to the coming war as a "racial war" and readily used verbs such as "eradicate" (*ausradieren*) and "annihilate" (*vernichten*) to describe his ultimate objective. On October 4, 1939, the Führer put out a directive granting all troops "amnesty" for any "atrocities" (*Greuel*) that they committed in Poland. Hitler reissued that directive on May 13, 1941, and expanded it also to include Soviet prisoners of war. Thereby, he effectively set aside the Geneva Convention on the treatment of prisoners of war, as well as the Hague Convention on the rights of civilians in war.[10]

On the last day of July 1940, having defeated France, Hitler again returned to this theme in announcing to the military his "irrevocable decision" to destroy the Soviet Union. General Franz Halder, chief of the General Staff, noted the gist of the Führer's speech in his war diary: "Decision: Russia must be finished off in the course of this confrontation. Spring 1941. The sooner we destroy Russia, the better. Operation makes sense only if we seriously cripple the state in one blow."[11] Yet again, Hitler left no doubt that the campaign was to destroy both the Soviet regime and the "Jewish-Bolshevik conspiracy" that he believed it entailed. The army registered no protests against this policy.

Both the genesis and the design of Operation Barbarossa (launched June 22, 1941) can be gleaned from the historical record. Hitler, in his addendum of March 3, 1941, to "Directive No. 21" (December 18, 1940), instructed General Alfred Jodl, chief of operations of the Supreme Command of the Armed Forces (OKW), that the war with the Soviet Union "would be more than simply a clash of arms"; rather, it was to be waged as "an ideological struggle between two *Weltanschauungen.*" It was to end with the "elimination" (*Beseitigung*) of the "Jewish-Bolshevik intelligentsia." The conquered territory was to be "dissolved into states, each with its own government."[12] How did the military respond? The Supreme Command submitted Hitler's directive to its staff for implementation within forty-eight hours of its issue. On March 13 the OKW's staff identified itself fully with Hitler's suggestion that the conquered territories be "dissolved" at once according to the geographical thrust of the German attack (north, center, and south)—that is, into Reichs-Commissariats Baltic, White Russia, and Ukraine. Additionally, the Supreme Command agreed that Heinrich Himmler and the Schutzstaffel (SS) be placed in charge of executing "special tasks at the direction of the Führer."[13] That this was a euphemism for the "liquidation" of "undesired" peoples is borne out by Hitler's further instructions to his generals on March 27, 1941. "Stalin's appointed intelligentsia must be eradicated. The ruling machinery of the Russian Empire must be destroyed. Application of the most brutal power [will be] necessary in the Great Russian Empire."[14]

On March 26, 1941, the Wehrmacht and the SS signed a draft agreement parceling out areas of responsibility for the coming war of annihilation. One day later, Field Marshal Walther von Brauchitsch, commander in chief of the army, instructed the designated commanders of Armies East to view the German-Soviet struggle as a racial war ("the struggle of race against race") and to use all possible harshness to conduct it.[15] Four days later, Hitler again lectured his military paladins on the nature of the war to be fought. General Halder recorded the Führer's instructions.

> *Struggle between two world views:* decimating evaluation of Bolshevism; akin to asocial criminality. . . . We must distance ourselves from notions of soldierly camaraderie. The Communist is no comrade from the start and will be no comrade in the end. We are here dealing with a war of extermination. . . . We are not conducting this war in order to preserve the enemy. *Struggle against Russia:* annihilation of Bolshevist commissars and of the communist intelligentsia.[16]

Once more, Hitler stated his intention to destroy the Soviet state and replace it with subservient client states, each "without its own intelligentsia." The war in the east was to be one of annihilation and racial extermination.

Hitler translated what a handful of scholars still dismiss as ideological musings into binding orders (edited and approved by Halder) shortly before the invasion of the Soviet Union. The "Decree concerning the Exercise of Military Jurisdiction" of May 13, 1941, and the "Guidelines for the Treatment of Political Commissars" of June 6, 1941, set the tone for the coming war. Troops were ordered to shoot suspected guerrillas "while fighting or escaping." Officers were admonished to submerge "feelings of justice" in favor of "military necessity." "Partisans" were to be "ruthlessly liquidated." Villages that harbored partisans were to be subjected to "collective execution of force," that is, to harsh reprisals. SS-General Erich von dem Bach-Zelewski, who knew the Nazi occupation policies in the east from firsthand experience, later conceded that the term *partisans* became "an excuse to carry out other measures, such as the extermination of the Jews and Gypsies, the systematic reduction of the Slavic people by some 30,000,000 souls . . . and the terrorisation of civilians by shooting and looting."[17]

Hitler and his military elite identified political commissars as "carriers of the Jewish-Bolshevist system" and agreed to liquidate them as such. Final battle orders to the Wehrmacht called for "ruthless and rigorous measures" against Bolsheviks and guerrillas, Jews and Russian civilians. Hitler and his later reich minister for agriculture, Herbert Backe, in February 1941 fully expected up to 30 million Russians to starve to death as a result of the planned invasion.[18] Both Hitler and General Wilhelm Keitel, head of the Supreme Command of the Armed Forces, justified these draconian policies with references to the past—to the legendary Russian army's "rape" of East Prussia in 1914 and to the allegedly "Bolshevik-inspired" German revolution of 1918. Both events, they argued, had represented nothing less than the imposition of "Asiatic customs" on to the "Germanic cultural state."[19]

Germany attacked the Soviet Union on June 22, 1941, with 3.6 million men and 3,648 tanks, arrayed along a broad front stretching from Finland to Romania, in what became the greatest single campaign of the European war. The official assessment was that Germany would win a decisive victory over the Soviet Union in the summer of 1941; accordingly, no plans were made for a follow-up winter campaign. Instead, Hitler and his generals fixed their gaze on the time after Barbarossa even before the Red Army had been destroyed. Hitler first indicated his plans for the Soviet Union to his inner circle on July 16, 1941: "Basically, it comes down to dividing up the giant cake [USSR] so that we can first rule it, second administer it, and third exploit it."[20]

Once across the Soviet border, this gigantic force of 150 divisions quickly fanned out: Army Group North headed for Leningrad, Army Group Center for Moscow, and Army Group South into Ukraine. The Wehrmacht, in cooperation with the SS, fought precisely the kind of campaign that Hitler had ordered. Unit commanders perfectly understood the Führer's earlier sinister instructions. General Joachim Lemelsen, head of General Heinz Guderian's Forty-seventh Panzer Corps, in his battle reports openly referred to "the Führer's calls for ruthless action against Bolshevism," and stated that Communist officials and their sympathizers should be "taken aside and shot."[21] General von Reichenau instructed Sixth Army that the "essential goal of the campaign" was to destroy Bolshevik power and to "eradicate" Asian influence on Western civilization. In the process, Reichenau decreed, the army would also eliminate "Jewish subhumanity."[22] General Erich von Manstein, head of Eleventh Army, demanded the "eradication" of the "Jewish-Bolshevik system" in the Soviet Union and exhorted his soldiers to show no mercy as the new "carrier of a racial conception."[23] General Hermann Hoth, chief of Seventeenth Army, called on his "racially superior" German soldiers "to save European culture from Asian barbarism," that is, from "an Asiatic mode of thinking and primitive instincts."[24] And Field Marshal Fedor von Bock, commander of Army Group Center, decreed that every German soldier had the right to gun down "from in front or from behind" any Russian suspected of guerrilla activities.[25]

Countless similar citations could be repeated from divisional commanders as well, thereby showing that such orders did not languish in army group archives. But perhaps a final word on the nature of the campaign in the east should go to General Erich Hoepner, head of Panzer Group 4.

> The war against Russia . . . is the old battle of the Germanic against the Slavic peoples, of the defense of European culture against Muscovite-Asiatic inundation and the repulse of Jewish Bolshevism. This battle must . . . therefore be conducted with unprecedented severity . . . [and] must be guided . . . by an iron resolution to exterminate the enemy remorselessly and totally.[26]

The nature of the "clash of civilizations" in the east in 1941 can easily be recognized from these selections. And while we do not always have the records to detail the mass murder down to the divisional level, Jürgen Förster has documented the case of the 707th Infantry Division, which in Belorussia in a single month in 1941 shot 10,431 out of a total of 10,940 "captives."[27] Nor will we ever have reliable figures on the number of "bandits," "agents," "saboteurs," "spies," and "resisters" shot by the SS or the Wehrmacht under the euphemism of "partisans" during Operation Barbarossa.[28] Scholars concur that their numbers were in the tens, if not hundreds, of thousands.

The Stalin "First-Order Counterfactual"

The spectacular German victories of 1941 shook Joseph Stalin to the core. He ordered Soviet factories in the German line of advance to be evacuated at once to sites beyond the Ural Mountains. On October 17–18 he convened an emergency meeting of his innermost ruling circle at the Kremlin. He ordered that antitank and anti-infantry defenses were to be built on all roads leading to Moscow and that explosive charges were to be laid at all important buildings in case the capital was lost to the Germans. Anticipating that Moscow might indeed fall to the enemy, Stalin ordered the government to prepare to evacuate to Kuibyshev and the General Staff to Arzamas. He also arranged for antiaircraft batteries to be installed in the birch forest of his dacha at Kuntsevo on a high bank of the Moscow River, which was now a mere day's drive away from the German panzers. Stuka dive-bombers were attacking Moscow. Crimson flashes on the horizon bore witness to both the intensity and the proximity of the war.

Within hours, the evacuation of Moscow was in full swing. Stalin decided to leave the capital temporarily for the relative safety of Kuntsevo. According to Dmitri Volkogonov, a recent biographer of Stalin, L. P. Beria, deputy prime minister and head of the Soviet Secret Service, nervously cautioned against the trip. Stalin was not amused by this intercession and shot Beria an irritated look. Beria stood his ground, explaining in his native Georgian that the dacha had been mined and was ready to be blown up.[29] To this point, I have relied on the known historical record. I now insert what is frequently called a "close-call counterfactual." What if Stalin would have had none of this caution and instead demanded to be transported to Kuntsevo?

Under my scenario, early in the evening of October 25, 1941, the dacha exploded in an inferno of flame and fire. The great dictator was dead. Thus, I argue that a weak and quarreling Politburo formed a ruling troika consisting of Beria, V. M. Molotov, and G. M. Malenkov. Panicked by the menacing approach of the German army, they, like V. I. Lenin and L. D. Trotsky before them at Brest-Litovsk in March 1918, sought to maintain at least a Bolshevik toehold—this time in Asiatic Russia (the area stretching from Perm, Magnitogorsk, and Chelyabinsk in the Urals to Krasnoyarsk and Novosibirsk in Siberia) by way of a peace with Germany. Without Stalin, the Red Army ceased to be an effective weapon. While some of the recent security studies literature casts doubt on the efficacy of "decapitation" (mainly through air power), serious scholars on the Soviet Union and the Red Army fully agree that Stalin was absolutely central to that system—indeed, its all-powerful head.[30] With the great dictator gone, partisan and nationalist groups that refused to bow to Hitler retreated into the mountains of the North Caucasus and the forests of Belorussia and Ukraine.

Hitler had, in fact, expressed a willingness to end Operation Barbarossa—on his terms. Already in August 1941 he had informed Propaganda Minister Joseph Goebbels of his willingness to accept a "capitulation" even from Stalin. To be sure, this would come about only on the basis of "vast territorial securities" and Bolshevik disarmament "down to the last rifle." Hitler assured Goebbels that the fate of bolshevism thereafter was of no concern to him. "It may develop [again] however it wishes once it has been hurled back into Asiatic Russia; for us that will then be of only marginal interest."[31] And in mid-September Hitler had startled his diplomats by announcing, "The war very surprisingly will end suddenly."[32] Now, on the basis of the Stalin first-order counterfactual that I have inserted, Hitler had his victory. I suggest that this is a plausible world counterfactual—the proverbial "historical near miss."

Almost immediately, Hitler set about to realize his further ambitions in the east. The official war diary of the Supreme Command provides precise insight into Hitler's military plans for the post-Barbarossa period. Thus, shortly after the Soviet collapse, Hitler ordered the Wehrmacht to reorganize and refit sixty divisions to serve as an occupation and exploitation army along the Archangel-Kazan-Astrakhan line, with forward outposts along the Ural Mountains.[33] Hitler's aim was straightforward: "Expansion and consolidation of the European–West African core base against the Anglo-American coalition."[34] There was no question in the Führer's mind that "the USA will, by 1942, be in a position to intervene" in European affairs.[35] Already, the Americans were escorting convoys to Britain and patrolling their side of the Atlantic with warships. On July 7, 1941, U.S. Navy Task Force 17 had occupied Iceland as a forward bastion against Nazi-dominated Europe. By August, the first American air squadrons had arrived at Reykjavik, and an airbase, humorously nicknamed Camp Snafu, had been scratched out of a treeless, rock-strewn field south of the capital. The move, coming while the Wehrmacht was fully engaged in Russia, had infuriated Hitler. "We cannot get around the reckoning with America," he lectured the Japanese ambassador to Berlin, General Hiroshi Oshima. "The Americans would have to get out, even if he [Hitler] would have to fight for years."[36] In other words, the war with the United States, which Grand Admiral Erich Raeder, commander in chief of the Kriegsmarine, had asked Hitler to proclaim already on July 9, 1941, was simply postponed until after the victory over the Soviet Union.

But that war would not wait. On December 7, 1941, Japanese naval air units operating off aircraft carriers bombed the U.S. Navy's battleship fleet in Pearl Harbor, Hawaii. Hitler heard the news via BBC Radio London. While his generals and admirals rushed to the map room of the Führer headquarters near Rastenburg, East Prussia, to find out where Pearl Harbor lay, Hitler "slapped his thighs, jumped to his feet as if electrified, and shouted 'Finally!' "[37] In a venom-laden speech to a hastily assembled Reichstag, "the world's largest male glee club," as Berlin wags called it, Hitler declared war on the United States. Two days later, he assured Ambassador Oshima that Pearl Harbor had constituted "the proper declaration of war!" By attacking the United States, Japan had made the struggle global. Its entry into the war constituted "a great relief" for Germany since the United States could not now concentrate its forces against Nazi-dominated Europe.[38] Already in November 1940,

Hitler had drawn a bold pencil down the spine of the Urals on the globe in his study to demarcate the dividing line between the German and Japanese "share" of the Soviet Union.

Hitler next returned his attention to the conquered East. Again, the historical record is rich. Hitler and General Keitel reorganized the vast majority of the army and air force units that had just won Operation Barbarossa—but for radically different purposes than was the case with the occupation forces. Numerous infantry divisions were dissolved and their officers and men incorporated into new panzer armies. As documented in General Halder's war diary, Hitler as early as April 1941 had ordered the Wehrmacht after Barbarossa to revamp into 24 panzer divisions, 12 motorized assault divisions, 66 "normal" infantry divisions, 10 alpine divisions, and 24 "mobile" divisions (including 8 for the tropics).[39] Now work on the Kriegsmarine's massive "Z-Plan" fleet of 684 ships was set in motion once again. The fleet was to be ready by 1948 for deployment against "the Anglo-Saxon maritime powers."[40] As revealed by Alfred Rosenberg's political diary, the Ministry for the Occupied Eastern Territories began work on a vast expansion of the navy's new Atlantic base at Trondheim, Norway. It was to become a port of 250,000 inhabitants and, in Hitler's words, would relegate Singapore to mere "child's play" by comparison.[41] In the rush of victory in the east, the navy asked Hitler for a "global" blue-water fleet of 3.3 million tons, including 20 battleships, 31 aircraft carriers, 100 cruisers, and 500 U boats![42] Shortly after the Japanese attack on Pearl Harbor, Tokyo in fact informed Berlin of its plans to divide the world at a line running north to south at 70 degrees longitude. Even General Halder found this early division of the globe—analogous to Pope Alexander VI's division of the world between Portugal and Spain in 1494—bombastic: "These people dream in continents."[43] For the moment, top priority in rearmament was accorded the Luftwaffe—both for its ongoing terror campaign against British cities and for future transatlantic sorties against America's East Coast cities.

The new mobile army became the spearhead for a "global blitzkrieg."[44] The war diaries of both the Supreme Command of the Armed Forces and the Naval High Command provide evidence for the Führer's plans. The blueprint, "Directive No. 32: Preparations for the Period After Barbarossa," penned already on June 11, 1941—that is, eleven days before Barbarossa—called for three major German assaults in the Middle East, the Mediterranean, and North Africa. In the west, German and Spanish forces seized the pivotal British naval base at Gibraltar (in Operation Felix) in the winter of 1941–42. Concurrently, seven German divisions embarked from southern French ports and landed in Spanish Morocco (in Operation Felix-Heinrich), from where they reinforced Vichy French possessions in North and West Africa. Hitler moved substantial Kriegsmarine and Luftwaffe units into the new West African bases to "seize Atlantic islands with offensive stance against America." From yet to be built air bases on the Azores, Hitler planned shortly "to deploy long-range bombers against the United States."[45] He ordered German armaments plants to step up production of the Focke-Wulf 200C four-engine bombers and to rush into production the new Heinkel 177 and Messerschmitt 264 long-range "America bomber," which could be deployed against U.S. targets as far inland as the Great Lakes. To remind the Bolsheviks in Asiatic Russia of their subordinate role in world affairs, Luftwaffe General Walther Wever pushed ahead with series production of what he called the new "Ural bomber."[46]

Hitler's projected occupations of Gibraltar and Spanish Morocco were but the precursors to what the Führer, in "Directive No. 32," called the "resettlement of the Mediterranean Sea area." German naval and parachute units were to assault Malta and Cyprus. Concurrently, General Erwin Rommel's reinforced Afrika Korps was to seize the important fortress and port of Tobruk[47] and then mount plans to break out of Libya into Egypt, effectively severing Britain's "windpipe" to India. The Mediterranean was to become a German, rather than an Italian, "lake."

In the fall of 1942 the victorious Hitler went on the offensive again, this time with a three-pronged blitzkrieg to seize Britain's Middle East positions. Under the actual "Directive No. 32," the Afrika Korps advanced from western Egypt to the Suez Canal. Another panzer force drove from Bulgaria through Turkey to Vichy French Syria and then to Palestine. A third panzer formation stormed out of "Transcaucasia" through Iran and into Iraq as far as Basra. The Anglo-Iranian Oil Company's wells and its major refinery at Abadan fell into German hands. Saudi Arabia, and with it the world's largest known oil reserves, lay within reach.[48] Hitler established a "Special Staff F" within the Supreme Command to foment Muslim uprisings around the world against their British overlords and thereby further destabilize the British Empire. Early in 1943 Hitler ordered the Wehrmacht to undertake a last offensive under the same "Directive No. 32": into Afghanistan and thus against India, the "jewel in the crown."[49] The *furor teutonicus* was to be the first battlefield test for Hitler's new hundred-ton "Maus" panzers.

The operation was never completed. The immediate threat to India sufficed, I suggest, to bring down Prime Minister Churchill's government.

With no hope of defeating Hitler on the Continent now that Soviet leaders had come to terms with the dictator, and with its major imperial vestige, India, threatened, London accepted the Führer's mastery of continental Europe. At Hitler's "suggestion," an interim government was formed, headed by Lord Halifax, Sir Samuel Hoare, and David Lloyd George. At a lower level, Sir Oswald Mosley's reinvigorated British Union of Fascists ruled the streets and William Joyce ("Lord Haw-Haw") the airwaves as director general of the BBC.[50] With King George VI safely escorted to Canada, Hitler returned the duke of Windsor to the throne to maintain a semblance of continuity. Halifax, a former viceroy of India and foreign secretary, in July 1938 during a visit to Germany had reportedly informed Captain Fritz Wiedemann, Hitler's adjutant, that he would regard as the culmination of his life to be at the Führer's side greeting the king at Buckingham Palace amid the "cheerios of the English people."[51] He now agreed to cooperate with the Germans in hopes of thereby maintaining the British Empire.[52] Of course, Hitler in "Directive No. 32" reserved the right to invade the British Isles at some future point if the new government failed to meet his expectations.[53] In the west, only the United States remained to carry on the struggle against Nazism.

While his armies were conducting their *Weltblitzkrieg* from Gibraltar to Afghanistan, Hitler set about to establish the new order in European Russia. His historical inspiration was the Raj, the British Empire in India. The historical record—especially the Führer's "secret conversations" with small groups of his inner circle—allows insight into those policies. By any standard, the occupation policies in the east were staggering in their scope. "The Slav people," the Führer informed his inner circle, "are not destined to lead an independent life." It would be "a great mistake" to allow them to return to Christianity, as this would permit them "to reorganize." There was to be no independent status for either the Baltic states or Ukraine; both became German satellites. The Slavs were not taught to read, not taught technical skills. Their task was simply "tilling the soil." Hitler saw absolutely no reason to distribute the land to the Russian peasantry. Decollectivization would lead to reduced productivity and endless ownership quarrels. Instead, German megafarms replaced the former collective farms and supplied "grain to all in Europe who depend on grain." The Crimea, renamed Gothengau, became an exclusive German colony and yielded its "citrus fruits, rubber (with 40,000 acres [of plantation] we will ensure our independence) and cotton." In return, Hitler provided the Slavs "with scarves, glass beads as jewelry and everything that colonial peoples like." No medical care, no vaccinations, no soap for the local populations. Above all, there was to be no talk of eternal peace. *Kampf* (struggle) remained the byword of the new Ministry for the Occupied Eastern Territories. "I would rather wage war for ten years," Hitler had boasted in September 1941," than be cheated of the spoils of victory." His "demands" in the east, he cheerily noted, were "hardly exorbitant."[54]

Month after month, Hitler pursued his monstrous goals with regard to the Slavs with dogged determination.[55] His "New India," as the Führer called the Germanic East of 150 million people, was being reconstructed by "helot armies" composed of 3 million former Soviet prisoners of war, recruited for twenty years of slave labor. By August 1942, the new order in the East began to take shape. Ukraine and the Volga Basin became "the granaries of Europe." In every "center of importance" Rosenberg's Ministry for the Occupied Eastern Territories set up markets. German brokers bought up the grain and fruit they needed for the Reich and in return sold the natives "the more trashy products of our own manufacture." German textile firms found "a splendid market for cheap cotton goods" in the east. German agricultural machinery factories, transport companies, and producers of household goods likewise secured "an enormous market for their goods." Rosenberg's ministry gradually "assimilated" the "best" of the Ukrainian women (about 400,000 to 500,000) into the Reich's racial stock, as they were "bursting with health"; "the rest can remain there."

Conversely, by a gradual policy of not inoculating the Slavs against disease, compelling them to live in swamps and marshes, and forcing countless males to undergo sterilization, the population was "weeded out" and replaced with Nordic stock. Hitler reveled in the monstrous nature of the occupation policies. The "laughable (*lächerliche*) hundred million Slavs," he mused, would become human raw material. And anyone who suggested that the indigenous population be uplifted, the Führer trumpeted, went "straight off into a concentration camp!" At first, Hitler argued that "Saint Petersburg" was to "disappear utterly from the earth's surface. Moscow, too. Then the Russians will retire to Siberia." But he later relented—in part. While Leningrad was battered into submission by German artillery and air strikes, for administrative purposes the Führer opted to leave a much reduced Moscow as the seat of government for the "Commissariat Muscovy."

European Russia became a German colony. Exploitation was the order of the day. "Timber we have in abundance," Hitler gushed with excited anticipation, "iron in limitless quantities, the greatest manganese-ore deposits in the world; oil—all is awash in it! German man-power deployed there; O Dear God!" The future was limitless. "No one will ever drive us out of the East!" Germans began to visit their new colonies by driving their Volkswagen cars on superhighways that stretched from Trondheim to the Crimea, or by heading east on the new double-decker, four-meter-gauge railroads that ran from Upper Silesia to Maikop and on to Rostov.[56]

Hitler rejected all suggestions that he collaborate with local ethnic, separatist, or religious groups. He had come not as a liberator but as a conqueror.[57] He dissolved the anti-Soviet Kaminski Brigade and General Andrei Vlasov's Liberation Army. Cossack, Kalmyk, and Tatar leaders who came to pay their respects were curtly ordered to submit to Rosenberg's Ministry for the Occupied Eastern Territories. Muslim Balkars and Tats (or Mountain Jews) were similarly informed.

To be sure, the administration and exploitation of the east on such a gigantic scale demanded a suitable "world" capital. For that, Hitler turned to his architect, Albert Speer, whose 1969 *Memoirs* are a rich source on the Third Reich's building plans. Speer set out at once to demolish and then rebuild the core of five so-called Führer cities by 1950. Three stand out by their vastness of scale. Nuremberg became the permanent site of the annual Nazi rallies; the new Congress Hall for 60,000 of the most faithful was to dwarf the Coliseum in Rome and to house the rallies "for the next 800 years." The Olympic Games, Hitler ordered, were to become the "Germanic" games, for which he instructed Speer to build a stadium for 405,000 spectators.[58] Munich, the "capital of the movement," was accorded its own grandeur: a new opera three times the size of the Vienna Opera, a new central train station six times the combined size of Saint Peter's Church and Saint Peter's Square in Rome, and a "victory memorial for the party" twice the size of the city's Frauenkirche.[59]

The greatest planning, of course, went into the new world capital of "Germania" (formerly Berlin), now with 10 million inhabitants. It was, in Hitler's words, to radiate the "magic" of Mecca or Rome.[60] The centerpiece was to be a four-mile-long north-south boulevard, more than twice the length of the Champs Élysées in Paris. Hitler planned the first "world parade" to be held on it for 1950. Two train stations, each larger than Grand Central Terminal in New York, were to set off both ends of the axis. A Triumphal Arch twice as grand as its Parisian model was to remind the nation of its victories. A Congress Hall seven times the size of Saint Peter's in Rome was to become a fitting venue for foreign potentates arriving to offer allegiance to the new "master of the world." The hall was to be crowned by a giant eagle clutching a globe, "whose possession," Speer later recalled, "Hitler did not seek merely symbolically."[61] Money, the Führer assured Speer, was of no concern; the conquered territories were being plundered to meet building costs. As well, Speer sought tens of thousands of Russian prisoners of war to work on the project.

In all Hitler and Speer undertook, their single, obsessive aim was gigantomania. Tempelhof in Berlin was to become the world's largest airport. Rügen Island was to receive the world's largest outdoor swimming pool, Herzberg the world's most powerful radio transmitter, and Hamburg the world's highest and longest bridge (to rival the Golden Gate Bridge in San Francisco). Berlin's 120-meter-wide east-west axis was to become the broadest in the world (surpassing the Avenida del Libertador in Buenos Aires). All monuments and halls were to be built of granite and marble and were to last three to four hundred years. "I am building for eternity," Hitler boasted, "because this will be the last Germany."[62]

But the ephemeral building boom of the Nazi regime soon collapsed. Not even the vast labor pool of the Germanic East could provide the skilled craftsmen needed for such monumental projects. The marble and granite quarries of Denmark, France, Italy, and Sweden could not keep pace with demand. As well, some fifty German cities, each jealous of the attention lavished on the five Führer cities, rallied to outdo one another in monumental buildings. This, in turn, encouraged each regional party leader (*Gauleiter*) to try to immortalize his role in the Nazi movement by way of massive memorials and residences. Naturally, each branch of the armed forces demanded its own memorials and heroic cemeteries. In the former Slavic East, Hitler had Wilhelm Kreis design gigantic monuments to the dead (*Totenburgen*), as well as war memorials (*Soldatenhallen*). Labor unrest became common at many of the construction sites, as workers rebelled against the forced pace of construction, which included mandatory Sunday work.[63]

The "victorious" Hitler showed no mercy toward the Jews of Nazi-occupied Europe. Once more, the historical record is rich. Already on the last day of July 1941, Hitler, by way of Hermann Göring, had instructed Reinhard Hedyrich of the Sicherheitsdienst (SD) "to carry out all the necessary preparations with regard to . . . bringing about a complete solution of the Jewish question in the German sphere of influence in Europe." On August 1, Hedyrich informed his superior, Reichsführer-SS Himmler, "that in the future there will be no more Jews in the annexed Eastern territories."[64] Still, Goebbels rushed to the Führer's headquarters late in August to complain about the "lenient" treatment of Berlin's Jews, only one-third of whom, he lamented, were manually employed. Hitler, Goebbels recorded in his private diary, was most sympathetic and immediately promised "to push the Jews off to the east as soon as the first transport possibilities became available." There, Hitler assured Goebbels, "we will lay our hands on them under much harsher conditions."[65]

In fact, Heydrich scheduled a meeting in Berlin to deal with the "Jewish question" for December 9, 1941. It had to be postponed for three weeks because of the Japanese attack on Pearl Harbor and the Führer's hasty declaration of war on the United States two days later. On January 20, 1942, the meeting took place at a villa on the shores of the Wannsee in Berlin. In what was now officially called the "final solution" of the Jewish question, Heydrich proposed to murder "some eleven million Jews"— including those in Britain, Switzerland, Sardinia, and Sweden. The largest group to be killed was in Ukraine (3 million) and the next largest in the General Government in Poland (2.3 million). The Jews would be worked to death; those who survived, Heydrich stated, would be "dealt with appropriately," that is, murdered.[66] The entire German governmental apparatus—Chancery, Foreign Office, Ministry of Justice, Ministry of the Interior, Ministry for the Occupied Eastern Territories, Plenipotentiary for the Four Year Plan—bought into the genocide. Central and eastern Poland became the killing ground: Auschwitz, Belzec, Chelmno, Majdanek, Sobibor, Treblinka. Satellite camps were quickly established in the Germanic East. Day after day, the "cattle trains," each loaded with 1,000 Jews, rolled into the extermination camps. The final solution was on track. During the first nine months of the Russian occupation alone, the SS Einsatzgruppen (execution squads) murdered more than 1 million Jews, Gypsies, and other "undesirable elements." And at a top-secret meeting (*Tagung*) convened at Posen on October 4, 1943, attended by senior SS leaders, as well as by Armaments Minister Speer and Grand Admiral Karl Dönitz, Himmler addressed what he called "a difficult chapter" in German history but one that his listeners understood. "I mean now the evacuation of Jews, the extirpation of the Jewish people." That policy constituted "a glorious page of our history," Himmler beamed, but one "which has never been written and never will be."[67]

Following his victory in the east, Hitler offered new "arrangements" to the lesser European powers. Some, such as Switzerland, were simply conquered (in Operation Tannenbaum) and divided among their neighbors. Others, such as Sweden, were brusquely informed that any disruption of raw materials shipments would trigger invasion (in Operation Polar Fox). As revealed in General Halder's war diary, Hitler ordered "in clear and uncertain terms" that client states, such as Vichy France, were to adhere to the new order unquestioningly.[68] As for Fascist Italy, Hitler had informed his staff already in May 1941 that after the defeat of the Soviet Union, "he would no longer have to take Italy into his considerations!"[69] A few steadfast allies were rewarded: Romania received Bessarabia and the Bukovina, Finland was handed Karelia, Japan was allowed to seize oil- and coal-rich North Sakhalin, and Turkey was given Armenia as a reward for not having opposed Hitler.[70] The various client states and newly subservient satellites—with the notable exceptions of Bulgaria and Denmark—sent the Jews residing within their borders to Hitler as "tribute."

The new order constituted rebirth and regeneration for a Europe, Hitler claimed, that had gone "soft" after the Thirty Years' War (1618–48). "Europe and no longer America," he predicted, "will be the land of unlimited opportunities." Thousands if not millions of Europeans who had left the Continent to seek better opportunities abroad would flood back to join the new order. They would "resettle" the Germanic East, bolster European military power, and conversely weaken the United States. Especially American engineers, two-thirds of whom Hitler discerned to be of German descent, would lead the hegira. The 130 million Americans remaining at home would face a Greater Germanic Empire encompassing 130 million Germans within the borders of the old Reich and 90 million in Ukraine, as well as the Nordic stock in the rest of Europe—in all, about 400 million. And this new Europe would be protected by a "German Monroe Doctrine."[71] Hitler was on the threshold of realizing the cherished "thousand-year Reich."

To the victors went the spoils. The Führer established a special Adolf Hitler Fund to reward his new elite. Having already been morally corrupted by their racial and occupation policies in the Germanic East, the Third Reich's paladins now added financial corruption to the list. Under the auspices of Himmler's office of Reich Commissioner for the Strengthening of German Nationhood, established shortly after the occupation of Poland, Hitler insisted that members of the new elite establish themselves on large estates in the conquered eastern lands and awarded them special tax-free cash "gifts" (*Dotationen*) to realize these ambitions.[72] Thus, at a time when an army major earned 8,400 reichsmarks (RM) per year, SS-General of Police Karl Daluege received 600,000 RM (3 million euros today)[73] to purchase Rittergut Ilsenau in the Warthegau; Waffen-SS Generals Sepp Dietrich and Theodor Eicke likewise received large grants. Field Marshal Erich Milch and Grand Admiral Erich Raeder each were handed 250,000 RM (1.1 million euros). Alfred Rosenberg was rewarded for his labors as Reich minister for the occupied eastern territories with a similar *Dotation,* while labor leader Robert Ley, whose Reich Tractor Factory in Waldbröl supplied all the tractors for the East, was handsomely compensated with 1 million RM (5 million euros). Foreign Minister Joachim von Ribbentrop was accorded 500,000 RM (2.5 million euros) and then "accidentally" handed a second check in the same amount. Goebbels and Göring annually submitted "wish lists" to industry to support their lavish lifestyles. Himmler was content with just enough money to build his mistress a villa in Berchtesgaden.

The list was endless. General Guderian received 1.24 million RM (6.2 million euros) to purchase the former family estate, Deipenhof, in the Warthegau; its Polish owner was simply evicted. General von Reichenau's family (after his death in January 1942) was given 1.01 million RM (5 million euros) to secure a manorial estate in the East. Wilhelm Ritter von Leeb was handed 888,000 RM (4.4 million euros), Wilhelm Keitel 764,331 RM (3.8 million euros), Gerd von Rundstedt and Hans-Günther von Kluge each 250,000 RM (1.25 million euros), and Ewald von Kleist 192,300 RM (1 million euros).[74] In every case, Himmler "suggested" that the money be invested in the Germanic East. Nor did Hitler, the former "Bohemian," forget his artists and architects, who, he insisted, "live like princes." Hitler chided a bureaucrat who objected to lavish grants to artists, "But you have no qualms when a manufacturer of toilet seats becomes a millionaire!"[75] While Speer received an estate in the Mark Brandenburg, Arno Breker took 800,000 RM (4 million euros) in cash.[76] The Führer could well afford to be generous: apart from the royalties for *Mein Kampf,* which by 1944 had sold more than 6 million copies, he charged the German Post for permission to use his image on stamps. Reich Post Minister Wilhelm Ohnesorge (who received a *Dotation* of 250,000 RM) each year presented Hitler on his birthday (April 20) a royalties check—which reportedly was around 50 million RM (250 million euros) per annum.[77]

The Hitler "Second-Order Counterfactual"

But the war in the east, the following *Weltblitzkrieg,* and the frenetic pace of "rebuilding" Germany had taken their toll on Hitler. To cope with his deteriorating physical condition, he had turned to Dr. Theodor

Morell, who administered a staggering array of tablets and dragées, leeches and bacilli, uppers and downers, and hundreds if not thousands of injections—of iodine, calcium, vitamins, glucose, and hormones, as well as heart- and liver-extract, seventy-four "medications" in all.[78] Hitler, ever concerned about his imminent death, insisted that he was suffering from rapid progressive coronary sclerosis (actually, it was angina pectoris). At the height of Operation Barbarossa in the summer of 1941, he was weakened by dysentery. For three years, Dr. Morell provided an ever-growing array of pills and injections to keep his patient content. By 1944, Hitler's health had deteriorated dramatically. That summer he was wracked with stomach spasms and cramps. Morell stepped up the customary lethal combination of strychnine and atropine, both deadly poisons. Hitler's physical condition continued to deteriorate rapidly under the steady dosages of poisons. On July 20, 1944, a group of General Staff officers—mostly the scions of German noble families who were concerned that Germany was rapidly heading toward catastrophic defeat—attempted to assassinate Hitler by exploding a bomb in his field headquarters while the Führer was inspecting a Maus panzer division. Hitler survived, but his already failing health further deteriorated due to the aftereffects of the blast. He next experienced throat and recurring coronary problems. By September, the Führer had become nauseous and was once more plagued by cramps, his face yellow and his urine "brown as beer."

That winter Hitler was bedridden with hepatitis. By early 1945, he was a physical wreck. Morell suspected Parkinson's disease. Hitler's left arm trembled uncontrollably. His right hand could barely scratch out a signature. His spine had lost its symmetry. His right eye was beset with conjunctivitis. Morell applied more of the same: strychnine and atropine. Late in April 1945 Captain Heinz Assmann of the Kriegsmarine left a vivid portrait of the Führer, one seconded by Albert Speer: "His handshake was soft and flabby, his gestures were those of an old, old man." Hitler's back stooped horribly. He could barely walk with a shuffling gait, his right leg dragging. His head shook constantly. His left hand, dangling from a limp arm, trembled violently. For his efforts, Dr. Morell was rewarded with a "gift" of 100,000 RM (500,000 euros).[79]

Hitler, I posit in my second-order counterfactual, died (iatrogenically) of natural (and drug-induced) causes in late summer 1945. As with the Stalin first-order counterfactual, I argue that this also is a "probable world counterfactual," one based on medical evidence that might well have led to the outcome I am about to suggest.

In his "Last Will and Political Testament," Hitler selected Grand Admiral Dönitz, a sycophantic Nazi, to succeed him. The new head of the navy (since January 1943) had fully embraced Hitler's vision of apocalyptic war, and his U-boat crews had died by the thousands to press the war against the "Anglo-Saxon maritime powers." The putative second in command, Reichsmarschall Göring, had retired to his estate, Karinhall, disabled by obesity and crippled by heroine addiction. For Dönitz, there remained but one coworker and possible rival: Reichsführer-SS Himmler. While Dönitz doggedly pursued his "tonnage war" against American merchant shipping out in the Atlantic Ocean, Himmler in cold blood pursued Hitler's final solution in the Germanic East to its ultimate end—a Europe without Jews (*judenfrei*). Day in and day out, the Auschwitz extermination camp alone "processed" about 3,500 human beings.[80] By late 1945, 8 million European Jews had been murdered. Step by step, Himmler also expanded his black empire. After the attempted assassination of Hitler, the SS was elevated to parity as an independent branch of the armed forces. The Nazi party salute became mandatory for military personnel. Political "observers" were attached to non-SS military formations. As the Wehrmacht began to downsize after its three-pronged *Weltblitzkrieg*, Himmler expanded his forces. In addition to the Waffen-SS of 100,000 men, he tightly ruled a cohort of 300,000 members of the normal police and a special "state defense corps." A further 120,000 SS men were in the regular armed forces, at Himmler's beck and call. In the summer of 1944 Himmler reorganized the SS into twelve armored divisions and an additional thirty "pan-European" volunteer divisions—a force greater than that with which the SS had invaded the Soviet Union. He even established a model "Germanic" SS tank corps (III SS Panzerkorps) as an elite armored unit charged with maintaining order and discipline in the occupied eastern territories.[81]

Back home, the Greater German Reich was a beehive of military and industrial activity. Firms such as I. G. Farben, Flick, Krupp, Mannesmann, and Thyssen took over Stalin's giant state factories. The Krupp conglomerate, for example, availed itself of the human labor pool at the Reich's disposal. By 1944, Krupp employed 54,990 foreign workers, 18,902 prisoners of war, and countless unnumbered concentration camp inmates provided by Himmler. Alfried Krupp expanded the number of labor camps just at his home base in Essen to fifty-five. He also constructed an automatic-weapons plant outside Auschwitz to take advantage of the cheap and plentiful labor there and reached an agreement with Himmler to "exchange" injured, sick or exhausted laborers for "fresh" camp inmates. Finally, he combed Nazi-occupied territories for additional forced labor.[82]

The SS sustained the Nazi building boom as well as armaments production through its vast slave labor empire.[83] Specifically, Himmler created the German Earth and Stone Works (*Deutsche Erd- und Steinwerke*) to realize the Führer's building mania. Concentration camps were purposefully sited near stone quarries such as Flossenbürg, Natzweiler, Gross-Rosen, and Mauthausen for this purpose; Neuengamme was situated near tile and brick manufactories. Plentiful and cheap labor came not only from the camp inmates but also from the "helot armies" of Slavic *Untermenschen* and former Soviet prisoners of war. German occupation authorities in the east cold-bloodedly calculated that the 6 million Wehrmacht soldiers sent there would produce 1.5 million illegitimate births—and decreed that this offspring would be returned to Germany as slave labor.

In fact, Himmler had rehearsed his ultimate plans for the Germanic East in Poland already in the summer of 1940. A leaderless labor force was put to work in quarries and on roads. The helots received only a rudimentary education—the ability to count up to five hundred and to write their names. In the countryside, Polish farmers built new villages and markets for their German overlords and planted and harvested crops. In Berlin, SS-Oberführer Konrad Meyer drafted a document, "Planning Fundamentals for the Reconstruction of the Eastern Territories," that called for the "deportation train by train" of about 3.4 million Poles and Jews to the extermination camps sited in the General Government. By the end of 1940, already roughly 325,000 people had been "deported" in accordance with Meyer's plan; another 100,000 followed between November 1942 and August 1943.[84]

But we know from surviving records that Himmler's plans went far beyond "deportation." Just two days after the start of Operation Barbarossa, he instructed the Reich Main Security Office of the SS to draft a "Generalplan Ost" to be implemented in the eastern lands over the next thirty years. Completed in May 1942, it surpassed anything proposed to date. Himmler's minions ordered the "deportation" of 31 to 45 million indigenous people (or about 70 to 85 percent of the inhabitants) from the Baltic states, Poland, White Russia, the Crimea, and parts of Ukraine to western Siberia—a "gift" to the Bolshevik government there. In fact, taking the native birthrate into account, the figure would be closer to 60 to 65 million people slated for "deportation." Whatever the total, the numbers included 5 to 6 million Jews to be "got rid of" before the trek began, their places to be taken by about 10 million new German settlers, as well as "related" Nordic stock from Denmark, Norway, Sweden, and the Netherlands. Accordingly, the Germanic East now began to take shape as a series of "racial belts" of soldier-settlers designed to keep out the "storm flood of Asia for all time." The outer rings featured "marcher settlements" of 50 percent German colonists (especially tough SS war veterans), linked to inner rings at 100-kilometer intervals by thirty-six "settlement strong points" whose residents would be 25 percent German. Himmler selected SS-Obergruppenführer Otto Globocnik, the erstwhile *Gauleiter* of Vienna, to implement the first stage of the plan in the Zamosc district of the General Government.[85] In time, Globocnik ordered the murder of 2 million human beings. The SS had found its proper role in the new Germanic East.

There remained the "America problem." Dönitz, who maintained his hands-on conduct of the Battle of the Atlantic, had but one solution: more U-boats. Yet again the historical record allows us to detail the admiral's program. Already in June 1943 he had wrung from Hitler a "Führer Directive" to refound the German navy: 11,134 new warships, including 2,400 submarines, were to be built by 1948![86] There was but one enemy for the "gray sharks": the United States. But lack of steel inhibited progress toward this new fleet. For the second quarter of 1943 alone, the navy was short 62,000 tons. Torpedoes were also in short supply; the U-boats received only 440 of the requested 600 G 7a and 730 of the required 1,400 G 7e "eels." Dönitz was able to raise the service's annual allotment of steel only by surrendering the navy's jealously guarded independence in appropriations to Armaments Minister Speer. "The year 43 was a hard nut to crack," he lectured his senior naval commanders in June 1943, "but the years 44, 45, 46, 47 will be better."[87]

At the same time, Donitz demanded qualitative improvements. Back in the 1930s, the Hamburg engineer Hellmuth Walter had developed a hydrogen-peroxide gas turbine that theoretically could drive a U-boat at thirty knots submerged. The Dutch had perfected a *Schnorchel* that allowed a submarine to take in air while submerged at minimal depths. The Kriegsmarine now melded these two innovations into a new prototype XXI boat; series production was to begin in April or May of 1945.[88] Dönitz combed Nazi-occupied Europe for skilled shipyard workers and pressed Himmler to release at least twelve thousand healthy and skilled concentration camp inmates as well.

In February 1945, as recorded in the Navy High Command's war diary, Dönitz assured an ailing Hitler that he was ready to launch a "new U-boat war." The Type XXI "electro" boats, he claimed, could travel from Germany to Japan without surfacing. By the end of the month, the head of the navy estimated that he had at his disposal a fleet of 551 U-boats, of which 350 could sally against the Americans. "The U-boat once more can operate successfully even in areas of the strongest escorts."[89] The time to deal with the United States finally was at hand. Dönitz's primary concern was that the United States could at any moment land forces in Great Britain—as it had done in Iceland in July 1941—and patrol the Atlantic in force now that the war against Japan apparently was winding down in Washington's favor. The "rebirth of the U-boat war," he boasted at a conference with Hitler, was "significant for the overall war situation"[90] vis-à-vis America. In fact, the first 1,600-ton Type XXI boat (range 15,500 miles) did leave Bergen, Norway, on April 30, 1945. Lieutenant Commander Adalbert "Adi" Schnee, outbound for the Caribbean Sea, gleefully reported that U-2511's submerged speed of seventeen knots allowed him to operate in and out of convoys with near impunity. A new "happy time" had dawned for Dönitz's gray sharks.

While the admiral was resuming the U-boat campaign out in the Atlantic, Wernher von Braun and his team of fifteen hundred engineers and scientists at Peenemünde on Usedom Island in the Baltic Sea rapidly moved forward with the development of a new A9/10 two-stage intercontinental ballistic rocket. This weapon was to be used against the United States. Braun personally went to Buchenwald to recruit skilled labor and eventually brought fourteen hundred concentration camp inmates, as well as three thousand "eastern laborers," into the program. The forced laborers drilled and blasted bombproof production halls into the Harz Mountains at KZ Mittelbau-Dora, where they built the parts for the A9/10 rocket.[91] These were then transported to Peenemünde for final assembly. American bomber flyovers apprised Washington of this new development.

In fact, the "new U-boat war" and Braun's rocket program greatly alarmed Washington. By late summer 1945, imperial Japanese forces had been driven back across the Pacific to their home islands. There was no question of Japan winning the war, but the human cost of invading the home islands was expected to be horrendous. Thus, on August 6, 1945, the United States exploded "Little Boy," a 4.5-ton nuclear bomb, over

Hiroshima. Three days later, a second nuclear bomb, "Fat Man," exploded over Nagasaki. Japan sued for an end to the war on August 14; the formal instrument of surrender was signed in Tokyo Bay on September 2, 1945.

Departing from actual historical developments and returning to my Hitler second-order counterfactual, I argue that the two nuclear explosions did not deter Dönitz from pursuing his *Götterdämmerung*. In fact, Germany continued to pose a "clear and present danger" to the United States from its continental "Fortress Europe" even after the Japanese surrender. Washington now focused on Berlin. There is no question today, on the basis of the documentary record of the Manhattan Project, that the European émigré scientists at the Los Alamos Laboratory in New Mexico—Leo Szilard, Enrico Fermi, Hans Bethe, Victor Weisskopf, Eugene Wigner, James Franck, and Niels Bohr—were convinced from the start that Germany had a stable of first-rate scientists—Otto Hahn, Werner Heisenberg, Max von Laue, and Carl F. von Weizsäcker—who understood the destructive possibilities of nuclear fission. Thus, they, along with American and British colleagues such as Glenn Seaborg, David Kawkins, and J. Robert Oppenheimer, were united in the conviction that the atomic bomb was to be used next against Nazi Germany.[92] General Leslie R. Groves, director of the Manhattan Project, also harbored no prejudices against targeting Germany. As he later recalled: "President [Franklin Delano] Roosevelt asked if we were prepared to drop [atomic] bombs on Germany if it was necessary to do so and we replied that we would be prepared to do so if necessary." The only (superfluous) caveat was that, at the insistence of General H. P. "Hap" Arnold, commander of the U.S. Army Air Forces, an American-made airplane should carry the bombs.[93]

The Boeing B-29 "Superfortress" heavy bomber was such an American-made airplane. First tested in flight in 1943, it had a range of 3,250 miles and a payload of 20,000 lbs. The B-29 was the bomber of choice used to pound Japan into surrender, and now a few units were shifted to Iceland. Fully fueled and precisely piloted, the B-29 could make the 2,970-mile round trip from Reykjavik to Germany. As a result of my second-order counterfactual, in September 1945 a B-29 manned by a specially trained composite crew took off from the American runway at Camp Snafu outside Reykjavik on a heading of 106.1 degrees east-southeast. Payload: a 4.5-ton nuclear bomb. Target: Hamburg. It exploded 1,800 feet over the city with a force equal to 13,000 tons of TNT. An immense reddish-purplish mushroom cloud boiled upward from ground zero. Two powerful shock waves violently shook the B-29. Immediate deaths on the ground were estimated at between 100,000 and 130,000 civilians. A week later, a second nuclear bomb exploded over Munich. It devastated more than two square miles of the Bavarian capital and killed approximately 100,000 people.

Still the Dönitz successor government refused to surrender. President Harry S. Truman, who had succeeded Roosevelt in April 1945, warned Dönitz that more bombs would come should Germany continue the war. In fact, the United States was producing two atomic bombs per month in the second half of 1945. After the first two nuclear bombings, the Dönitz regime responded with a series of countermeasures, ranging from the destruction of occupied cities to putting hostages (captured Allied airmen) in vulnerable German cities to test-firing the A9/10 prototype rockets at cities on the Eastern Seaboard of the United States. Washington reacted angrily with a further half dozen atomic bombings (Augsburg, Bremen, Essen, Frankfurt, Hanover, and Mannheim). Early in 1946 Berlin sued for an end to the war.

A pax Americana ensued. In this counterfactual thought experiment, World War II ended not with an Allied, but rather with an American, victory. The United States emerged from the conflict with virtual global hegemony, with sole possession of the atomic bomb, and with all potential rivals either in ruin or reduced to second-rate powers. Germany had been decimated by atomic bombings. Britain struggled to regain international legitimacy and reestablish its empire. The Bolsheviks emerged from beyond the Urals to reclaim as much as they could of the former Soviet Union. They posed no serious threat to the United States, and hence there was no immediate cold war, no division of either Germany or Berlin. And there was little need for a Marshall Plan; Europe was left to recover on its own.

Over time, I suggest, the world would have emerged along today's lines. But it would have been a long journey and a difficult one. Without the polarization of the world between Moscow and Washington, European states would have been left alone to sort out the past. Passions, hatred, and lust for revenge would have been high on the agenda. Most Europeans would have sought some form of retribution against the former Third Reich. Germany's borders would have been redrawn. Germans, in turn, would have resented the use of atomic weapons against them and been far less willing to accept Western notions of capitalism and parliamentarism.

Yet, once on the road to recovery, the European states would of necessity have banded together to form a counterweight to American hegemony. Some form of "common market" or "European community" would have come about. The transition from production to service industries would have taken place—as coal yielded to oil, steel declined, and high technology came to dominate the market. The U.S. dollar would have remained the global currency, English the global language of business and banking, science and technology. There would have been no pressing need to establish NATO, but some form of a European "mutual defense force" would have come about to keep the Bolsheviks in check. China would have developed as it did under Mao Zedong. And eventually Japan would have rebuilt its industries and taken its place as a Pacific economic player. What today we euphemistically refer to as globalization—read Americanization—would have come about much earlier. In other words, the American pursuit of open global markets from Woodrow Wilson to Franklin D. Roosevelt to Ronald Reagan would have been realized probably by the 1950s. With but a single superpower, the United Nations would not have emerged as a strong voice of the so-called third world; rather, it would have become a clearinghouse for American initiatives. Far beyond that, I dare not venture. The farther we extend our counterfactual world into the future, the more opaque and frailer the connecting assumptions and principles become. Differing branching points and vast and unpredictable probabilities cloud our vision.

Finally, I want to point out that the "Hitler Wins but Germany Loses" counterfactual thought experiment reveals both the fragility and the resilience of the West. A Nazi victory in 1941 would have constituted a triumph over all that we associate with the term *Western civilization.* While the Nazis at times claimed to be defending that culture against what they called "Asiatic barbarism," in fact the brown revolution of 1933 was a victory against Western civilization. The Nazis viewed themselves as counterrevolutionaries insofar as their revolution was designed to undo the "negative" effects of both the French Revolution of 1789 and the Bolshevik Revolution of 1917. Hitler had little in common with, and cared little about, egalitarianism, pacifism, internationalism, liberalism, or capitalism. His revolutionary dynamic was driven by racial conflict. Its operative was first exclusion and then annihilation. The regime's anti-intellectualism and primitive tribalism were in deep tension with core Western values. Joseph Goebbels perhaps best expressed the political-cultural character of a Nazi Europe during a national radio broadcast as early as April 1, 1933: "We will erase the year 1789 from the pages of history."[94] For a brief period after 1941, the Nazi "victory" resulted in a more brutal West. It brought into play the darker side of the Western heritage—hatred, racism, expansionism, and state-inspired mass murder.

That Nazi victory failed to come about because of the other side of the coin—the West's incredible resilience. Nazi Germany was defeated—both in reality and in this counterfactual thought experiment—by the Western values of science and tolerance. Nazi notions of "Aryan" versus "Jewish" science blinded the Third Reich's leadership to the potential military use of atomic weaponry. Failure to understand the concept of operations research meant that the West rather than the Third Reich developed radar, high-frequency director-finders, and the computer. Moreover, Nazi tribalism carried the intellectual seeds of its own destruction. The West was simply too resilient and entrenched for the Nazis to achieve a radical transformation of its cultural and intellectual character. Their occupation policies in the Germanic East, however radical, eventually proved to be transitory.

Conclusion

We return to the basic question: what is the value of a counterfactual thought experiment? The historian who has thus "altered" the past needs to pause and take stock. I fully concur with the commonsense view that even the plausible counterfactual has to take into account the historical antecedent. I could not imagine a plausible scenario in which Hitler at a particular spot in his career—say, July 1940—simply decided to stop his plans of conquest in the east and to establish a lasting system of German hegemony in Europe (a special kind of "norm-restoring counterfactual"). To be sure, a durable German hegemony at that point was feasible. Some of Hitler's professional diplomats put forth such a possibility. But that would have gone against every word that the Führer had ever written or spoken and would have been diametrically opposed to his racial and annexationist beliefs. Likewise, to have Hitler invade the Soviet Union in June 1941 as a liberator and to have him restore the land to the peasants, churches to the clergy, independence to Ukraine, and autonomy to the Tatars would have violated all that we know about the nature of that campaign. At a general level, such a norm-restoring counterfactual simply plays into the hands of the critics. It is not grounded in reality. While world leaders do change (dare I say, mature) over time, as in the case of

Menachem Begin and Anwar al-Sadat, they rarely change their spots, from Chinggis Khan to Mother Theresa. To have Hitler behave after the fall of France like a "traditional" German statesman such as Otto von Bismarck or Gustav Stresemann would border on the miraculous.

Therefore, I stuck to two less problematical counterfactual thought experiments. I argue that Stalin had to be "removed" by way of a first-order counterfactual for there to have been any chance of a Nazi victory. Thereafter, Hitler had to be counterfactually removed for the war to have ended, as I suggest; his rapidly deteriorating physical condition (even before the attempted assassination in July 1944) rendered a further five or ten years' rule highly improbable.

The Stalin first-order counterfactual seemed most credible, most plausible. Few scholars will dismiss offhand the fact that chance (assassination, change in travel plans, oversight, unanticipated error) and random events do occur and that they are bound by no political or social science theory. The "death" of Stalin in October 1941 due to an explosion at his dacha (as feared and relayed to Stalin by Beria) does not require a miracle explanation. Nor does such a close-call counterfactual make mandatory an alternative world—a much more brutal, aggressive West. Nor does it "stop" history. It does, however, extend both the intensity and the geographical reach of the Holocaust. It puts into play Hitler's maniacal occupation policies in the east, which are well documented in his speeches and "secret conversations," as well as in the actual occupation policies. It documents the unbounded arrogance and gigantomania of the Third Reich's master architect. It reveals Hitler's obsession first with Britain (the *Weltblitzkrieg* to seize its Middle and Near East possessions) and second with the United States (the use first of long-range bombers from Atlantic bases and then of A9/10 rockets from Peenemünde against American cities and the plan to confront the U.S. Navy with the "Z-Plan" fleet by 1948). And it allows for the "normal" course of events to proceed: the Japanese assault on Pearl Harbor and Hitler's subsequent declaration of war against the United States in December 1941, and even the attempted assassination of the Führer in July 1944.

The Hitler second-order counterfactual, then, undoes the Stalin close-call counterfactual and brings history fairly well back on track. By way of reasonable extrapolations of a well-established medical history, my second-order counterfactual has Hitler die in late 1945. Again, this conjures up no miracle counterfactual but rather a scenario well documented by Dr. Morell, Hitler's personal physician. It requires but a minimal rewrite of the history of that tumultuous year, 1945. It meets Robyn Dawes's test that counterfactual inferences are valid only if they are "embedded in a system of statistical contingency for which we have reasonable evidence."[95]

The rest of the story of the resulting Germanic East is also grounded in what we reasonably know of those murderous months. Hitler *did* press what already in 1933 he had called the "ruthless Germanisation" of the east to its brutal but logical conclusion—the ultimate political correctness in terms of social engineering. Dönitz *did* promise his Führer a "new U-boat war" for April–May 1945 and pressured German shipyards to test and then mass produce a new series of Type XXI boats for deployment in the Atlantic against U.S. shipping. Many expatriate European scientists associated with the Manhattan Project at Los Alamos *did* want the atomic bomb to be used against Nazi Germany. The United States *did* have a delivery system (the B-29 Superfortress) capable of dropping atomic bombs on Germany from advanced air bases on Iceland, and, according to General Groves, President Roosevelt *was* prepared to use the weapon against Germany.

Finally, the editors requested that contributors identify what they may have learned, or what may have surprised them, while wrestling with their counterfactual thought experiment. First, stark fear overcame me at the thought of "rewriting" the history of 1941. Second, a sense of revulsion grew in me at the prospect of describing the monstrous parameters of a Nazi victory in 1941 and a subsequent Germanic East. Third, a bewildering choice of possible counterfactuals confused me. Which to choose? Hitler triumphant and yet "content" and "norm restoring" after the fall of France? Hitler crossing the English Channel to hook up with Lord Halifax? Hitler invading the Soviet Union as a liberator? Hitler driving southeast for the oil of the Middle East? And fourth, a final cruel counterfactual choice: the American decision to drop the bomb on Germany, which would have killed me (then a baby in Hamburg)!

My counterfactual thought experiment does not suggest for one moment that history can be reduced to "chaostory" (Niall Ferguson) with its simplistic scale of kaleidoscopic contingency and chance. Nor does it show that historical figures at all times are free to act as they like. All major players are bound to varying degrees by circumstances, economic and material constraints, time, and situation. All are products of their intellectual and psychological makeup and predisposition (antecedent). But a naive pragmatic empiricism also does not serve historians well. For there is room for contingency, for choice, chance, accident, fate, and luck at every turn of the wheel of history. Even a person such as Hitler—that is, someone about whom we assume an unerring, steady, course-driven determinism—constantly calculated, recalculated, and posed to his inner self the question "what if?" to move his strategy forward. Admiral Raeder in his memoirs left a vivid portrait of Hitler's thought processes, eventually concluding that the Führer was a "master of dialectic and bluff," of vast knowledge and effective "evasions," to the point that Raeder "gave up trying to solve the enigma."[96]

In the end, on the issue of the value of counterfactual thought experiments, I come down on the side of contingency and choice. I respect the extent, as well as the limits, of the experiment's range of possibilities. I depict history as unfolding in an indeterminate way, the end result of unpredictable human actions and physical circumstances. To put this squarely within the context of this essay, I accept a modicum of determinism with regard to the broad contours of the eastern policies of Hitler and his inner circle. They shared a radical annexationist and racial "solution" to both *Lebensraum* and *Untermenschen*. Removing one or the other actor from a position of power would not have altered Germany's occupation policies in the east. Nor was timing critical. I argue that the removal or death of Hitler in early 1944 or late 1945 would have caused little disruption in that murderous action. Nor would it have seriously altered the assault in the Atlantic against America. It is inconceivable that either Dönitz or Himmler would have abandoned the regime's raison d'être.

But I strongly argue that there was contingency within the range of possibilities concerning the conduct of that policy. There was always a plethora of choice. This, perhaps, was the greatest surprise of the experiment. In July 1940, after the fall of France, Albert Speer has argued that Hitler was embarrassed by the richness of choice open to him. He seemed to commune with himself during those lonely walks on the Obersalzberg high above Berchtesgaden.[97] Should he now reach out and achieve an "understanding" with Britain on the basis of Europe for Germany, the empire for Britain? Or should he invade Britain and thus clear his front in the west? Should he occupy the Balkans? Should he unleash an offensive into the Middle East? And when should he launch the invasion of the Soviet Union? I suggest that the same richness of choice confronted Hitler in late summer 1941, as he became certain of victory over Stalin. To that end, and unlike 1940, he had his military staff draft the breathtaking "Directive No. 32: Preparations for the Period after Barbarossa." This was to focus his mind and sharpen his thoughts, to lay down the broad contours of policy in a new world of contingency, and to decide in the face of uncertainty how to maintain the edge, the momentum in the war. This document alone shows that a counterfactual thought experiment concerning a possible Germanic East is much more than a "parlor game."

If this conclusion waffles somewhat on the *precise* value of counterfactual thought experiments, and merely acknowledges that this process can force historians to rethink long-accepted positions and tweak out possible alternatives, then that is the extent of my intellectual dexterity. I am, in the words of Sir Isaiah Berlin (borrowing from Leo Tolstoy), a fox rather than a hedgehog. Unlike the hedgehog, I do not relate everything to a "single, universal, organizing principle in terms of which alone all . . . has significance." Rather, as a fox, I pursue many ends, "often unrelated and contradictory" and connected "by no moral or aesthetic principle." I analyze historical actors and ideas as centrifugal rather than centripetal, their thoughts "scattered or diffused, moving on many levels, seizing upon the essence of a vast variety of experiences and objects . . . without, consciously or unconsciously, seeking to fit them into, or exclude them from, any one unchanging, all-embracing, sometimes self-contradictory and incomplete, at times fanatical, unitary inner vision."[98] In short, I believe in choice, in contingency, in coterie.

Last but not least, this counterfactual thought experiment provides chilling insight into what even a temporary Nazi victory would have meant. A victorious peace in October 1941 would have given Hitler years in which to complete the final solution of the Jewish question. It would have allowed him to launch a monstrous policy of racial "cleansing" (to use a contemporary term) against what he derisively termed the "laughable hundred million Slavs." It would have allowed him to "reorder" Europe into a vast camp of subservient German client states. It would have given him control of the world's major reserves of crude oil (in the Middle East) and two of its maritime choke points (Gibraltar and Suez) through a *Weltblitzkrieg* from Spain to Afghanistan. And it would have positioned Germany to execute Hitler's final aim, a gigantic confrontation between Nazi Europe and the United States for control of the western hemisphere. Even alone, this reminder of what the world was spared by the German failure to win the war in the fall of 1941 makes the counterfactual thought experiment worthwhile. For the contingencies were catastrophic by comparison.

NOTES

1. Robert Cowley, "Introduction," in *What If? Military Historians Imagine What Might Have Been,* ed. Robert Cowley (New York: Putnam, 1999), xii.

2. Ibid., xiii.

3. Max Weber, "Objective Possibility and Adequate Causation in Historical Explanation," in *The Methodology of the Social Sciences* (Glencoe, IL: Free Press, 1949), 164–88.

4. Winston S. Churchill, *My Early Life: A Roving Commission* (London: Leo Cooper, 1989), 246.

5. Gerhard L. Weinberg, *The Foreign Policy of Hitler's Germany: Diplomatic Revolution in Europe, 1933–36* (Chicago and London: University of Chicago Press, 1970), 27.

6. Cited in Klaus-Jürgen Müller, *The Army, Politics, and Society in Germany, 1933–1945* (Manchester: Manchester University Press, 1987), 34 (comments in the winter of 1935).

7. Gerhard L. Weinberg, *The Foreign Policy of Hitler's Germany: Starting World War II, 1937–1939* (Chicago and London: University of Chicago Press, 1980), 35–40.

8. Hitler's "program" was most clearly reconstructed in Andreas Hillgruber, *Hitlers Strategie. Politik und Kriegführung 1940–1941* (Frankfurt am Main: Bernard und Graefe Verlag, 1965). See also Michael Geyer, "German Strategy in the Age of Machine Warfare, 1914–1945," in *Makers of Modern Strategy from Machiavelli to the Nuclear Age,* ed. Peter Paret (Princeton: Princeton University Press, 1986), 574.

9. *Heeresadjutant bei Hitler, 1938–1943: Aufzeichnungen des Majors Engel,* ed. Hildegard von Kotze (Stuttgart: Deutsche Verlags-Anstalt, 1974), 45.

10. Militärgeschichtliches Forschungsamt, *Das Deutsche Reich und der Zweite Weltkrieg,* vol. 4: *Der Angriff auf die Sowjetunion* (Stuttgart: Deutsche Verlags-Anstalt, 1983), 431, 433.

11. Entry for July 31, 1940, in Franz Halder, *Kriegstagebuch: Tägliche Aufzeichnungen des Chefs des Generalstabes des Heeres, 1939–1942,* ed. Hans-Adolf Jacobsen, 3 vols. (Stuttgart: W. Kohlhammer, 1962–64), 2:49.

12. See Militärgeschichtliches Forschungsamt, *Das Deutsche Reich und der Zweite Weltkrieg,,* 4: 414.

13. Ibid., 415.

14. Ibid., 416.

15. Ibid., 416–7.

16. Halder, *Kriegstagebuch,* 2: 336–7. Italics in the original. Halder's postwar attempts to "cleanse" his role in Barbarossa have been exposed by Bernd Wegner, "Erschriebene Siege. Franz Halder, die 'Historical Division' und die Rekonstruktion des Zweiten Weltkrieges im Geiste des deutschen Generalstabes," in *Politischer Wandel, organisierte Gewalt und nationale Sicherheit. Beiträge zur neueren Geschichte Deutschlands und Frankreichs. Festschrift für Klaus-Jürgen Müller,* eds. Willi Hansen, et al. (Munich: R. Oldenbourg, 1995), 287–302.

17. Bach-Zelewski's deposition, November 27, 1945, in *Nazi Conspiracy and Aggression,* 8 vols. (Washington, DC: Government Printing Office, 1946), 6:427.

18. See Jürgen Förster, "New Wine in Old Skins? The Wehrmacht and the War of 'Weltanschauungen', 1941," in *The German Military in the Age of Total War*, ed. Wilhelm Deist (Leamington Spa, Warwickshire, and Dover, NH: Berg, 1985), 310–13. See also Helmut Krausnick and Hans-Heinrich Wilhelm, *Die Truppe des Weltanschauungskrieges: Die Einsatzgruppen der Sicherheitspolizei und des SD, 1938–1942* (Stuttgart: Deutsche Verlags-Anstalt, 1981); and Christian Gerlach, *Kalkulierte Morde: Die deutsche Wirtschafts- und Vernichtungspolitik in Weißrussland, 1941 bis 1944* (Hamburg: Hamburger Edition, 1999).

19. Militärgeschichtliches Forschungsamt, *Das Deutsche Reich und der Zweite Weltkrieg*, 4:431.

20. *Der Prozess gegen die Hauptkriegsverbrecher vor dem Internationalen Militärgerichtshof Nürnberg 14. November 1945–1. Oktober 1946* (Munich: Delphin Verlag, 1949), 38:88.

21. Cited in Omer Bartov, *Hitler's Army: Soldiers, Nazis, and War in the Third Reich* (New York and Oxford: Oxford University Press, 1991), 86.

22. Order of October 10, 1941, in ibid., 129–30.

23. Order of November 20, 1941, in ibid., 130.

24. Order of November 25, 1941, in ibid., 131.

25. Cited in Militärgeschichtliches Forschungsamt, *Das Deutsche Reich und der Zweite Weltkrieg*, 4:435.

26. Cited in Förster, "Old Wine in New Skins?" 310.

27. Ibid., 318.

28. See Matthew Cooper, *The Phantom War: The Struggle against Soviet Partisans, 1941–1945* (London: Macdonald and Janes, 1979), 59–76.

29. Dmitri Volkogonov, *Stalin: Triumph and Tragedy* (London: Weidenfeld and Nicolson, 1991), 434–35.

30. On "decapitation," see Robert A. Pape's latest statement, "The True Worth of Air Power," *Foreign Affairs* 83 (March–April 2004): 116–30. John Erickson, *The Soviet High Command: A Military-Political History, 1918–1941* (London: Macmillan, 1962), 372, makes the case for Stalin's centrality. Even Defense Commissar Marshal K. E. Voroshilov, he writes, "did not forbear to consult Stalin even on the smallest point."

31. Entry for August 19, 1941, in *Die Tagebücher von Joseph Goebbels*, part 2: *Diktate 1941–1945*, vol. 1: *Juli–September 1941*, ed. Elke Fröhlich (Munich: K. G. Sauer, 1996), 262.

32. Entry for September 16, 1941, in *Die Weizsäcker Papiere, 1933–1950*, ed. L. E. Hill (Frankfurt: Propyläen, 1974), 270.

33. Hillgruber, *Hitlers Strategie*, 378.

34. Entry for June 4, 1941, in *Kriegstagebuch des Oberkommandos der Wehrmacht (Wehrmachtführungsstab)*, ed. Percy-Ernst Schramm et al., 4 vols. (Frankfurt am Main: Bernard und Graefe, 1961–65), 1:400ff.

35. Cited in Andreas Hillgruber, "Der Faktor Amerika in Hitler's Strategie, 1938–1941," *Aus Politik und Zeitgeschichte. Beilage zur Wochenzeitung "Das Parlament,"* vol. b19/66, 15.

36. Speech of July 14, 1941, cited in *Staatsmänner und Diplomaten bei Hitler: Vertrauliche Aufzeichnungen über Unterredungen mit Vertretern des Auslandes,*

1939–1941, ed. Andreas Hillgruber, 2 vols. (Munich: Deutscher Taschenbuch Verlag, 1969), 1:299, 303.

37. Max Domarus, ed., *Hitlers Reden und Proklamationen*, 4 vols. (Würzburg: Schmidt, Neustadt, 1963), 4:1791.

38. Cited in *Staatsmänner und Diplomaten bei Hitler*, 1:337–39.

39. Entry for April 7, 1941, in Halder, *Kriegstagebuch*, 2:354.

40. See Michael Salewski, *Die deutsche Seekriegsleitung 1935–1945*, 3 vols. (Frankfurt am Main: Bernard und Graefe, 1970–73), 1:57ff.

41. Entry for April 30, 1940, in *Das Politische Tagebuch Alfred Rosenbergs aus den Jahren, 1934/35 und 1939/40*, ed. Hans Günther Seraphim (Göttingen: Musterschmidt, 1956), 110. See also Albert Speer, *Erinnerungen* (Berlin: Propyläen, 1969), 196.

42. Naval Construction Department, Bundesarchiv-Militärarchiv (hereafter BA-MA), Freiburg, Germany, K 10–2/21.

43. Entry for June 12, 1942, in Halder, *Kriegstagebuch*, 3:455.

44. The *Weltblitzkrieg* concept is in *Hitlers Weisungen für die Kriegführung, 1939–1945: Dokumente des Oberkommandos der Wehrmacht*, ed. Walther Hubatsch (Munich: Deutscher Tachenbuch Verlag, 1965), 151–62.

45. BA-MA, Naval War Diary, PG 32185, case 240, I SKL, part C VII, 117–18; Naval War Diary, May 22, 1941, PG 32185, case 240, I SKL, part C VII, 103 (italics in the original).

46. See Olaf Groehler, "Globalstrategie der Luftwaffe. Ein Dokument aus den Akten des Reichsluftfahrtsministeriums aus dem Jahre 1942," *Militärgeschichte* 11 (1972): 445–59.

47. *Hitlers Weisungen*, 152.

48. Ibid., 153; Hillgruber, *Hitlers Strategie*, 381–82. John Keegan, in "How Hitler Could Have Won the War: The Drive for the Middle East, 1941," in Cowley, *What If?* 295–305, posits such a drive as an *alternative* to Operation Barbarossa. I have rejected such a probable (and reasonable) counterfactual because I remain convinced that for Hitler there never was an alternative strategy to the invasion of the Soviet Union in 1941.

49. *Hitlers Weisungen*, 153, 157; Halder, *Kriegstagebuch*, 2:292; *Kriegstagebuch des Oberkommandos*, 1:328.

50. Andrew Roberts and Niall Ferguson,"Hitler's England: What If Germany Had Invaded Britain in May 1940?" in *Virtual History: Alternatives and Counterfactuals*, ed. Niall Ferguson (London: Picador, 1997), 313–14.

51. Fritz Wiedemann, *Der Mann der Feldherr werden wollte. Erlebnisse und Erfahrungen des Vorgesetzten Hitlers im 1. Weltkrieg und seines späteren Persönlichen Adjutanten* (n.p., 1964), 164. Andrew Roberts, in *"The Holy Fox": A Biography of Lord Halifax* (London: Weidenfeld and Nicolsen, 1991), 103, 313, wrongly attributes Wiedemann's comment as stemming from German official documents. See Auswärtiges Amt, *Documents on German Foreign Policy, 1918–1945: Series D (1937–1945)*, 13 vols. (Washington, DC: Government Printing Office, 1949–64), 2:515, no. 315.

52. Roberts (*"The Holy Fox,"* 304) claims that Halifax would have gone to Canada if Hitler had actually *invaded* Britain.

53. This is stipulated in "Directive No. 32," in *Hitlers Weisungen,* 154. Fictional representations of a "German Britain" include Noël Coward's play *Peace in Our Time* (London: W. Heineman, 1947); C. S. Forester, *If Hitler Had Invaded England* (London: Pan, 1971); and Len Deighton, *SS-GB: Nazi-Occupied Britain, 1941* (London: Cape, 1978). On the broader subject of a Nazi victory, see the eclectic collection *Hitler Victorious: Eleven Stories of the German Victory in World War II,* ed. Gregory Benford and Martin H. Greenberg (New York and London: Garland, 1986).

54. Entry for September 17 and 18, 1941, in *Adolf Hitler: Monologe im Führer-Hauptquartier, 1941–1944,* ed. Werner Jochmann (Hamburg: Knaus, 1980), 63–64. See also the entry for July 27, 1941 (47–48).

55. The next three paragraphs are based on ibid., 109–10, 330–31, 335–36, entries for October 26–27, 1941, and August 6 and 9, 1942.

56. Jochen Thies, *Architekt der Weltherrschaft: Die "Endziele" Hitlers* (Düsseldorf: Droste, 1976), 77.

57. Michael Burleigh, "Nazi Europe: What If Nazi Germany Had Defeated the Soviet Union?" in Ferguson, *Virtual History,* 327–29, reverses this order in his counterfactual thought experiment. This is a case of a miracle counterfactual, as it runs against everything that we know about Hitler's racial and occupation policies in the east.

58. Speer, *Erinnerungen,* 84.

59. Thies, *Architekt der Weltherrschaft,* 93–94.

60. Adolf Hitler, *Mein Kampf* (Munich: Zentralverlag der NSDAP, 1939), 381.

61. Speer, *Erinnerungen,* 525. See pages 148ff., 159ff., and 168ff. for Speer's architectural megalomania.

62. Thies, *Architekt der Weltherrschaft,* 79–81, 86, 90.

63. Ibid., 100.

64. Cited in Martin Gilbert, *The Holocaust: A History of the Jews of Europe during the Second World War* (New York: Holt, Rinehart, and Winston, 1985), 176–77.

65. Entry for August 19, 1941, in *Die Tagebücher von Goebbels,* part 2, vol. 1, 266.

66. Gilbert, *The Holocaust,* 280–82.

67. Cited in Hans-Ulrich Thamer, *Verführung und Gewalt: Deutschland, 1933–1945* (Berlin: Sieder, 1986), 703.

68. Entry for December 5, 1940, in Halder, *Kriegstagebuch,* 2:212.

69. Cited in Thies, *Architekt der Weltherrschaft,* 175.

70. See Dmitry Oleinikov and Sergei Kudryashov, "What If Hitler Had Defeated Russia?" *History Today* 45 (May 1995): 68–69.

71. Thies, *Architekt der Weltherrschaft,* 171. See also Lothar Gruchmann, *Nationalsozialistische Großraumordnung: Die Konstruktion einer "deutschen Monroe-Doktrin"* (Stuttgart: Deutsche Verlags-Anstalt, 1962).

72. These, and the following figures for *Dotationen,* are from Gerd R. Ueberschär and Winfried Vogel, *Dienen und Verdienen: Hitlers Geschenke an seine Eliten* (Frankfurt am Main: Fisher Taschenbuch, 2000), 127–40, 145, 150–59, 163–67, 172, 180. See also Norman J. W. Goda, "Black Marks: Hitler's Bribery of

His Senior Officers during World War II," *Journal of Modern History* 72 (June 2000): 413–52.

73. Given the Nazis' notorious manipulation of the reichsmark both before and especially during the war, equivalency figures in today's euro currency are approximations at best.

74. For Leeb's particularly egregious demands, see Gerhard L. Weinberg, "Zur Dotation Hitlers an Generalfeldmarschall Ritter von Leeb," *Militärgeschichtliche Mitteilungen* 26 (1979): 97–99.

75. Cited in Arno Breker, *Im Strahlungsfeld der Ereignisse* (Preussisch-Ohlendorf: K. W. Schütz, 1972), 100.

76. Ueberschär and Vogel, *Dienen und Verdienen,* 118–19, 133.

77. Ibid., 92, 126–27.

78. The following medical details on Hitler's rapidly deteriorating condition are from Theodor Morell, *Adolf Hitler, the Medical Diaries: The Private Diaries of Dr. Theo Morell* ed. David Irving (London: Sidgwick and Jackson, 1983), 17, 190, 197, 262, 265, 272. See pages 304–10 for a summary. The original German edition was entitled *Die geheimen Tagebücher des Dr. Morell: Leibarzt Adolf Hitlers* (Munich: Goldmann, 1983).

79. Ueberschär and Vogel, *Dienen und Verdienen,* 184; Speer, *Erinnerungen,* 474–75.

80. *The Holocaust: The "Final Solution" in the Extermination Camps and the Aftermath* (New York: Garland, 1982), 99.

81. Bernd Wegner, "'My Honour Is Loyalty': The SS as a Military Factor in Hitler's Germany," in Deist, *The German Military in the Age of Total War,* 234–35.

82. *Trial of the Major War Criminals before the International Military Tribunal,* 42 vols. (Nuremberg: Government Printing Office, 1948), 1:136.

83. Jan Erik Schulte, *Zwangsarbeit und Vernichtung: Das Wirtschaftsimperium der SS—Oswald Pohl und das SS-Wirtschafts- und Verwaltungshauptamt* (Paderbon: F. Schöningh, 2001), 379ff.

84. See Burleigh, "Nazi Europe," 334–35, 339.

85. Ibid., 336–99.

86. Guntram Schulze-Wegener, *Die deutsche Kriegsmarine-Rüstung, 1942–1945* (Hamburg: Mittler, 1997), 127–28.

87. Speech of June 8, 1943, BA-MA, III M 1005/7; see also, Salewski, *Die deutsche Seekriegsleitung,* 2:294.

88. See Werner Rahn, "Die Entstehung neuer deutscher U-Boot-Typen im Zweiten Weltkrieg: Erprobung und erste operative Erfahrungen," *Militärgeschichte* 2 (1993): 13–20.

89. Entry for February 28, 1945, in *Kriegstagebuch der Seekriegsleitung, 1939–1945,* ed. Werner Rahn and Gerhard Schreiber, 68 vols. (Herford and Bonn: Mittler, 1988–97), 66:342.

90. Entry for February 17, 1945, in *Lagevorträge des Oberbefehlshabers der Kriegsmarine vor Hitler, 1939–1945,* ed. Gerhard Wagner (Munich: Lehmann, 1972), 656.

91. See Jens-Christian Wagner, *Produktion des Todes—Das KZ Mittelbau Dora* (Göttingen: Wallstein, 2001).

92. See Arjun Makhijani, "'Always' the Target?" *Bulletin of Atomic Science* 51 (May–June 1995): 23–24; Barton J. Bernstein, "Compelling Japan's Surrender without the A-bomb, Soviet Entry, or Invasion: Reconsidering the US Bombing Survey's Early-Surrender Conclusions," *Journal of Strategic Studies* 18 (June 1995): 101–48, offers an intriguing counterfactual. Of course, the Heisenberg group had not transformed uranium research from a laboratory into an industrial undertaking and thus had not achieved a self-sustained chain reaction, much less an atomic bomb. See Alan D. Beyerchen, *Scientists under Hitler: Politics and the Physics Community in the Third Reich* (New Haven and London: Yale University Press, 1977), 189.

93. Cited in Gregg Herken, *The Winning Weapon: The Atomic Bomb in the Cold War, 1945–1950* (New York: Knopf, 1980), 13n; Makhijani, "'Always' the Target?" 25.

94. Cited in Thamer, *Verführung und Gewalt,* 26.

95. Robyn Dawes, "Counterfactual Inferences as Instances of Statistical Inferences," in *Counterfactual Thought Experiments in World Politics: Logical, Methodological, and Psychological Perspectives,* ed. Philip E. Tetlock and Aaron Belkin (Princeton: Princeton University Press, 1996), 301–8.

96. Erich Raeder, *My Life* (Annapolis: U.S. Naval Institute, 1960), 241–44.

97. Speer, *Erinnerungen,* 97ff.

98. Isaiah Berlin, *The Hedgehog and the Fox: An Essay on Tolstoy's View of History* (New York: Simon and Schuster, 1966), 1–2. For the original, see the second epilogue of Leo Tolstoy in *War and Peace,* 2 vols. (New York: Heritage Press, 1938), vol. 2, esp. 800–843.

PART 4

Conclusions

The majorities in Congress in [17]74 on all the essential points and principles of the Declaration of Rights were only one, two, or three. Indeed, all the great critical questions about men and measures from 1774 to 1778 were decided by the vote of a single state, and that vote was often decided by a single individual.

—John Adams, second president of the United States,
to Benjamin Rush, June 12, 1812

Historical studies are turning to a theme which promises an historical rehabilitation, the theme of counterfactual analysis. It is this, above all, which has freed our vision of the world from the overdetermination which underlies all stadial theories, whether modernist or postmodernist. It reminds us that all historical episodes have prehistories, but those prehistories are prehistories of the many things which might have happened as well as of the fewer, but still hugely diverse, things which did. No mere listing of "preconditions" can reconstruct within the past a highroad leading in only one direction. A prehistory is not a set of determinants that exist long before their outcome, but a set of circumstances that make a particular outcome possible.

—Jonathan Clark, Our Shadowed Present

The Spur of Fame: Dialogues of John Adams and Benjamin Rush, 1805–1813, ed. John A. Schutz and Douglass Adair (San Marino, CA: Huntington Library, 1966), 225; Jonathan Clark, *Our Shadowed Present: Modernism, Postmodernism, and History* (Stanford: Stanford University Press, 2004), 28–29.

CHAPTER 12

Counterfactual History

ITS ADVOCATES, ITS CRITICS, & ITS USES

Geoffrey Parker and Philip E. Tetlock

The Counterfactual Enterprise Reconsidered

Hundreds of historical studies treat the rise of Nazism as a near-inevitable consequence of Germany's defeat in World War I, of the disastrous reparations policy imposed on the vanquished, as part of an irresistible pan-European tide of fascism, or as an unavoidable consequence of the great crash and the global economic depression. On New Year's Day, 1933, however, an editorial in the prestigious *Frankfurter Zeitung* saw things very differently: it jubilantly informed readers that "The mighty Nazi assault on the democratic state has been repulsed." On the same day, *Vorwärts,* the newspaper of the Social Democratic Party, entitled its editorial "Hitler's Rise and Fall," while a writer for the *Berliner Tageblatt* looked forward to telling his future grandchildren that during the previous year, "Everywhere throughout the whole world people were talking about—what was his first name?—Adalbert Hitler. Later? Vanished!" Strange though it may now seem, these German newspapers had good reasons for their confidence. In spring 1932, Hitler ran for president of the republic and lost; in summer, he demanded that President Hindenburg make him chancellor but failed; and in autumn his party lost 15 percent of its parliamentary seats in a general election. Badly shaken, the

Nazi leader told a confidant: "If the party falls apart, I'll finish myself off with a pistol within three minutes." Nevertheless, on January 30, 1933, Hindenburg swore in Adolf Hitler as chancellor.[1]

Politics is particularly susceptible to the influence of chance and Henry Ashby Turner filled his close study of "Hitler's thirty days to power"—the month of January 1933—with the improbable coincidences and circumstances that turned Nazi defeat into victory. He argued that just three men "held Germany's future in their hands" at that time, while three others "had lesser but also significant parts in what happened. Compared with the roles of these men, Hitler's was essentially reactive. He played the hand they dealt him with great cunning, but the cards were theirs, not his, to deal." In such situations, Turner concluded:

> When the disposition of power in a great nation rested with [a] small circle of individuals, some of the most elementary of human sentiments—personal affinities and aversions, injured feelings, soured friendships, and desire for revenge—had profound political effects.[2]

War is perhaps even more subject to chance. According to the eminent military theorist Carl von Clausewitz in the 1820s, no other human activity is so "continuously or universally bound up with chance." Two centuries before, a Dutch general argued against commanders risking a battle because "the outcome of war depends on fortune, as in a game of dice" while, thousands of miles away, the founder of the Manchu dynasty that would rule China for almost three centuries made exactly the same point. "Giving battle," he told an ally, "is like throwing knuckle-bone dice: they can fall on one side or the other."[3] Thus, as in politics, so in war: the "most elementary of human sentiments"—including an individual's fear, courage, rashness and prudence—often exert a disproportionate impact.

Not surprisingly, therefore, most of the chapters in this book deal with either politics or war. Two more deal with religion and the other two with science and technology, fields that likewise afford wide opportunity for "chance." "The study of technological progress," Joel Mokyr has observed, is "a study of exceptionalism, of cases in which as a result of rare circumstances, the normal tendency of societies to slide toward stasis and equilibrium was broken."[4] Religion, too, is by definition dominated by "exceptionalism." It may be self-evident to true believers looking back in time why a certain individual's vision of God and humanity's relationship to God would prevail over competing visions. But it most assuredly was not obvious to historical observers of the day, and sometimes it was not obvious to the messianic figures who would subsequently leave such profound imprints on history (recall Christ's despairing question from the cross: "My father, why have you forsaken me?). Mokyr sums up the analytical problem for students of both technology and religion when he compares searching historical archives for the seeds that gave root to the Industrial Revolution to "studying the history of Jewish dissenters between 50 A.D. and 50 B.C. What we are looking at is the inception of something which was at first insignificant and even bizarre, albeit destined to change the life of every man and woman in the West."[5]

All four subjects—politics, war, technology, and religion—are particularly appropriate for counterfactual analysis. Each of them offers enormous room for chance to channel us down historical paths that once seemed quite improbable, and once we are on a certain path, it becomes progressively harder to get off because those potential paths often multiply in nonlinear—even exponential—fashions. And yet most academics lack firsthand experience of politics, war, science, and (especially) messianism, and few are versed in the intricacies of path-dependency theory. Perhaps this is why so many of them have followed the advice of E. H. Carr and begun their "examination of historical events at the event itself, and then [worked] backward to discern the decisions and turning-points that seemingly led to that event through an imaginary straight-line sequence of cause and effect." And yet, as the chapters in this book demonstrate, many events do not unfold that way. Instead, individuals and organizations eventually take decisions that

> reflect personal idiosyncrasies and organizational cultures. . . . Historical actors often take correct decisions for reasons that appear bizarre in retrospect. And commanders and military organizations are rarely wholly honest—whether in the aftermath of victory or that of defeat—about what actually happened.[6]

When we concentrate our explanatory efforts on the great impersonal forces that push history onto one particular path, we unavoidably slight alternative paths that, ex ante, may have seemed every bit as plausible.

Hindsight bias blurs this crucial distinction, however. Knowledge of what subsequently happened can systematically distort which causal antecedents we deem worthy of our attention and can be safely relegated to the dustbin of history. The more retrospectively obvious we can convince ourselves the outcome was, the more difficult it becomes to achieve the central mission of the historian: to acquire the capacity to see the world as it once appeared to those alive at the time.

As argued in chapter 1, we believe that the best antidote to excessively deterministic thinking is granting greater academic license to explore counterfactual possibilities. To prevent our world from completely blocking our view of worlds that could have been, we need to loosen the tight disciplinary constraints on "what-if" thinking. How much it is reasonable to loosen, of course, remains a judgment call on which reasonable people—including our authors—can disagree. Some contributors created what-if scenarios that had such narrative zest that they took on a life of their own, even causing their inventors to rethink their starting assumptions about cause and effect, whereas other contributors felt little need to modify their prior worldviews as a result of their excursions into what-if history. This does not, of course, mean that they are closed minded; they may have been correct before the exercise and correct afterward as well. Nonetheless, we may imagine the skeptics snickering in the background: in their view, the phrase "counterfactual thought experiment" was always just an affectation, a linguistic sleight of hand meant to obfuscate what sensible people knew all along. "Some experiments," the skeptics may scoff, "when the results are known in advance."

Here a nuanced appraisal is critical. Surprising oneself—self-subversion—is a high standard, implying a reversal of the author's prior opinion. We should not expect to observe it often, and, when we do, we should not assume that authors have moved to a more "correct" reading of historical forces than they possessed before. The more appropriate epistemological standard is not, in any case, what is going on inside the minds of authors but rather: "do the exercises sensitize us, the readers, to aspects of reality that we otherwise would have overlooked?"

"Close Calls" versus "Reversion"

Our choice of the magnification lens through which to view the past has important consequences. The stronger the magnification of our lens, it would seem, the more likely that plausible opportunities for redirecting events down different paths will suggest themselves. Historians who focus on close-call counterfactuals involving specific people at specific times and places face a vast variety of possible rerouting points. By contrast, those who favor counterfactuals that bring history back on track more commonly use a weaker lens and focus on impersonal forces—the underlying balance of power, the advance of technology, the restraints imposed by the prevailing culture. In short, what historians find depends in large part on how closely they look.

- Victor Davis Hanson's consideration of the consequences for Greek civilization had Salamis ended in a Persian victory enters into great detail on the circumstances surrounding the battle—what did and did not happen as well as what might have happened—because he sees the events of that day as a unique node of uncertainty, a point at which events could have taken several different turns. By contrast, Barry Strauss's chapter includes relatively little about the encounter because he favors a "second-order" explanation: even had the Persians won the battle of Salamis, they would still eventually have lost the war.

- For Jack A. Goldstone, the exact moment of William III's death possesses great significance because he believes it would have unleashed a totally different and irreversible course for British, European, and even global history. Carla Gardina Pestana believes it scarcely matters because William would have been succeeded, first, by his wife Mary and, if she had predeceased William, by her sister Anne (as happened in 1702.)[7]

Those who favor "reversionary" counterfactuals thus tend to see detailed "unpacking" of chronology and events as a waste of time, while those who favor close-call counterfactuals see them as essential.

Perhaps the most satisfying case studies contain elements of both "revision" and "reversion." For instance, Holger H. Herwig allows Hitler to conquer virtually all of Europe and to develop long-range weapons of extraordinary sophistication with which to defeat his more distant enemies, but his regime nevertheless perishes in 1945 because he failed to develop atomic weapons. The United States, therefore, still becomes the dominant geopolitical and economic power in the second half of the twentieth century.

Outstanding Analytical Challenges

We do not wish to leave the misleading impression that we think our analytical guidelines provide the final word on how to do counterfactual history—clearing up all possible reservations that reasonable people might have toward this form of scholarship. Although we strongly disagree with E. H. Carr's and Richard Evans's wholesale dismissal of counterfactual history, we think it critical not to "oversell": we, like them, have no time for "miracle counterfactuals." In chapter 1, we therefore urged readers to approach counterfactual thought experiments in the same spirit in which they approach any other form of inquiry, with an open-minded willingness to change their minds as long as they cannot spot critical flaws in the evidence and logic marshaled to support a conclusion. And we highlighted three procedural directives issued to our contributors to render their counterfactual thought experiments proof against the three objections advanced by each genre. We exhorted our contributors to think hard about the following.

- How they chose the antecedents for their thought experiments (those things that, if different, might have put us—at least temporarily—on a different historical path)
- How they forged the connecting principles between their antecedents' starting points and the projected consequences of those starting points
- How they determined how far they could plausibly project events into the futures of their hypothetical worlds

Our contributors clearly gave deep thought to each question, but inevitably our directives remained incomplete; in addition, even the most scrupulously careful investigator cannot foresee all potential counterattacks. Let us illustrate some of the challenges that will confront future efforts in counterfactual history (for we are confident that counterfactual history will remain an essential part of historical study) by revisiting each of our procedural guidelines and some of the deeper complexities of implementing them.

Procedural Request 1: How Historians Choose Antecedents as Starting Points for Thought Experiments

We observed earlier that our contributors showed a strong preference for the minimal-rewrite rule in deciding which antecedents provided the most appropriate starting points for thought experiments. They sought to avoid counterfactuals that required rewriting a great deal of existing history: we cannot equip the Persian vessels at Salamis with torpedoes. They also tended to gravitate toward counterfactuals that undid *unusual* antecedents in the actual record, things that were out of the ordinary, such as the distinctively good or bad leadership skills of Themistocles or James II.

These intuitive guidelines for the selection of antecedents are both historically and logically defensible, but they by no means provide a blueprint for how historians and social scientists should sample and select antecedent starting points for counterfactual thought experiments. Indeed, even if scholars who favor more deterministic interpretations of history accept the validity of speculative what-if rerouting scenarios, they can still argue that the antecedents for the first-order counterfactuals were chosen selectively. For instance, when a counterfactual historian focuses on "averting" a war that in fact occurred, the critic can object:

> You looked for ways in which war might have been averted when war finally came, but you didn't look equally hard for ways in which war could easily have been triggered in those earlier crises that were resolved peacefully. If you had sampled from the set of conceivably alterable antecedent conditions in an unbiased manner, you would have discovered that there are far more counterfactual paths (in addition to the one actual path) that lead to war than there are counterfactual paths to peace.

This is a legitimate criticism; but we can point to sophisticated counterfactual thought experiments that explicitly address such objections. A good illustration is a recent influential article in which Paul W. Schroeder tried to "avert" World War I but failed for three reasons—one of them precisely addressing the concerns of our hypothetical critic. First, Schroeder asserted, Archduke Franz Ferdinand was so obstinate and self-willed that, even had he not been assassinated by a Bosnian terrorist connected with Serbia in Sarajevo in June 1914, he would doubtless have perished the next time he took similar risks, leading the Austro-Hungarian leaders to issue an ultimatum to Serbia that they knew could not be met. Second, Schroeder argued that the war also stemmed from the deep-seated (and well-founded) fears of the imperial government in Vienna that, unless it struck Serbia soon, its position in the Balkans would become untenable. These two reasons explained the outbreak of war; but Schroeder's third ground for regarding a major international conflict as inevitable addressed the breakdown of peace. After all, Austria-Hungary had faced Serbian provocation before but had stopped short of war (in 1904–5, 1908–9, and 1912–13). Why, he asked, did the other European powers not intervene to restrain Serbia in 1913–14 at exactly the same time they exerted themselves to keep the peace between Russia and its rivals competing for control of the Straits of Constantinople?

For almost a month after the assassination (June 28–July 23 [1914]), the powers did absolutely nothing in concert to deal with the possible or likely consequences of this sensational incident. Everyone knew that Austria-Hungary and Serbia were mortal enemies, that they had gone to the brink of war at least four times in the past five years, three of them in the past year, and that Russia was Serbia's ally and protector and Austria-Hungary's main enemy. Yet when something occurred that anyone could see might set off this long-expected war, the Entente powers averted their eyes, went about their other business, waited for the Austro-Hungarian and German reaction, and hoped for the best—while Austria-Hungary and Germany planned and took the action that started the war.

World War I *really* broke out, Schroeder concluded, because none of the powers truly cared any longer about Austria-Hungary's humiliation: not Russia, which had resolved to protect the Balkan Slavs at all costs; not Germany, which feared that Russia's impressive rearmament program would leave it vulnerable; not France or Britain, which feared German aggression and therefore would do nothing to weaken their entente with Russia. Hence, his counterfactual examination of the July Crisis of 1914 ended on a reversionary note: Balkan instability seemed almost certain to produce a general European war around 1914 with or without the assassination of the archduke. By then, almost no counterfactual path led to peace.[8]

Procedural Request 2: On Potential Logical Contradictions between the Connecting Principles Needed to Link Our Antecedents to Conclusions

Whenever a counterfactual historian contends that "if *x* had been different, then *y* or *z* would have resulted," it is perfectly fair for critics to ask: "well, what else would have had to be different at the outset to permit *x* to be different?" Sticking to the minimal-rewrite rule makes it fairly easy to answer this challenge: slightly different assumptions about, say, the health of a key player should do the job. But counterfactual historians sometimes pose what-if questions that require more dramatic revisions in starting points, such as Robert Fogel's famous conjecture that if American railroads had been introduced twenty years later than they were, the net impact on American economic growth would have been tiny. Putting to one side the highly technical debate that followed, historians may not argue that (since necessity is the mother of invention) the counterfactual fails because, if railroads had been delayed, the resourceful Americans would have developed cars and highways earlier than they did. They may not do so because a logical tension exists between the lack of societal innovativeness posited for slowing down railroads and the surge of innovativeness posited for speeding up the introduction of cars and highways. The two assertions are not cotenable.

Counterfactual thought experiments are almost bound to fail this cotenability test if historians suppose that, once they enter their hypothetical world and make their first change (even when it is a minimal rewrite), everything else will remain the same as actual history. Consider the first "major counterfactual" advanced by Holger H. Herwig for World War II: if Stalin had died in December 1941 and Soviet forces had withdrawn into Siberia, is it reasonable to expect that a crucial battle would have occurred at Stalingrad (or anywhere on the Volga) over the winter of 1942–43? No, because German troops would already have gained control of Russia up to the Urals and the Caucasus. The two assertions are not cotenable. Likewise, with victory in the east as well as in the west, opposition to Hitler within the German military would no doubt have abated, rendering the assassination attempt of July 1944 unlikely. Thus an overwhelming German victory in 1941 and a plot by disaffected Wehrmacht officers three years later are also not cotenable.

This constitutes an important limitation of the minimal-rewrite rule. Although that rule is obviously needed to screen out preposterous antecedents as starting points for counterfactual exercises (such as "if Hitler had possessed operational command of a sizable arsenal of nuclear weapons in 1940, he could have dominated the world"), the rule was never intended to preclude us from exploring the causal implications of the initial alteration in the hypothetical world. Indeed, it would require a massive rewrite of the history of the counterfactual world to suppose that the Battle of Stalingrad in 1942–43 or the assassination plot in July 1944 would have unfolded on the same schedule in the hypothetical Hitler-conquers-Russia world as it did in the actual one.

Procedural Request 3: How Far into Hypothetical Futures Is It Possible to See?

The simple, and far from facetious, answer is that there is no reason to suppose historians and social scientists can see farther into hypothetical futures than they can see into the actual future—and that generally means not very far at all. Here we need to be alert to the constraints of logic—in particular, the impact of probability theory on counterfactual sequences. This means that if an author constructs a chain of ten links from a node of uncertainty to a significantly different outcome, and that the probability of each stands at 80 percent—remarkably good odds—the cumulative probability diminishes over the ten links to 80 percent, or 0.8 to the tenth power: a total probability of only 0.107![9]

Nevertheless, this argument may be unduly pessimistic in one key regard: it assumes that each event in the sequence is independent, that it has no effect on those that follow—that historical sequences have "no memory," that they resemble a succession of tosses of a coin (albeit, in this case, a coin that lands "heads" 80 percent of the time). History is rarely, if ever, like coin tossing: rather, it is a path-dependent system with positive feedback. It resembles a vortex in which what has already happened quickly accentuates the probability of certain events and reduces that of others, making escape from the new path difficult. This counterargument suggests that historians may be on more secure ground in sometimes extrapolating action-reaction scenarios in their counterfactuals.[10]

The positions that historians take in this debate will reveal much about their deepest assumptions about the causal dynamics at work in their domains of expertise. Those who subscribe to the view that history is for the most part "just one damned thing after another," with minimal inteconnectedness among the various causes that shape events, should be especially wary of aggressive extrapolations of trends into counterfactual worlds (some of our contributors try, albeit gingerly, to peer hundreds of years into their fictitious futures). By contrast, those who believe that there is a systemic logic to how history unfolds—be it a positive-feedback logic that propels us, ever accelerating, in a particular direction or a negative-feedback logic that keeps us locked into a particular present—should be more supportive of what-if speculations that aggressively lay out visions of distant hypothetical futures.

Can "Synergy" Undo the Rise of the West?

It is worth stressing once more that this volume does not aim to provide a historical overview of the increasing power of the West; rather, it uses the rise of the West as a vehicle to test the strengths and weaknesses of counterfactual thought experiments in history. Nevertheless, the various tipping points examined in the foregoing chapters suggest a final "test" of our project.

Most of the nodes of uncertainty considered by the authors leave the rise of the West largely "on track." Victor Davis Hanson sees a Persian victory at Salamis as the "last chance" to derail it. For Carlos M. N. Eire, Rome without Christianity would have been even stronger; he also argues that a Catholic England might have accelerated European overseas expansion. Robin D. S. Yates and Kenneth Pomeranz can envisage scenarios in which China resisted the West more effectively but not Chinese expansion to global dominance. Only Jack A. Goldstone and Joel Mokyr argue that the crucial transition to industrialization was (in Mokyr's word) "contingent" and that therefore a relatively minimal rewriting of history could prevent it—and with it, the power of the West to gain global economic mastery.

Perhaps, however, it is possible to identify synergistic interactions among turning points, so that (without violating either the minimal-rewrite rule or cotenability) a combination of counterfactuals might leave the West permanently crippled, either incapable of expanding or even at risk of collapse. Before the sixteenth century, the synergy would simply have to cripple the West, since it controlled under 10 percent of the land surface of the earth: just Europe. It is easy, for example, to imagine a yet more lethal visitation of the plague in the mid–fourteenth century, one that killed one-half (or more) of the population rather than just one-third, perhaps coupled with a new wave of Mongol invasions (see pages 378–79 below.) It is also easy to envisage "social filters" that might have prevented the adoption of inventions that played a crucial role in Western expansion—such as the compass, printing, and gunpowder (just as social filters" in the medieval Muslim world froze out block printing, harnessing draft animals for plowing, and the oxcart).[11] Without the development of the "full-rigged ship," the most complex machine to emerge in medieval Europe, without a sophisticated system of navigation, and without a means to install broadsides of heavy artillery on sailing ships, Western domination of Asian waters would have been impossible. This would inevitably have delayed the creation of the European seaborne empires in Asia (though not in America), perhaps allowing the "gunpowder empires" of Asia time to develop warships capable of excluding Western vessels when eventually they attempted to break into the market. By contrast, as noted earlier, after 1800 and the Industrial Revolution, it is hard to imagine any combination of factors derailing the rise of the West, for by then the share of the world it controlled had increased to 35 percent of the land and all of its oceans. By 1914, the Western powers ruled 85 percent of the land and almost all of its oceans.

(Japan's naval victory at Tsushima in 1905 set a temporary limit to Western dominance of East Asian waters.) In addition, by then the West boasted far better material resources with which to deal with challenges (even biological challenges thanks to the development of vaccination and industrially manufactured quinine).

"Unmaking the West" through the synergy of several minimal rewrites therefore only makes sense between the sixteenth and nineteenth centuries, when the important structures of empire were either unformed or relatively malleable. Out of the myriad of counterfactual combinations, we will consider the possible synergy between just three: the collapse, long before it actually happened, of the Hapsburg monarchy; the failure of the Iberian colonists to export vast quantities of gold and silver from America; and the prevention (or significant delay) of the creation of a British empire in India.

It is a curious paradox that Christendom lost substantial territory in southeastern Europe just as it began to acquire new territory overseas. Belgrade fell to Ottoman Sultan Süleyman the Magnificent in 1521, allowing a rapid advance to Budapest, which fell in 1526. That same year, he defeated a large Christian army and turned Hungary into a protectorate. From then on, in his correspondence with Christian rulers, Süleyman adopted the title Distributor of Crowns to the Monarchs of the World. In 1529, he laid siege to Vienna, the capital of Habsburg Austria, and, although it resisted successfully, Turkish garrisons lay within one hundred miles of both Vienna and Venice for the rest of the century. At the same time, the sultan's fleet gained control of the eastern and southern shores of the Mediterranean, from which it picked off Christian island outposts: Rhodes in 1522, Chios in 1566, Cyprus in 1570–71. Probably only the sultans' simultaneous efforts to conquer Persia, on the eastern frontier, prevented further Turkish gains in the West.

What, then, if the Ottoman advance, perhaps thanks to a truce with Persia, had *not* petered out before Vienna? The resources of the Hapsburg empire were not infinite, and its rulers experienced considerable difficulty in raising money in one area to pay for their wars elsewhere. In 1520, the taxes levied by Emperor Charles V had provoked a major rebellion in both Castile and Valencia, the richest provinces of Spain. Ten years later, he confessed to his brother Ferdinand, who commanded Hapsburg forces in Austria, "You must realize, brother, that in Spain they abhor all their resources that I have spent [abroad]."[12] Had the Turks taken and held Vienna, Charles would have required far more money from Spain even as he shifted his base of operations to either Italy or the Netherlands. This might well have provoked a further revolt in Spain—something his advisers feared—leading to a collapse of Hapsburg power in Europe and the loss of control over Spanish America and its resources.

But what if Spanish America had lacked not only a strong bond with Spain but also its principal economic resource: gold and silver mines? These two reroutings of history would have directly influenced another aspect of Western expansion: the rise of European power in Asia, since American silver largely financed Europe's outposts and operations in the East. Thus the English East India Company exported £750,000 in silver to Asia between 1601 and 1624, and the total rose steadily thereafter, surpassing £700,000 in the fiscal year 1700–1701 alone, while the Dutch East India Company also exported huge amounts silver: over £100,000 annually in the early seventeenth century and almost £300,000 annually by the end. Almost all of it came from Spanish America. Early modern Europe simply could not produce at competitive prices the manufactured goods that Asian consumers desired, only silver, mined by slave labor in America so cheaply and in such prodigious quantities that even after traveling halfway round the world it still seemed a bargain. Without it, European merchants would not have been able to acquire the Asian spices, silks, and other luxury goods that they desired.

America remained crucial to the survival of a European presence—both colonial and commercial—in Asia until the late eighteenth century. Nevertheless, until the mid–eighteenth century, the Europeans made little military or political impact on Asia. The predominant power in India remained the Mughal empire, which had expanded rapidly in the course of the sixteenth and seventeenth centuries and (so its ministers boasted) could mobilize four million soldiers against its enemies. The centralizing policies of the Mughals alienated several groups of rural gentry, which began to ally with the court nobles sent to govern them, until by the 1720s several regions—especially Bengal—had become semiautonomous. Although imperial armies retained the power to intervene in succession disputes or to expand in marginal zones, this changed abruptly in 1739. Nadir Shah, who had seized power in Iran and conquered Afghanistan, invaded India, defeated the Mughal emperor, and briefly ruled Hindustan in his name. Although Nadir unexpectedly led his army back to Iran, his spectacular success fatally undermined Mughal authority. The emperor lost his power to intervene in the northeast, whether to discipline recalcitrant subordinates or to drive out the British when they intervened in Bengal after 1757.

The Europeans fully recognized the significance of Nadir Shah's incursion: one of the first British accounts of Mughal India took as its turning point the "total subversion of the empire" in 1739.[13] Had Nadir remained in Delhi, as previous Afghan and Iranian conquerors had done, British power would surely have remained confined to coastal enclaves in the south. In any case, the directors of the East India Company in London always sought to avoid military activity—defensive as well as offensive. In 1750, they reproached their subordinates: "You seem to look upon yourselves rather as a Military Colony than [as] the factors and agents of a body of merchants"; nine years later they dismissed the strategic designs of their officials in India on the grounds that "were we to adopt your several plans for fortifying, half our capital would be buried in stone walls."[14] Local commanders therefore set their own subimperial agenda and seized the initiative. In 1757, the governor of Madras sent a small army to Bengal, which by 1765 had secured lands that yielded over £1,000,000 in annual profit, all paid in silver, more than enough to allow the British to maintain an army of over 115,000 men in India. With this, they could (and did) intervene in Burma, East Africa, and, above all, East Asia. The Western armies that invaded China in 1839–42 and 1859–60 included important Indian contingents. After the suppression of the Boxer rising in 1900, Sikh policemen even directed the traffic of Beijing. In the words of the distinguished sinologist Louis Dermigny, "It was as if the British had subjugated the Indian peninsula simply in order to use its resources against China."[15]

In the opinion of Sanjay Subrahmanyam, author of a perceptive and subtle analysis of Nadir Shah's remarkable exploit in 1739, a minimal rewrite—Nadir's decision to stay in Hindustan rather than return after his crushing victory—would have rerouted all this. Nadir commanded the only well-supplied, directly paid, obedient army in South Asia, boasting an efficient combination of firepower and cavalry far superior not only to any other native state in the subcontinent but also to any European army in India: "In military terms, none of the company's armies until the 1790s came even faintly close to the degree of efficiency that Nadir Shah's forces possessed already in the 1730s." Neither the British nor the French—who went to war against each other in the 1740s anyway—would have possessed the military strength to break into Bengal, and without Bengal they would have lacked the resources to project Western power farther afield.[16]

Interestingly, Subrahmanyam's minimal rewrite initially changes little in either Indian or European history. In Hindustan, Nadir and his advisers already possessed the administrative expertise to run the empire they had won; they also spoke the same language (Persian) and shared the same religion (eclectic Islam) as the Mughals. The dominant state of Hindustan would have remained monarchical, with its economy still resting mainly on peasant agriculture with significant artisanal production and considerable foreign trade. But the centrifugal tendencies would have ceased. The new state would surely have brought Bengal back under its control and managed "to protect itself politically for at least three-quarters of a century longer from British imperialism than the Mughal empire in fact did." Furthermore, had the British not acquired Bengal and its other eighteenth-century conquests in India, "the British Empire in much of South Asia and even elsewhere (based as it was on using Indian troop-levies, and financed in good part by Indian capital-markets) would have been inconceivable."[17]

A stronger state in Hindustan might not at first have affected Britain's economy significantly either, since the early stages of industrialization there did not depend on colonial supply or demand. So economic and social changes in England and Scotland might well have proceeded unaffected by events in India until about 1800. Thereafter, however, the rapid rise of British industrial and commercial power would have been blighted in two crucial ways. First, economic expansion depended not only on new machinery but also on manipulating markets. By the 1780s, a Lancashire machine spinner took two thousand hours to produce one hundred pounds of cotton thread; one decade later, with the introduction of steam power, the same Lancashire operative required only three hundred hours. An Indian hand spinner, by contrast, required fifty thousand hours. Nevertheless, even such a colossal advantage did not satisfy nineteenth-century Lancashire mill owners. To maximize their profits, they therefore mobilized superior power as well as superior production, pressuring the government of India to abolish all import duties protecting native manufactures, to undertake public works (such as building railways) that would open up the interior to their products, and to liberalize the marketing of cotton. If Nadir Shah had remained in India, none of this would have been possible, reducing Britain's economic might.[18] Second, as Kenneth Pomeranz argues, a delay in the massive drain of silver caused by the opium trade with British India might have allowed China to experience at least some of the growth associated with the early phases of industrialization based on domestic coal, iron, and steam and thus acquire the means to keep Western competitors at arm's length.

In chapter 10, Joel Mokyr argues that Europe undoubtedly possessed such a remarkable pool of scientific talent, and so many incentives to translate abstractions into technology, that by 1688 "the culture that created the growth of the epistemic bases of technology that led to the Industrial Revolution was in place, and it would have required more than a minimal rewrite to dislodge." True. But a West without Spanish America and British India would have been far less likely to translate that "epistemic basis" into global dominance. Severing (or even seriously weakening) the link between Spain and its American colonies, coupled with a decision by Nadir Shah to remain in Hindustan after defeating the Mughals, therefore leads (at least partially) to "unmaking the West." Some might feel, however, that such a run of "alternative histories" goes far beyond the realms of plausibility.[19]

Why the West Rose

Readers might now wonder, finally, what light counterfactual thought experiments shed on why the West *did* rise. Our contributors, like most other historians, make three important assumptions: the absence of a successful invasion of Europe; the resilience of most Westerners to most non-Western diseases, combined with the susceptibility of non-Westerners to diseases such as smallpox; and Western military and naval superiority. What happens if we change each of these?

Europe Invaded

What if, after the defeat of the Persians in the fifth century BC, some *other* region of the world expanded into Europe and destroyed it? At least three later civilizations possessed an ideology that envisaged indefinite expansion: the Aztecs, the Muslims, and the Mongols. The first stood little chance of conquering Europe—or indeed of expanding beyond the Central Valley of Mexico: lacking wheels, draft animals and sailing ships, Aztec expansion was limited to what humans could carry. The other two civilizations were very different.

Both the Arabs in the eighth century and the Ottoman Turks in the sixteenth viewed themselves as inheritors of the Roman tradition and developed an imperial ideology that sought to regain the "lost provinces" in Europe. Their failures, the first at Tours in 732 and the second at Vienna in 1529, were by no means preordained. In neither case, however, would victory by itself have destroyed or even permanently maimed the West. In the eighth century, the frontier conquests would no doubt have split off into a plethora of small states (as happened in Spain) and commercial capitalism would still have developed (with greater resources, since none would have been diverted into crusading). In the sixteenth century, too, political fragmentation would no doubt have followed conquest, as happened with the Ottomans' gains in North Africa. Everywhere the Christians (and other "Peoples of the Book" protected by Islamic teaching) would have retained their distinctive culture and commercial privileges, as they did in those areas actually conquered and held by the Turks (e.g., Cyprus, Greece, and the Balkans). Admittedly, under Islam, the search for collective well-being would have eclipsed the individual profit motive as the primary economic goal, but the obligation of Muslims actively to advance the cause of their faith both at home and abroad would have led to further expansion. As it was, European missionaries and merchants arrived in the Philippine and Indonesian archipelagoes somewhat later than their Muslim counterparts.[20]

The Mongol challenge in the thirteenth century was different again. By 1250, the Mongol khans had created the most extensive land empire the world has ever known. It stretched into eleven of the world's twenty-four time zones, from the Pacific Ocean to the Black Sea, and included Mesopotamia, parts of Anatolia, and the areas today occupied by Afghanistan and Iran. To travel from one end of the Mongol empire to the other was a journey of eight thousand miles—about the distance that separates London from Vancouver. The empire differed markedly from that of the Arabs or the Aztecs because, like other peoples who lived by herding (such as the Masai of East Africa or the Native Americans of the Great Plains), the Mongols despised all sedentary cultures. They therefore destroyed, initially at least, what they could not take with them; they razed towns and cities; and they massacred farmers, whom they regarded as competitors for their grazing lands. Unlike other peoples who lived by herding, the Mongols excelled in acquiring military technology from their enemies in one area and using it against those in another: for example, the first military use of gunpowder weapons in Russia and the Near East was by Mongol generals, who had acquired them, and skilled practitioners, in their conquest of China.

In the 1250s, the Persian historian Juvaini, who served the grandson of Chinggis Khan, called his study of the Mongol onslaught "The History of the World Conqueror" because the Mongols both aspired to universal domination and possessed the means to achieve it. He recorded, with a combination of sorrow and admiration, the desolation that followed the conquest. The Mongol rules of war were simple: they accepted those who surrendered instantly as their slaves, and the rest they killed. According to Juvaini, those areas around Bokhara and Samarkand that had submitted to Chinggis Khan forty years before "have in some cases attained their original levels and in others have closely approached it," but "it is otherwise with Khorasan and Iraq" (his own homeland), which had tried to resist. There:

> Every town and village has been several times subjected to pillage and massacre and has suffered this confusion for years, so that even though there be generation and increase until the Resurrection the population will not attain to a tenth part of what it was before.[21]

In 1235, having subdued Central Asia and northern China, the Mongols made plans to conquer Europe. The rulers nearest to the Mongol line of advance made frenzied attempts to forge alliances with their neighbors but in vain: when the Mongol army hit southern Russia in the winter of 1237–38, it destroyed the unprepared and disunited principalities one by one. In 1240, it stormed and sacked the cultural and political capital of Russia, Kiev, leaving it in ruins.[22] Next, the Mongols divided their forces as they advanced westward: one invaded Poland, while the other devastated Hungary. The first corps crossed the Oder and swept down the river valley until, in April 1241, it met and annihilated a combined army of German and Polish knights in Silesia. A few days later the second army routed the Hungarians and advanced through Budapest to the gates of Vienna before moving southeast to ravage the Balkans. At just this moment, when the Mongols seemed poised to press on into Western Europe, news arrived that the Great Khan had died and the Mongol generals led their armies back to Central Asia to take part in the election of his successor.

In 1245, the pope sent an envoy after the invaders to try and discover what they wanted. He returned with a letter announcing that the khan was the sole messenger of God on earth, charged with establishing the world order decreed by heaven, in which the Mongols ruled and everyone else either obeyed or died. The king of France also sent an envoy, but he too returned with a peremptory demand for unconditional surrender to the world conqueror. Luckily for Europe, the Mongols decided to move next on the Near East, followed by southern China.[23]

Could the Mongols have conquered Europe? Without doubt: they overran the vast Song empire, the northern part in the 1230s and the rest in the 1270s, and in between they conquered the Islamic states of the Near East, culminating in 1258 with the capture of Baghdad, the capital of the caliphs. The victors burned down the palace of the caliph, the Great Mosque, and most other public buildings and piled the heads of thousands of the vanquished in huge pyramids. They then ruled their new conquests until the mid-fourteenth century (in the case of China and Persia) or even longer (in the case of southern Russia). Yet China and Persia boasted by far the most advanced civilizations of the thirteenth-century world, and their wealth, economy, and literate populations far surpassed those of all of Europe; their ability to withstand the Mongol onslaught was therefore much greater.[24]

Could a Mongol conquest of Europe have prevented the rise of the West? After all, Mongol rule did not last forever in Russia, China, or Persia: native dynasties eventually regained control and drove out the invaders, and most of the devastated cities—even Kiev and Baghdad—rose from their ashes. The process of recovery, however, took decades and in some cases centuries. Although Kiev eventually recovered, the center of Russian civilization moved permanently northward, and its new rulers continued to pay tribute to the descendants of Chinggis Khan until the 1470s. Those descendants continued to sack Moscow, the new capital, until 1571. The expansion of early modern Europe by either land or sea is therefore not cotenable with a devastating Mongol invasion of the Continent similar to those of Russia and the Near East. Protection from invasion was indeed a vital precondition for the rise of the West.

Microbes

A second critical advantage favored the rise of the West: the relative resistance of Europeans, and people of European descent, to most non-Western diseases, whereas European germs devastated several of the societies with which they came into contact. *Relative* here means that, like all premodern societies, Europe prior to the eighteenth century suffered extremely high mortality rates: above all, one child in every four died within its first year, and one in every two died before the age of twenty. Some died of neglect and malnutrition, and others through accidents, but the majority died of disease. Bubonic plague affected considerable parts of Europe once every decade between the mid-fourteenth and mid-sixteenth centuries and once every two decades for another century. Some epidemics halved a region's inhabitants in a single year. Although less spectacular than plague, smallpox killed even more early modern people.

The smallpox virus spreads rapidly and easily by inhalation, especially in the cooler and drier periods of the year, and once a community reached a certain size the disease became endemic. It therefore thrived in towns, where everyone eventually caught it. Statistics reveal that smallpox killed almost one-quarter of all those infected and ended the lives of roughly one-tenth of all children—although all who survived contact with the disease acquired lifelong immunity.[25]

Communities that had never been exposed to smallpox (or had not been exposed for a generation or more) suffered far higher mortality when they first encountered the disease. The indigenous inhabitants of the Americas offer the best-known example: they suffered catastrophic declines shortly after the Europeans made contact and experienced a smallpox epidemic every five to eight years throughout the early modern period. Although the strikingly high figures from the Valley of Mexico in the sixteenth century—a mortality rate of 80 percent and sometimes more—rest on impressionistic data, more reliable statistics from New Mexico in the seventeenth century also suggest losses of 80 percent—so high as to suggest that the indigenous populations of the New World had a genetic code that made their case fatality to diseases such as smallpox much higher.[26]

In many areas, the colonists also systematically killed, mistreated, and overworked Indians, and disrupted their economic and social systems, but similarly dramatic demographic losses also occurred far beyond the reach of colonial cruelty. For example, although few Europeans settled in Brazil during the sixteenth century, the indigenous population suffered some of the highest depopulation rates of the entire continent. The same occurred later in Australia.[27] Without question, the epidemics greatly assisted the European invaders: they encountered fewer adversaries, and the survivors were often demoralized. Whereas Cortés remained in command of his followers throughout the conquest of Mexico, and most of his lieutenants and cadres also survived the campaign, the Aztecs lost two emperors and 40 percent of their population within a year.

In the eighteenth century, the Europeans consciously and callously began to "use" their biological advantage to wage germ warfare. In 1763, the commander in chief of British forces in America, Jeffrey Amherst, ordered his lieutenants "to send the small pox among the disaffected tribes of Indians." The idea had already occurred to the commander of Fort Pitt, at the junction of the Ohio, Allegheny, and Monongahela rivers. Three weeks before receiving Amherst's order, he summoned the local native American chiefs for a parley and callously presented them, as a token of esteem, with two blankets and two handkerchiefs from infected members of his garrison specifically "to convey the small-pox to the Indians."[28] Another outbreak of the deadly disease swiftly reduced their numbers.

But what if the Native Americans had been able to protect themselves against smallpox? This is not as far-fetched as it seems for two reasons. First, by the sixteenth century if not before, some Chinese doctors had already perfected "variolation," the technique of administering to children a mild form of the virus that conferred immunity, and published books describing their methods. Pre-Columbian America also possessed medical experts of great skill, who might, like their Chinese contemporaries, have stumbled on the technique. Second, in the mid–seventeenth century, a group of invaders who had little or no previous contact with smallpox quickly adjusted when they first encountered it: the Manchu conquerors of China. At first, fear of the disease dominated Manchu strategy. They created special "shelters for keeping smallpox at bay," to which members of the ruling elite who had not had the disease could escape, and they entrusted field commands only to generals and princes who had survived smallpox, leaving the rest in charge of garrisons in the rear. Nevertheless, in 1661 the Manchu emperor himself died of the disease. Not surprisingly, his successor, Kangxi (who had caught and survived smallpox as a child) took a keen interest in variolation. Having "had it tested on one or two people," despite some strong opposition, he insisted on inoculation for his children and grandchildren and later for his elite warriors. "This is an extremely important thing, of which I am very proud," Kangxi wrote later in a testament for his family. "[This] practice has saved the health of millions of men." From China, the technique spread to the Ottoman Empire and, in the 1720s, to Western Europe.[29]

What if the Aztec leaders had displayed the same ingenuity and tenacity as Kangxi? Could Cortés and his two thousand followers—or any later expedition—have prevailed against more healthy and numerous enemies (who had come into contact with smallpox long before its propagators arrived in the Valley of Mexico)? It seems unlikely. Although the Spaniards could have continued to exploit the resources of the Caribbean, those of the American mainland—above all its silver—would have remained beyond their grasp, and, according to the synergy model described earlier, no American silver would mean no dominion in Asia.[30]

The Western Way of War

Every culture develops its own way of war. Societies located where land is plentiful but manpower scarce tend to favor a ritualized conflict in which only a few "champions" actually fight but their fate decides that of everyone. The "Flower Wars" of the Aztecs and the "amok" combats of the Indonesian islanders caused relatively little bloodshed because they aimed to seize people rather than territory, to increase each warlord's available manpower rather than waste it in bloody battles. In China, too, strategy aimed to achieve victory without battle. According to the most revered military theorist, Sun-Tzu (writing in the fourth century BC), "To subdue the enemy without fighting is the acme of skill."[31] Many non-Western military traditions have displayed great continuity over time: thus even in the 1960s anthropologists could study the wars of the highland peoples of Irian Jaya in Indonesia, who still settled their disputes in the same ritualized way as their ancestors did. By then, however, most other military cultures had been transformed by that of the West—of Europe and the former European colonies in the Americas.

The "Western way of war" (to use the felicitous phrase coined by Victor Davis Hanson), which also boasts great antiquity, rests on five principal foundations. First, the armed forces of the West have always placed heavy reliance on superior technology, usually to compensate for inferior numbers. That is not to say that the West enjoyed *universal* technological superiority. Until the advent of musketry volleys and field artillery in the seventeenth century, the recurved bow used by horse archers all over Asia proved far more effective than any Western weaponry, but with few exceptions the horse archers of Asia did not directly threaten the West and, when they did, the threat was not sustained. Nor did all the advanced technology originate in the West: many vital military and naval innovations, including the stirrup, the compass, and gunpowder, came from Asia.

Now military technology is usually the first to be borrowed by every society, because the penalty for failing to do so can be immediate and fatal, but the West seems to have been preternaturally receptive to new technology, whether from its own inventors or from outside. Technological innovation, and the equally vital ability to respond to it, soon became an established feature of Western warfare. A "technological edge," however, has rarely been sufficient in itself to ensure victory. As the Swiss military writer Antoine-Henri Jomini wrote in the early nineteenth century: "The superiority of armament may increase the chances of success in war, but it does not of itself win battles."[32] Even in the twentieth century, the outcome of wars has been determined less by technology than by better war plans, the achievement of surprise, greater economic strength, and, above all, superior discipline. The critical element of discipline is the ability of a formation to stand fast in the face of the enemy, whether attacking or being attacked, without giving way to the natural impulses of fear and panic. (The same was true of war at sea; whether resisting boarding parties on a galley or enduring a cannonade aboard a ship of the line, discipline and training proved essential.) Western military practice has always exalted discipline—rather than kinship, religion, or patriotism—as the primary instrument that turns bands of men fighting as individuals into soldiers fighting as part of organized units. This, like technology, helped to compensate for numerical inferiority, for whether defending Europe from invasion (as at Salamis in 480 BC or at Vienna in AD 1529) or subduing the Aztec and Mughal empires, Western forces were always outnumbered by at least two to one and often by far more. Without superior discipline and technology, such odds would surely have proved overwhelming.

Reinforcing these two elements, and indeed refining them, was a remarkable continuity in military theory. The history of the *Epitome of Military Matters,* a compendium of Roman military practice first composed by Flavius Renatus Vegetius around the year AD 390 (and revised into its final form about fifty years later), offers perhaps the most remarkable example. In the eighth century the Northumbrian scholar Bede, on the northwestern fringe of the former Roman world, possessed a copy; a hundred years later, a Carolingian emperor commissioned an abridgment of the work to help him devise a successful strategy for resisting the Scandinavian invasions; and later manuscript copies appeared in English, French, German, Italian, Spanish, and perhaps Hebrew. In the eighteenth century, the young George Washington possessed and annotated his own printed copy of Vegetius. Other classical works on military affairs also enjoyed continuing popularity and influence. In the late sixteenth century, the leaders of the Dutch Republic studied accounts of the stunningly successful tactic of encirclement attributed by Roman writers to Hannibal at the battle of Cannae in 216 BC. Three centuries later, Count Alfred von Schlieffen and his successors in the Prussian General Staff expressly modeled their strategy for destroying France in the "next war" on Cannae, and in AD 1914 it came within an ace of success.

The steady spread of Western military power rested on far more than the triad of technology, discipline, and a tradition of unlimited aggression toward outsiders, however. Many other military cultures (such as those of China and Japan) also placed a high premium on technology and discipline, and the teachings of Sun Tzu strikingly anticipated many positions later developed by (say) Jomini. The Western way of war possessed two further unique features: first, its ability to change, as well as to conserve its military practices as the need arose; and, second, its power to finance those changes.

Areas dominated by a single hegemonic power, such as Aztec Mexico or Mughal India, faced relatively few life-threatening challenges, and so military traditions changed slowly if at all. In areas contested by multiple polities, by contrast, the need for military innovation could become extremely strong. Admittedly, when the states remained relatively underdeveloped, with backward political and economic institutions and infrastructures, the tension between challenge and response seldom resulted in rapid and significant change. But where the major competing states were both numerous and institutionally strong, the challenge and response dynamic could become self-sustaining, with growth (in effect) begetting growth.

The ability to reproduce unfamiliar military techniques and strategies required more than changes in the art of war, however. Above all, a military system based on maintaining a technological edge is, by definition, expensive: labor-intensive systems, which rely for their impact on concentrating an overwhelming number of men, may only require a society to mobilize its adult males—probably only for a brief period—equipped with traditional weapons (sometimes, as in the case of Japanese or early medieval European swords, weapons of considerable antiquity that could, like Excalibur, be used again and again). The financial burden of fighting may therefore be spread over a wide social group and even over several generations. A capital-intensive military system, by contrast, requires the stockpiling of a panoply of weapons that, however expensive, may soon become outdated. Its attraction, paradoxically, lies precisely in the combination of high initial cost with low maintenance: thus Harlech castle, one of Edward I's magnificent fortifications to control Wales, cost almost an entire year's revenue to build, but in 1294 its garrison of only thirty-seven soldiers successfully defended it against attack. The king's strategic vision anticipated that of the Manhattan Project, which spent two billion dollars on the production of two distinct types of atomic device, which, delivered on two August mornings in 1945 by just two airplanes, precipitated the unconditional surrender of imperial Japan and its five million troops still in arms within a week.

The emphasis on technology caused the cost of each war waged by the West to increase significantly beyond that of the last, until military hardware became so expensive that only centralized states could afford to buy it. Creating the means to fund such an expensive form of warfare clearly enhanced the power of the state, since each change in the size or equipment of armed forces required both new efforts to extract resources from the subject population and an expanded bureaucratic structure to handle them.

Imitating the Western way of war thus involved adaptation at many levels. Simply copying weapons picked up on the battlefield could never suffice; it also required the "replication" of the whole political, social, and economic structure that underpinned the capacity to innovate and respond swiftly. "Westernizing war" depended on the ability of warriors, traditionally one of the most conservative groups, to accept both the need for change and the need for instruction from "inventors" of a different (and normally inferior) social background. It also presupposed the state's ability to mobilize resources rapidly, in large quantities, and often for long periods, so that any technological shortcomings revealed in the course of a conflict could be remedied swiftly. Naturally, the less developed the economy, the less easily the cost of military preparedness could be absorbed.

Mobilizing credit to finance wars, however, rests not only on the existence of extensive private credit but also on a convergence of interest between those who make money and those who make war, for public loans depend both on finding borrowers willing to lend and on finding taxpayers willing and able to provide ultimate repayment. In England, tax revenues increased sixfold in the century following William of Orange's invasion in 1688. As an alarmed member of Parliament exclaimed:

> Let any gentleman but look into the statute books lying upon our table, he will there see to what a vast bulk, to what a number of volumes, our statutes relating to taxes have swelled. . . . It is monstrous, it is even frightful to look into the Indexes, where for several columns together we see nothing but Taxes, Taxes, Taxes.

And yet most members, who paid the taxes themselves, accepted their necessity, and so did the majority of the political nation.[33] By 1783, when the unsuccessful American War came to an end, Great Britain's national debt stood at £245 million, equivalent to more than twenty years' revenue, yet many of the loans had been contracted at just 3 percent interest. "Who pays and why" is as important, in the Western way of war, as "who fights and why;" and the ability to organize long-term credit (and therefore the existence of a secure and sophisticated capital market) to fund government borrowing needs in wartime represented a crucial "secret weapon" of the West.

Thus even in the strict military sense, the rise of the West rested on multiple foundations. For its financial edge, it required elites prepared to trust the state and contribute or lend huge sums of money voluntarily, and that in turn normally required the limited executive governments and responsible legislatures that first developed in Britain and the Netherlands in the seventeenth century. For its technological edge, it required both innovation and emulation, a process that depended on streams of cultural and political diversity that flowed in northwestern Europe but initially not elsewhere. And so on. But what if its enemies had managed to "replicate" the Western way of war? Then probably Western expansion would have ceased. Yet this begs an important question because relatively few states proved able to remain in the arms race for long due to the huge cost of keeping abreast of changing technology and of maintaining the resources to deploy it effectively. Japan offers almost the only counterexample, thanks to the vital combination of discipline, doctrinal flexibility, and a sophisticated financial structure that permitted not only the acquisition of expensive military and naval technology but also the equally expensive successive adaptations necessary to keep abreast, if not ahead, of all rivals. Even so, it seems unlikely that Japan could have defeated Russia in 1904–5—which marked its emergence as a Great Power—without the £82 million raised by selling Japanese treasury bonds at low interest issued to subscribers in Britain, Germany, and the United States by Jewish financiers eager to humble the Russian government, which had persecuted their coreligionists.[34]

In a sense, therefore, we have returned to E. H. Carr's "big battalions." The rise of the West becomes "by and large a record of what people did, not of what they failed to do: to this extent it is inevitably a success story." This is true but with one important difference. This volume has traveled the "roads not taken" in order to study and evaluate the road actually followed and thus to distinguish more clearly the true causes from the merely contingent. We have not extracted "from the multiplicity of sequences of cause and effect . . . those, and only those, which are historically significant," nor have we dragged "into prominence the forces which have triumphed and [thrust] into the background those which they have swallowed up" (page 29 above). To the contrary, by seeking various nodes of uncertainty at which Western hegemony might have been halted or undone, and by examining how easy it would be to change particular developments in both the West and elsewhere, we have revealed the extreme complexity of the process we call the rise of the West. It involved the coming together of a large number of changes and processes in Western and global history that jointly produced the modern world. Our counterfactual, at the very least, makes us appreciate the multitude of paths that led into this world.

We stand unequivocally with those historians who maintain that what happened acquires its full significance only in the context of what could have happened and with those cognitive scientists who warn that the best way to prevent hindsight from distorting our view of the past is to make a good faith effort to explore what could have happened on the counterfactual roads not taken. You, our persevering readers, will have to judge how well our pursuit of alternative paths and the use of counterfactual reasoning to interpret the past in order to understand the present have clarified one of the major and most puzzling developments in world history—the rise of the West—as well as how central counterfactual framing should be to serious historical research.

NOTES

For helpful comments and suggestions, we thank Richard Ned Lebow, Paul Schroeder, and especially Jack Goldstone and Jonathan Clark.

1. German newspapers published on January 1, 1933, and the entry from Goebbels's *Tagebücher* are cited and translated in Henry A. Turner Jr. *Hitler's Thirty Days to Power: January 1933* (New York: Addison-Wesley, 1996), 1, 28. One wonders what fate awaited the journalists quoted after January 30.

2. Ibid., 166, 168. The three major figures were President Hindenburg, Chancellor Schleicher, and former chancellor Papen; the others were Hindenburg's son Oskar, Otto Meissner, and Alfred Hugenburg.

3. Alison Anderson, *On the Verge of War: International Relations and the Jülich-Kleve Succession Crisis (1609–1614)* (Boston: Humanities Press, 1999), 178–79, William Louis of Nassau to his cousin Maurice, August 4, 1614; Nicola di Cosmo, "Military Aspects of the Manchu Wars against the Caqars," in *Warfare in Inner Asian History (1500–1800)* (Leiden: Brill, 2002), 351, Nurhaci to a Mongol ally, September 18, 1625; C. von Clausewitz, *On War* (written in the 1820s), ed. and trans. M. Howard and P. Paret (Princeton: Princeton University Press, 1984), 85. See also the point made by John Adamson: "War is inevitably premised on a series of contemporary exercises in 'virtual history.' For each belligerent party only takes up arms because, if defeated, it expects a malign future that it is

the purpose of victory to render counterfactual" ("King Charles I wins the English Civil War," in Andrew Roberts, ed., *What Might Have Been: Leading Historians on Twelve "What Ifs" of History* (London: Weidenfeld and Nicholson, 2004), 49.)

4. Joel Mokyr, *The Lever of Riches: Technological Creativity and Economic Progress* (Oxford: Oxford University Press, 1990), 16.

5. Joel Mokyr, *The Economics of the Industrial Revolution* (Totowa, NJ: Prentice-Hall, 1985), 55–57.

6. Williamson Murray, "May 1940: Contingency and Fragility of the German RMA," in *The Dynamics of Military Revolution, 1300–2050*, ed. Macgregor Knox and Williamson Murray (Cambridge: Cambridge University Press, 2001), 156. This book, a collection of essays on "revolutions in military affairs" in the West, bristles with examples of chance and contingency changing the course of history. As the editors and many of the authors realize, it provides ample justification for counterfactual history.

7. Nevertheless, although England developed plans to secure a "Protestant succession," none existed in the Dutch Republic. When William died in 1702, the Republic managed to fight France, in alliance with England and several German states, without him. William had spent most of the 1690s creating Anglo-Dutch-German cadres capable of fighting (and winning) as a coalition. Had he died in 1688 or 1690, before achieving this, the Republic's ability to withstand France would have been seriously diminished.

8. Paul W. Schroeder, "Embedded Counterfactuals and World War I as an Unavoidable War," in Paul W. Schroeder, *Systems, Stability and Statecraft: Essays on the International History of Modern Europe*, ed. David Wetzel, Robert Jervis, and Jack S. Levy (New York: Palgrave, 2004), 158–91.

9. Philip E. Tetlock and Richard N. Lebow, "Poking Counterfactual Holes in Covering Laws: Cognitive Styles and Historical Reasoning," *American Political Science Review* 95 (2001): 829–43.

10. See chapters 1 and 10 in this volume for further discussions of this point.

11. On the social filters that stifled inventions in large parts of the medieval Islamic world, see Richard W. Bulliet, "Determinism and Pre-industrial Technology," in *Does Technology Drive History? The Dilemma of Technological Determinism,* ed. Merritt R, Smith and Leo Marx (Cambridge: MIT Press, 1994), 201–15. For another example—the rejection of handheld gunpowder weapons by the Mamluks of Egypt for social reasons, which doomed them to defeat by the Ottoman Turks in 1517, see David Ayalon, *Gunpowder and Firearms in the Mamluk Kingdom: A Challenge to Medieval Society* (London: Valentine, Mitchell, 1956).

12. Karl Lanz, *Correspondenz des Kaisers Karl V,* 3 vols. (Leipzig: F. A. Brockhaus, 1846), 2:368, Charles to Ferdinand, January 11, 1530.

13. William Bolts, *Considerations on India Affairs, Particularly Respecting the Present State of Bengal and Its Dependencies* (London: J. Almon, 1772), chaps. 2 ("On the Mogul Empire before the Invasion of Nader Shah") and 3 ("On the State of Hindostan since the Total Subversion of the Empire"). Our thanks to Sanjay Subrahmanyam for drawing this work to our attention.

14. Quotations are from East India Company records reproduced in Gary J.

Bryant, "The East India Company and Its Army, 1600–1778," PhD thesis, University of London, 1975), 74, 138. We are most grateful to Dr. Bryant for permission to use his excellent thesis.

15. Louis Dermigny, *La Chine et l'Occident: Le commerce à Canton au XVIIIe siècle, 1719–1833*. 4 vols. (Paris: SEVPEN, 1964), 2:781.

16. Sanjay Subrahmanyam, "'Un grand dérangement': Dreaming an Indo-Persian Empire in South Asia, 1740–1800," *Journal of Early Modern History* 4 (2001): 337–78 (quotation from 372).

17. Ibid., 374, 377.

18. See the fascinating information in two classic studies: Eric R. Wolf, *Europe and the People without History* (Berkeley: University of California Press, 1982), 273 (on p. 402, Wolf notes that he grew up in the textile belt along the German-Czech border, which explains his sensitivity to such figures); and Peter Harnetty, *Imperialism and Free Trade: Lancashire and India in the Mid-nineteenth Century* (Vancouver: University of British Columbia Press, 1972).

19. We can think of only one "single-shot" counterfactual that might derail the rise of the West "from within." The dramatic reduction in mortality achieved by the conquest of smallpox (through Jenner's vaccination process) after 1798 allowed rapid population growth. As it happened, the Industrial Revolution created jobs and wealth sufficient to absorb much of the increase, but had industrialization been delayed, the West would surely have suffered a series of subsistence crises (as happened in other parts of the world) that would have precluded its takeoff into self-sustained growth. However, delaying or aborting the Industrial Revolution scarcely qualifies as a minimal rewrite.

20. Our thanks to Ira M. Lapidus and Richard W. Bulliet for help in framing this paragraph. See also chapter 8 of this volume for further thoughts by Robin D. S. Yates on the Mongols.

21. J. A. Boyle, ed., *The History of the World Conqueror by 'Ala-ad-Din 'Ata-Malik Juvaini,* 2 vols. (Manchester: Manchester University Press, 1958), 1:96–97 (and see another description at 2:533). See also Thomas Allsen, "The Circulation of Military Technology in the Mongol Empire," in di Cosmo, *Warfare in Inner Asian history,* 272–82.

22. The Mongol achievement is all the more remarkable when one considers the fate of the winter campaigns conducted by Western armies in 1812, 1941, and 1942. It was the only successful invasion of Russia.

23. E. Voegelin, in "The Mongol Orders of Submission to European Powers, 1245–55," *Byzantion* 15 (1940–41): 378–413, published eight known letters from the Mongols to the West and demonstrated their uncompromising philosophy.

24. One might object that the Mongols lacked the means to achieve universal domination by sea since their two attempts to conquer Japan (using ships built and manned by Koreans) failed. Later, however, during the early Ming period, an Arab-speaking admiral, Zheng He, with Arab-speaking crews, developed impressive techniques of maritime expansion that allowed the Chinese to reach Arabia and Africa. Arthur Waldron sees these as a continuation of the policies pursued by Mongol rulers such as Kublai Khan (personal communication, February 1997).

25. See the excellent historical discussions of smallpox in Ann B. Jannetta,

Epidemics and Mortality in Early Modern Japan (Princeton: Princeton University Press, 1987), 61–107; and Joseph Needham, Gwei-Djen Lu, and Nathan Sivin, *Science and Civilization in China,* vol. 6, pt. 6 (Cambridge: Cambridge University Press, 2000), 115–40.

26. Daniel T. Reff, "Contact Shock in Northwestern New Spain," in *Disease and Demography in the Americas,* ed. John W. Verano and Donald H. Ubelaker (Washington, DC: Smithsonian Institution Press, 1992), 265–76. A vast and contradictory literature exists on the impact of disease on Latin America. For a helpful introduction, which stresses and explains regional differences, see Linda A. Newson, "Indian Population Patterns in Colonial Spanish America," *Latin American Research Review* 20 (1985): 41–74. For a recent overview, see Jared Diamond, *Guns, Germs, and Steel The Fates of Human Society* (New York: Norton, 1997), pt. 4, "Around the World in Five Chapters."

27. Noel G. Butlin, *Our Original Aggression: Aboriginal Populations of Southeast Australia, 1788–1850* (Sydney: Allen and Unwin, 1983), 20–22, considers whether the first British colony in Australia unleashed the deadly smallpox epidemic that decimated the aboriginal population in 1789—a population that had not suffered smallpox for at least a century—but found no "smoking gun."

28. Francis Jennings, *Crowns, Colonies, and Tribes in the Seven Years War in America* (New York: Norton, 1988), 447 and n. 26, presents prosaic but irrefutable proof of this atrocity. The garrison's account book records the cost of "sundries got to replace in kind those which were taken from people in the hospital to convey the small-pox to the Indians." Jennings also established that the fatal parley with the Delaware leaders took place on June 23, 1763, whereas Amherst issued his order on July 7 (received at Fort Pitt on the thirteenth).

29. See Chang Chia-Feng, "Disease and Its Impact on Politics, Diplomacy, and the Military: The Case of Smallpox and the Manchus (1613–1795)," *Journal of the History of Medicine and Allied Sciences* LVII/2 (2002); and Needham, Lu, and Sivin, *Science and Civilization in China,* 140, for Kangxi's boast. They estimate that the emperor carried out his tests "in 1681 or slightly later." In the 1690s, English men and women residing in China and Turkey sent home reports of the technique, but it was not tried out in Europe until the 1720s (145).

30. See also the interesting essay of Ross Hassig, "Counterfactuals and Revisionism in Historical Explanation," *Anthropological Theory* 1 (2003): 57–72. Our thanks to Richard Fitzsimmons for bringing this item to our attention.

31. Sun Tzu, *The Art of War,* ed. S. B. Griffith (Oxford: Oxford University Press, 1963), 77.

32. Antoine-Henri Jomini, *The Art of War,* ed. G. H. Mendell and W. P. Craighill (Westport, CT: Greenwood, 1977), 47.

33. The quotations are from John Brewer, *The Sinews of Power: War, Money, and the English State, 1688–1783* (Cambridge: Harvard University Press, 1988), 91.

34. Richard J. Smethurst, "Russian Anti-Semitism and Japanese Fundraising during the Russo-Japanese War, 1904–5," in *Anglo-Japanese Economic Relations 1900–2000,* ed. Philip Towle and Nobuko Margaret Kosuge (London: Anthem, 2005).

Notes on the Contributors

CARLOS M. N. EIRE is Riggs Professor of History and Religious Studies at Yale University, where he earned his PhD in 1979. Before joining the Yale faculty in 1996, he taught at Saint John's University and the University of Virginia and resided for two years at the Institute for Advanced Study in Princeton. He is the author of *War against the Idols* (Cambridge, 1986), *From Madrid to Purgatory* (Cambridge, 1995), and *Reformations: Early Modern Europe, 1450–1700* (forthcoming, Yale, 2007). He is also coauthor of *Jews, Christians, Muslims: An Introduction to Monotheistic Religions* (Prentice-Hall, 1997). His memoir of the Cuban Revolution, *Waiting for Snow in Havana* (Free Press, 2003), won the National Book Award for nonfiction and is being translated into many languages.

JACK A. GOLDSTONE is Hazel Professor of Public Policy at George Mason University. After receiving AB, AM, and PhD degrees from Harvard University, he taught at Northwestern University and the University of California, Davis, before coming to George Mason and has been a visiting scholar at the University of California, Los Angeles; the University of California, Berkeley; Cambridge University; and the Australian National University. He has held research fellowships from the American Council of Learned Societies, the Canadian Institute for Advanced Research, the Center for Advanced Studies in the Behavioral Sciences, and the MacArthur Foundation. His book *Revolution and Rebellion in the Early Modern World,* published by the University of California Press, was awarded the 1993 Distinguished Scholarly Publication Award of the American Sociological Association. He has written or edited nine books on the topic of revolutions and social change, including *Revolutions* (now in its third edition, from Wadsworth Publishers) and the forthcoming *A Peculiar Path: The Rise of the West in Global Context, 1500–1850,* from Harvard University Press.

VICTOR DAVIS HANSON was educated at the University of California, Santa Cruz (BA, classics), Stanford University (PhD, classics), and the American School of Classical Studies. He is the author of sixteen books, among them *The Western Way of War* (Knopf, 1989), *The Other Greeks* (Free Press, 1995), *The Soul of Battle* (Anchor, 2000), and most recently *Carnage and Culture* (Doubleday, 2001), *An Autumn of War* (Anchor, 2002), *Ripples of Battle* (Random House, 2003), and *Between War and Peace* (Random House, 2004). He is Professor of Classics Emeritus at California State University, Fresno, and has been a fellow at the Center for Advanced Study in the Behavioral Sciences, a visiting professor at Stanford University, and has served as the Shifrin Chair of Military History at the U.S. Naval Academy, Annapolis. Currently he is Senior Fellow in Military History and Classics at the Hoover Institution, Stanford University. He writes a weekly column for both *National Review Online* and the *Chicago Tribune* and is a frequent contributor to the *Wall Street Journal, Commentary, Daily Telegraph, American Heritage,* and *City Journal.* In 2002 he received the Eric Breindel Award for opinion journalism. He has been an Onassis Fellow, National Endowment for the Humanities Fellow, and Distinguished Teaching Fellow in History at Hillsdale College, as well as the recipient of the American Philological Association's Teaching Award for creating a classics program at California State University, Fresno.

HOLGER H. HERWIG, born in Hamburg, Germany, on September 25, 1941, is Canada Research Chair in Military and Strategic Studies at the University of Calgary. He received his BA (1965) from the University of British Columbia and his MA (1967) as well as his PhD (1971) from the State University of New York at Stony Brook. He taught at Vanderbilt University in Nashville, Tennessee, from 1971 until 1989, then served as Head of the Department of History at the University of Calgary from 1991 to 1996. He was Visiting Professor of Strategy at the Naval War College, Newport, Rhode Island, in 1985–86 and the Andrea and Charles Bronfman Distinguished Visiting Professor of Judaic Studies at the College of William and Mary, Williamsburg, Virginia, in 1998.

A Fellow of the Royal Society of Canada and of the Alexander von Humboldt Foundation in Bonn, Germany, Herwig has held major research grants from the Humboldt Foundation, the National Endowment for the Humanities, NATO, the Rockefeller Foundation, and the Social Sciences and Humanities Research Council. He has published more than a dozen books on German military and naval history, 1871 to 1945. His works have been translated into Chinese, Czech, German, Polish, and Spanish. They include the prize-winning *The First World War: Germany and Austria-Hungary, 1914–1918* (London, 1997); and *The Destruction of the Bismarck* (Toronto, 2001; New York, 2001; London, 2002), coauthored with David J. Bercuson.

RICHARD N. LEBOW is James O. Freedman Presidential Professor of Government at Dartmouth College. He is also a Fellow of the Centre of International Studies, Cambridge University. He is the Past President of the International Society of Political Psychology. His most recent single-authored book is *The Tragic Vision of Politics: Ethics, Interests, and Orders* (Cambridge, 2003), which won the Alexander L. George Award for the best book in political psychology. His most recent edited volumes include *Ending the Cold* (Palgrave, 2004) and *The Politics of Memory in Postwar Europe* (Duke, forthcoming).

JOEL MOKYR is Robert H. Strotz Professor of Arts and Sciences and Professor of Economics and History at Northwestern University and Sackler Professor (by special appointment) at the Eitan Berglas School of Economics at the University of Tel Aviv. He specializes in economic history and the economics of technological and population change. He is the author of *Why Ireland Starved: An Analytical and Quantitative Study of the Irish Economy*, *The Lever of Riches: Technological Creativity and Economic Progress*, *The British Industrial Revolution: An Economic Perspective*, and his most recent *The Gifts of Athena: Historical Origins of the Knowledge Economy* (Princeton University Press, 2002). He is currently working on a new book, *The Enlightened Economy*, to be published by Penguin in 2006. He has authored more than 70 articles and books in his field. He served as Senior Editor of the *Journal of Economic History* from 1994 to 1998 and is Editor in Chief of the *Oxford Encyclopedia of Economic History* (Oxford, 2003) and the *Economic History of the Western World*. He served as President of the Economic History Association in 2003–4 and is a Director of the National Bureau of Economic Research and a member of its Executive Committee. He served as Chair of the Economics Department at Northwestern University between 1998 and 2001 and was a Fellow at the Center for Advanced Studies in the Behavioral Sciences at Stanford University between September 2001 and

June 2002. Professor Mokyr has an undergraduate degree from the Hebrew University of Jerusalem and a PhD from Yale University. He has taught at Northwestern University since 1974 and has been Visiting Professor at Harvard University, the University of Chicago, Stanford University, the Hebrew University of Jerusalem, the University of Tel Aviv, University College of Dublin, and the University of Manchester. He is a Fellow of the American Academy of Arts and Sciences and a Foreign Fellow of the Royal Dutch Academy of Sciences and the Accademia Nazionale dei Lincei. His books have won a number of important prizes, including the Joseph Schumpeter Memorial Prize (1990), the Ranki Prize for the best book in European economic history, and most recently the Donald Price Prize of the American Political Science Association. In 2005 he was awarded the biennial Heineken Prize for History awarded by the Royal Dutch Academy of Science. His current research is an attempt to apply insights from evolutionary theory to long-run changes in technological knowledge and economic history, and he is completing a book entitled *The Enlightened Economy*.

GEOFFREY PARKER was born in Nottingham, England, and holds BA, MA, PhD and LittD degrees from Cambridge University. He taught at the University of Saint Andrews, Scotland; the University of British Columbia, Vancouver; the University of Illinois at Urbana-Champaign; and Yale University before joining Ohio State University in 1997, where he teaches undergraduate and graduate courses on the Reformation, European history, and military history. He has written, edited or coedited thirty-two books, of which the best known are *The Military Revolution: Military Innovation and the Rise of the West, 1500–1800* (Cambridge, 1988), the winner of two prizes (a third, expanded edition was published in 2000, with Chinese, French, Italian, Japanese and Spanish translations); and *Philip II* (1978), now in its fourth edition (Chicago, 2001), with translations into Spanish (multiple editions since 1984), Czech, Dutch, Italian, and Polish. In 1984 he became a Fellow of the British Academy, the highest honor open to scholars in the humanities in Great Britain. In 1992, the king of Spain named him a Knight Grand Cross of the Order of Isabella the Catholic in recognition of his work on Spanish history.

CARLA GARDINA PESTANA was born in Burbank, California, and received her MA and PhD degrees from the University of California, Los Angeles. She is the W. E. Smith Professor of History at Miami University, a position she has held since 2003. Prior to accepting that position she taught at Ohio State University. She is the author of *Quakers and Baptists in Colonial Massachusetts* (Cambridge, 1991), and she continues to write and speak on the Quakers in particular. Her *The English Atlantic in an Age of Revolution, 1640–1661,* was published by Harvard University Press in 2004. She has just completed a manuscript entitled "Religion in the British Atlantic World, 1530–1800." Her current project is on the origins of English imperialism. She is the winner of the Colonial Society of Massachusetts' Walter Muir Whitehill Prize in Colonial History, and she has been awarded fellowships from the National Endowment of the Humanities and the American Philosophical Society, among others.

KENNETH POMERANZ was born in New York. He has a BA from Cornell University and an MA, M.Phil, and PhD from Yale University. He is currently Chancellor's Professor of History and Professor of East Asian Language and Literature at the University of California, Irvine, where he has taught since 1988. He teaches courses on the history of China, comparative economic history, environmental history, and world history and is Director of the University of California's Multi-campus Research Unit in World History. He has written three books and numerous articles. His first book, *The Making of a Hinterland: State, Society, and Economy in Inland North China, 1853–1937* (University of California Press, 1993), won the John King Fairbank Prize from the American Historical Association for the year's best book in East Asian history. His most recent book, *The Great Divergence: China, Europe, and the Making of a Modern World Economy* (2000), won the Fairbank Prize again and was a cowinner of the World History Association's book of the year prize; several translations are in print or under way. His other book is *The World That Trade Created* (1999; 2nd ed., 2005), coauthored with Steven Topik. He is also coeditor of *The History of World Trade* (2005). He is a Fellow of the American Academy of Arts and Sciences.

BARRY STRAUSS is Professor of History and Classics at Cornell University. The *Washington Post* listed his *Battle of Salamis: The Naval Encounter That Saved Greece—and Western Civilization* (Simon and Schuster, 2004) as one of the best books of 2004. His *The Trojan War: A New History,* will be published by Simon and Schuster in 2006. He has written or edited eight books and is the author of numerous scholarly papers and reviews. He is Past Director of Cornell University's Peace Studies Program. Educated in History at Cornell (BA) and Yale University (PhD), he studied archaeology at the American School at Athens as a Heinrich Schliemann Fellow. He also holds fellowships from the National Endowment for the Humanities, the MacDowell Colony, the German Academic Exchange Service, the Korea Foundation, and the Littauer Foundation. He holds Cornell University's Clark Distinguished Teaching Award. He has been interviewed on the History Channel, PBS, Discovery, and the BBC World Service. His op-ed pieces have appeared in such newspapers as the *Washington Post, Los Angeles Times,* and *Newsday.*

PHILIP E. TETLOCK (PhD from Yale University 1979) currently holds the Mitchell Endowed Professorship in the Haas School of Business at the University of California, Berkeley (with affiliations to the psychology and political science departments). He has received numerous awards from professional and scientific organizations, including the American Psychological Association, the American Political Science Association, the American Association for the Advancement of Science, the International Society of Political Psychology, the Sage Foundation, the MacArthur Foundation, and the National Academy of Sciences. He has published more than 150 articles in peer-refereed journals and has edited or written nine books. He has special research interests in the political psychology of counterfactual reasoning: the role that prior beliefs and emotional sympathies can play in shaping our opinions about alternative paths that history could have taken. His most recent book is *Expert Political Judgment: How Good Is It? How Can We Know?* (Princeton, 2005). *Expert Political Judgment* won the American Political Science Association's 2006 Robert E. Lane Award for Best Book in Political Psychology.

ROBIN D. S. YATES (BA and MA, Oxford University; MA, University of California, Berkeley; PhD, Harvard University) is Professor of History and East Asian Studies and James McGill Professor at McGill University, Montreal. He is currently Chair of the Society for the Study of Early China and Editor of the journal *Early China.* In the last ten years, he has published many articles and presented more than fifty papers on various topics at international academic conferences and as an invited guest speaker. He is a specialist on Warring States and early imperial China, including the Qin and Han dynasties, early Chinese philosophy, the history of science and technology in China (particularly military science and technology), and the history of women. He has published three books, including *Science and Civilisation in China,* vol. 5, pt. 6: "Military Technology: Missiles and Sieges," with the late Joseph Needham (Cambridge, 1994; Chinese translation, 2002); and *Five Lost Classics: Tao, HuangLao; and Yin-Yang in Han China* (Ballantine Del Rey Fawcett, 1997). He has been the recipient of numerous fellowships and research grants over the years and has acted as a consultant and interviewee on television documentaries and radio programs on Chinese history, science, and technology. He was also Scientific Adviser for the exhibition "Xi'an: La Capitale Éternelle," Musée de la Civilisation, Quebec City, December 2001 to September 2002.

Index